DISABILITY, SPACE, ARCHITECTURE

Disability, Space, Architecture: A Reader takes a groundbreaking approach to exploring the interconnections between disability, architecture and cities. The contributions come from architecture, geography, anthropology, health studies, English language and literature, rhetoric and composition, art history, disability studies and disability arts and cover personal, theoretical and innovative ideas and work.

Richer approaches to disability – beyond regulation and design guidance – remain fragmented and difficult to find for architectural and built environment students, educators and professionals. By bringing together in one place some seminal texts and projects, as well as newly commissioned writings, readers can engage with disability in unexpected and exciting ways that can vibrantly inform their understandings of architecture and urban design.

Most crucially, *Disability, Space, Architecture: A Reader* opens up not just disability but also ability – dis/ability – as a means of refusing the normalisation of only particular kinds of bodies in the design of built space. It reveals how our everyday social attitudes and practices about people, objects and spaces can be better understood through the lens of disability, and it suggests how thinking differently about dis/ability can enable innovative and new kinds of critical and creative architectural and urban design education and practice.

Jos Boys trained in architecture and has worked as a journalist, researcher, academic and community-based practitioner. As a non-disabled person she is particularly interested in how architects and other built environment professionals can act creatively and responsively as designers and policy-makers without misrepresenting or marginalising disabled people. Her previous book, *Doing Disability Differently: An Alternative Handbook on Architecture, Dis/ability and Designing for Everyday Life*, grew out of a series of collaborations between disabled artists and architects, through a group she co-founded called Architecture-Inside Out. Previously Jos has written extensively about feminism and architecture. She was co-founder of Matrix, a feminist architectural design and research practice, and has been a member of the TakingPlace art and architecture collective.

'This diverse collection of essays proposes creative and critical ways of engaging in disability studies within the field of architecture. From rethinking technologies and design practices to reframing dis/ability across the theoretical and historical discourses of architecture, it challenges dominant assumptions about the embodied occupation of designed environments. Instead of simply framing disability as a problem to be solved by way of regulations and universal spatial solutions, embodied dis/abilities are explored as opportunities rather than impediments to design thinking and socio-spatial awareness.'

— Dr Hélène Frichot, KTH (Royal Institute of Technology), Sweden

'*Disability, Space, Architecture: A Reader* is a critical and thought provoking collection of essays broadening the potential of dis/ability studies for designers, educators and academics. Seeking to radically relocate disability front and center within architectural discourse, the Reader positions disability as a transformative place to design and educate from. For the built environment to become more responsive and inclusive, we must not only acknowledge but also conceptualize differently the relationship between heterogeneous bodies and space as far more complex and intersectional, providing a trove of under examined spatial potential.'

— Lori A. Brown, Professor, School of Architecture, Syracuse University, USA

DISABILITY, SPACE, ARCHITECTURE

A Reader

Edited by Jos Boys

Routledge
Taylor & Francis Group

LONDON AND NEW YORK

First published 2017
by Routledge
2 Park Square, Milton Park, Abingdon, Oxon OX14 4RN

and by Routledge
711 Third Avenue, New York, NY 10017

Routledge is an imprint of the Taylor & Francis Group, an informa business

British Library Cataloguing in Publication Data
A catalogue record for this book is available from the British Library

Library of Congress Cataloging in Publication Data
Names: Boys, Jos, editor.
Title: Disability, space, architecture : a reader / edited by Jos Boys.
Description: New York : Routledge, 2017. | Includes bibliographical references and index.
Identifiers: LCCN 2016036334| ISBN 9781138676428 (hb : alk. paper) | ISBN
9781138676435 (pb : alk. paper) | ISBN 9781315560076 (ebook)
Subjects: LCSH: Barrier-free design. | Architecture--Human factors. |
Architecture and society. | City planning--Social aspects.
Classification: LCC NA2545.A1 D57 2017 | DDC 725/.53--dc23
LC record available at https://lccn.loc.gov/2016036334

ISBN: 978-1-138-67642-8 (hbk)
ISBN: 978-1-138-67643-5 (pbk)
ISBN: 978-1-315-56007-6 (ebk)

Typeset in Bembo
by HWA Text and Data Management, London

MIX
Paper from
responsible sources
FSC™ C013985

Printed in the United Kingdom
by Henry Ling Limited

Dedicated to Tobin Siebers, who is sorely missed

CONTENTS

FIGURES

CONTRIBUTORS

Peter Anderberg graduated from Lund University, Sweden, and then undertook his PhD in Rehabilitation Engineering at the Center for Rehabilitation Technology (CERTEC), part of the Department of Design Sciences, Faculty of Engineering at Lund. His doctoral research – exploring the impact of the internet on people with significant mobility/physical impairments – brings together a theoretical background in disability studies and a critical engagement in the social model of disability, the independent living movement, and rehabilitation engineering and design processes. Peter is currently senior lecturer at Blekinge Institute of Technology Karlskrona, Sweden, with responsibility for applied health technology studies.

Jos Boys trained in architecture and has worked as a journalist, researcher, academic and community-based practitioner. As a non-disabled person she is particularly interested in how architects and other built environment professionals can act creatively and responsively as designers and policy-makers without misrepresenting or marginalising disabled people. Her previous book, *Doing Disability Differently: An Alternative Handbook on Architecture, Dis/ability and Designing for Everyday Life* (2014), grew out of a series of collaborations between disabled artists and architects, through a group she co-founded called Architecture-Inside Out. Previously Jos has written extensively about feminism and architecture. She was co-founder of Matrix, a feminist architectural design and research practice, and has been a member of the TakingPlace art and architecture collective.

Todd Byrd serves as lead writer and editor at Gallaudet University in Washington, DC, USA, which provides higher education for deaf and hard-of-hearing students. His role supports research and international affairs, and ensures that the written output of the university's Research Support and International Affairs (RSIA) unit and its programme specialists is timely, clear and effective. He supervises staff and students who are involved in the unit's writing for websites or print publications for campus or external readership, and provides editing assistance to scientific personnel who are writing research grant proposals. He was previously a contributor to the university's newspaper, and involved in its DeafSpace project.

Amanda Cachia is an independent curator from Sydney, Australia, and is currently completing her PhD in Art History, Theory and Criticism at the University of California, San Diego, focusing on the intersection of disability and contemporary art. She is the 2014 recipient of the Irving K. Zola Award for Emerging Scholars in Disability Studies, issued by the Society for Disability Studies (SDS). Amanda held the position director/curator of the Dunlop Art Gallery in Regina, Saskatchewan, Canada, from 2007 to 2010, and has curated approximately forty exhibitions over the last ten years in various cities across the USA, England, Australia and Canada. She serves on the College Art Association's (CAA) Committee on Diversity Practices (2014–2017).

Liz Crow is an artist-activist, based in Bristol, UK, who works with performance, film, audio and text. Interested in drama, life stories and experimental work, she is drawn to the potential of storytelling to trigger change. Liz's work has shown at Tate Modern and the Smithsonian Institution, as well as on television and at festivals internationally. Through a four-year National Endowment for Science, Technology and the Arts (NESTA) fellowship, she explored ways to combine her creative practice and political activism. Liz is a graduate of the Skillset Guiding Lights scheme where she was mentored by Peter Cattaneo (*The Full Monty*), an Associate of the Centre for Cultural Disability Studies at Liverpool Hope University, UK, and is currently a doctoral candidate on a practice-led PhD at the University of the West of England.

Jay Dolmage is an associate professor of English at the University of Waterloo in Ontario, Canada. He is the founding editor of the *Canadian Journal of Disability Studies*. His book, *Disability Rhetoric*, was published in 2014 by Syracuse University Press and won a PROSE award from the American Publishers Association. His essays on rhetoric, writing and disability studies have appeared in several journals and edited collections, including *Cultural Critique*, *Disability Studies Quarterly* and *Rhetoric Review*. Jay grew up in the disability rights movement in Canada and remains committed to promoting greater access within higher education and across society.

J. Kent Fitzsimons is an architect, associate professor at the Ecole Nationale Supérieure d'Architecture et de Paysage de Bordeaux, France, and director of the PAVE research laboratory (Profession Architecture Ville Environnement). He teaches architectural design, architecture theory and research seminars. His architectural research considers the relationship between social phenomena and the notions of lived experience deployed in architectural design, with a focus on body-based issues such as life phases, gender and impairment. At the urban scale, he is interested in spatial practices and their representation in public policy, with particular attention to mobility and urban form.

Aimi Hamraie is assistant professor of medicine, health and society at Vanderbilt University, Nashville, Tennessee, USA. They are a feminist historian and epistemologist whose work focuses on the intersections of disability, design and technoscience. Aimi's essays on universal design, disability history and the politics of access appear or are in press in *Disability Studies Quarterly, Hypatia, Foucault Studies* and *Age Culture Humanities.* Their forthcoming book, entitled *Building Access: Disability, Universal Design, and the Politics of Knowing-Making* (2017), focuses on the history of universal design in the US and argues that the concept and practice of universal design took shape as an epistemological and material intervention.

Sophie Handler is a research–practitioner, currently based in Manchester, UK. She works at the intersection of urban theory, social policy and creative practice. She has spent the last ten years exploring the spatial politics of ageing through participative urban interventions, creative writing, research and policy development. She is author of *The Fluid Pavement* (2007) (a large print psychogeographic novel on ageing), an *Alternative Age-friendly Handbook (for the socially engaged practitioner)* (2014) and is chair of the Royal Institute of British Architects (RIBA) working group on Research and Ageing. Her practice-based work operates under the platform Ageing Facilities.

Sara Hendren is an artist, design researcher and professor based in Cambridge, Massachusetts, USA. She makes material and digital artworks, writes and lectures on adaptive and assistive technologies, prosthetics, inclusive design, accessible architecture and related ideas. Her work has been exhibited in the US and abroad and is held in the permanent collection at the Museum of Modern Art (MoMA), and her writing and design work have appeared in the *Boston Globe, The Atlantic Tech, FastCo Design* and on National Public Radio (US), among others. She teaches socially engaged design practices, adaptive + assistive technologies, and disability studies for engineers-in-training in her role as assistant professor at Olin College. She writes and edits the Abler website.

Paul Hunt was an extremely influential British disability activist, renowned as co-founder with Vic Finkelstein of the Union of the Physically Impaired against Segregation (UPIAS) when he wrote a letter to *The Guardian* in 1972 inviting disabled people to join in campaigning against discrimination. UPIAS was the first organisation to reject 'compensatory' and tragic or medical approaches to disability. As an alternative, UPIAS developed attention to the social and structural barriers that oppress people with impairments, rendering them 'disabled', what is now usually called the social model of disability. The group developed a Fundamental Principles of Disability manifesto, as well as being important in the Independent Living Movement and other campaigns for disability rights.

Rob Imrie is visiting professor of sociology in the Department of Sociology at Goldsmiths, University of London, UK, and director of an European Research Council (ERC) project on universal design. His research is focused on disability, design and embodiment with an interest in exploring the shaping of design through the intersections of the sensual nature of body–environment interactions. With a background in geography, sociology and planning studies, Rob has written extensively on disability and the built environment.

S. Lochlann Jain is an associate professor in the Anthropology Department at Stanford University, USA, and is an expert in medical and legal anthropology. Her most recent book, *Malignant: How Cancer Becomes Us* (2013), reads across a range of material to explain how a national culture that simultaneously aims to deny, profit from and cure cancer entraps us in a state of paradox – one that makes the world of cancer virtually impossible to navigate for doctors, patients, caretakers and policy-makers alike. The book has won numerous prizes. Lochlann is currently researching urban planning and transportation and experimental methods in anthropology.

Katie Lloyd Thomas is a senior lecturer in architecture at Newcastle University, UK, where she co-directs ARC, the Architecture Research Collaborative, and is an editor of the international journal *arq*. Her research is concerned with materiality in architecture and with feminist practice and theory, with a particular interest in how technologies and building have the capacity to transform relations, as explored in 'Between the Womb and the World: Building Matrixial Relations in the NICU' in *Architectural Relational Ecologies*, edited by Peg Rawes (Routledge, 2013). Katie edited *Material Matters* (2007) and with Tilo Amhoff and Nick Beech, *Industries of Architecture* (2015).

Thea McMillan is design director at Chambers McMillan Architects based in Edinburgh, Scotland. Their Ramp House won the 2013 Chairman's Award for Architecture, Scottish Design Awards amongst others. It was exhibited at The Lighthouse, Glasgow, and has been extensively published in the architectural press. Thea co-led first year architecture at the University of Edinburgh for seven years, and was co-chair for the consultation and engagement group at Edinburgh's new Royal Hospital for Sick Children, where she instigated a programme of architectural engagement workshops with children hospital users and their siblings and advised on design. Her aims are to make architecture accessible to all through communication and engagement.

Rod Michalko recently retired from teaching sociology and disability studies at the University of Toronto, Canada. He is author of numerous articles and books, including a co-edited book with Dr Tanya Titchkosky titled, *Rethinking Normalcy* (2009). Almost all of Rod's work originates in his blindness and is explored at the intersections of narrative and disability theory. He is author of *The Mystery of the Eye and the Shadow of Blindness* (1998), *The Two-in One: Walking with Smokie, Walking with Blindness* (1999) and *The Difference that Disability Makes* (2002).

Ingunn Moser is professor and principal at VID Specialized University, Oslo, Norway. She has published extensively on disability, subjectivity and embodiment in relation to new technologies and material environments. Her more recent research deals with elderly care and dementia care in particular, and also in relation to new technologies and other material conditions and built environments.

Margaret Price is an associate professor of rhetoric/composition and disability studies at The Ohio State University, Columbus. Her book, *Mad at School: Rhetorics of Mental Disability and*

Academic Life (2011), won the Outstanding Book Award from the Conference on College Composition and Communication. She is a member of the Black Disability Studies Coalition and coordinator of the website Composing Access (http://composingaccess.net). She is now at work on a book titled, *Crip Spacetime.*

David Serlin is associate professor of communication and science studies at the University of California, San Diego, USA. His books include *Replaceable You: Engineering the Body in Postwar America* (University of Chicago Press, 2004), *Imagining Illness: Public Health and Visual Culture* (editor; 2010), *Keywords for Disability Studies* (co-editor; 2015) and *Window Shopping with Helen Keller: Architecture and Disability in Modern Culture* (forthcoming). He is a member of the editorial collective for the *Radical History Review,* an editor-at-large for *Cabinet,* and a founding editor of the online journal *Catalyst: Feminism, Theory, Technoscience.*

Tobin Siebers was professor of English language and literature, and art and design at the University of Michigan, USA, and also co-chair of the University of Michigan's Initiative on Disability Studies. He was author of two seminal volumes, *Disability Aesthetics* (2010) and *Disability Theory* (2008), as well as a wide range of other papers in disability studies.

Tanya Titchkosky is a professor at the University of Toronto, in the Department of Social Justice Education. Making use of her lived experience of dyslexia and her commitment to interpretive sociology, Tanya's work examines how the meaning of disability is made in relation to the built environment, knowledge production and other forms of interaction and cultural production. She is author of three books: *The Question of Access: Disability, Space, Meaning* (2011); *Reading and Writing Disability Differently: The Textured Life of Embodiment* (2007); and *Disability, Self and Society* (2003). With Rod Michalko, she has co-edited *Rethinking Normalcy: A Disability Studies Reader* (2009).

Stefan White is a Senior Enterprise Fellow at the Manchester School of Architecture (MSA), Manchester, UK. He directs the centre for Spatial Inclusion Design-research (cSIDr) alongside the post-graduate MSA Projects atelier (MSAp). An architect with a specialism in social and environmental sustainability, his research and practice explore the ethics of design.

Aaron Williamson is an artist whose interdisciplinary engagement with performance, objects, place and space is inspired by his experience of becoming deaf and by a politicised, yet humorous sensibility towards disability. During the last twenty years he has created over 300 performances, interventions, videos, installations and publications, for galleries, museums and festivals. A monograph, *Aaron Williamson – Performance, Video, Collaboration,* was published by the Live Art Development Agency in 2007. His awards include: the Helen Chadwick Fellowship at the British School at Rome; Artist Links, British Council, China; Three-Year Arts and Humanities Research Council (AHRC) Fellowship, Birmingham Institute of Art and Design, University of Central England (UCE); Adam Reynolds Memorial Bursary; Acme Studios Stephen Cripps Award; in addition to project funding through Arts Council

England, the British Council, Henry Moore Foundation and Esmée Fairbairn Foundation. Williamson holds a DPhil in critical theory from the University of Sussex (1997).

Bess Williamson is assistant professor, art history, theory and criticism at the School of Art Institute of Chicago, USA. She is a historian of design and material culture, focusing on social and political concerns in design, including environmental, labour, justice and rights issues as they shape and are shaped by spaces and things. Her current book project, *Designing an Accessible America*, traces the history of design responses to disability rights from 1945 to recent times. Her writing has appeared in *Winterthur Portfolio* and *American Studies*, with reviews in *Design and Culture* and *Design Issues*.

ACKNOWLEDGEMENTS

The editor and publisher gratefully acknowledge the following for permission to reproduce written material in this book.

David Serlin (2006) Excerpt from 'Disabling the *Flâneur*', *Journal of Visual Culture* 5: 2, 193–202, 206. Reprinted by permission of Sage Publications.

Rob Imrie (1999) Excerpt from 'The Body, Disability and Le Corbusier's Conception of the Radiant Environment', in Butler, R. and Parr, H. (eds) *Mind and Body Spaces: Geographies of Disability, Illness and Impairment*, London and New York: Routledge, pp 25–45. Reprinted by permission of Routledge.

Paul Hunt (1966) 'A Critical Condition', originally published in Hunt, P. (ed.) *Stigma: The Experience of Disability*, London: Geoffrey Chapman, pp 1–10. Reprinted by permission of Judy Hunt and The Disability Archive UK, University of Leeds Centre for Disability Studies. Available for free download at http://disability-studies.leeds.ac.uk/files/library/Hunt-critical-condition.pdf.

Liz Crow (2013) 'Lying down Anyhow: Disability and the Rebel Body', in Swain, J., French, S., Barnes, C. and Thomas, C. (eds) *Disabling Barriers – Enabling Environments*, 3rd edition, London: Sage. Reprinted by permission of Sage Publications.

Rod Michalko (2015) Originally presented in draft at the Canadian Association of Cultural Studies conference at McGill University in Montreal, 2011. By permission of the author.

Tobin Siebers (2006) 'Disability Aesthetics', *Journal for Cultural and Religious Theory* (*JCRT*) 7: 2, Spring/Summer, 63–72. Reprinted by permission of Jill Siebers.

Tanya Titchkosky and Rod Michalko (2012) 'The Body as a Problem of Individuality: A Phenomenological Disability Studies Approach', in Goodley, D., Hughes, B. and Davis, L. (eds) *Disability and Social Theory: New Developments and Directions*, Basingstoke: Palgrave Macmillan. Reprinted by permission from Palgrave Macmillan.

Aimi Hamraie (2013) Excerpt from 'Designing Collective Access: A Feminist Disability Theory of Universal Design'. Reprinted from *Disability Studies Quarterly* (*DSQ*) 33: 4 (online). Open Access Journal available for free download from http://dsq-sds.org/article/view/3871/3411. Reprinted by permission from the author.

J. Kent Fitzsimons (2016) 'More than Access: Overcoming Limits in Architectural and Disability Discourse'. This chapter was developed from an unpublished paper delivered at the Disability and Public Space conference in Oslo, Norway, in April 2011. A slightly different version of the discussion of Peter Eisenman's Memorial may be found in J. Kent Fitzsimons, 'Seeing Motion Otherwise: Architectural Design and the Differently Sensing and Mobile', *Space and Culture* 15: 3, August 2012. Printed by permission of the author.

Aaron Williamson (2010) 'The Collapsing Lecture', in Butt, G. (ed.) *Performing/Knowing*, Birmingham: ARTicle Press. Printed by permission of the author and ARTicle Press.

Jay Dolmage (2016) 'From Steep Steps to Retrofit to Universal Design, From Collapse to Austerity: Neo-Liberal Spaces of Disability'. This chapter was developed from a 2012 conference presentation for the Society of Disability Studies (SDS). Earlier work towards it is published in Dolmage, J. (2008) 'Inviting Disability in the Front Door', in Tassoni, J. and Reichert-Powell, D. (eds) *Composing Other Spaces*, Cresskill, NJ: Hampton Press, pp 121–144. Printed by permission of the author.

Peter Anderberg (2006) 'Where Does the Person End and the Technology Begin?' Excerpt from doctoral thesis, 'FACE: Disabled People, Technology and the Internet', Center for Rehabilitation Technology (CERTEC), Division of Rehabilitation Engineering Research, Department of Design Services, Lund University. Available for free download at: http://www.arkiv.certec.lth.se/doc/face/Anderberg_Peter_FACE-doctoral_thesis.pdf. Reprinted by permission from the author.

S. Lochlann Jain (1999) Excerpt from 'The Prosthetic Imagination: Enabling and Disabling the Prosthetic Trope', *Science, Technology and Human Values*, Winter 24: 1, 31–33, 38–40. Reprinted by permission from Sage Publications.

Bess Williamson (2012) 'Electric Moms and Quad Drivers: People with Disabilities Buying, Making, and Using Technology in Postwar America', *American Studies* 52: 1, 5–29. Reprinted by permission from *American Studies Journal*.

David Serlin (2010) 'Pissing without Pity: Disability, Gender, and the Public Toilet', in Molotch, H. and Norén, L. (eds) *Toilet: Public Restrooms and the Politics of Sharing*, New York: New York University Press, pp 167–185. Reprinted by permission of New York University Press.

Ingunn Moser (2006) 'Disability and the Promises of Technology: Technology, Subjectivity and Embodiment within an Order of the Normal', *Information, Communication & Society*, 9: 3, 373–395. Reprinted by permission of Taylor & Francis.

Todd Byrd (2007) 'Deaf Space' in *Gallaudet Today: the Magazine*, Spring. Reprinted by permission of Gallaudet University. Also available for free download from: http://www.gallaudet.edu/university_communications/gallaudet_today_magazine/deaf_space_spring_2007.html.

Amanda Cachia (2016) 'Along Disabled Lines. Claiming spatial agency through installation.' Some of this content appears in 'The Alterpodium: A Performative Design and Disability Intervention' in *Design and Culture: Journal of the Design Studies Forum*, Vol. 8, No. 3, Routledge/Taylor & Francis.

Sophie Handler (2008) 'Public Seating'. 'Resistant Sitting: The Pensioner's Alternative Street Furniture Guide' *Project Report*, London: RIBA/Ice McAslan Bursary. Reprinted by permission of the author.

FIGURE CREDITS

Chapter 1

Figures 1.1 and 1.2: From the collection of David Serlin.

Chapter 2

Figure 2.1 and 2.2: Photographs by Colin Bisset.

Chapter 4

Figure 4.1: © Matthew Fessey/Roaring Girl Productions. By permission of Liz Crow.

Chapter 6

Figures 6.1 and 6.2: © Paul McCarthy. Courtesy Paul McCarthy and Hauser & Wirth.
Figures 6.3 and 6.4: Leon A. Borensztein. With thanks to the CGAC.

Chapter 9

Figure 9.1: Photograph by Stephan Czuratis (Jazz-face), Creative Commons https://commons.wikimedia.org/w/index.php?curid=1288384.
Figure 9.2: Photograph by Mike Peel (www.mikepeel.net). Creative Commons https://commons.wikimedia.org/w/index.php?curid=32824026.
Figures 9.3 and 9.4: Drawing and photographs reprinted by permission of SANAA.

Chapter 10

Figure 10.1: Photograph by Ken MacLeod.
Figure 10.2: Photograph by Will Henderson-Nold. Reprinted by permission of Ed Roberts Campus.

Chapter 11

Figures 11.1, 11.2, 11.3 and 11.7: Table, drawing and diagrams by Stefan White.
Figure 11.5: Collage by Kat Timmins, Manchester School of Architecture.
Figures 11.6 and 11.7: Diagrams and photograph by Stefan White.

Chapter 12

Figures 12.2 and 12.3: Sketches by Thomas Carpentier.
Figure 12.4: Diagram reprinted by permission of UN Studio.
Figures 12.5 and 12.6: Table and sketch by Jos Boys.
Figures 12.7 and 12.8: Architectural drawings by Thomas Carpentier. Figure 12.8 reprinted with permission of Fondation Le Corbusier.

Chapter 13

Figures 13.1, 13.2 and 13.3: Photographs by Margaret Price.

Chapter 14

Figure 14.1: By permission of Aaron Williamson.
Figure 14.2 (top): Photograph by Manuel Vanson. Reprinted by permission of Aaron Williamson.
Figure 14.2 (bottom): Photograph by Warren Orchard. Reprinted by permission of Aaron Williamson.

Chapter 17

Figures 17.1, 17.2 and 17.3: Re-printed by permission of Post-Polio Health International.

Chapter 18

Figures 18.1 and 18.2: Photographs licensed under the Creative Commons Attribution 4.0 International License, http://creativecommons.org/licenses/by/4.0/.
Figures 18.3 and 18.4: Photographs by David Serlin.

Chapter 20

Figure 20.1: Reprinted by permission of Hansel Bauman.

Chapter 21

Figure 21.1: Photographs by courtesy of Corban Walker.

Figure 21.2: From the Collection of Gallerie dell'Accademia, Venice.

Figure 21.3: © ARS, NY. Photographic credit: Banque d'Images, ADAGP / Art Resource, New York.

Figures 21.4, 21.5 and 21.6: Photographs by courtesy of Wendy Jacob.

Figure 21.7: Gift of Jacqueline, Paul and Peter Matisse in memory of their mother Alexina Duchamp. 13-1972-9(303) Philadelphia Museum of Art. Marcel Duchamp: © Succession Marcel Duchamp / ADAGP, Paris / Artists Rights Society (ARS), New York 2016. Photographic Credit: The Philadelphia Museum of Art / Art Resource, New York.

Chapter 22

Figures 22.1 and 22.2: Photographs by Thea McMillan.

Figure 22.3: Photograph by David Barbour.

Chapter 23

Figures 23.1 and 23.2: Photographs by Verity-Jane Keefe.

Chapter 24

Figure 24.1: Reprinted by permission from Ehrmann Estate and with thanks to Chloe Parent. © DACS 2016.

Figures 24.2, 24.3, 24.4: Photographs by Justin Knight.

INTRODUCTION

Jos Boys

Disability sits in a peculiar position within architecture and urban design. Whilst readers and anthologies already exist that explore architecture and other identities of difference – such as gender (Matrix 1984, Weisman 1994, Massey 1994, Agrest et al. 1996, Hughes 1998, Borden et al. 1999), sexuality (Colomina 1992, Sanders 1996, Betsky 1997) and race (Lokko 2000, Barton 2001, Wilkins 2007) – disability as a concept, and disabled people as a constituency, continue to be assumed as completely separate from social or cultural politics. Within the discipline of architecture disability remains predominantly framed by design guidance and building regulations on the one hand, and by a 'common sense' language of accessibility and inclusive/universal design on the other. Neither of these approaches is wrong. What is extraordinary is that both because of and despite these existing framings, disability has somehow remained consistently stuck in a non-historical, atheoretical and – most crucially – *seriously underexplored* category in relationship to building design practices. It is invisible in both avant-garde and mainstream architectural theories and discourses, just as it is a persistent absence in critical and cultural theory more generally (Davis 2002, Davidson 2008). Perhaps this illustrates just how deeply disability remains widely avoided, compared to other disadvantaged identities. Unlike gender, race or sexuality then – and the feminist, post-colonial and queer studies which underpin associated scholarship and debate – it seems that we assume 'disability' to be unable to bring any kind of criticality or creativity to the discipline of architecture.

This Reader, then, is long overdue. It aims to break new ground by refusing to think of disability as an obvious and straightforward category – as mostly a design problem demanding a design solution. Rather, the many different contributors to this book understand disability *and* ability as ambiguous and relational; as shaped as much by everyday social and spatial practices as by specific impairments; and as a potentially powerful means to critically and creatively investigate, speculate about, and generate designs for built space. In fact, a big claim underpins these texts across their diverse perspectives and approaches – a belief that *starting from disability* can open up innovative and unexpected understandings across the whole range of architectural education and practices; its histories and theories; its attitudes towards, and deployment of, technologies; and in its design processes and practices.

What can architecture learn from disability?

To begin to do this, *Disability, Space, Architecture: A Reader* introduces students, educators and practitioners of architecture, planning and other built environment disciplines to some important emerging work that tries to think differently about disability *and* ability – dis/ability – and built space. In fact a rich seam of theoretical and critical thought already exists, but seems to have had almost no impact on architectural and related discourses, a huge gap for the subject. Through the developing field of disability studies, disability arts practice and disability activism, there are now many scholars, artists and advocates examining how disability intersects with social, spatial and material practices. Many of these studies and projects have a direct relevance to architecture. Most immediately this is because recent design thinking has increasingly re-centred the body. There has been a renewed interest in theories such as phenomenology, materialism, post-humanism and Deleuzian philosophy that help us to think harder about embodied experiences and what these mean for the design of built space. In moving away from modernist architecture and its dreams of a universal user (see Imrie this volume) there has been much concern with how to articulate bodies-in-space in a more sensual, dynamic and non-deterministic manner. Here, disability studies is both critiquing assumptions about what kinds of bodies *matter* in contemporary theories and commentaries, and opening up innovative kinds of critical and creative investigation of dis/ability as an embodied experience (Boys 2014, see also Serlin, Chapter 1, this volume). This is a wide-ranging engagement, intersecting with many of the theoretical frameworks currently influencing architectural thinking, as well as offering new insights into how social, spatial and material practices operate between and across dis/ability, race, sexuality, gender and class (see, in particular, Titchkosky and Michalko, Hamraie, White, and Serlin (Chapter 18), this volume). In addition, with contemporary shifts towards bio-mimicry, intelligent building and augmented reality in architecture, understanding the shifting inter-relationships between bodies and technologies are also becoming central. Here too, critiques and engagements with dis/ability can open up new ways of thinking (see Jain, Bess Williamson, Moser, and Serlin (Chapter 18), this volume).

Architecture and urban design can also learn by thinking differently about dis/ability through acknowledging, and engaging with, the considerable expertise of disabled people – as scholars, activists and as especially experienced users of built space. As Tobin Siebers puts it:

> disabled people have to be ingenious to live in societies that are by their design inaccessible and by their inclination prejudiced against disability. It requires a great deal of artfulness and creativity to figure out how to make it through the day when you are disabled, given the condition of our society.
>
> (From interview with Mike Levin, 2010 online)

Rather than, as too often happens, disabled people being treated as passive users of buildings and services, we need to realize that starting from the many diverse perspectives and experiences of disability and impairment offers something powerful back to architects and other built environment professionals. Taking notice of the narratives of disabled people themselves (see for example, Hunt, Crow, Michalko, Aaron Williamson, Anderberg, and Byrd this volume) offers new and creative ways of articulating how built space works from the perspective of 'unruly bodies' (Mintz 2007) and 'misfits' (Garland-Thompson 2011) rather than assumed normal and unnoticed forms of embodiment.

This is not only in terms of working towards more inclusive design improvements, but also about revealing architecture's deepest assumptions about what is valued and noticed, and what is marginalized and forgotten, in the processes of design. There are now many writers and artists specifically exploring inter-relationships between dis/ability, space and aesthetics in ways that connect very directly into debates and projects currently going on within architecture and other built environment disciplines (see Siebers, Dolmage, Price, and Cachia this volume). Some of this work is coming out of architectural education and practice itself, as well as from associated design fields. There is clearly an emerging interest in going beyond the reductivist logic of design guidance and building regulation, providing some productive explorations of what can happen when you start explicitly from differently abled bodies in built space (see Fitzsimons, White, Boys, McMillan and Lloyd Thomas, Handler, and Hendren this volume).

About this anthology

The contributors to *Disability, Space, Architecture: A Reader* come from a wide range of disciplines including architecture, geography, anthropology, health studies, English language and literature, rhetoric and composition, art history, disability studies and disability arts and performance. They produce work in diverse ways, from the personal to the theoretical, offering a range of perspectives and attitudes, which this anthology hopes to reflect in its overall selection of pieces. This has not aimed to be comprehensive, but instead to capture the flavours of an emerging set of intersections between and across disability, space and architecture.

The most immediate aim has been to bring together in one place some important and relevant texts and projects about dis/ability and built space, as well as expanding the field by commissioning new writing. Disability studies is an increasingly strong area of study, but one that remains fragmented and under-recognized, with its scholars spread worldwide and across many different university departments. Disabled artists who make creative work exploring aspects of dis/ability – like people interested in disability within architecture – are also often invisible or marginalized within these disciplines. The uneven global spread of scholars, artists and activists is equally expressed in where the reprinted pieces were originally published, often in non-mainstream or unexpected journals and publications. Nonetheless, there is clearly an expanding body of innovative and engaging work going on, which I hope will be as appealing and enlightening to you, the reader, as it was for me when I first discovered it. There are also, without a doubt, many important examples left out; and hopefully many more to be written and created. Some seminal publications are also listed in the 'recommended reading' section at the end of this introduction, to enable readers to place the pieces here in their broader context.

Disability, Space, Architecture: A Reader is divided into five parts – histories/narratives, theory and criticism, education, technologies/materialities and projects and practices. This is partly to demonstrate the considerable potential of dis/ability in asking interesting questions across the whole discipline of architecture; and partly to make it easier for readers to engage with preferred areas of interest. However, many of the pieces also 'cross-over' in their concerns, so these divisions can also be ignored, if preferred.

1   Histories/narratives aims to open up new spaces in architectural history, theory and design by introducing a number of both interpretative and personal disability histories. In a variety of ways these each critically engage with both assumptions of what constitutes a 'normal' body and what it means to start from disabled perspectives and experiences of impairment.

2   Theory and criticism explores some approaches that enable disability, space and architecture to be thought about together in innovative and challenging ways. It illustrates some of the kinds of critical and creative critiques that starting from dis/ability can offer to architectural and design theory and criticism.

3   Education offers examples of where rethinking dis/ability beyond design guidance and building regulations has the potential to generate alternative ways of teaching architectural design and of imagining different kinds of built space.

4   Technologies/materialities explores the critical and creative disruptions enabled by starting from dis/ability when thinking about augmented bodies and smart spaces and materials. Rather than be seduced by 'cyborg' technologies, the selected pieces reveal the more complex and nuanced understandings that come from both investigating the more 'debased' technologies usually associated with disabled people, and by taking notice of disabled perspectives on living with prosthetics.

5   Projects and practices brings together examples of work that illustrate some of the vibrant new projects being undertaken at the creative intersections between dis/ability and built spaces.

One final note. Most of the writers and practitioners here follow one of the central tenets of disability studies – research and practice must be more than an academic endeavour: it must also aim to improve the position of disabled people in society. Whilst architecture as it is taught and practised also has a strong underlying social commitment, this usually remains too vague and generalized to have any recognizable mainstream impact. This is particularly true of dis/ability that – as I noted at the beginning of this introduction – remains under-theorized and under-developed, across both mainstream and radical and community-based architecture. This concern for real change and improvement is also an aim of *Disability, Space, Architecture: A Reader*. By enabling easy access to a previously unknown or ignored body of work, the ultimate intention is to open up debate, and to generate new kinds of conversations, attitudes and approaches. By offering productive and interesting ways of engaging with dis/ability, all the contributors to this anthology hope to increasingly make it a *normal* part of architectural discourse and practices, rather than something to be avoided, feel awkward about, or 'contain' within the category inclusive design, or a merely regulatory demand. Longer term, the intended impact on the discipline is not only about making more accessible places (although this remains essential), but also about rethinking the very shape of architecture itself – finding ways to shift attitudes and approaches to disability *and* ability, and expanding explorations of what the critical and creative implications of this might be for architectural education, scholarship and practice.

Recommended further reading

Boys, J. (2014) *Doing Disability Differently: An Alternative Handbook on Dis/Ability, Architecture and Designing for Everyday Life,* London and New York: Routledge.

Corker, M. and Shakespeare, T. (eds) (2002) *Disability/Postmodernity: Embodying Disability Theory,* London: Continuum.

Davis, L. J. (1995) *Enforcing Normalcy: Disability, Deafness, and the Body,* London: Verso.

Davis, L. J. (ed.) (1997) *The Disability Studies Reader,* London: Routledge.

Michalko, R. (2002) *The Difference that Disability Makes,* Philadelphia, PA: Temple University Press.

Seibers, T. (2008) *Disability Theory,* Ann Arbor, MI: University of Michigan Press.

Seibers, T. (2010) *Disability Aesthetics,* Ann Arbor, MI: University of Michigan Press.

Snyder, S. L., Brueggemann, B. and Garland-Thomson, R. (2002) (eds) *Disability Studies: Enabling the Humanities,* New York: Modern Language Association of America.

Titchkosky, T. (2011) *The Question of Access: Disability, Space, Meaning,* Toronto: University of Toronto Press.

Titchkosky, T. and Michalko, R. (eds) (2009*) Re-thinking Normalcy: A Disability Studies Reader,* Toronto: Canadian Scholars' Press Inc.

PART I
Histories/narratives

I suggested in the introduction that disability tends to be mainly treated within architecture in a completely ahistorical way. This may be by assuming that disabled people can be defined through a series of unproblematic and unchanging categories such as wheelchair user, deaf, blind or visually impaired. Or that disability itself, and its relationship to the built environment, has no history (or not one that is worth investigating) but is simply a matter of technicalities – design guidance and legal requirements. Or that explicitly introducing disability as a concept and/or disabled people's perspectives and experiences into architectural history is too problematic or marginal to consider.

Yet, looking at disability through time (both through historical study and via personal narratives) reveals a considerable amount about how particular kinds of bodies become normalised in different periods and places; how what comes to be considered normal depends equally crucially on the framing and marginalisation of *non-normal* bodies; how built space is implicated in these processes; and how 'what is normal' changes – that is, comes to be implemented, perpetuated, adapted, contested and transformed through time.

A central thread within disability studies has been to unravel the interrelationships between changing concepts of the ideal/normal/average body and the disabled body – with its persistent naming as monster and freak, that is, as less than human (Davis 1997; Garland-Thomson 1996; Stiker 2000; Stephens 2011). This is often a horrifying history for disabled people, linked as it has been to ideas about perfectible versus degenerate bodies in eugenics (leading for example to the mass murder of disabled people by the Nazis – see Silberman 2015) and to the continuing enforced incarceration and maltreatment of those with disabilities in many countries (Ben-Moshe et al. 2014; Soldatic et al. 2014). Definitions of what constitute 'good' and 'bad' bodies also underpin our assumptions about work, both assuming and demanding a specific type of productive and competent body, which act to marginalise the more fragile and vulnerable as non-productive and thus without value (Ervelles 1996, 2011). Importantly, discrimination and de-valuing of disabled people is not something that can be relegated to the past. Paul Hunt's eloquent analysis of his situation as a disabled man – 'A critical condition' originally published in 1966 and reprinted here – not only reminds us that disabled people have been segregated and institutionalised until very recently (and still are in many places and contexts), but also how crucial disabled people themselves have been to campaigns for accessibility and universal/inclusive design; in his case through the founding of the Union of Physically Impaired Against Segregation (UPIAS).

Understanding the contested history of bodily norms also means looking more critically at how these have been translated into 'standard' architectural practices – that is, have become part of everyday common sense designers' assumptions about bodies-in-space. What, for example, are the links between earlier eugenic beliefs and the typical ergonomic and anthropometric data that are still used mechanically in architectural education and practice today, based as these are on standardised and 'average' bodies (Lambert 2012; Lambert and Pham 2015)? Or we can ask what kinds of bodies are assumed in campaigns for shared spaces (Imrie 2012, 2013), active design guidance (Price, this volume; see also Keller 2016) or sustainability and environmentalism (Kafer 2013)? The first essay in this section, by David Serlin, explores how we can trouble a particular kind of figure – the *flâneur* – that continues to have a lot of resonance within architectural education and practice as well as across other disciplines. Serlin argues that this concept of a leisured street-walker, who has been an icon of urban modernity since the 19th century, needs to be made problematic and re-evaluated from a disability perspective. He does this by opening up the intersections between and across the sensorial and tactile experiences of disabled people, thus challenging the able-bodied privileges embodied in *flanerie* (for an equivalent feminist critique see, for example, Wolff 1985, 2008).

The second piece in this section is by geographer Rob Imrie, one of the very few people who has been exploring over many years how to think critically about disability and the built environment in relation to its design and regulatory practices. 'The body, disability, and Le Corbusier's concept of the radiant environment' from 1999, is a seminal example of such an approach, and critically engages with the problematic norm of the 'modern' body.

Both Liz Crow and Rod Michalko, in their essays in this anthology, also aim to trouble assumptions about what 'proper' bodies do, and what 'improper' bodies should not do. In 'Lying down anyhow: disability and the rebel body' Crow reminds us of some of the taken-for-granted everyday social, spatial and material practices about what is acceptable to do and where. In public spaces, to be ordinary and normal (and therefore to be both someone who takes no notice and who can go unnoticed) is to be independent, autonomous, mobile and have the appearance of mental competence. Lying down in public, on the other hand, aligns you with 'suspect' types – homeless, vagrant, mentally suspect – and with shirking, with not working in the normal manner. In her artistic practice, Crow has also explored this assumption of a clear private/public divide in acceptable behaviours as experienced by disabled people through her ongoing project, Bedding Out (http://www.roaring-girl.com/).

For Rod Michalko, the experience of going blind has also been about the experience of sighted peoples' unease. Michalko has written extensively and brilliantly about blindness and disability in ways that intertwine personal narrative with theoretical investigation (1998a, 1998b, 2002). In 'Blinding the power of sight' he details just one everyday encounter to unravel two interrelated aspects. This is, first, how 'normal' social and spatial practices – the assumptions of the sighted – are confused and disrupted by disability; and second, the gap between living with and knowing blindness as a *normal* life, and its common sense amongst the non-disabled as a difference so fearful as to be worse than death, so terrible as to freeze up their ordinary social interactions. Crucially, in both these pieces, the 'problem' is not disability per se, but operates in the complex and contested encounters between disability *and* ability. Histories and narratives, then, need to expose the ableism embodied in everyday 'common sense' about how the world works, just as much as it increases our understandings of disability history (Campbell 2009).

As the next part, theory and criticism, shows in more depth, much of the work in disability studies has been informed by an interest in theories of the everyday; in ways of better understanding how particular types of bodies come to be normalised through specific social, spatial and material practices that not only affect how we talk about dis/ability but are also embodied and situated, that is, are constantly enacted through the 'ordinary' things we *do*. If architecture as a discipline is also to better understand how built space intertwines with such everyday practices which 'just happen' to locate normal bodies and disabled bodies *differently and differentially,* then we need to begin to critically and creatively interrogate the many histories of how social, spatial and material practices have operated across and through the design of built space. And we need to pay attention to narratives that start from the perceptions and experiences of disability. The recommended further reading here suggests some routes, both through existing disability histories (of which there are still far too few) and by paying attention to diverse disabled perceptions and experiences, of which there are already many powerful and relevant stories written.

Finally, it should be noted that whilst the readings in this collection are all centrally concerned with analysing how dis/ability 'works' to articulate conceptual, social and material spaces in particular ways rather than others, there is also an emerging disability history and theory that starts from disability as a means to interrogate beyond itself. This, as Galis argues, does 'not involve the privileged study of either impaired bodies or socio-material constructions, but the analysis of situations where the interactions of bodies and materiality/culture produce action or inaction, ability or disability' (Galis 2011: 830–831). A recent example is Rebecca Sanchez's *Deafening Modernism: Embodied Language and Poetics in American Literature* (2015) that explores the history of modernist literature from the perspective of Deaf critical insight. This is not about deafness per se. It is about starting from deaf culture as a means to investigate cultural modernism differently, so as to discover new and alternative insights. Sanchez's study also demonstrates the emergent potential of starting from the 'non-normal' as an exploratory tool that could offer new kinds of critical and creative understandings of aspects of art, design and architectural history, as well as cultural history more generally.

Recommended further reading

Bradshaw, M. (ed.) (2016) *Disabling Romanticism*, London: Palgrave Macmillan.

Corker, M. and French, S. (eds) (1999) *Disability Discourse*, Buckingham: Open University Press.

Davis, L. J. (1997) 'Constructing Normalcy: The Bell Curve, the Novel and the Invention of the Disabled Body in the Nineteenth Century', in L. Davis (ed.) *The Disability Studies Reader*, New York: Routledge, 9–28.

Davis, L. J. (2015) *Enabling Acts: The Hidden Story of the Americans with Disability Act Gave the Largest US Minority its Rights*, Boston, MA: Beacon Press.

Essaka, J. (2011) 'The Drifting Language of Architectural Accessibility in Victor Hugo's *Notre-Dame de Paris*', *Disability Studies Quarterly* 31 (3) (online), available at: http://dsq-sds.org/article/view/1677

Grandin, T. (2006) *Thinking in Pictures: My Life with Autism*, New York: Vintage, Reissue Edition.

Guffey, E. (2015) 'The Scandinavian Roots of the International Symbol of Access', *Design and Culture* 7(3): 357–376.

Guffey, E. (2017) *Ab/Normal: History of a Mis-fit Symbol*, London: Bloomsbury Academic.

Hamraie, A. (2016) 'Universal Design and the Problem of Post-Disability Ideology', *Design and Culture* 8(3): 1–25.

Hockenberry, J. (1995) *Moving Violations: A Memoir. War Zones, Wheelchairs, and Declarations of Independence*, New York, Hyperion.

Imrie, R. (2013) 'Buildings That Fit Society: The Modernist Ideal and The Social Production of Ableist Spaces', in Model House Research Group (ed.) *Transcultural Modernisms*, Berlin and New York: Sternberg Press, 208–219.

Linton, S. (2015) *My Body Politic: A Memoir*, Ann Arbor, MI: University of Michigan Press.

Jain, S. L. (2013) *Malignant: How Cancer Becomes Us*, Oakland, CA: University of California Press.

Mairs, N. (1996) *Waist-High in the World: A Life Among the Nondisabled*, Boston, MA: Beacon Press.

Michalko, R. (1998) *The Two in One: Walking with Smokie, Walking with Blindness*, Philadelphia, PA: Temple University Press.

Michalko, R. (2002) *The Difference that Disability Makes*, Philadelphia, PA: Temple University Press.

Millet-Gallant, A. and Howie, E. (Eds)(2016) *Disability and Art History*, London & New York: Routledge.

Mintz, S. (2009) (ed.) *Unruly Bodies: Life Writing by Women with Disabilities*, Oakland, CA: California University Press.

Morris, J. (1996) (ed.) *Encounters with Strangers: Feminism and Disability*, London: The Women's Press, 206–226.

Samuels, E. (2014) *Fantasies of Identification: Disability, Gender, Race*, New York: NYU Press.

Sanchez, R. (2015) *Deafening Modernism: Embodied Language and Visual Poetics in American Literature*, New York and London: New York University Press.

Schweik, S. M. (2010) *The Ugly Laws: Disability in Public*, New York: New York University Press.

Serlin, D. (2012) 'On Walkers and Wheelchairs. Disabling the Narratives of Urban Modernity', *Radical History Review* 114, 19–28.

Serlin, D. (forthcoming) *Window Shopping with Helen Keller: Architecture and Disability in Modern Culture*, Chicago, IL: University of Chicago Press.

Silberman, S. (2015) *Neurotribes. The Legacy of Autism and How to Think Smarter About People Who Think Differently*, Sydney and London: Allen and Unwin.

Stiker, H.-J. (2000) Translated by Sayers W. *A History of Disability*, Ann Arbor, MI: University of Michigan Press.

Titchkosky, T. (2003) *Disability, Self and Society*, Toronto: University of Toronto Press.

Williamson, B. (2012) 'Getting a Grip: Disability in American Industrial Design of the Late Twentieth Century', *Winterthur Portfolio* 46 (4): 213–236, Winter.

Williamson, B. (2017) *Designing an Accessible America: A History of Design and Disability in the United States*, New York: New York University Press

1

DISABLING THE *FLÂNEUR*

David Serlin (2006)

Excerpt reprinted from Journal of Visual Culture *(2006)
5: 193–206, pp 193–200, 206.*

On 29 January 1937, an editor for *Le Soir*, one of Paris's many competing daily newspapers, made arrangements to photograph Helen Keller window-shopping on the fashionable avenue des Champs-Élyseés. Keller, the world's most famous – and, arguably, most photographed – deaf-blind person, visited Paris during a brief tour of Europe before preparing for her historic journey to Japan in the spring. The following morning, on 30 January, Keller and Polly Thomson – Keller's assistant for over two decades and primary traveling companion after Anne Sullivan's death just three months earlier in October 1936 – took breakfast at the Hotel Lancaster on the rue de Berri and went out promenading on the avenue, stopping long enough for one of *Le Soir*'s photographers to preserve the moment for posterity (Figure 1.1). Later that day, Keller recorded the event, with self-conscious delight, in the journal that she kept of her daily activities: 'Polly and I walked out with [the photographer] and he took pictures of us on the Champs-Élysées beside a shop window resplendent with Paris hats and gowns…Seeing everybody here in the pink of fashion doesn't tend to lull my feminine vanity' (Keller 1938, 164).

In the photograph, Keller and Thomson stand side by side in front of a boutique window showcasing a selection of belted and embroidered dresses, patterned chemises with cravats, and form-fitting cloche hats in delicate, light fabrics, suggestive of the coming spring, which stand in enormous contrast to the textured, heavy winter coats worn by the two passers-by. Their apparent delight in and longing for the consumer goods that have captured their attention is marked not only by the message that Keller communicates directly into Thomson's hand, the paleness of which is centered against the backdrop of their black winter coats, but also by the reflections of both women mirrored in the window's glass that seem to haunt the shop's interior and our reception of the event. Indeed, the sumptuous display behind glass serves as a kind of visual analogue for Keller herself, who experiences the clothing in the shop window not through tactile means but through virtual projection as mediated through Thomson's gaze and subsequent description. Keller, who was fifty-seven when the photograph was taken, clearly had more than a passing interest in clothes,

FIGURE 1.1 Helen Keller (left) and her companion, Polly Thomson, window-shopping on the Avenue des Champs-Élysées, Paris. Originally published in *Le Soir* (Paris), 31 January 1937

Photograph from the collection of the author

which gave her the space to engage the tactile pleasures of the phenomenological world while simultaneously satisfying her own 'feminine vanity.' The day after posing for *Le Soir*'s photographer, for instance, Keller described in her diary a visit to the atelier of the *grande couturieuse* Elsa Schiaparelli, who was only too happy to have her material creations linked to the world's most famous deaf-blind person, a person who wanted to be recognized as disabled but also irreducibly female. 'I was sorry that [one of Schiaparelli's dresses] could not be made for me in a day,' she wrote disappointedly, 'but my hands were crammed with loveliness as one robe after another appeared' (Keller 1938, 169).

One could also argue that, for all of its putative playfulness, the photograph's two mutually constitutive subjects – the two women on the one hand and the boutique's goods on the other – are divided practically down the middle, suggesting a symbiosis of theme and form as well as a distinct separation, if not a potential gulf, between its two halves. Such a division is not an insignificant insight into Keller's own biography. As Kim E. Nielsen has argued, representations of Keller in the popular media during the course of her life tended to embody the dialectic between nineteenth-century gestures of sentimental womanhood and twentieth-century instantiations of the New Woman. Images of Keller equivocate between the 'publicly pitied deaf and blind young virgin' and 'the politically safe, but glorified, superblind saintly spinster' (Nielsen 2004, 50). Nielsen argues that, trapped within this gendered logic of comprehensibility, Keller frequently tempered her public persona by fulfilling expectations of what the public wanted her to be and, when necessary, taking the appropriate measures to distance herself from other disabled people in order to assert claims to a more normative subjectivity. Keller's desire to be seen as special and on her terms, however, was not incompatible with the editorial goals of a daily newspaper like *Le Soir*, which sought to present Keller and Thomson as special yet also infinitely capable of performing the predictable rituals of female conspicuous consumption. Is it not unseemly, then, to ask: for what audience(s) was this photograph intended, and for what purposes? If the photograph is simply a news item lifted from daily life in Paris during the late 1930s, then *what*, exactly, is newsworthy about it, and what elements of urban culture does it document?

Perhaps the photograph's explicit commercial power and unapologetic consumerism – both the convention of window-shopping and the adaptation of Keller and Thomson within it – capture the imagination precisely because they confirm the promise of a certain kind of normative subject position that under the right circumstances the disabled person, for whom Keller serves metonymically, might perform in public. As Rosemarie Garland-Thomson has written, 'Realist disability photography is the rhetoric of equality, most often turned utilitarian…Realism domesticates disability' (Garland-Thomson 2002, 69). Unlike photographs of disabled figures in the urban milieu such as Paul Strand's famous *Blind Woman* (1917), for instance, a watershed moment in a genealogy of 'high' modern figurations of disability, the image of Keller and Thomson might have functioned somewhat differently within early-twentieth-century French popular media (Mirzoeff 1995, 51–53). The blind figure in traditional eighteenth and nineteenth-century French art, as Nicholas Mirzoeff has argued, was almost always gendered male, though exceptions – as in the case of the female 'blind justice' – conceded more to mythological tropes than to social realities. A categorical icon in the pantheon of Western cultural fantasies, from Tiresias onward, of the blind person whose judicious inner eye can 'see' beyond the superficial distractions of the external world, such figures were used in the political iconography of the early republic to demonstrate the Enlightenment triumph of humanist reason in order to build a new egalitarian society that would replace old aristocratic corruption. Well into the twentieth century, however, the blind were far more accustomed either to social isolation in institutions far from the public view or, in more dire circumstances, survival through street begging, than the metaphorical insight endowed upon them by artists and philosophers. Indeed, if there is common thread within disability history in the nineteenth and early twentieth centuries, it is not that people with physical and cognitive impairments went traipsing down the Champs-Élysées but instead were deliberately segregated from their fellow citizens, occupying domestic or rehabilitative or institutional spaces where they might be cared for (if they were cared for at all), and routinely excluded and often prohibited from public spaces. The vaunted promises of French republican values, in other words, rang hollow for the disabled and instead barred them from cultural recognition and political participation except, perhaps, for those whose wealth or status effectively neutralized the reductive equation of bodily difference with social incompatibility.

The most obvious, and most regularly sustained, exception to this disparity between the promise of republican values and the exclusion of the disabled was provided by photographic representations of *les mutilés de guerre* (disabled war veterans), the wholesale bombardment of which French newspaper readers and newsreel viewers had become accustomed to in the interwar years (Figure 1.2). One news photograph, taken approximately two years earlier in December 1934, depicts a demonstration by disabled veterans of the First World War who are marching down the sidewalk of the Champs-Élyseés and waving French flags to attract the attention of pedestrians and automobile drivers. The powerful iconographic value of this procession of middle-aged veterans moving slowly across cold, wet pavement on canes and crutches, many sporting berets and decorations in deference to their military service as well as mustaches often cultivated to conceal battle scars, makes a dramatic visual contrast with the elegant, *beaux arts* shapes of the storefront façades, apartment buildings, and shiny sedans that seem to be moving, as if with teleological certainty, in an entirely different direction. This is a markedly different strategy for representing disability than that used in the photograph of Keller and Thomson. In early-twentieth-century France, wounded veterans were seen as symbols of enormous personal sacrifice to the nation-state, and as such occupied an esteemed position in the social hierarchy of disability since their bodily difference was equated with tropes of patriotic citizenship and domestic care giving (Panchasi 1995; Sherman 1999). Furthermore, French war veterans with disabilities – the image of which is crystallized by the amputee in the foreground perched resignedly on crutches – were at the forefront of what might be called anachronistically a disability rights movement, forming extensive networks

FIGURE 1.2 Disabled veterans of the First World War demonstrating for increased pensions and benefits on the Avenue des Champs-Élysées, Paris. Photograph taken ca. December 1934

Photograph from the collection of the author.

of military fraternities and mutual aid societies, demanding improved pension and health benefits from the French government, and organizing protest marches on symbolic (and tourist-heavy) thoroughfares like the Champs-Élyseés (Prost 1992).

Perhaps this is why, in the end, the photograph of Keller and Thomson remains so striking. It presents a gendered alternative to displays of bodily difference by forging connections between the public representation of disability and its heretofore-unrealized corollaries in the realms of paparazzi, fashion, and documentary photography that so characterized visual culture in Paris during the 1930s. The image of Keller and Thomson challenges the male-defined public culture of disability by invoking the kind of gendered images of consumption and urban pleasure with which the French public was well acquainted during the interwar years including the New Woman, the androgynous *garçonne*, and the single working girl (Roberts 1994; Stewart 2001; Chadwick and Ladimer 2003). Yet the photograph's deliberate blurring of the visual codes of window-shopping with the visual codes of public disability also has the effect, intentional or otherwise, of distinguishing Keller not only from disabled veterans but also from images of women that, historically, saturated the French popular imagination. Indeed, the photograph depicting a deaf-blind woman window-shopping may have been a point of ironic juxtaposition with the complex public iconography of the *Parisienne*, the single girl-about-town who inhabited *fin-de-siècle* urban culture as memorialized in the graphic poster art of Henri de Toulouse-Lautrec, which combined coquettish playfulness and robust sexuality two decades before the emergence of the New Woman (Nesbit 1992).

Rather than codifying – and, to some degree, essentializing – the differences between the masculine terrain traversed by protesting veterans and the feminine terrain traversed by Keller and Thomson, perhaps it would be more productive to see the two women and the parade of men as independent but dialectically linked actors within the complex and highly contested epistemological terrain of urban modernity. In other words, how might we make space for Helen Keller, veterans, and other disabled urbanites in the voluminous literature on the *flâneur*?

Scholarship devoted to the enduring significance of *flânerie*, from its historical origins in early-nineteenth-century Paris to its most well-known iterations by Charles Baudelaire, Walter Benjamin, and a host of writers and critics throughout the twentieth century, is something of a cottage industry in contemporary visual and cultural studies as well as within historical studies of modern and postmodern urban cultures (Baudelaire 1972; Benjamin 1978; Buck-Morss 1991; Tester 1994; White 2001). Priscilla Parkhurst Ferguson, for instance, has argued that the *flâneur* is not a singular urban type but a multivalent urban icon, developing from the lazy, unproductive figure of the 1830s to the mid-century mock-artist to the famously perambulating gadfly-about-town of the 1870s to the anachronistic figure of urban modernity whose primary association with enclosed shopping arcades Benjamin so lovingly delineated in writings that overlapped chronologically with Keller's appearance on the streets of Paris (Ferguson 1994). Such shifting tides of meaning across a century and a half track a constant recalibration of the *flâneur* from aloof observation to conspicuous consumption. The phenomenological inspiration derived from *flânerie* has played a central component in genealogies of modern experience that can be traced to late-nineteenth-century urban visual spectacles such as window displays, wax museums, and early cinema (Crary 2001; Charney and Schwartz 1996; Friedberg 1994; Schwartz 1999). In all of these scholarly explorations, however, there is a constant and, arguably, almost tacit commitment to the normative elements of the *flâneur*'s physical experience – betrayed implicitly by what some critics have rightly insisted as modernism's tendency toward ocularcentrism or the 'hegemony of vision' – that is not factored into discussions of *flânerie* nor, for that matter, the codes of urban modernity that are assumed to crystallize around certain kinds of acts (observing, shopping, collecting) or sensorial experiences (listening, moving, gazing) associated with the *flâneur*'s body (Levin 1993). Despite its adoption within a range of academic disciplines and theoretical approaches, scholars continue to preserve the notion of the *flâneur* as a paradigmatic example of the modern subject who takes the functions of his or her body for granted.

Certainly, there are more nuanced exceptions to this paradigmatic approach to *flânerie*. As early as 1841, for example, Louis Hart's *Le Physiologie du flâneur* implied that the *flâneur*'s foppish caprice carried all of the sexual (and, often, homosexual) connotations of physical and social difference found in nineteenth-century pseudoscientific tracts on physiognomy and phrenology (Ferguson 1994, 26). A century and a half later, in the 1980s and 1990s, feminist scholars in urban studies and visual culture studies carved out space for the *flâneuse* in order to problematize the male privilege implicit in discussions of *flânerie* and inscribe women's place in the social etiologies of nineteenth- and twentieth-century urban modernity (Parsons 2000; Pollock 1988; Wilson 2001; Wolff 1985). Yet even within such groundbreaking studies, making claims for the *flâneur* or the *flâneuse* as agents of modern experience already presumes that the codes of urban modernity – what really counts as urban and/or modern – are organized around narratives of normative able-bodiedness. The shopping adventures of Keller and Thomson and the protest activities of disabled veterans on the streets of Paris in the mid-1930s may point to the different semiotic registers in which public definitions of disability were communicated and understood in the popular imagination, but they also point to the reasons why the liberal, autonomous subject of modernity must be able-bodied for canonical understandings of *flânerie* to survive (Breckenridge and Vogler 2001). If we define modernity only through a recognizable set of compulsory able-bodied acts such as walking, looking, and hearing, then we exclude a sizeable proportion of the population, both in historical perspective as well as in contemporary experience. In the literature on urban modernity, disabled people – regarded by dominant discourses as tragic and dependent upon paternalistic forms of care and attention – hardly ever get to drink absinthe, let alone relish the opportunity to hold the crystal goblet.

Such limited interpretations of the urban subject clearly had little or no lasting effect on Keller, a person who believed not only that one could experience modernity through senses other than sight or hearing but that one could appear modern, act modern, feel modern, and *be* modern without relying upon any of the meanings attached to bodily difference as either proscribed by her contemporaries or codified retrospectively by historians of urban modernity. Keller, for one, did not think that she herself was excluded from the boulevards of modernity. As she wrote in her diary, on the same day that she posed for *Le Soir*, she and Thomson

> went alone for a stroll…The air was soft, the moon was snowing its loveliness upon the city. The traffic was at a low ebb. We went as far as the Rue Royale, passing

Maxim's, looking in the shop windows which are the undoing of unwary mortals, Polly noticing especially the jewelry, rare antiques, and Lalique glass. Everywhere I recognized the odor peculiar to Paris – perfumes, powders, wines, and tobacco agreeably blended…. This is the real Paris in winter, and the more I see of it the better it pleases me…

(Keller 1938, 169)

As any connoisseur of modernist literature will confirm, engagement with the phenomenological world through smell, taste, and touch was deemed a standard component of urban *flânerie*, enabling one to experience modern cityscapes through senses other than sight and sound (Hammergren 1994). Anthony Vidler has argued that the august pronouncements of Le Corbusier, the French avatar of modernist architecture during the early twentieth century who claimed that the disorderly and unhealthy body was an analogue to the disorderly and unhealthy city, were merely products of fantasy that held bodily difference and thus social difference in thrall (Vidler 1992). Yet such fantasies have not prevented scholars from writing about the experiences of the disabled in cities like Paris, when they are considered at all, as examples of the perceived incommensurability between disorderly bodies and rectilinear architectural experiments, Art Deco façades, or the ironic pre-postmodern reveries of the *flâneur*. Keller's pleasurable tactile and olfactory sensations of the modern city help reconstitute elements of her biography, especially for the ways in which touch and smell functioned in her immediate environment and enabled her to negotiate geographical and physical spaces as well as social and political ones (Fuss 2004; Feld 2005).

Perhaps the willful exclusion of disabled bodies from the literature on *flânerie* has something to do with how the embodied experience of disability challenges and even thwarts cultural expectations of the firm division between public and private spheres. Victor Burgin has written that, 'The *flâneur* who turns the street into a living room commits an act of transgression which reverses an established distinction between public and private spaces…[and makes visible] the survival of precapitalist social forms that had not yet succumbed to the modern segregation of life into public and private zones' (Burgin 1996, 145). Burgin's observation echoes that of Benjamin, who wrote in 1936 that the *flâneur* has a tendency to 'turn the boulevard into an *interieur*,' and that 'The street becomes a dwelling for the *flâneur*; he is as much at home among the facades of houses as the citizen is in his four walls' (Benjamin 1978, 37). One could argue that this is precisely what the body of the disabled *flâneur* does when it circulates or is visibly represented in public spaces. The disabled *flâneur* visibly alters perceptions of public space by exposing that which has typically pertained to the '*interieur*' – visible bodily differences as well as the invisible effects of institutionalization or, in more contemporary circumstances, networks of care giving and mutual support – to the outside world in ways that are anathema to narratives of modern autonomy. The routine institutionalization of people with mental or physical disabilities certainly contributed to the limitation of some disabled bodies in public space, especially those regarded as social dangers, whereas different categories of impairment may have been supported by different categories of freedom. In the mid-1930s, the disabled body of the veteran was a highly visible, and highly gendered, component of the French public sphere, sustained by correlations between male bodily sacrifice and the impassioned defense of French civility under duress. In one account published in a French journal for war veterans in 1917, for example, an officer riding on the Paris metro observes a disabled ex-serviceman board the metro car. Noticing that none of the passengers are willing to vacate their seats for the veteran, the officer accosts a 'young man of robust appearance' and implores him, 'Come on, young civilian, give up your seat to this wounded man.' The young man tilts his hat deferentially to the officer and awkwardly replies, 'Excuse me, Captain, but I have lost a leg' (Prost 1992, 30).

The nuanced negotiations between private and public spheres that disabled bodies endured in the 1930s took multiple forms, emboldened not only by the sensorial experiences identified with urban modernity but through the innovations of space-time compression identified as hallmarks of technological modernity. As Rebecca Scales has written, 'In 1928, just a few years after the first radio broadcast from the Eiffel Tower, two new radio charities, *Radio for the Blind* and *Wireless at the Hospital*, took up the task of distributing free radios to invalids and the blind, with the goal of putting these "brave and poor people into contact with *exterior* life" and ending their "isolation" in the private sphere' (Scales 2006, 2). By 1939, Theodor Adorno recognized radio technology as making possible a kind of aural *flânerie*, thereby identifying airspace as one in which virtually all citizens could spatially perambulate and discover new narrative experiences of modern life (Buck-Morss 1985, 105). The disabled person that emerges from isolation to ride across urban space via city streets, underground trains, or radio waves inverts the perceived distinction between private and public by using his or her private body as the crucible in which he or she forges public identity, and thus challenges the presumption that disability is the antithesis of modernism's programmatic functionalism.

For scholars of modernism, the multiple urban subjectivities of the disabled remain largely unintelligible because the dynamic textures of sensory and psychic experience are too regularly subordinated to, and held captive by, the valorized gaze of the *flâneur*. Even with the best of intentions, such a critical predilection effectively naturalizes the presumptive link between modern subjectivity and the privileges of the visual. One could argue that an ocularcentric epistemology follows directly from the canonical work on bodily difference provided by early- and mid-twentieth-century photographers, such as August Sander and Weegee, who sought out both formal and informal methods for documenting urban typologies (Serlin and Lerner 1997). In French visual culture of the 1920s and 1930s, images of racial and ethnic types, homeless men, itinerant families, and those with bodily differences were regularly exploited by the camera and spanned a range of both commercial products and avant-garde experiments, used to demonstrate either humanist narratives of endurance in the face of adversity or else, in the case of the surrealists, used to explore the uncanny textures of the urban unconscious (Walker 2002). In this context, the image of Keller and Thomson window-shopping in late January 1937 represented both an epistemological challenge to the ocularcentric conventions of *flânerie* as well as a distinct shift in the generic conventions used to depict bodily difference. For some, the photograph may have suggested that the reveries associated with conspicuous consumption could be no longer naturalized as the exclusive purview of the able-bodied, and that such reveries might be indulged by anyone, regardless of bodily difference, perhaps even by a famous deaf-blind female tourist. The photograph confirms the presence of a disabled female body that was not only capable of promenading openly on a famous Parisian thoroughfare but one whose subjective experience as an autonomous modern subject who derives pleasure from window-shopping had the capacity to transform the meaning of disability in the popular imagination.

2

THE BODY, DISABILITY AND LE CORBUSIER'S CONCEPTION OF THE RADIANT ENVIRONMENT

Rob Imrie (1999)

Excerpt reprinted from R. Butler and H. Parr (eds) (1999)
Mind and Body Spaces: Geographies of Disability, Illness and
Impairment, *London and New York: Routledge, pp 25–45.*

> Proportion is the commensuration of the various constituent parts with the whole.
> For no building can possess the attributes of composition…unless there exists that
> perfect conformation of parts which may be observed in a well formed human body.
>
> (Vitruvius 1960)

One of the critical contexts for the perpetuation and reproduction of social inequalities is
the built environment (Crowe 1995; Knox 1987; Laws 1994a, 1994b). For disabled people
in particular, the built environment is often encountered as a series of hostile, exclusive and
oppressive spaces. Examples abound of discriminatory architectural design, including steps
into shops and public buildings, inaccessible transport, and the absence of colour coding and
induction loops. Indeed, most housing in the United Kingdom is not wheelchair accessible,
yet for the House Builders Federation (1995) this is barely an issue. As they state, 'if a disabled
person visits a homeowner, it is to be expected that they can be assisted over the threshold'
(HBF 1995:1). Moreover, in the 1997 British general election, 75 per cent of polling offices
were inaccessible to people in wheelchairs, while few contained the technical aids to permit
visually impaired and/or blind people to mark their vote on the polling papers. In Lefebvre's
(1968) terms, such representations of space project the dominant values of specific body-
types, that is, the 'able-bodied', or bodies characterised by a 'statically balanced symmetrical
figure with well defined limbs and muscles' (McAnulty 1992:181).

Ableist bodily conceptions underpin architectural discourses and practices, and there
is evidence to suggest that the specific mobility and/or access needs of disabled people

rarely feature in the theories and practices of designers or architects (Davies and Lifchez 1987; Hayden 1981; Weisman 1992). In this sense, one of the sources and sites of disabled people's marginalisation and oppression in society relates to architects and architecture (also see Dickens 1980; Imrie 1996; Knesl 1984; Knox 1987). In particular, architectural conceptions of the body are premised upon abstract theories of the self, or what Lester (1997:481) refers to as 'a largely disembodied self which is held to be outside of time, space, outside of culture and gender'. Yet, as Lester (1997) comments, the presumption of a disembodied self is impossible and what generally has been presented through the context of architecture, art, and other mediums is less a body in a neutered state but one infused with (male) gender, class, and the embodiment of health and normality (see Probyn 1993).

In this chapter, I develop the proposition that modern architectural conceptions of architectural form and the built environment are simultaneously ableist and disablist by ignoring and/or denying the multiplicities of the human body. I suggest that such conceptions are premised upon a decontextualised, disembodied, ideal of the body which is at the core of disabled people's oppression within the built environment. In pursuing such themes the chapter is divided into three. The first part is a brief discussion of architectural modernism and the emergence of what some have referred to as disembodied architecture (Colomina 1994; Gray 1929; Grosz 1994, 1995; Mumford 1968; Whiteman et al. 1992). In the second section, I relate such ideas to a consideration of the architectural theories and practices of one of the most influential architects of the twentieth century, Le Corbusier. How, for example, did Le Corbusier conceive of the human body and of its possible multiplicities and how did such conceptions of body/mind inform, if at all, his architecture and approaches to urbanism and urban planning? I conclude by discussing the possibilities for the development of non-ableist, embodied, architectural discourses and practices.

Modernity, technology and decontextualised/disembodied architecture

The theories and practices of architects in Western society are underpinned by what Grosz (1995:127) refers to as 'epistemic domains where the neutrality, transparency, and universality of the body is all assumed'. Such epistemic conceptions are connected to modernist values which have been highly influential in twentieth-century architecture (Le Corbusier 1900, 1925a, 1967; Sullivan 1947; also, see Ward 1993). For Sullivan (1947), for example, such values involved the search for a 'true normal type' and for universal laws of human habitation and behaviour. Underpinning this was the propagation of an engineering aesthetic based on the idea that pure, distilled, design could be produced which was fixed and absolute, singular, transcontextual, and grafted from the essence of the human being. Such essentialism has its roots in classical ideas where the body was conceived of in naturalistic terms or what Grosz (1995) refers to as the cause and motivation for the design of cities (also see Colomina 1994; Frampton 1980, 1991; Sennett 1994). Indeed, as McAnulty (1992:182) notes, 'the unified body of the Vitruvian image was taken as the model for classical architecture' in that buildings were to replicate its order, harmony, and proportions.

[…] The essentialist depiction of such bodies is of geometric proportion and symmetry, or, in this instance, of a body seemingly able-bodied, taut, upright, male, an image projected as self-evidently invariable, normal, vigorous and healthy. The body (to be built for) was conceived of, in classical terms, as being constituted prior to its projection into the world, comprising what McAnulty (1992:182) refers to as a 'figural self sufficiency'. In this sense, the body was posited as a purity, prior to, and beyond, socialisation or culture (on this theme see, for example, Bordo 1995; Grosz 1995; Shilling 1995). Such bodies were either seen as being reducible to organic or technical and instrumental matter, that is, machine-like or, as Grosz (1995:8) notes, 'merely physical, an object like any other'. Thus, such bodies are without sex or gender, or class or culture. They are, in Hall's (1996) terms, objective entities to be dissected, manipulated, treated, and utilised as instruments and/or objects.

Such conceptions, in informing the values and practices of architects, are also premised upon a body assumed to be an organic system of interrelated bits, pieces of matter alike in functioning and form. For architects, the body, as somehow inert, passive, and pliable, is a pre-given which permits its (geometric) proportions to define the possibilities of design and building form. The body, then, as pre-formed, fixed, and known, has led some to refer to the ideas and practices of architects as necessarily leading to the production of 'standard-fit' design, that is, decontextualised, one-dimensional, architecture (Colomina 1994; Grosz 1995; Tschumi 1996). Thus, as Gray (1929, in Nevins 1981:71) commented, in referring to the rise of the abstractions of modern or avant-garde architecture:

> avant-garde is intoxicated by the machine aesthetic… But the machine aesthetic is not everything… Their intense intellectualism wants to suppress everything which is marvellous in life… Their desire for rigid precision makes them neglect the beauty of all these forms… Their architecture is without soul.

For Gray (1929, in Nevins 1981), the machine aesthetic was premised on universalising the essence of the body by a denial of the (contextual and contextualised) differences in bodily experiences and form. As Ward (1993:43) suggests, the rationality underpinning such meta-narratives 'erases differences, standardises experiences, drains the world of colour and texture, and precludes the richness and quality of life'. This, then, is a world which seeks to normalise. Such conceptions of architecture and bodies are also problematical for conceiving of buildings, bodies, and environments as discrete, rather than constitutive, entities. Indeed, for Knox (1987:355) architecture, buildings, and the wider built environment have been assigned the roles of independent variables 'explaining everything from people's perceptual acuity to their social networks'. In this sense, form is seen as shaping space and, in turn, space is conceived of as giving shape to social relations. Such determinism was underpinned by what Gray (1929) referred to as the vain arrogance of architects in their popularisation of the aesthestic, or form, over the (bodily) use of buildings, so conceiving of the idea that the architect as artist is instilling critical capacities into buildings. And, as Tschumi (1996) notes, bodies have been regarded as problematical in the architect's wider, critical, endeavours, in being seen in Platonic terms as impure, degenerate and for their potentially disruptive influence on aesthetic and/or design considerations (also see Frampton 1980; Ghirardo 1991).

A slippage between the categories of mind/body, art/craft, architect/craftsperson, purity/impurity, etc., is important in supporting and sustaining the position of architects as artists or purveyors of beauty and truth. For Le Corbusier, and others, there was little doubt as to the elevated status of the architect over those without the requisite critical capacities (Sullivan 1947). As Le Corbusier (1925a:137) stated: 'architecture is there, concerned with our home, our comfort, and our heart. Comfort and proportion. Reason and aesthetics. Machine and plastic form. Calm and beauty.' [T]he rationality of the avant-garde was sustained by the conception of the architect as the mindful and ethereal purveyor of good taste, or as those who were able to create the rational disposition of spaces beyond the contamination of the earthy impurities of society. Yet, as Caygill (1990:261–2) notes, such claims, to represent the wider world, necessarily depend on abstracting 'from individual idiosyncrasies and differences in order to reduce them to complexes of universal human needs and rights'.

While such conceptions have been difficult to sustain in the wider social sciences and humanities, they still underpin many of the theories and practices of architects (see, for example, accounts and critiques by Jencks 1987; Knox 1987; Venturi 1966; Wolfe 1981). The abstract premises of modernism are, in Caygill's (1990) terms, particularly problematical for divorcing conceptions of building form (body) and design (mind) from its use. This, for Caygill (1990), is implicated in the production of insensitive, decontextual, design. For others, the limitations of the avant-garde are expressed through the materiality of designed body-spaces premised on conceptions of standard body sizes and shapes, that is, the body as objectification. However, for Merleau-Ponty, and other theorists, the body is not an object per se 'but it is the condition and context through which an embodied person is able to have a relation to objects' (Merleau-Ponty 1962, quoted in Grosz 1995:5; also see Ghirardo 1991; Probyn 1993). In this sense, the body constructs, and is constructed by, 'an interior, a psychical and a signifying viewpoint, a consciousness or perspective' (Grosz 1995:8).

However, such critiques, and reformulations of body/mind, have had little effect on the writings and practices of most architects and there is no evidence to suggest that architectural schools teach trainee architects about the problems and limitations of decontextual conceptions of the body and architecture. Moreover, there has been little written about the specificity of bodies in the ideas and practices of the more influential architects and architectural traditions (although, for notable exceptions, see Colomina 1994; Tschumi 1996; Whiteman et al. 1992). Little or nothing has been documented about whether or not architects and their practices are self-consciously sensitised to diverse conceptions of, for instance, disabled bodies. In seeking to redress, in part, this research lacuna, the rest of the chapter is a preliminary exploration of the writings of one of the most influential architects of the twentieth century, Le Corbusier. The objective is twofold. First, by referring to the earlier work of Le Corbusier, between 1924 and 1933, I provide a brief documentation of the ways in which he wrote about, and conceived of, the human body. Second, I relate Le Corbusier's conceptions of the human body to examples of his architecture. [...]

In documenting aspects of Le Corbusier's writings and architectural practices, two qualifications should be made. First, following Jencks (1987), the life of Le Corbusier was characterised by significant changes in perspectives and modes of thinking. By the second half of his career, from the early 1940s, Le Corbusier's conceptions of the interrelationships between body/mind and design had shifted to a degree that it is impossible to gauge any temporal unity and/or consistency to his thinking on such matters. Second, Le Corbusier's writings are idiosyncratic and obscure, seemingly half-formed, yet full of detail and contradiction. In this sense, this chapter is a small contribution to a wider research agenda in which much remains to be done to excavate the meanings, materialities, and processes of bodies in Le Corbusier's architectural spaces.

Spatial perfectibility, Le Corbusier and the radiant environment

The architect Le Corbusier was characterised by Mumford (1962:34) as a 'crippled genius' who 'warped the work of a whole generation, giving it arbitrary directives, superficial slogans, and sterile goals'. Others have noted the one dimensional conception of the body propagated by Le Corbusier, the portrayal of people as asexual, and his pre-occupation with the establishment of an 'able bodied' standard in order to face what Le Corbusier characterised as the problem of perfection (Colomina 1994). Le Corbusier was influenced by modernism and the emergent avant-garde of the 1920s and with the search for what Tschumi (1996) refers to as the specificity of architecture. Such specificity, for Le Corbusier (1927:220), was conceived of, in part, as an art of geometric volumes or, as he argued, 'there is nothing but pure forms in precise relationships'. Le Corbusier was influenced by classical design and by the desire to conceive of architecture as a 'process based on standards' (1980:37). Such standards were, for Le Corbusier, based upon the 'truths and emotions of a superior mathematical order' (1927:221).

Le Corbusier rejected what he saw as the disequilibria of curved lines and jagged edges for what he characterised as 'the classical equilibrium of rectangles and pure volumes' (1980:23). His inspiration was connected to the specificity of precision. Such precision, for Le Corbusier (1980:18), was evident in classical architecture:

> the Parthenon, the Indian Temples, and the cathedrals were all built according to precise measures which constitutes a code, a coherent system: a system which proclaimed an essential unity.

Le Corbusier was, as Jencks (1987:112) notes, 'propelled by a single vision of technology as a progressive force which, if guided by the right ideals, might reinstate a natural and harmonic order'. Underpinning such conceptions of architectural form and process was purism, a system of thinking which was concerned about 'the laws of natural selection which inevitably produces the pure forms of standardised objects' (Le Corbusier 1925a:74). Purism was also obsessed with the typical or, as Curtis (1986:50) argues, 'the purist thought that neither the human figure nor landscapes were relevant to their aims…they wished to portray familiar everyday objects and to raise them to the levels of symbols by extracting their most generalised features'. Thus, purism was important in leading Le Corbusier to a distillation of the body's essence, of a thing, and of conceiving the body in ideal-typical terms. Such conceptions are evident in Le Corbusier's writings and, as he notes:

> the establishment of a standard involved evoking every practical and reasonable possibility and extracting from them a recognised type conformable to all functions with a maximum output and a minimum use of means and workmanship and material, words, forms, colours, sounds.
>
> (Le Corbusier 1980:27)

The idea of a type is also evident in La Peinture Moderne, where Le Corbusier (1900:83) develops the notion that 'mechanical evolution leads at once towards the universal and the geometrical culminating in the slogan that man is a geometrical animal'. For Le Corbusier (1900:83) such geometric specificity could be related to the search for the human type or a form of 'universal symbolism that would be trans-historical' (also see Jencks 1987; King 1996). As Le Corbusier (1925a:72) suggested:

> to search for the human scale, for human function, is to define human needs. They are not very numerous; they are very similar for all mankind, since man has been made out of the same mould from the earliest times known to us…the whole machine is there, the structure, the nervous system, the arterial system, and this applies to every single one of us exactly and without exception.

Such conceptions of the body were recurrent in the writings of Le Corbusier in the 1920s and early 1930s. Throughout this period, Le Corbusier's conceptions of the body were derived from the Newtonian idea of the body as a machine, that is, in Sennett's (1994:7) terms, 'a closed system, mechanical, with all of its parts rigid and pre-given to interaction'. For Colomina (1994:136), Le Corbusier conceived of the body as a 'surrogate machine in an industrial age'. Indeed, there are clues in Le Corbusier's writings which support Colomina's contention, that is, of the body as analogous to a type reducible to specific, interlocking, mechanical parts.

Thus, as Le Corbusier (1925a:76) intimated:

> If our spirits vary, our skeletons are alike, our muscles are in the same places and perform the same functions: dimensions and mechanism are thus fixed…human limb objects are in accord with our sense of harmony in that they are in accord with our bodies.

The fixity of the (physical) body for Le Corbusier reaffirmed the underlying essentialist terms in which he wrote about the interconnections between bodies and architecture. For instance, in referring to the human (bodily) organism as a machine, Le Corbusier (1947:22) conceived of biology as the determinant of human need or, as he said: 'since all men have the same biological organisation, they all have the same basic needs'. As Le Corbusier (1925a:71) suggested, the specificity of the body was 'a man, a constant, the fixed point'. The body, for Le Corbusier, was, therefore, a biology and/or a physiology of parts which did not vary. For example, in a typical flourish, Le Corbusier (1925a:33) comments about his conception of the standard body:

> the climates, the suns, the regimes, the races, everything is classified in terms of its relationship to man. A typical, standardised, normal man: two legs, two arms, a head. A man who perceives red, or blue, or yellow, or green.

His architecture was, so some argue, based on a world which seemingly denied the relevance of difference or the vitality of the knowing (individual) subject (see, for example, Frampton 1980; Colomina 1994; King 1996; Wigley 1992). In an interchange between Le

Corbusier and an unnamed individual, Le Corbusier's views, on the potentially complex interrelationships between the body and architectural form, reinforced his belief in the possibilities of generic solutions to fit the standard or constant-type. Thus, as Le Corbusier (1925a:72) commented:

> nevertheless, one of the big names of the 1925 Exhibition recently violently disagreed; with his heart set on multifold poetry, he proclaimed the need of each individual for something different claiming different circumstances in each case; the fat man, the thin man, the short, the long, the ruddy, the lymphatic, the violent…he sees the character of an individual as dictating his every act.

However, in dismissive terms, Le Corbusier (1925a:72) noted: 'let us recognize the practical impossibility of this dream of an individual sentient object, in all its intimate multiplicity'. He reinforces this further on in the text when commenting that 'in all things that are in universal use, individual fantasy bows before human fact' (76). For Le Corbusier, then, the distillation of bodily essence was critical in developing systems of standards and measures which, in turn, were to be used in designing the built environment. In rejecting the individual sentient-object, Le Corbusier conceived of a world where the (standardised) measurements of the body would be critical in giving shape to the objects, decorations, and materials of everyday (human) use.

Reclaiming context and developing self-conscious embodied architecture: concluding thoughts

One of the challenges for architecture and architects is to transcend what Grosz (1995:127) refers to as 'the standard assumptions, the doxa, the apparent naturalness, or rather, the evolutionary fit assumed to hold between being and buildings'. Such assumptions underpin many contemporary architectural ideas and practices and are rooted, historically, in the theories and conceptions of influential architects and architectural traditions. Architecture has also been beset by major tensions, or, as Crawford (1991:41, quoted in Imrie 1996:96) suggests, 'the restricted practices and discourse of the profession have reduced the scope of architecture to two equally unpromising polarities: compromised practice or esoteric philosophies of inaction'. For disabled people, such tensions have worked their way into hostile and oppressive buildings and built environments, underpinned by self-serving ideas which have failed to challenge the hegemonic position of key actors within the wider design and building industries.

As this chapter suggests, architects' conceptions of bodies in space, such as, for example, those propagated by Le Corbusier, are connected to the estrangement of disabled bodies in the built environment (Figure 2.1). However, it is difficult to derive any easy or definite characterisation of Le Corbusier's feelings and thoughts concerning architecture and the body. In particular, some of his writings hint at conceptions of the human body which are sensitised to the possibilities of flux, change, and difference. In one part of *The Radiant City* (1933 (1967)), Le Corbusier conceives of the body as an interconnection between body/mind, that is, the body as a holistic socio-psychological and biological entity:

contingencies are the environment: places, peoples, cultures, topographies, climates…contingencies should only be judged as they relate to the entity – man – and in connection with man, in relation to us, to ourselves: a biology, a psychology.

(Le Corbusier 1967:1)

By the end of the 1940s, Le Corbusier (1948:38) was conceiving of body spaces in the following terms:

society being in man's image, the nation's wealth in building must be similar to the human body. Man is carried by a temporal flux in which he is immersed body and soul; but the flow does more than carry him physically; it models and remodels him, loosening this, allowing that to form, operating in a thousand linked ways.

These views seem to have stemmed from his recognition of the disruptive, contextually specific ways in which clients and/or users of architecture were able to transform the meanings and materialities of the architects' design conceptions and intentions. Others have also noted the disruptive interrelationships between architectural ideas and practices. For Colomina

FIGURE 2.1   Le Corbusier's Unité d'Habitation, Marseille, completed in 1952. Also known as *Cité radieuse* (Radiant City) and colloquially as *La Maison du Fada* (French – Provençal, "The Nutter's House").

Photo: Colin Bisset (see also Bisset, C. (2015) *Loving Le Corbusier* Amazon Digital).

(1994:126), for instance, 'a theory of architecture is a theory of order threatened by the very use it permits'. Moreover, as Tschumi (1996) notes, architecture is never autonomous but is necessarily constitutive as well as constituted by social processes. For Tschumi (1996), the fluidity and erratic motions of bodies underpins the possibilities of new and unexpected spaces being constituted in ways never anticipated by the architect. Le Corbusier, for instance, recognised the limitations of the application of an architecture premised upon standards determined by logical analysis and experimentation in noting the subversive nature of people's idiosyncrasies. As Le Corbusier (1925b, quoted in Banham 1960:270) argued:

> but in practice things do not happen so; man's sensibilities intervene even in the midst of the most rigorous calculation…intervention of an individual task, sensibility, and passion.

These comments were particularly directed at workers' houses designed by Le Corbusier in Pessac, south of Paris, in 1925 where he witnessed the inhabitants transforming the geometric textures and forms of the dwellings (Figure 2.2). In interpreting Le Corbusier's

FIGURE 2.2 Contemporary photo of workers' housing at Pessac, built 1925: showing an example of how Le Corbusier's standardised design has been altered; in this case by filling-in of the strip windows, and addition of window mouldings – so subverting, according to Le Corbusier, the original design conceptions which underpinned the scheme.

Photo: Colin Bisset.

contradictory feelings about Pessac, Jencks (1987:74–5, quoted in Imrie 1996:86) comments:

> Starting with the idea of resolving two incompatibilities like the individual and the group, it was not surprising that Le Corbusier could end up, as at Pessac, by admiring the way personalisation was destroying his own architecture. All the arguments for a geometrical civilisation…were countered by the barbaric actions of the inhabitants at Pessac, and yet, according to the supreme dialectician, these barbarians were still right.

However, Le Corbusier's notion of 'rightness' was still circumscribed by the idea that people, by transforming their living spaces, were somehow, in his terms, subverting and undermining the ideals and purity of the architect. Tschumi (1996:123), in reinforcing Le Corbusier's observation on the interrelations between buildings and users, notes:

> the human body has always been suspect in architecture: it has always set limits to the most extreme architectural ambitions. The body disturbs the purity of architectural order. It is equivalent to a dangerous prohibition… architecture, then, is only an organism engaged in constant intercourse with users, whose bodies rush against the carefully established rules of architectural thought.

Tschumi's views are important for drawing attention to the intersections between bodies and architecture and, in particular, to what he regards as the potentially violent relationship between the two. For disabled people many dimensions of the built environment are disruptive and violent precisely because buildings are underpinned by the embodied ideal of a body which fails to conform with the complexities of bodily interactions in space. Others, in recognising the complexity of such interactions, argue for some reconception of the interrelationship between people and architecture in ways which recognise the fluidity and transformative nature of bodies in space (Grosz 1995; Weisman 1992). For Weisman (1992:32, quoted in Imrie 1996:91), for example, universal design offers a direction given its recognition that the built environment should be 'demountable, reasonable, multifunctional, and changeable over time'. Likewise, Davies and Lifchez (1987) conceive of buildings as much more than a physical, bodily, experience or a matter of logistics, but as a quality of sociopsychological experiences.

This suggests that one pre-requisite for a non-ableist architecture is for architects to confront the social psychology of design by considering the interactions between bodies/ minds in the context of specific building use. How do particular buildings and built environments feel to different types of disabled people? Indeed, how do disabled people's feelings interconnect with their bodies' experiences of movement and mobility in specific types of places? What do architects know about this and where do they get their knowledge from and in what form? Moreover, architects need to confront the ideology of art over function and seek to privilege use over aesthetics or pretensions to poetics. This, then, calls for a demystification and systematic critique of ideas and ideals within particular architectural traditions, theories, and practices and for architects to (re)connect themselves to social and economic concerns. This might involve asking who architecture is for, in what ways, and with what effects, potentially sensitising architects and their clients to the possibilities of architecture which is inclusive and emancipatory rather than exclusive and oppressive.

The democratisation of architectural and building practices is also connected to the wider task of developing non-ableist design by moving beyond Le Corbusier's conception of the architect as above and beyond the client and/or user. Few architects in Britain are registered as disabled people while the Royal Institute of British Architects has done little to encourage architects to think about the specific architectural requirements of disabled people (see Imrie 1996; also Knox 1987; Wolfe 1981). However, one also needs to look beyond what Weisman (1992) refers to as failed architecture or prejudiced architects towards the totality of structures framing the social oppression and marginalisation of disabled people within the built environment. Architects are connected to wider cost and material imperatives which inhibit or restrict the scope for design beyond prescribed limits (see Knox 1987). In this sense, an explication of architects' conceptions of bodies in space is only part of a wider endeavour to understand the interrelationships between design theory, practice, and people's experiences of buildings and the built environment.

3

A CRITICAL CONDITION

Paul Hunt (1966)

Reprinted from P. Hunt (ed.) Stigma: The Experience of Disability, *London: Geoffrey Chapman, pp 1–10, http://disability-studies.leeds.ac.uk/files/library/Hunt-critical-condition.pdf.*

All my adult life has been spent in institutions amongst people who, like myself, have severe and often progressive physical disabilities. We are paralysed and deformed, most of us in wheelchairs, either as the result of accident or of diseases like rheumatoid arthritis, multiple sclerosis, muscular dystrophy, cerebral palsy and polio. So naturally this personal experience forms a background to the views on disability that follow. I do not mean to exclude altogether the large number of people who today are able to lead a more or less normal life in the community; those with relatively light disabilities, or with such handicaps as defects in sight, speech or hearing, epilepsy, obesity, heart disease, and so on. I hope that much of what I say will be relevant to this latter group since they have many problems in common with us. But apart from the obvious value of writing from my own direct knowledge, it is also true that the situation of 'the young chronic sick' (as we are officially and rather unpleasantly termed) highlights, or rather goes to the depths of, the question of disablement. Our 'tragedy' may be only the tragedy of all sickness, pain and suffering carried to extremes. But disabilities like ours, which often prohibit any attempt at normal living in society, almost force one to consider the basic issues, not only of coping with a special handicap, but of life itself.

Being cheerful and keeping going is scarcely good enough when one has an illness that will end in an early death, when one is wasting away like some Belsen victim, maybe incontinent, dependent on others for daily needs, probably denied marriage and a family and forced to live out one's time in an institution. In these circumstances the most acute questions arise and the most radical answers are called for. I am not suggesting that all of us with such devastating handicaps probe deeply into the meaning of life, nor that we automatically gain great wisdom or sanctity. We have our defences like anyone else. But it does seem that our situation tends to make us ask questions that few people ask in the ordinary world. And it also means that to some extent we are set apart from, or rather have a special position *within*, the everyday society that most people take it for granted they belong to.

I want to look at this special situation largely in terms of our relations with others, our place in society. This is essentially related to the personal aspect of coping with disablement, which I hope it will at the same time illuminate, since the problem of disability lies not only in the impairment of function and its effects on us individually, but also, more importantly, in the area of our relationship with 'normal' people. If everyone were disabled as we are, there would be no special situation to consider. This focus on the ways in which we are set apart from the ordinary does not mean that I see us as really separated from society. In fact the reverse assumption underlies everything I write. We *are* society, as much as anybody, and cannot be considered in isolation from it. I am aware of the danger of concentrating on the ways in which disability makes us like each other and unlike the normal, and thus being trapped into the common fault of viewing people in terms of one characteristic to the exclusion of all others. Disabled people suffer enough from that kind of thing already. But whatever the differences between us, we do have certain sets of experiences in common.

In dealing with this aspect of our lives I have tried not to forget two others – our uniqueness as persons and the human nature we share with the rest of mankind. I think the distinguishing mark of disabled people's special position is that they tend to 'challenge' in their relations with ordinary society. This challenge takes five main forms: as *unfortunate*, *useless*, *different*, *oppressed* and *sick*. All these are only facets of one situation, but here it seems worth taking each in turn. The first way in which we challenge others is by being *unfortunate*. Severely disabled people are generally considered to have been unlucky, to be deprived and poor, to lead cramped lives. We do not enjoy many of the 'goods' that people in our society are accustomed to. The opportunity for marriage and having children, authority at home and at work, the chance to earn money, independence and freedom of movement, a house and a car – these things, and plenty more, may be denied us. Underprivileged as we are in this sense, one point seems to be clear. If the worth of human beings depends on a high social status, on the possession of wealth, on a position as parent, husband or wife – if such things are *all-important* – then those of us who have lost or never had them are indeed unfortunate. Our lives must be tragically upset and marred for ever, we must be only half alive, only half human. And it is a fact that most of us, whatever our explicit views, tend to act as though such 'goods' are essential to a fully human existence. Their possession is seen as the key to entry into a promised land of civilized living.

But set over against this common sense attitude is another fact, a strange one. In my experience even the most severely disabled people retain an ineradicable conviction that they are still fully human in all that is ultimately necessary. Obviously each person can deny this, and act accordingly. Yet even when he is most depressed, even when he says he would be better off dead, the underlying sense of his own worth remains. This basic feeling for the value of the person *as such* becomes fully operational, as it were, when those with severe disabilities live full and happy lives in defiance of the usual expectations. An increasing number of people do seem to overcome their misfortunes like this, and it is they who present the most effective challenge to society. When confronted with someone who is evidently coping with tragic circumstances, able-bodied people tend to deny the reality of the adjustment. The disabled person is simply making the best of a bad job, putting a good face on it. There may be some truth in this. But when it becomes obvious that there is also a genuine happiness, another defensive attitude is taken up. The 'unfortunate' person is assumed to have wonderful and exceptional courage (although underneath this overt canonization there is usually a degree of irritation and hostility which comes to light at moments of stress). This devalues other disabled people by implication, and leaves the fit person still with his original view that disablement is really utterly tragic.

Such reactions appear to be caused by the need to safeguard a particular scale of values, where someone's sense of security depends on this being maintained. He almost *wants* the disabled person to suffer, as a confirmation that the values denied him are still worthy and important and good. If he shows no obvious sign of suffering, then he must challenge people whose own worth seems to them to be bound up with their more fortunate position in life.

So if those of us who are disabled live as fully as we can, while being completely conscious of the tragedy of our situation – this is the possibility when one has an alert mind – then somehow we can communicate to others an awareness that the value of the human person transcends his social status, attributes and possessions or his lack of them. This applies however much we recognize these 'accidents' as important, and however much we regard the 'goods' I have mentioned as the normal elements in a full life. What we oppose is only the assumption that makes them absolutely indispensable for a completely human existence. Perhaps we can help prepare people for the almost certain day when they themselves lose, at least in old age, some of the advantages that are so highly valued. But anyway, those who implicitly believe that a man's worth depends on his good fortune must be building their lives on rather inadequate foundations, and they will perhaps find contact with us a thought-provoking experience.

A second aspect of our special position in society is that we are often *useless*, unable to contribute to the economic good of the community. As such, again we cannot help posing questions about values, about what a person is, what he is for, about whether his work is the ultimate criterion of his worth, whether work in the everyday sense of the word is the most important or the only contribution anyone can make to society.

There is no doubt that we do put great stress on the individual's economic contribution. Most people are wrapped up in a workaday, utilitarian world, and regard anything not visibly productive as expendable. Contemplation, philosophy, wisdom, the liberal arts, get short shrift from the average man. Those who cannot work, such as the sick, aged or unemployed, are subject to a tremendous pressure to feel useless, or at least of less value than the breadwinner.

I am not indicting some abstract society for getting its priorities wrong; each of us shares responsibility for the prevailing attitudes. Also I am far from saying that work, in the sense of contributing to the wealth of the community, is unimportant. Of course willingness to pull one's weight is an essential part of a healthy and balanced outlook on life and other people. But I am concerned that we should not elevate the idea of work in our minds to the point where it dominates values that ought to transcend it. It is important not to do this, if only because it causes the most acute suffering in those of us who cannot help being parasites on the economic body. Obviously we who are disabled are deeply affected by the assumptions of our uselessness that surround us. But it is vital that we should not accept this devaluation of ourselves, yearning only to be able to earn our livings and thus prove our worth. We do not have to prove anything.

If we have a basic willingness to contribute to the community, yet cannot do an ordinary job, we may certainly contribute in less obvious ways; even, and perhaps especially, if these seem insignificant beside the 'real world of work'. Our freedom from the competitive trappings that accompany work in our society may give us the opportunity to demonstrate its essential elements. Also we can act as a symbol for the pre-eminent claims of non-utilitarian values, a visible challenge to anyone who treats his job as a final end in itself. And we do of course afford people the chance to be generous in support of the needy, thus enabling them to give practical expression to their desire to go beyond the acquisitive instinct.

At the ultimate point we may only be able to suffer, to be passive through complete physical inability. Just here we have a special insight to offer, because our position gives us an extra experience of life in the passive aspect that is one half of the human reality. Those who lead active lives are perhaps especially inclined to ignore man's need to accept passivity in relation to so many forces beyond his control. They may need reminding sometimes of our finiteness, our feminine side in the hands of fate or providence. We are well placed to do this job at least.

The next challenging characteristic of the disabled is that we are *different*, abnormal, marked out as members of a minority group. Normality is so often put forward as the goal for people with special handicaps, that we have come to accept its desirability as a dogma. But even if one takes a common sense meaning for the word – being like most people in our society – it is doubtful if this is what we should really fix our sights on. For one thing it is impossible of achievement, at certain levels anyway. Obviously we cannot be physically normal, are doomed to be deviants in this sense at least. Also we must be affected psychologically by our disabilities, and to some extent be moulded into a distinct class by our experiences. But more important, what kind of goal is this elusive normality? If it does mean simply trying to be like the majority, then it is hardly a good enough ideal at which to aim. Whether they are physically handicapped or not, people need something more than this to work towards if they are to contribute their best to society and grow to maturity.

Of course there is a certain value in our trying to keep up with ordinary society, and relate to it; but it is essential to define the sense in which this is a good thing. Once more I am not rejecting in a sour-grapes spirit the many excellent normal goals that may be denied us – marrying, earning one's living, and so on. What I am rejecting is society's tendency to set up rigid standards of what is right and proper, to force the individual into a mould. Our constant experience of this pressure towards unthinking conformity in some way relates us to other obvious deviants and outcasts like the Jew in a gentile world, a Negro in a white world, homosexuals, the mentally handicapped; and also to more voluntary rebels in every sphere – artists, philosophers, prophets, who are essentially subversive elements in society. This is another area where disabled people can play an important role.

Those we meet cannot fail to notice our disablement even if they turn away quickly and avoid thinking about us afterwards. An impaired and deformed body is a 'difference' that hits everyone hard at first. Inevitably it produces an instinctive revulsion, has a disturbing effect. Our own first reaction to this is to want to hide ourselves in the crowd, to attempt to buy acceptance on any terms, to agree uncritically with whatever is the done thing.

Feeling excessively self-conscious we would like to bury ourselves in society away from the stares of the curious, and even the special consideration of the kindly, both of which serve to emphasize our difference from the majority. But this very natural impulse has to be resisted. We must try to help people accept the fact of our unavoidable difference from them which implies that we are attempting to integrate it within ourselves too. However, this does not mean just creating a comfortable atmosphere of acceptance around ourselves, building up a circle of able-bodied friends who treat us right, and trying to leave it at that. It is imperative that the effort should be followed through to the point where we, and those we come into contact with, understand that it is not just a case of our minds compensating for our disabilities, or something like that.

We can witness to the truth that a person's dignity does not rest even in his consciousness, and certainly that it does not rest in his beauty, age, intelligence or colour. Those of us with unimpaired minds but severely disabled bodies, have a unique opportunity to show other people not only that our big difference from them does not lessen our worth, but also that *no* difference between men, however real, unpleasant and disturbing, does away with their right to be treated as fully human.

We face more obviously than most the universal problem of coming to terms with the fact of man's individuality and loneliness. If we begin to accept our own special peculiarity, we shall be in a position to help others accept even their own difference from everyone else. These two acceptances are bound up together. People's shocked reactions to the obvious deviant often reflect their own deepest fears and difficulties, their failure to accept themselves as they really are, and the other person simply as 'other'. The disabled person's 'strangeness' can manifest and symbolize all differences between human beings. In his relations with more nearly normal people he may become a medium for reconciling them to the fact of these differences, and demonstrate their relative unimportance compared to what we have in common.

The fourth challenging aspect of our situation follows inevitably from our being different and having minority status. Disabled people often meet prejudice, which expresses itself in discrimination and even oppression. Sometimes it seems to us that we just can't win. Whatever we do, whether good or bad, people put it down to our being disabled. Meeting this kind of attitude constantly can be depressing and infinitely wearing. You may produce the most logical and persuasive arguments only to have them dismissed, without even the compliment of counter-argument, as products of your disability. The frustrating thing is that there is no appeal against this. If you point out what is happening you are assured it isn't, that you are imagining a prejudice which does not exist. And immediately you know you are branded again as being unrealistic and impossibly subjective. So many people take it for granted that what you say can be explained by a crude theory of compensation, and therefore is of no account or self-evidently false. And they tell themselves that you can't really help having these ideas, poor thing.

One rather doubtful pleasure is to discover that this 'poor thing' attitude does not survive a determined rejection of the able-bodied person's assumption of inherent superiority. He admits equality as a theory, but when you *act* as though you *are* equal then the crucial test comes. Most people are good-willed liberals towards us up to this point, but not all of them survive close contact with disability without showing some less attractive traits. Of course it is not only the 'fit' who are like this. I know I have instinctive prejudices against lots of people; against the able-bodied to start with. It is a basic human characteristic to fear and put up barriers against those who are different from ourselves. Without for a moment justifying any of its manifestations, it seems to me just as 'natural' to be prejudiced against someone with a defective body (or mind) as it is to have difficulty in accepting the members of another racial group. Maybe it is invidious to compare our situation with that of racial minorities in any way. The injustice and brutality suffered by so many because of racial tension makes our troubles as disabled people look very small. But I think there is a connection somewhere, since all prejudice springs from the same roots. And there stirs in me a little of the same anger as the Negro writer James Baldwin reveals in *The Fire Next Time* (1964) when I remember the countless times I have seen disabled people hurt, treated as less than people, told what to do and how to behave by those whose only claim to do this came from prejudice and their power over them.

In the hospitals and homes I have lived in one rarely sees any physical cruelty. But I have experienced enough of other kinds of subtly corrupting behaviour. There are administrators and matrons who have had people removed on slight pretexts, who try to break up ordinary friendships if they don't approve of them. There are the staff who bully those who cannot complain, who dictate what clothes people should wear, who switch the television off in the middle of a programme, and will take away 'privileges' (like getting up for the day) when they choose. Then there are the visitors who automatically assume an authority over us and interfere without regard for our wishes. Admittedly some of these examples are trivial, and I have not mentioned all the excellent people who make any sort of life possible for us. But still I think it is true that we meet fundamentally the same attitude which discriminates against anyone different and shades off into oppression under the right – or rather wrong – conditions.

In the wider community the similarity is even clearer. Employers turn away qualified and competent workers simply because they are disabled. Restaurants and pubs give transparent excuses for refusing our custom. Landladies reject disabled lodgers. Parents and relations fight the marriage of a cripple into their family – perhaps with more reason than with a black African, but with many of the same arguments. And it's not hard to see the analogy between a racial ghetto and the institutions where disabled people are put away and given enough care to salve society's conscience.

Of course there are vast differences between our situation and that of many other 'downtrodden' people. One of these is that we are not a potential threat to lives and property. For this reason alone we can be hopeful that at least our freedom from open discrimination can be achieved even though we shall never have sufficient power in the community to ensure this. It also gives us a good chance of avoiding the ever-present danger for those who are oppressed – that they will pay homage to the same god of power that is harming their oppressors.

The elimination of prejudice is not really possible: a helpful social climate can only do so much, and each individual and generation has to renew a fight that cannot be won. It is true that we still have to solve the problem of means and ends; of whether, or rather in what way, we should oppose evil. But perhaps precisely because violence and power-seeking are not really practical possibilities for us, we are well placed to consider other ways of achieving freedom from injustice. However, we should be careful that our weakness here does not become an excuse for sterile resignation. One reason why we must resist prejudice, injustice, oppression, is that they not only tend to diminish us, but far more to diminish our oppressors. If you try to care about people you cannot be indifferent to what is happening to those who treat you badly, and you have to oppose them. If this opposition is to be by means of patience and long-suffering, then they must be directed at the abolition of evil or they are just forms of masochism.

In this section I have not only been drawing an analogy between our position in society and that of racial minorities, but also pointing out the connection between all the manifestations of prejudice and discrimination. This connection means that although we cannot directly assist the American Negro, for instance, in his resistance to oppression, in one way we can help everyone who suffers injustice. We do this above all by treating properly those we meet. There are always people we feel superior to or resent – the mentally ill, the aged, children, those who patronize us or hurt us. If we do not try to treat all these as fully human beings, then it is certain we would not be able to help the Negro or anyone else in a similar predicament. Here, as in so many instances, it is true that what we do is a symbol of what we would do. Not only can we do no more than to let an act substitute for a more splendid act, but no one can do more. This is the reconciliation.

The last aspect of our challenge to society as disabled people is that we are *sick*, suffering, diseased, in pain. For the able-bodied, normal world we are representatives of many of the things they most fear – tragedy, loss, dark and the unknown. Involuntarily we walk – or more often sit – in the valley of the shadow of death. Contact with us throws up in people's faces the fact of sickness and death in the world. No one likes to think of such which in themselves are an affront to all things, our aspirations and hopes. A deformed and paralysed body attacks everyone's sense of well-being and invincibility. People do not want to acknowledge what disability affirms – that life is tragic and we shall all soon be dead. So they are inclined to avoid those who are sick or old, shying from the disturbing reminders of unwelcome reality.

Here I would suggest that our role in society can be likened to that of the satirist in some respects. Maybe we have to remind people of a side of life they would sooner forget. We do this primarily by what we are. But we can intensify it and make it more productive if we are fully conscious of the tragedy of our situation, yet show by our lives that we believe this is not the final tragedy. Closely involved with death and dark in the unconscious and subconscious, though really distinct, is the idea of evil. An almost automatic linkage is made not only between a sick body and a sick mind, but also undoubtedly between an evil body and an evil mind, a warped personality.

There is a definite relation between the concepts of health and holiness. So many of the words used about health are moral ones – we talk of a good or bad leg, of being fit and unfit, of walking properly, of perfect physique. And disabled people find that the common assumption of good health as a natural thing often comes over to us as an 'ought', carries with it undertones of a moral failure on our part. 'If only you had enough will-power...' is the modern-dress version of the idea that we are possessed by an evil spirit.

Then there are traces of a desire to externalize evil, to find a scapegoat, in attitudes to the sick. Sometimes people are evidently trying to reassure themselves that they are 'saved', justified, in a state of grace. I do not mean just the feeling of gaining merit from charitable works, but rather a satisfaction got from their 'good' selves juxtaposed with the 'unclean', the untouchables, who provide them with an assurance that they are all right, on the right side. No doubt this process works the other way too. Our experience of subjection as sick people may give us a sense of being holy and predestined in contrast to our condescending, prejudiced fellow men. But such attitudes, whether in ourselves or others, have to be constantly resisted and rooted out. They are simply products of our own fears and weaknesses, and any temporary security they give is false and dangerous.

I have dealt briefly with five interrelated aspects of disabled people's position as a challenge to some of the common values of society: as *unfortunate, useless, different, oppressed* and *sick*. A paradoxical law runs through the whole of the situation I have been describing. It is that only along the line of maximum resistance to diminishment can we arrive at the required point for a real acceptance of what is unalterable. We have first to acknowledge the value of the good things of life – of prosperity, usefulness, normality, integration with society, good health – and be fully extended in the search for fulfillment in ordinary human terms, before we can begin to achieve a fruitful resignation. Nowadays many disabled people will have nothing to do with resignation as it used to be understood. Thriving in a climate of increasing public tolerance and kindness, and on a diet of pensions and welfare, we are becoming presumptuous. Now we reject any view of ourselves as being lucky to be allowed to live. We reject too all the myths and superstitions that have surrounded us in the past. We are challenging society to take account of us, to listen to what we have to say, to acknowledge us as an integral part of society itself. We do not want ourselves, or anyone else, treated as second-class citizens and put away out of sight and mind. Many of us are just beginning to *refuse* to be put away, to insist that we are part of life too. We are saying that being deformed and paralysed, blind or deaf – or old or mentally sick for that matter – is not a crime or in any meaningful sense of the words a divine punishment. Illness and impairment are facts of existence, diminishment and death are there to be thought about and must be taken account of in any realistic view of the world. We are perhaps also saying that society is itself sick if it can't face *our* sickness, if it does not overcome its natural fear and dislike of unpleasantness as manifested by disability.

We are asking of people something that lies a lot deeper than almsgiving. We want an extension of the impulse that inspires this, so that it becomes a gift of self rather than the dispensing of bounty (material and other kinds) from above. To love and respect, treat as equals, people as obviously 'inferior' as we are, requires real humility and generosity. I believe that our demand to be treated like this is based on a truth about human beings which everyone needs to recognize – which is why we have a particularly important function here. But there is also no doubt that acquiring and maintaining such an attitude runs contrary to some of people's most deep seated impulses and prejudices. The quality of the relationship the community has with its least fortunate members is a measure of its own health. The articulate person with a severe disability may to some extent represent and speak on behalf of all those who perhaps cannot interpret their predicament, or protest for themselves – the weak, sick, poor and aged throughout the world. They too are rejects from ordinary life, and are subject to the same experience of devaluation by society.

This linkage with other 'unfortunates', with the shadow side of life, is not always easy to accept. For the disabled person with a fair intelligence or other gifts, perhaps the greatest temptation is to try to use them just to escape from his disabledness, to buy himself a place in the sun, a share in the illusory normal world where all is light and pleasure and happiness. Naturally we want to get away from and forget the sickness, depression, pain, loneliness and poverty of which we see probably more than our share. But if we deny our special relation to the dark in this way, we shall have ceased to recognize our most important asset as disabled people in society – the uncomfortable, subversive position from which we act as a living reproach to any scale of values that puts attributes or possessions before the person.

Note

Paul Hunt was founder of the Union of the Physically Impaired Against Segregation (UPIAS) in 1972, which invited disabled people to form a group to confront disability issues, based on the ideas developed in work, like this essay, written whilst he was living in an institution. UPIAS was one of the first Disability Rights organisations in the UK. It challenged the charitable model of disability support, and argued for recognition of disabled peoples' own expertise and rights of self-determination. The group were instrumental in developing the terms 'medical' and 'social model' of disability and in making new differentiating definitions between impairment and disability. You can find the UPIAS Founding Statement here: http://disability-studies.leeds.ac.uk/files/library/UPIAS-UPIAS.pdf

The campaigning that developed from these initiatives, as well as equivalent organisations in other countries, formed the basis of government legislation improving accessibility for disabled people in the UK, the US and elsewhere.

4

LYING DOWN ANYHOW

Disability and the rebel body

Liz Crow (2013)

Chapter 12, reprinted from J. Swain, S. French, C. Barnes and C. Thomas (eds) (2013) Disabling Barriers – Enabling Environments, *3rd edition, London and New York: Sage, pp. 85–91.*

In this chapter, I begin with a short autobiographical piece about lying down in public places. This is followed by an exploration of the influences involved in the process of *Lying Down Anyhow*.

> We sip from glasses of orange juice and half-pint lagers on a cool afternoon in autumn, a gentle rise and fall of conversation, and I nudge off my shoes to lie upon the cushioned window seat. From behind the bar, the landlord hurls himself towards me, his face as livid as the velvet beneath me. "Get up, get up, get out. This is a *respectable* establishment."

★★★

> When I lie down, it is clean mountain air, cool water in blistering summer, soft rains of release. Sit up, and I am fragile as ice, a light breeze might shatter me. Sitting up, I am beyond my body; lying down, cradled by gravity, I creep back in to occupy my self.
>
> In the privacy of home, I move from bed to sofa, sofa to floor, pillow, rugs and hardwood boards. I lie down wherever I happen to be, with the ease of twenty years' practice, freely.
>
> But in the world outside, I am censored. I seek out-of-the-way spaces: corridors and empty classrooms, fields and first aid rooms and once, even, a graveyard. I wait to be alone, tuck myself from sight and then, only then, as though it is a thing of shame, I recline.

To be a part of the social world, I must sit: brace myself, block body from mind, steel will. To lie down is to absent myself from ordinary spaces. I wonder how many of us there are skulking in the in-between spaces. And I wonder at how such an everyday action, a simple thing born of necessity, became a thing to conceal. What taught us our shame?

★★★

"Lie down on the job" and we purposely neglect our work. "Let something lie" and we decline to take action. A "layabout" slacks and skives and shirks. The English language tells me my shame. Is that why, when I look around, I see lying down in public places only in the merest snatches and swatches of life, as though those of us who lie down have been written out?

Work hard enough, and I may recline, guiltless, in the green of summer parks or bake on sun-kissed beaches. With degrees of censure, young enough, slim enough, pretty enough, I can enter a young love's tryst, entwined on grassy banks. I can child's play Sleeping Lions and make angels in the snow, or pose as death on a yoga mat until body and self dissolve.

Ill enough, and I can lie down on doctor's couch or in hospital bed, a properly licensed space. In extremis – grand mal and hypo, knife attack and heart attack – I can make the street my bed; although, mistaken for drunk or overly-dramatic, my saviour might just "let it lie" and cross over the road.

Human beings do not, apparently, much lie down and, if they must, then they tempt accelerated demise. In the annals of research, lying down is all let-this-be-a-warning treatises on the dangers of bedrest, of bone demineralisation and blood clots. Yet for me, lying down is my holding together; far from demise, this is my way to life.

In well-earned leisure, in pleasure, play and extremes, we may lie down in public places. In carefully controlled circumstances, we will not be judged for idleness and sloth. But why is it, as adults, to lie down amongst others, we must either be productive or chasing death? It is as though, in permitting ourselves to lie down in carefully sanctioned spaces, we have become convinced of our autonomy, when all we have proved is the strength of its prohibition.

Out in the urban jungle, edgy young designers create street furniture to dissuade the populace from lying down: benches divided by armrests, rails for perching, seats which revolve to prevent extended idling (Lockton 2008). New laws in multiple cities around the world make it an offence to lie down in public places. If Westminster Council prevails, lying down could cost me £500 (Bullivant 2011); in San Bruno it could earn me six months in jail (Municipal Code 2011). This is not, you understand, a bid to address the social costs of homelessness, just to move on, design out, that which does not conform. Lying down in public spaces is no longer merely invisible; it is to be *disappeared*.

It seems it will take a brave woman to undertake public lying down. I intend to be her. I will not be disappeared.

I vowed to write lightly because I am writing of something so simple: of stretching out my legs, reclining my body, resting my head, amongst people. Lying down, for me, *is* lightness. But this is not light. To lie down, in social spaces, is not a simple act of physiology; it is a statement. In the midst of codes that say *you do not do this*, to lie down in public is confrontation.

Perhaps if it did not matter so much, it would be easy.

Still, I worry about the small things.

To lie down in front of others feels so *exposed*. The bed exists in private space; it is sleep and sex, intimacy and guard let down. In public, reclined, I have *so much body*; it unfolds and unravels on the horizontal plane, taking up more than its share of space. It flaunts itself, "look at me," and eclipses face and mind. I watch myself through the eyes and ideas, the anxieties and judgements of others; danger lurks in being misread. And I wonder: shall I keep my boots on or tuck them neatly to one side? There is no guidebook.

Lying down in public places demands portion control, dress sense and, in summer months, attention to the calluses on my feet. If I am to become a poster girl for the disappeared, I'd like to look my best.

The absence of a guidebook could yet become my freedom. If the rules cannot be kept, then they are there for the breaking. And so I shall search for better ways.

★★★

Tying my bootlaces by the front door, I glance up and see anew a picture that has hung so long it had blended to invisibility. A black-and-white engraving from the 1893 *Graphic* celebrates the fashionable seaside resort of Brighton where wealthy society brought ailments for salt-water cures. A gentleman, pale faced in bowler hat and waxed moustache, reclines upon a bath chair. His arm rests languidly upon the furs that swathe him and his fingers grip tight upon a cigarette. Well-wishers smile and hang upon his every word: a lady admirer takes him by the hand, a gentleman rests an arm tenderly on the hood of the chaise, and a large dog stands sentinel. He is, the title tells us, *An Interesting Invalid*, and, though the chair's canopy frames him like a halo, he better describes a more fabulous, dissipated, dolce vita of invalidism. Perhaps this is a sensibility to aspire to.

Closer to nirvana, the Reclining Buddha rests his head upon a lotus flower. He lies feet together, long toes aligned, adorned in offerings of oranges and marigolds. In Thailand, the Buddha lies vast in stone, wrapped Christo-like in saffron folds (Visbeek 2009), which billow in the breeze. There are four "respect-inspiring forms" (Tophoff 2006) in Buddhism, and the fourth of these is lying down. A lighter expression of being, it shifts us "out of the way of the Way" (Vassi 1984), so that we may more readily find the path to an authentic self. Is there revelation in this for me? Lie down and I am freed from the distraction of physicality to reoccupy my self; transcending the tethers of the social world, I find there are other ways to be.

The reclining figures of Henry Moore survey the landscape with a gaze that is far-seeing. Rooted in this earth, organic, monumental, they cast aside the myth of beauty to embrace the energy, barely contained, of the static form. His figures rise from stone so embodied, so absolutely *present*, they almost breathe. I read of the themes of the sculptor's work – truth to the material, form-knowledge, resurrection (Wilkinson 2002) – and I smile. I respond to my own materiality, shaping myself to its truth and find, for me, that lying down is life restored. And, just as the figures echo the contours of the Yorkshire in which they belong, when I lie down, I come home.

Moore would "give everything" to chisel figures "more alive than a real person" (Wilkinson 2002), though few could outdo the *cojones* of Frida Kahlo. All passion and flesh, she painted her very *self*. From her bed, reflecting her gaze in a ceiling-mounted mirror, she described the play of gravity on the contours of a body lying down. I see her now, muddying the bed sheets with oil and turpentine, lust and rebellion hand-in-hand. Always one for the grand entrance, she is photographed lying in state at the opening of a solo show, the paintings hastily rearranged to accommodate her bed (Herrera 1983) until Frida herself became a work of art. No fears holding her back. Even after she had left the room, her bed remained.

When he was ill, Christopher Newell would have his bed wheeled to the front of the tiered lecture theatre in Hobart Hospital, from where he would address future-doctors on the ethics of their profession, urging his audiences to "dare to encounter the muckiness of everyday ethical decision making" (Newell 2002). As associate professor, he lay down with authority, and he lay down knowingly. He unfolded and unravelled his body amongst people in a bid to move his students from "other to us" (Newell 2006) to bring them to a point of knowing deep down the humanity of those they would meet in their later professional lives. He lay down for both his comfort and his campaign.

In the sand dunes of Kijkduin, on the North Sea coast of the Netherlands, lies a crater, 30 metres across, entered through an underground passage (Frank 2011). At its core lies a bench of stone built for lying down, in sculpture that can only ever be appreciated prone. Supporting the whole of the body, it tips the head back until your gaze is cast upwards, beyond the circle of the crater's rim, from where you fall up up up into a canopy of sky. We believe we know the sky, arched above us in the everyday, but Turrell's sculpture of light wraps it, traces its edges, and the world looks different from here.

I vowed to write lightly because lying down, for me, *is* lightness and Turrell's *Celestial Vault* begins to uncover a lighter way. When I gaze up, does his sky fall in upon me, or does it fall away? Does it threaten to come hurtling down, or can I reach up to touch it? When I lie down, transgressing my society's norms, should I brace myself for disapproval or shall I lean towards it in curiosity and embodied exploration? Is lying down an act, or is it a process of discovering the people who surround me? There are many ways to be in the world.

And now I remember. I lay down another time in public. In Covent Garden, cobbles unyielding, I dragged a large foam cushion behind me. Oh, this time it was *good*. We were a festival of artists with rebel bodies and an outsider view. For that day, we occupied the space, discovering who we might be in a world that was ours. I lay down amongst people and it felt just fine.

So here is my choice: I can absent myself from the social world, or I can lie down anyhow. If there is no guidebook, I shall write one for myself. I will not "take this lying down".

My guide is not about managing shame or the troubled body. My guide is about seizing some small courage and breaking rules that cry out to be broken. It is about laughing with the results and going back for more. And it's about realising that, when I push the boundaries, others find their courage too: that time, that conference, where I sat on the floor and, two days later, amidst sighs and wry smiles, at least half the people there had made themselves more comfortable too.

My guide shows me that lying down is not a simple act of physiology but my marking out a place in the world. Sitting up is about my body, but lying down is a declaration of liberty, the soft rain of release.

And so, I see it now; here is my freedom: I shall be fabulous in my dissipation, delight in the earth-mother voluptuousness of a Henry Moore, get out of the way of the Way in my drapes of gold and protest from the very heart of body and soul. I shall be Frida Kahlo, has she no shame, brazen hussy, wearing her wounds with pride. And my boots I shall tuck neatly to one side.

And every time I venture out and lie down, it will be a fanfare for the disappeared, a toast to the rebel body, and I will say, *we are here and we are here and we are here*.

Lying Down Anyhow begins in the physicality of the body, the freedom that is, for me, the act of lying down. Yet, when I ask why lying down in public is so very hard to do, it transforms to a story about external codes and constraints, those emotional, social, political and cultural influences that shape the body's way of being. *Lying Down Anyhow* is less the story of a troubled body than of its interface with the language, values and physical structures that limit the possibilities of lying down in public places.

Those codes and constraints permeate my internal world, shaping my thinking and behaviour. Internalising external sanctions and their attendant shame, I censor myself, believing that lying down in public places cannot be done. But, when I question their validity, I find there are other ways to respond. *Lying Down Anyhow* extends from a story of why it is so difficult to lie down in public to a decision that the constraints cannot be allowed to limit my life or the life of others; it is a decision not to be "disappeared".

In changing my response, I shift to the role of activist. Since there is no guidebook, I write my own, producing a counter-narrative to say beyond doubt that "we are here". I find myself in a process of freeing the imagination to new ways of being in the world. Setting out to make sense of my own world, I find I am also drafting a map for others to follow. My response is an antidote to the constraints and, even as they continue to hold me back, I begin to reform them in return.

I tell a story of lying down despite the constraints, to spite the constraints. And whilst such prohibitions become apparent only in collision with bodies which do not, or cannot, conform, I realise that theirs is an influence exerted upon us all. *Lying Down Anyhow* begins with my body but is, more truthfully, a tale for every body in a social world.

I begin to question whether this is a story of disability at all. In writing *Lying Down Anyhow*, increasingly I find the difficulty of lying down in public to be a symbol of the universal constraints that impact upon us all. It is a symbol of the collective need to find courage to break those myriad rules that cry out to be broken. *Lying Down Anyhow* becomes a story of the larger human condition and our need for better ways of being in the world.

In passing the text onwards, I ponder what it might set in motion. I hope there will be readers who recognise their own experience in mine and, in doing so, find "some small courage" too. Perhaps they will not lie down in public, but find from inside themselves the capacity to confront other constraints that hold them back. In questioning who we are and how we want to be, *Lying Down Anyhow* opens up possibilities for celebrating the rebel body and finding a more curious way of living.

FIGURE 4.1 Liz Crow (2012–13) *Bedding Out*, a live durational performance (Salisbury Arts Centre). Photo: Matthew Fessey/Roaring Girl Productions. By permission of the artist

Bedding Out was a durational performance which emerged from the current welfare benefits overhaul in the UK, which threatens many with poverty and a propagandist campaign that has seen a doubling in disability hate crime. The project had artist-activist Liz Crow taking her private bed-oriented life and placing it in the public arena for all to see over a 48-hour period in order to show that what many see as contradiction, or fraud, is simply the complexity of life. The work was livestreamed to 10,000 people in over 50 countries.

Members of the public were invited to participate in "Bedside Conversations", gathering around the bed to talk about the work, its backdrop and its politics, while those unable to attend in person were invited to take part virtually, through social media.

5

BLINDING THE POWER OF SIGHT

Rod Michalko (2015)

It is easier, Fredric Jameson (2003) suggests, to imagine the end of the world than it is to imagine a different one. Without treating what Jameson says as an empirical claim or a stipulation, I will explore one of the possibilities that flows from what Jameson says. In doing so, though, I will heed his call for us to imagine. Imagining Jameson's words as a call, and thus as a provocation, I will begin, to borrow from Thomas King (2003) "back in imagination."

It is not that it is impossible to imagine a different world or to imagine difference, for we sometimes do. While not impossible, imagining a different world is difficult, at least it is more difficult than imagining the end of the world. Easier for us to imagine, the end of the world comes more rapidly to us than does a different one. We seem to be closer to the end than we are to difference. But, what is this temporal and spatial connection we have to the end of the world and what makes our connection to a different world more distant and thus more difficult?

It is easy to imagine the end of the world and, therefore, such an imagining brings with it a sense of ease. Imagining a different world, in contrast, brings a sense of unease. We are relatively at ease with an image of a world that ends and not so at ease with an image of a world that is different.

Images of a different world may be disruptive and even scary. A different world, if it is truly different, must surely disrupt the world we know as ours, the world in which we now live. The science fiction genre, for example, has been disrupting and scaring us for decades. Such images of different worlds, of course, rely upon a current understanding of "a world" as a key source for the generation of disruption. Without a current image of the world, a different one is impossible or, put differently, without sameness, no difference. So different from the sameness of our current world, the science fiction world is scary. It is not easy to imagine such a world, let alone to imagine living in it and, thankfully, the category "fiction" gets us out of doing either. Nonetheless, the image of even fictional worlds of difference often generates unease. Imagining a non-fictional world of difference is not as easy as imagining a fictional one. It is very difficult to imagine living in such a world, and a mere glimpse at such an image generates not only unease but trepidation and, at times, even horror.

The end of the world is often more appealing than its continuation in difference. A different world, and again, if it is truly different, means not only the end of the current one (something relatively easy to imagine), but it also means living in difference (something not so easy to imagine). A different world is difficult to imagine and living in it is even more difficult to imagine and sometimes, even, unimaginable. The images of difference and life in difference come to us, conjoined as they are with a veil of unease and we resort to imagining the end of the world since…it is easier.

Let me try to illustrate what I have been saying. Sometime ago, I was having a beer in a bar, a bar with which I am very familiar. At one point, I decided to move to the bar's patio to smoke a cigarette. I did what I normally do; I unfolded my white cane and proceeded to locate the floor mat directly in front of the door. Finding the mat, I located the door and passed through. With my cane in my right hand in front of me I moved slightly left and found the second door. I moved through it and onto the patio. I moved to my left once again and began to walk the three or four steps to where I knew I would find a wooden ledge. I could then do what I always did – lean on the ledge, light and smoke a cigarette.

But, something happened that didn't always happen, in fact, it had never happened before. Cane in my right hand and with my left hand extended slightly forward and a little to the left so that I could locate the sandwich board that always stood there, I took the first step of the three or four that would lead me to the wooden ledge. Two steps later, my left hand found the sandwich board and I proceeded to move the final couple of steps to the ledge.

To my surprise, though, my left hand touched something; it was soft, clothing perhaps, and I quickly withdrew my hand thinking that it might be a person even though no voice came from what I had touched. Still, imagining that the unaccountable soft object might be a person, I said "Sorry." Framed in a nervous sounding laugh, the words "Oh, it's okay," came from the soft object. Sure enough, it was a person whose voice I heard as that of a woman. Laughing a little too, I again said that I was sorry and moved slightly to my right to locate the wooden ledge.

To my surprise again, another voice – a voice I heard this time as male: "You're good to go straight out now," he said. "I was coming out here for a cigarette," I said, "are you people smoking?" The male voice spoke – "No, no we're going into the bar. We were just waiting out of your way so you could get out." I said that maybe they could move around me and go into the bar and that I would lean against the ledge, pointing to it, and have a cigarette. The woman laughed again, the man said "Great," and I heard them move around me to the bar. The man spoke once more, though, and I supposed that the two of them had reached the first door of the bar and, since the man lowered his voice, I was quite certain that he thought I wouldn't hear what he said. "I could never be blind," he said, but I heard.

Now, if I heard what the man said as an empirical claim, I could dismiss what he said as simply wrong. He could, after all, "go blind"; anyone could. This means, however, that I would have to hear "I could never be blind" as "I could never go blind." But, he said that he could never "be blind." Perhaps only slightly, but there is a difference between "going blind" and "being blind."

What could "being blind" have meant to the man, given he could never be it? The man couldn't imagine "being blind," at least it wasn't easy for him to do so. "Going blind" would be horrible – imaginable, but horrible – "being blind," though, could never be, it is simply unimaginable. And yet, the experience of "being blind" was exactly what the man confronted on the patio of the bar. The unimaginable was right there in front of him. And, the man could not imagine himself in what he confronted.

What was it that the man confronted? Blindness, of course, but also something else. He confronted a "blind being," a being… "being blind." Going blind is one thing; being blind is another. The former may be easier to imagine than the latter. The shudder that often comes from imagining going blind lies in the unease of imagining being blind.

The man and the woman were headed toward the bar as I was coming out. What did they see, or better, what did they imagine when they saw me? White cane, dark glasses – we are looking at a blind man. But, what did they see – what did they imagine?

Surely, they imagined that I couldn't see. I lacked sight. They, on the other hand, didn't since they saw me. They imagined that I didn't see them and also imagined that I was leaving the bar. They were in the way, though, and I would almost certainly bump them with my white cane. The best thing that could be done, they imagined, was to get out of my way. Move quickly to the right, out of my way, and let me proceed straight through the patio, past the wooden ledge and out onto the sidewalk. Then, the unimaginable – I moved left, headed directly for them, headed to where they were standing "out of my way." Stand still; don't move; don't speak; maybe he'll move slightly right and find his way out. But he didn't; he touched her; stand still; don't speak.

Anxious as they must have been, this experience wasn't the end of the world for the man and the woman, at least not the end of their world, but…it certainly was a different one. It is easier to imagine blindness as the end of sight than it is to imagine it as a different way of being, as a different world. The man and the woman looked at blindness, something they could imagine, and when they looked at blindness that afternoon, they saw someone living blindness, living difference, and this was not so easy to imagine. It is easier to imagine the end of the world of sight than it is to imagine a different world of blindness. It is easier to see the end of sight than it is to see blindness. The power of sight is blinded by its own limit.

Sight (the man and the woman) stand still, quietly, not speaking; sight stands vanishing in the face of the end of sight and in the midst of the beginning of the difference of blindness. Sight moves quietly out of the way of on-coming blindness and stands very still, vanishing in the face of blindness and watching it move out-of-sight retreating to where it belongs – into the end of the world of sight. Ghostly figures, unseen by one another, blindness and sight stand together groping, one for an image of a different world, the other, for an image of the end of the world. The latter is easier to imagine and, at times, is so perhaps for both blindness and sight and is so when the power of sight is blinded by its own end.

PART II
Theory and criticism

Much critical and cultural theory across the arts and humanities is currently examining how to better conceptualise and articulate the intersections of individuals, society and space as situated, embodied, specific, partial and dynamic. Theorists across a multiplicity of disciplines such as Michel Foucault, Judith Butler, Luce Irigaray, Homa Bhaba, Karen Barad, Felix Guttari and Gilles Delueze, Isabelle Stengers, Maurice Merleau-Ponty and Bruno Latour have been challenging earlier modernist framing of ideas within simplistic binary relationships – man/woman, public/private, white/black, straight/gay – and shifting away from concerns with representation and cultural meaning (what things *say*) to the non-representational, to how life is performed (what things *do*). However, as many disability studies scholars have shown, the ability–disability pairing has often remained unnoticed in these theories or has simply been added 'on the end'. Starting from dis/ability has enabled interesting disruptions of some contemporary theoretical assumptions, as well as opened up how to better conceptualise disability as situated and embodied (Davis 1995, 2002, 2014; Michalko, 2002; Corker and Shakespeare 2002; Kafer 2013).

Theoretical explorations of disability are not new; whilst in geography, in particular, there have been explorations of disability and built space over many years (Imrie 1996, 2012; Imrie and Kumar 1998; Gleeson 1998; Butler and Parr 1999; Imrie and Edwards 2007; Chouinard et al. 2010). Studies of dis/ability have also overlapped with interrogations of art practice and aesthetics, and of disability representation (Garland-Thomson 1996; Siebers 2008, 2010; Haller 2010). One of the most renowned disability studies scholars in this field, Tobin Siebers, writes here about disability and aesthetics, and in particular how ideas about bodies come to be incorporated into art practices. He is particularly interested in how some contemporary artists refuse only to imagine beauty through picturing ideal, healthy bodies but instead explore dis/ability as a means of enriching and complicating our ideas of the aesthetic.

Other theorists and activists from disability studies have been engaging directly with space, and how this might be (re)conceptualised through dis/ability. In particular Tanya Titchkosky, Rod Michalko, Aimi Hamraie, Jay Dolmage and Margaret Price interrogate how built space *works*. This is through the social, spatial and material practices it perpetuates, so as to make everyday assumptions about disability and ability seem normal and obvious by the very concreteness of our surroundings, and by acting differently and *differentially* on disabled compared to abled bodies.

In 'The body as a problem of individuality: A phenomenological disability studies approach' Titchkosky and Michalko unravel how disability comes to be framed as a problem in need of solution – a common assumption behind much accessibility design guidance and regulation. They explore whose interests such an articulation supports; how it enables 'normal' bodies (and their privilege) to remain unnoticed, whilst disabled bodies are exposed only as 'difficult'; and how it perpetuates particular ideas of individuality. In this reading they turn to disabled students' experiences of the university, as a means of understanding the impact of such common sense framings. By articulating disability as different from, and simultaneously outside, 'normal' life, choosing to study becomes a problem of individual disabled students themselves, rather than a problem of the spatial and educational organisation of the university. In important related work Titchkosky shows how through such processes, disabled people come to be articulated as 'includable as excludable' (2011: 39), that is, included at the level of appearance (for example in policy papers or guidance notes) but ignored or marginalised in actual situations, and exposes some of the 'ordinary' justificatory narratives that defend such an approach (2008, 2011).

For Titchkosky and Michalko, as for many of the other writers here, though, making a critique of ableist framings, is only part of the story. This is because, as they say in their chapter here 'disability is ... ambiguity incarnate, a rupture in the clarity and unquestioned flow of daily life, and thus almost a "natural" starting place for thinking about the workings of culture'. Starting from disability, then, offers opportunities to trouble cultural theories and practices more generally.

The concepts of inclusive or universal design (UD) and accessibility are also garnering theoretical and critical attention. Rather than simplistically arguing for UD as a common sense – often oppositional – model to 'uncaring' mainstream design, the other three authors in this section, Aimi Hamraie, J. Kent Fitzsimons and Jay Dolmage instead explore how to critically unpick the complexities and difficulties of 'designing for the disabled'. In 'Designing collective access: A feminist disability theory of universal design', Hamraie is concerned that UD is often implemented at the level of appearances as a marketing strategy, rather than operating as it was intended by disability activists, as an important method of social justice activism. Through intersecting feminism and disability studies, Hamraie argues that treating UD theoretically and critically means more than just applying its principles; it means 'paying attention to how physical environments produce symbolic and material access or exclusion through their interactions with and knowledge about bodies'. As with Titchkosky and Michalko, the central problem is in assuming (and failing to acknowledge) that building design starts from a normal body, framed as independent, mobile and individual. Since this is set against disabled bodies as problematic dependencies, it also implies a refusal to accept the fundamental interdependence of all bodies for sustenance, community and care – that is, for what Hamraie calls collective access.

J. Kent Fitzsimons also critically engages with assumptions about access. In 'More than access: Overcoming limits in architectural and disability discourse' he is interested in how many ideas in contemporary architecture are potentially redefining what accessibility *is or could be*. By critically reviewing schemes by Peter Eisenman and SANAA, he argues that when access is taken purely functionally as a compensatory measure to help disabled people be more 'normal' it actually acts to 'distract from other aspects of the complex relationships between space design and the experiences of disability'. By this he means that being in built space is never just a matter of its functionality, of navigating mechanically from one place to another, but is also imbued with meanings and encounters; and that we need to think beyond such a limited assumption about the spatial 'needs' of disabled people, as a means to start imagining bodies-in-space differently. By showing how – in different ways – the Berlin Memorial to the Murdered Jews of Europe and SANAA's Rolex Learning Center in Lausanne disturb the common sense divisions in architecture between functional circulation and meaningful design, Fitzsimons is able to open up the idea of accessibility to both critical and creative questioning.

Jay Dolmage, in 'From Steep Steps to Retrofit to Universal Design, From Collapse to Austerity: Neo-Liberal Spaces of Disability' puts this into a broader context, by examining how accessibility and universal design are embedded in social, spatial and material practices that already create 'steep steps' for disabled people. He too looks at the university as a key site in enabling the privilege of some, and disabling others; and crucially how these two processes are completely intertwined both historically and in contemporary space. Dolmage also homes in on the underpinning logic of everyday building design that is explored throughout this section. This is that 'normal space' is first created and then *retrofitted* for disabled people. As he says, to

> retrofit is to add a component or accessory to something that has been already manufactured or built. This retrofit does not necessarily *make* the product function better, does not necessarily fix a faulty product, but it acts as a sort of correction – it adds a modernized part in place of, or in addition to, an older part. … [It] is a sort of cure, but half-hearted, thus leaving many people with disabilities in difficult positions.

Dolmage then explores his third metaphor – universal design. Like Hamraie he sees it not as a design solution but as an important *direction*. It too, can be aligned and overlap with retrofitting, can act as a easy cover for other policies that act against disabled people, and does not always challenge the independent, mobile and individual (also neo-liberal) body. He proposes that we might instead take the concept of collapse, not as a negative but as a deliberate mode of action – 'collapsing' as a means to reclaim and re-inhabit the role and nature of design in a neo-liberal world.

I started this section introduction by noting how usefully disability studies is critiquing many of the critical and cultural theories that are currently impacting on architectural discourses. It should be noted that disability scholars and activists are also exploring connections between disability and feminism, queer studies, post-colonial and critical race studies, and are generating emerging fields such as mad studies. This inter-sectionality is developing understandings of some important interrelationships, as well as generating creative and constructive scholarship and activism, which the pieces selected here cannot fully express. For this reason, the recommended readings for the theory and criticism part deliberately extends beyond disability studies, to include theorists for related areas who are also engaging with the including/enabling and excluding/disabling aspects of built space.

Recommended further reading

Ahmed, S. (2006) *Queer Phenomenology: Orientations, Objects, Others*, Durham, NC: Duke University Press.

Davidson, M. (2008) *Concerto for the Left Hand: Disability and the Defamiliar Body*, Ann Arbor, MI: University of Michigan Press.

Edwards, C. and Imrie, R. (2003) 'Disability and Bodies as Bearers of Value', *Sociology* 37(2): 239–256.

Erevelles, N. (2011) *Disability and Difference in Global Contexts: Enabling a Transformative Body Politic*, London: Palgrave MacMillan.

Galis, V. (2011) 'Enacting Disability: How Can Science and Technology Studies Inform Disability Studies?', *Disability and Society* 26(7): (December) 825–838.

Garland-Thomson, R. (2011) 'Misfits: A Feminist Materialist Disability Concept', *Hypatia Special Issue: Ethics of Embodiment* 26(5): 591–609, Summer.

Hamraie, A. (2012) 'Proximate and Peripheral: Ableist Discourses of Space and Vulnerability Surrounding the UNCRPD', in C. Certoma, N. Clewer and D. Elsey (eds) *The Politics of Space and Place: Exclusions, Resistance, Alternatives*, Newcastle-Upon-Tyne: Cambridge Scholars Press, 145–169.

Hamraie, A. (2015) 'Inclusive Design: Cultivating Accountability towards the Intersections of Race, Aging and Disability' *Age Culture Humanities: An Interdisciplinary Journal* Issue 2. Available for free download at: http://ageculturehumanities.org/WP/inclusive-design-cultivating-accountability-toward-the-intersections-of-race-aging-and-disability/

Hamraie, A. (2017) *Building Access: Disability, Universal Design, and the Politics of Knowing-Making*, Minneapolis, MN: University of Minnesota Press.

McRuer, R. (2006) *Crip Theory: Cultural Signs of Queerness and Disability*, New York: NYU Press.

Puwar, N. (2004) *Space Invaders: Race, Gender and Bodies Out of Place*, London: Bloomsbury Academic.

Siebers, T. (2001) 'Disability in Theory: From Social Constructionism to the New Realism of the Body', *American Literary History* 13(4): 737–754.

Seibers, T. (2006) 'Disability Studies and the Future of Identity Politics', in L. Martín Alcoff, M. Hames-Gárcia, S. P. Mohanty, and P.M. L. Moya (eds) *Identity Politics Reconsidered*, New York: Palgrave MacMillan, 10–30.

Seibers, T. (2008) *Disability Theory*, Ann Arbor, MI: University of Michigan Press.

Seibers, T. (2010) 'Disability and the Theory of Complex Embodiment – For Identity Politics in a New Register', in L. Davis (ed.) *Disability Studies Reader*, 3rd edition, New York: Routledge, 316–335.

Seibers, T. (2010) *Disability Aesthetics*, Ann Arbor, MI: University of Michigan Press.

Titchkosky, T. (2008) 'To Pee or Not to Pee? Ordinary Talk about Extraordinary Exclusions in a University Environment', Canadian Journal of Sociology 33(1): 37–60, http://ejournals.library.ualberta.ca/index.php/CJS/article/view/1526/1058

Titchkosky, T. (2011) *The Question of Access: Disability, Space, Meaning*, Toronto: University of Toronto Press.

6

DISABILITY AESTHETICS

Tobin Siebers (2006)

Reprinted from Journal for Cultural and Religious Theory (JCRT) *(2006) 7.2 Spring/Summer, pp 63–72.*

Aesthetics tracks the emotions that some bodies feel in the presence of other bodies. This definition of aesthetics, first conceived by Alexander Baumgarten, posits the human body and its affective relation to other bodies as foundational to the appearance of the beautiful – and to such a powerful extent that aesthetics suppresses its underlying corporeality only with difficulty (1954). The human body is both the subject and object of aesthetic production: the body creates other bodies prized for their ability to change the emotions of their maker and endowed with a semblance of vitality usually ascribed only to human beings. But all bodies are not created equal when it comes to aesthetic response. Taste and disgust are volatile reactions that reveal the ease or disease with which one body might incorporate another. The senses revolt against some bodies, while other bodies please them. These responses represent the corporeal substrata on which aesthetic effects are based. Nevertheless, there is a long tradition of trying to replace the underlying corporeality of aesthetics with idealist and disembodied conceptions of art. For example, the notion of "disinterestedness," an ideal invented in the eighteenth century but very much alive today, separates the pleasures of art from those of the body, while the twentieth-century notion of "opticality" denies the bodily character of visual perception. The result is a non-materialist aesthetics that devalues the role of the body and limits the definition of art.

There are some recent trends in art, however, that move beyond idealism to invoke powerful emotional responses to the corporeality of aesthetic objects (Siebers 2000a, 2003). Andy Warhol's car crashes and other disaster paintings represent the fragility of the human body with an explicitness rarely found in the history of art. Nam June Paik, Carolee Schneemann and Chris Burden turn their own bodies into instruments or works of art, painting with their face or hair, having themselves shot with guns, and exhibiting themselves in situations both ordinary and extraordinary. Other artists employ substances thought to be beyond the bounds of art: food stuff, wreckage, refuse, debris, body parts. Curiously, the presence of these materials makes the work of art seem more real, even though all aesthetics objects have, because of their material existence, an equal claim to being real. And yet such works of art are significant neither because they make art appear more realistic nor because they discover a new terrain for aesthetics. They are significant because they return aesthetics forcefully to its originary subject matter: the body and its affective sphere.

Works of art engaged explicitly with the body serve to critique the assumptions of idealist aesthetics, but they also have an unanticipated effect that will be the topic of my investigation here. Whether or not we interpret these works as aesthetic, they summon images of disability. Most frequently, they register as wounded or disabled bodies, representations of irrationality or cognitive disability, or effects of warfare, disease, or accidents. How is disability related to artistic mimesis – or what Erich Auerbach called "the representation of reality" (1953, Siebers 2004)? Why do we see representations of disability as having a greater material existence than other aesthetic representations? Since aesthetic feelings of pleasure and disgust are difficult to separate from political feelings of acceptance and rejection, what do these objects tell us about the ideals of political community underlying works of art?

What I am calling disability aesthetics names a critical concept that seeks to emphasize the presence of disability in the tradition of aesthetic representation. Disability aesthetics refuses to recognize the representation of the healthy body – and its definition of harmony, integrity, and beauty – as the sole determination of the aesthetic. It is not a matter of representing the exclusion of disability from aesthetic history, since such an exclusion has not taken place, but of making the influence of disability obvious. This goal may take two forms: 1) to establish disability as a critical framework that questions the presuppositions underlying definitions of aesthetic production and appreciation; 2) to establish disability as a significant value in itself worthy of future development. My claim is that the acceptance of disability enriches and complicates materialist notions of the aesthetic, while the rejection of disability limits definitions of artistic ideas and objects.

To argue that disability has a rich but hidden role in the history of art is not to say that disability has been excluded. It is rather the case that disability is rarely recognized as such, even though it often serves as the very factor that establishes works as superior examples of aesthetic beauty. Disability intercedes to make the difference between good and bad art – and not as one would initially expect. That is, good art incorporates disability. Distinctions between good and bad art may seem troublesome, but only if one assumes that critical judgments are never applied in the art world – an untenable assumption. My point is only that works of art for which the argument of superiority is made tend to claim disability. This is hardly an absolute formula, although some have argued it, notably Francis Bacon and Edgar Allan Poe, who wrote that "There is no exquisite beauty, without some strangeness in the proportion," or André Breton, who exclaimed "Beauty will be convulsive or it will not be at all" (Allan Poe 1978, Bacon 2007, Breton 1960).

Significantly, it could be argued that beauty always maintains an underlying sense of disability and that increasing this sense over time may actually renew works of art that risk to fall out of fashion because of changing standards of taste. It is often the presence of disability that allows the beauty of an art work to endure over time. Would the *Venus de Milo* still be considered one of the great examples of both aesthetic and human beauty if she still had both her arms? Perhaps it is an exaggeration to consider the Venus disabled, but René Magritte did not think so. He painted his version of the Venus, *Les Menottes de cuivre*, in flesh tones and colorful drapery but splashed blood-red pigment on her famous arm-stumps, giving the impression of a recent and painful amputation. The Venus is one of many works of art called beautiful by the tradition of aesthetic response that eschew the uniformity of perfect bodies and embrace the variety of disability (Quinn 2004).

To argue from the flipside, would Nazi art be considered kitsch if it had not pursued so relentlessly a bombastic perfection of the body? Sculpture and painting cherished by the Nazis exhibit a stultifying perfection of the human figure. Favored male statuary such as Arno Breker's *Readiness* displays bulked up and gigantesque bodies that intimidate rather than appeal. The perfection of the bodies is the very mark of their unreality and lack of taste. Nazi representations of women, as in Ivo Saliger's *Diana's Rest*, portray women as reproductive bodies having little variation among them. They may be healthy, but they are emotionally empty. When faced by less kitschy representations of the body, the Nazis were repulsed and launched their own version of a culture war: their campaign against modern art stemmed from the inability to tolerate any human forms except the most familiar, monochromatic, and regular. Specifically, the Nazis rejected modern art as degenerate and ugly because they viewed it as representing physical and mental disability. Hitler saw in paintings by Modigliani, Klee, and Chagall images of "misshapen cripples," "cretins," and racial inferiors when the rest of the world saw masterpieces of modern art (Mosse 1991, Seibers 2000b). Hitler was wrong, of course, not about the place of disability in modern aesthetics but about its beauty. Modern art continues to move us because of its refusal of harmony, bodily integrity, and perfect health. If modern art has been so successful, I would argue, it is because of its embrace of disability as a distinct version of the beautiful. The Nazis simply misread the future direction of art, as they misread many things about human culture.

What is the impact of damage on classic works of art from the past? It is true that we strive to preserve and repair them, but perhaps the accidents of history have the effect of renewing rather than destroying art works. Vandalized works seem strangely modern. In 1977 a vandal attacked a Rembrandt self-portrait with sulfuric acid, transforming the masterpiece forever and regrettably (Domberg 1987, 1988, Gamboni 1997, Siebers 2002). Nevertheless, the problem is not that the resulting image no longer belongs in the history of art. Rather, the riddle of the vandalized work is that it now seems to have moved to a more recent stage in aesthetic history, giving a modernist rather than baroque impression.

The art vandal puts the art object to use again, replicating the moment of its inception when it was being composed of raw material and before it became fixed in time and space as an aesthetic object. Would vandalized works become more emblematic of the aesthetic, if we did not restore them, as the *Venus de Milo* has not been restored? My point is not to encourage vandalism but to use it to query the effect that disability has on aesthetic appreciation. Vandalism modernizes art works, for better or worse, by inserting them in an aesthetic tradition increasingly preoccupied with disability. Only the historical unveiling of disability accounts for the aesthetic effect of vandalized works of art. Damaged art and broken beauty are no longer interpreted as ugly. Rather, they disclose new forms of beauty that leave behind a kitschy dependence on perfect bodily forms. They also suggest that experimentation with aesthetic form reflects a desire to experiment with human form.

Beholders discover in vandalized works an image of disability that asks to be contemplated not as a symbol of human imperfection but as an experience of the corporeal variation found everywhere in modern life.

Art is materialist because it relies on the means of production and the availability of material resources – as Marx understood. But art is also materialist in its obsession with the embodiment of new conceptions of the human. At a certain level, objects of art are bodies, and aesthetics is the science of discerning how some bodies make other bodies feel. Art is the active site designed to explore and expand the spectrum of humanity that we will accept among us.

Since human feeling is central to aesthetic history, it is to be expected that disability will crop up everywhere because the disabled body and mind always elicit powerful emotions. I am making a stronger claim: that disability is integral to aesthetic conceptions of the beautiful and that the influence of disability on art has grown, not dwindled, over the course of time. If this is the case, we may expect disability to exert even greater power over art in the future. We need to consider, then, how art is changed when we conceive of disability as an aesthetic value in itself. In particular, it is worth asking how the presence of disability requires us to revise traditional conceptions of aesthetic production and appreciation, and here the examples of two remarkable artists, Paul McCarthy and Judith Scott, are especially illuminating.

Paul McCarthy is well known in avant-garde circles for his chaotic, almost feral, bodily performances as well as his tendency to make art from food and condiments. One of the most significant fictions of disembodiment in the history of art is, of course, the doctrine of disinterestedness, which defines the power of an art work in direct proportion to the urgency of the desires and appetites overcome in the beholder. Hunger, sexual desire, and greed have no place in the appreciation of art works, despite the fact that these appetites are constant themes in art. McCarthy challenges the classic doctrine of disinterestedness in aesthetic appreciation by revealing that it censors not only the body but also the disabled body. He refuses to prettify the human body, reproducing the logic of the nineteenth-century freak show in the museum space with exhibits that stress bodily deformation. He also makes art out of food stuff, forcing beholders to experience his work with all their senses, not merely with their eyes. In short, his is a different embodiment of art, one expert in the presentation of differently abled bodies. For example, *Hollywood Halloween* pictures the artist tearing a Halloween mask from his head (Figure 6.1), but because the mask has been stuffed with hamburger meat and ketchup in addition to the artist's head, the effect is a kind of self-defacement.

The transformation of the artist from eerie able-bodiedness to the defacement of disability is the work's essential movement. The work reverses the apparently natural tendency to consider any form a corporeal transformation as driven by the desire for improvement or cure. In *Death Ship*, a crazed ship captain hands out sailor hats to the audience, inviting them on a voyage in which the boundaries between body, food, and filth dissolve, as the captain smears his body with ketchup and food and installs a feeding tube for himself running from his anus to his mouth. *Mother Pig* similarly plays out a self-sculpture using processed meats and condiments in which McCarthy, masked as a pig, wraps strings of frankfurters smeared with ketchup around his penis. In these typical

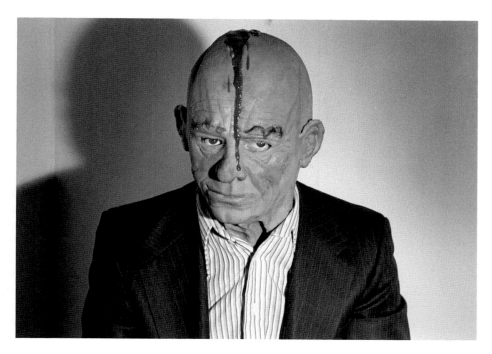

FIGURE 6.1 Paul McCarthy 1977, *Hollywood Halloween*, performance, Los Angeles, CA

© Paul McCarthy. Courtesy Paul McCarthy and Hauser & Wirth.

works, the smell of raw meat and pungent condiments permeate the air of the performance space, making it difficult for the audience to avoid reactions to foodstuff and flesh from its everyday life.

In addition to the challenge to disinterestedness perpetrated on the audience by McCarthy's stimulation of the appetite or gag reflex, as well as the assault on human beauty and form, is the representation of the mental condition of the artist. As the performances grow more intense and irrational, the audience begins to react to McCarthy as if he were mentally disabled. The video of *Class Fool* (1976), for example, shows the audience's reaction to his performance moving from amusement, to hesitation, to aversion. At some level, McCarthy's commitment to elemental behavior – smearing himself with food, repeating meaningless actions until they are ritualized, fondling himself in public – asks to be seen as idiocy, as if the core values of intelligence and genius were being systematically removed from the aesthetic in preference to stupidity and cognitive disorder. *Plaster Your Head and One Arm into a Wall* (Figure 6.2), in which McCarthy inserts his head and left arm into wall cavities and then uses his right hand to close the holes with plaster, provides a more obvious example of these values. McCarthy changes how art is appreciated by overstimulating his audience with a different conception of art's corporeality. He takes the analogy between art work and body to its limit, challenging ideas about how the human should be transformed and imagined. Moreover, the link between aesthetic appreciation and taste faces a redoubtable attack in his works because of their single-minded evocation of things that disgust.

The appreciation of the work of art is a topic well rehearsed in the history of aesthetics, but rarely is it considered from the vantage point of the disabled mind – no doubt because the spectacle of the mentally disabled person, rising with emotion before the shining work of art, disrupts the long-standing belief that pronouncements of taste depend on a form of human intelligence as autonomous and imaginative as the art object itself. Artistic production also seems to reflect a limited and well defined range of mental actions. Traditionally, we understand that art originates in genius, but genius is really at a minimum only the name for an intelligence large enough to plan and execute works of art – an intelligence that usually goes by the name of "intention." Defective or impaired intelligence cannot make art according to this rule. Mental disability represents an absolute rupture with the work of art. It marks the constitutive moment of abolition, according to Michel Foucault, that dissolves the essence of what art is (1973: 286).

The work of Judith Scott challenges the absolute rupture between mental disability and the work of art and applies more critical pressure on intention as a standard for identifying artists. It is an extremely rare case, but it raises complex questions about aesthetics of great value to people with disabilities. A remarkably gifted fiber artist emerged in the late 1980s in California named Judith Scott. Her work is breathtaking in its originality and possesses disturbing power as sculptural form (Figure 6.3). The sculptures invite comparisons with major artists of the twentieth century and allude to a striking variety of mundane and historical forms, from maps to the works of Alberto Giacometti, from Etruscan art and classical sculpture in its fragmentary state, to children's toys. What makes the fiber sculptures even more staggering as works of art is the fact that Scott has no conception of the associations sparked by her objects and no knowledge of the history of art. In fact, she

FIGURE 6.2　Paul McCarthy, 1973, *Plaster Your Head and One Arm into a Wall*, performance, Pasadena, CA

never visited a museum or read an art book, she did not know she was an "artist," and never intended to make "art" when she set to work, at least in the conventional understanding of these words. This is because Scott had Down's syndrome. She was also deaf, unable to speak, extremely uncommunicative, isolated, almost autistic. She was warehoused at age seven in the Ohio Asylum for the Education of Idiotic and Imbecilic Youth and spent the next thirty-five years of her life as a ward of the state, until her twin sister rescued her and enrolled her in the Creative Growth Center, a California program in Oakland designed to involve intellectually disabled people with the visual arts. Almost immediately, she began to make fiber sculptures six hours a day, and she maintained this relentless pace for over ten years.

Although materials were made available to her, Scott behaved as if she were pilfering them, and each one of her sculptures takes the form of a cocoon at the center of which is secreted some acquired object (Figure 6.3). The first hidden objects were sticks and cardboard spools used to store yarn and thread. Then she began to wrap other objects, an electric fan, for instance. Commentators have made the habit of associating her methods with acts of theft and a kind of criminal sensibility, acquired during thirty-five years in a mental institution. The association between Scott's aesthetic method and criminal sensibility, however, takes it for granted that she was unable to distinguish between the Ohio Asylum for the Education of Idiotic and Imbecilic Youth and the Creative Growth Center in Oakland, between thirty-five years spent in inactivity and neglect and her years involved intensively in the making of objects of beauty. The fact is that Scott's relation

FIGURE 6.3 Judith Scott, *Untitled*, 1989. 30 × 11 × 6 inches. Collection de l'Art Brut
Copyright: Creative Growth Art Center. Photograph by Leon A. Borensztein

to her primary materials mimics modern art's dependence on found art – a dependence that has never been described as a criminal sensibility to my knowledge. Her method demonstrates the freedom both to make art from what she wants and to change the meaning of objects by inserting them into different contexts. One incident in particular illuminates her attitude toward her primary materials. During a period of construction in the art center, Scott was left unobserved one day for longer than usual. She emptied every paper-towel dispenser in the building and fabricated a beautiful monochromatic sculpture made entirely of knotted white paper towels.

Scott's method always combines binding, knotting, sewing, and weaving different fiber materials around a solid core whose visibility is entirely occluded by the finished work of art. She builds the works patiently and carefully, as if in a process of concealment and discovery that destroys one object and gives birth to another mysterious thing. A number of aesthetic principles are clearly at work in her method, even though she never articulated them. She strives to ensure the solidity and stability of each piece, and individual parts are bound tightly to a central core (Figure 6.4). Since she had no view to

FIGURE 6.4 Judith Scott in action 1999. Oakland Studio, Creative Growth Center.

Photograph copyright: Leon A. Borensztein. With thanks to the Creative Growth Center.

exhibit her work, no audience in mind, her sculptures do not distinguish between front and back. Consequently, her work projects a sense of independence and autonomy almost unparalleled in the sculptural medium. Despite the variety of their shape, construction, and parts, then, Scott's sculptures consolidate all of their elements to give the impression of a single, unique body.

John MacGregor who has done the most extensive study to date of Scott poses succinctly the obvious critical questions raised by her work. "Does serious mental retardation," he asks, "invariably preclude the creation of true works of art? … Can art, in the fullest sense of the word, emerge when intellectual development is massively impaired from birth, and when normal intellectual and emotional maturation has failed to be attained?" The problem, of course, is that Scott did not possess the intelligence associated with true artists by the tradition of art history. What kind of changes in the conception of art would be necessary to include her in this history?

Despite the many attacks launched by modern artists, genius remains the unspecified platform on which almost every judgment in art criticism is based, whether about artistic technique, invention, or subversiveness. In fact, Thomas Crow claims that the campaign against autonomy and creativity in modern art gives rise to a cult of the genius more robust than any conceived during the Romantic period (1996). We still assume that creativity is an expression of inspiration and autonomy, just as we assume that aesthetic technique is a form of brilliance always at the artist's disposal. Intelligence, however, is fraught with difficulties as a measure of aesthetic quality, and intention in particular has long been condemned as an obsolete tool for interpreting works of art (Wimsatt and Beardsley 1954). Artists do not control – nor should they – the meaning of their works, and intentions are doubtful as a standard of interpretation because they are variable, often forgotten, improperly executed, inscrutable to other people, and marred by accidents in aesthetic production. If intention has uncertain value for interpretation, why should it be used to determine whether an action or object is a work of art?

Disability aesthetics prizes physical and mental difference as a significant value in itself. It does not embrace an aesthetic taste that defines harmony, bodily integrity, and health as standards of beauty. Nor does it support the aversion to disability required by traditional conceptions of human or social perfection. Rather, it drives forward the appreciation of disability found throughout modern and avant-garde art by raising an objection to aesthetic standards and tastes that exclude people with disabilities. The idea of disability aesthetics affirms that disability operates both as a critical framework for questioning aesthetic presuppositions in the history of art and as a value in its own right important to future conceptions of what art is.

7

THE BODY AS A PROBLEM OF INDIVIDUALITY

A phenomenological disability studies approach

Tanya Titchkosky and Rod Michalko (2012)

Excerpt reprinted from Dan Goodley, Bill Hughes and Lennard Davis (eds) (2012) Disability and Social Theory: New Developments and Directions, *Palgrave Macmillan, pp 127–129.*

Disability, as Paul Abberley (1998: 93) reminds us, is interesting often only as a problem. Or as Bill Hughes (2007: 673) puts it, 'almost by definition, [we] assume disability to be ontologically problematic, and many disabled people feel that many of the people with whom they interact in everyday situations treat them as if they are invisible, repulsive or "not all there".' What interests us from a phenomenological perspective, is that the contemporary scene of disability framed as a 'problem' typically generates the requirement for explanation and amelioration, but little else. Thus, this paper examines the hegemonic taken-for-granted character of the disability-as-a-problem frame.

We aim to show how this frame is produced against a background of a notion of the 'natural' or 'normal' body, that is, a body conceived of by science as in need, and worthy, of description – how does it work, what are its essential features? The disabled body, in contrast, is conceived of as requiring explanation – what went wrong, how can it be fixed and brought back to normalcy? Yet, the questions 'what went wrong and what should be done?' are based on the reproduction of the frame 'disability as a problem' and leave this frame completely unexamined. Questioning the 'facticity' (Heidegger, 1962) of the problem-of-disability means reflecting on the oft used, over-deterministic, and under-theorized frame 'disability is a problem in need of a solution' as itself a solution to some implicit problem. That disability is conceptualized as a problem is what we take to be our problem in need of theorizing. In other words, conceiving of disability as a problem in need of a solution may be treated as a response to an implicit version of disability, a response that acts as a solution to the question 'What is disability?' This approach permits us to ask, what sort of problem do contemporary times need disability to be? And, what is the meaning of human embodiment that grounds the unquestioned status of disability as a problem?

The field of disability studies says, and says often, that such frames constitute disability as an individual problem of tragic proportions requiring only individualized redress. But, from a phenomenological perspective, knowing this and showing this are not the same. We aim, then, to show how disability is made into an individual problem of tragic proportions and this returns us to the question of the normalized embodied contours of individuality itself. As disability is made into a problem, what is made of the human condition harnessed to the workings of a culture that seeks to service 'normal' individuals? A disability studies approach informed by phenomenology can contribute to understanding the consequences of the contemporary 'demand' on us to understand identity as our individual 'task' and 'duty' (Bauman, 2004: 18–19). We will further draw out these issues by conducting an exploration of how the phenomenon of disability-as-problem composes university life while teasing out how the language of the problem reflects the educational world views that arise through the lived bodies that we are. In so doing, we offer a reflection regarding what a phenomenological approach does in order to do what it does and to say what it says, and then show this at work in the university milieu.

Disability as problem

Framing disability as a problem in need of a solution takes many different forms. The biomedical world view, for example, conceives of disability as the 'body-gone-wrong' (Michalko, 2002: 120) and, if living a life of disability is to be achieved at all, this body should be treated in a way that permits it to 'look' and act as 'normal' as possible. This treatment, or better, this interpretive work, is achieved through such contemporary ideologies as medicine, rehabilitation and education, especially that of the 'special' kind.

Still another form of the disability-as-problem frame is the erasure of disability through the privileging of personhood – a framing of disabled people as 'like everyone else' but only *like* and not *as* everyone else since, within this frame, personhood is not located in disability but against it (Titchkosky, 2001). This frame suggests that disabled people can 'resemble' non-disabled others even though they are other to non-disability regardless of the fidelity of the resemblance. Disability may participate in normalcy, but it can never be normal let alone be valuable, enjoyable, or necessary.

Framed in these ways disability is represented and experienced as a kind of partially protected liability precariously perched on the edge of liveable life (Butler, 2009: 9, 43). The disciplinary infrastructures and technologies engaged in these ways of framing disability are powerful and global in their character and reach (Titchkosky and Aubrecht, 2009). The disciplinary research based regimes, such as medicine and education, do not typically address what it means to constitute the phenomenon of disability in this singular and unified way. The socio-political act of framing disability as a problem in need of a solution does not engage itself, it does not question what it makes when it makes disability a problem – this way of framing disability is not reflexive and this now becomes *our* problem.

Phenomenology is a way to frame disability as a scene (Butler, 1993: 23) where the meaning of the human condition of embodiment can be brought into consciousness for reflective consideration – a task we regard as essential to any political possibility of forging something new since the new is tied to rethinking our most basic ways of framing embodiment. The desire for something 'new' is grounded in the sense of the unexpected potentiality that resides in all forms of human action as well as in the politicalized sense that disabled people face extreme forms of devaluation within cultures animated by limited and limiting conceptions of embodiment that themselves leave much to be desired. The possibility of forging something new is intimately interwoven with questioning what is typically assumed to be beyond question; questioning what is otherwise taken as a given serves as a reflexive re-framing of our lives together as bodied beings.

We turn our analysis toward a fuller discussion of the phenomenological conception of the 'frame' and of framing with regard to disability.

Disability-frameworks and phenomenology

The world comes to us and we receive it always-already 'framed.' Like all other phenomena, disability comes to us in a frame and this frame 'works' as a guide and even as a rule for recognizing the phenomenon of disability. We recognize disability in others and in ourselves insofar as disability-frameworks guide us to these recognitions and work to rule them. Even though we recognize disability, we do not easily recognize its frames and the framework that provides for such recognition. Nonetheless, we are conscious of disability insofar as there are disability frames for and of such consciousness. Disability consciousness typically entails experiencing disability as always already a problem, located in individuals.

Edmund Husserl tells us that a function of understanding is '… ruling in concealment, i.e., ruling as constitutive of the always already developed and always further developing meaning-configuration "intuitively given surrounding world"' (Husserl, 1970: 104). The world surrounds us, according to Husserl, and it is intuitively given to us. The world comes to us always configured (framed) as meaning – the world always means. Or as Maurice Merleau-Ponty (1945: xxii) says, 'Because we are in the world, we are *condemned to meaning.*' Meaning is the rule and it constitutes a world, including all that belongs in and to it, which comes to us as 'given' and intuitively so. As such, we take the reality of the world for granted. It is this 'rule' of the taken-for-granted world that is concealed from us when we experience the world. We perceive the world that surrounds us but we do not 'see' the frameworks that constitute this world as configured in and by meaning. […]

Sustaining the 'given-ness' of the world, the sense that it is naturally just there for all to perceive, is an activity in which we are constantly involved (Sacks, 1984). The world, change and human agency are given to us and received by us as naturally occurring phenomena. These phenomena are seemingly so natural to us that we readily give an explanatory account for those times they do not occur. We make sense of the world even when it is disrupted and every disruption is remedied through the sense-making character of the natural attitude (Garfinkel, 1967; Weiss, 2008). 'I think you're in denial, you have to get past this and move forward.' 'Some people just don't see that things have to change, they're brainwashed by society and the media.' 'What you need is a reality check.' Despite the mundane character of these accounts, they do dramatically demonstrate how we act to sustain the taken-for-granted and natural character of the life-world.

We are continuously providing an account, albeit in a taken-for-granted way, for the existence and possibility of world views, different and conflicting as they may be. We all have a world view. We perceive the world from a perspective or 'standpoint.' We are socially positioned in the world and, from the perspective of contemporary versions of identity, for example, we are so positioned through categories such as race, gender, sexuality, social class, and sometimes even disability. These social categories position us and give us a standpoint, a perspective from which to view the world. We also view the world from the 'point of view' of our interests, concerns, anxieties, aspirations, and the like (Ahmed, 2004 a & b). The way people are positioned in the world, then, generates not only multiple perspectives but multiple realities.

While we do experience the world differently from one another, depending upon our sense of our social identity and upon our differences and interests, we also experience the world in common with one another insofar as we assume that everyone would 'see' the world as we do if they were in our position (standpoint) and that we would 'see' the world the way others do if we were in theirs. This means that frames reconcile difference by making the perception of a disruption or a difference into a signifier of the same, as originating in the intuitively given life-world. How we understand and know the world and its phenomena is potentially understood and known by 'everyone' – everyone, that is, who shares our social position, everyone who shares in our taken-for-granted sense of being anyone. People knowing the world 'in common' is provided for by the assumed potentiality of shareable perspectives, or what Schutz (1973: 11) calls, 'reciprocity of perspectives,' the 'interchangeability of standpoints,' or as what we have been calling frames or frameworks.

Schutz expands this phenomenological notion of shareable frames.

> What is supposed to be known in common by everyone who shares our system of relevances is the way of life considered to be the natural, the good, the right one by the members of the 'in group'; as such, it is at the origin of the many recipes for handling things (and each other) in order to come to terms with typified situations, of the folk ways and mores, of 'traditional behaviour,'… of the 'of course statements' believed to be valid by the in-group in spite of their inconsistencies, briefly, of the 'relative natural aspect of the world'.
>
> (Schutz, 1973: 13)

Living in the midst of others, at times we experience a sort of 'belongingness,' a sense of belonging in and to a group, a social space, not as someone marginal to this group and space, but as someone integral to them and thus as someone who is valuable. What we conceive to be relevant is now understood as a shared perspective and as relevant to everyone 'in the know' and thus what is relevant and valuable is understood under the rubric of a 'system' rather than that of 'individual idiosyncrasy.' In this way, our perspective of the world becomes understood, as Schutz tells us, as something natural, good and right. From this 'system of relevances,' socially put together or constructed through our assumption of the 'reciprocities of perspectives,' flows all other aspects of our individual and collective lives. And, perhaps most important, we come to understand ourselves as naturally belonging in and to this world.

It is, then, this taken-for-granted life-world and the natural attitude that represents, for us, the genesis of disability frameworks. It is within and from this conception of human life that disability experience, whether our own or that of others, springs and that frames disability as a meaning-full phenomenon. Disability is a frame that can, upon analysis, teach us much about the life-world that generates it. But herein lies an irony – disability is framed as a phenomenon located and locatable only outside of the taken-for-granted life-world as well as outside of the natural attitude. Disability is thus understood as marginal to the common-sense world and, as such, as outside of intuitively given reality. Disability is one source of what Schutz (1973: 228 [see also Michalko, 1998: 29–34]) calls, the 'fundamental anxiety' insofar as disability can, and often does, disrupt the taken-for-granted character of the world and our life in it.

Disability, framed as a problem, becomes one of the fundamental 'unnatural aspects' of the otherwise natural, good, and right way of being-in-the-world. Disability disrupts, and even threatens, what Schutz calls, 'the relative natural aspect of the world.' What disability often represents is the taken-for-granted sense of the unnatural, of the value-less and of that which does not belong – or, to take liberties with Schutz's words, disability is framed as the unnatural, the bad and the wrong way of being-in-the-world. With this framework as background, this chapter now turns to an examination of some of the ways disability is conceived of and treated as just this sort of radical and disruptive problem, a problem naturalized as such.

Disability as a problem in need of a solution

The perception of a problem brings with it the requirement for a solution even though, and somewhat paradoxically, the problem is an expected and taken-for-granted aspect of the life-world. Problems are inevitable (Butler, 1999: vii) and a life free of problems is inconceivable. Everyone has problems – some serious, some not so serious, some trivial and some catastrophic – but, everyone has problems. We are not required to search for problems, for they 'naturally' occur in the round of everyday life. In the face of our inevitable problems, we are, however, expected to search for solutions.

The search for a solution to the problem of disability is inevitable and not optional since disability is understood within this framework as generating the requirement for a solution and thus the search. Disability is understood as a problem insofar as it represents a disruption to the 'natural-order-of-things' with its concomitant requirement to restore this order, an activity understood as the 'need' to solve the problem of disability. Cure, of course, is the quintessential solution to disability conceived of as a problem. But, many disabilities resist curative measures and become, in the vernacular of the day, 'permanent.' Now, we have a more serious problem – what to do about and how to live with disability as a 'permanent problem,' or, how to solve the permanent problem of disability.

The solution to the permanent problem of disability, the one favoured today, is normalization which takes shape through remedial treatments such as rehabilitation, special education, and the like. Since the problem of disability is located in the world and is so often permanent, the solution becomes one of 'normalizing' disability thus 'making' it a 'normal' part of the natural-order-of-things. Normalizing disability is one way of making it identical with the taken-for-granted life-world where this act of 'making identical' serves to socially produce the life-world as identifying with disability as one of the many problems that are inevitable, again, naturally so. Through the social act of normalization, disability becomes *merely* a problem that some people have. Ironically, being 'merely' a problem requires that disability never comes to consciousness as anything but a problem. Thus, the rule of finding a solution to the always-already problem of disability is a singular unified response to disability with which individuals are routinely and ordinarily engaged. We already know, and obviously so, that disability simply *is* a problem in need of a solution and to admit an alternative approach can be as disruptive as is the onset of impairment or as is the attempt to manoeuvre in a world prepared only for a 'non-impaired carnality' (Hughes and Paterson, 1997: 607, 604).

The ubiquity of the frame of disability-as-problem for individuals means making disability identical not only as problem but also in its solution. Henri-Jacques Stiker speaks of the act of making disability identical in this way:

> This act [of identification and of making identical] will cause the disabled to disappear and with them all that is lacking, in order to assimilate them, drown them, dissolve them in the greater and single social whole.
>
> (Stiker, 1999: 128)

Making disability identical is not the same as making disabled people identical to those who are not disabled nor does it allow non-disabled people to identify with disabled people. Instead, the act of making identical generates the common-sense understanding of disability as part of the life-world and, as such, identifies disability as a phenomenon among the plethora of phenomena making up the taken-for-granted world. Making disability identical, however, does not make disability 'equal' to other phenomena; on the contrary, it makes disability one of the less favoured problems to have.

As one of the least favoured problems to have, the contemporary act of making identical – an act marked by the advent of rehabilitation and special education – seeks, in its identification with the world, to make disability disappear, particularly the lack that disability is thought to be. In this way, as Stiker says, disabled people can be assimilated or, more poignantly, be drowned, dissolved 'in the greater and single social whole.' Given that disability is merely a problem, any alternative interpretation is, like disability itself, also drowned, but with this annihilation of alterity comes the achievement of a 'normal' approach to the problem of disability. This is one reason why Hughes (2007: 680, 681) argues that, '[T]he real problem in this existential mire is not disability but non-disability… The normative, invulnerable body of disablist modernity [the greater and single social whole] that is the problem.' This interpretation, however, admits an alternative view, a view which is typically drowned in the single social whole by asking 'But what is your problem? What do you need? How can we help?'

[…]

Experiencing disability as a problem that some people have and simultaneously a problem that everyone has, represents the dominant ideological frame through which disability experience is mediated. Some of us are a problem to the society, its institutions and settings. That disabled people experience their lives in this way is crucial, if not essential, for the ways in which society and its institutions develop solutions to the problem of disability. Any solution developed within this framework, of course, serves to politically and socially sustain the cultural conception of disability as a problem and thus to make it disappear, to drown it, in the single social whole that contains the inevitability of problems as an integral feature of its social organization. It is important that we phenomenologically uncover the problem to which the conception 'disability is a problem in need of a solution' is a solution. To this end, and as a way to further exemplify our phenomenological approach, we turn to an examination of one way that the university formulates the problem that is disability.

Including 'them'

Like all other appearances, the appearance of disability must be noticed for its appearance to count as apparent. Noticing requires more than 'looking' insofar as it is taken-for-granted cultural frameworks that permit us to 'see' what we are 'looking at.' What do we 'see' when we experience someone using a wheelchair or someone who is blind or when someone tells us they have a learning disability? Typically, what we 'see,' is a problem. But, what sort of a problem and thus what sort of a solution do we perceive? The contemporary space of the university, in our case the University of Toronto, does have a way of 'seeing' and thus of noticing disability. As a way to explicate this 'way' we turn to an examination of how the university conceives of disabled students.

Accessibility Services, St. George Campus

The role of accessibility services is to facilitate the inclusion of students with disabilities into all aspects of university life. Our focus is on skills development, especially in the areas of self-advocacy and academic skills. Services are provided to students with a documented disability. It can be physical, sensory, a learning disability, or a mental health disorder.

Accessibility Services is responsible for facilitating the inclusion of students with disabilities into university life. Specifically, accessibility services is responsible for:

- Receiving and retaining documentation from a medical professional or specialist which identifies your disability. (This documentation is kept in confidence with the service.)
- Providing information and advice to students, student applicants, university departments, and individual staff members on accommodation strategies.
- Providing or facilitating services such as alternative test and examination arrangements, note-taking services.

- Assessment for adaptive equipment and assistive devices.
- Assessment for learning disabilities, coordination of interpreters and intervener services, and liaison and referral on and off campus.
- The office is also a resource for instructors who require information in order to meet the needs of students in their classes. The office also plays an educational role; raising the awareness of students with disabilities among staff, faculty, and students at the university and wider community.

(Accessibility Services, University of Toronto, 2010)

The role of accessibility services, as it understands it, is to 'facilitate' the 'inclusion of students with disabilities into all aspects of university life.' Students with disabilities are understood as *not* included into all aspects of university life despite the obvious 'fact' of their presence in university life. Present yet absent or included as an excludable type, is the way that accessibility services frames and subsequently characterizes the presence of disabled students in university life (Titchkosky, 2008). This frame constitutes disabled students as the problem of the lack of 'skills development' particularly those of self-advocacy and academic skills. Thus, the lack of skills marks the problem that disabled students are understood to be and skill development marks the solution. Disability thus becomes a technical problem in need of a technical solution and the problem of disability as a problem is itself a solution to the absent presence character of disability.

Accessibility services says that disability can be physical, sensory, a learning disability, or a mental health disorder, and that students are eligible for services only if their disability is 'documented.' Student documentation of their own disabilities does not count as such. It is only medical professionals or specialists who are permitted (legitimately) to provide such documentary evidence. Evidence of a disability, therefore, can come only from the legitimated source of biomedicine. The notion of 'expertise' is invoked as a way to establish a disabled student's eligibility for yet another form of expertise, namely, accessibility services. 'Documentation,' then, acts as an implicit social process to transform 'your disability' (point one above) into 'our disability' (see the remaining points above). This social process acts to delegitimize a disabled student as 'expert' and to legitimize professionals as such thus transforming disability into a problem that can be best remedied by 'expertise.' This represents yet another version of the problem-of-disability: disability is a 'thing' about which expertise can be gleaned and put into practice (Titchkosky and Michalko, 2009: 1–14). As an objective-problem-thing, a disabled student enters university life framed by the sensibility that there are those who 'know' his or her problem ...expertly. Knowing oneself *as* disabled, then, is illusory insofar as a disabled 'one' is not constituted as an 'expert' on disability and given that 'knowing disability' is framed, in contemporary times, as some 'thing' to be 'expertly known' making all other ways of knowing disability superfluous.

It is a medical professional or specialist, who provides documentation that, according to accessibility services, identifies your disability, but this does more than merely 'identify' a disability in a student. The documentation of disability and the subsequent accessibility services practices may be read as the constitution and re-constitution of expertise as the paramount framework, and framer, of the conception of disability-as-problem. This framework gives rise not only to legitimate individual problems understood as a disability but also to individuals legitimated as in possession of such problems understood as 'people with disabilities.'

Disabled students have a problem, an individual one, and now that they are applying for entry into university, or are already here, or, as we suggest, have always been here, disabled students are now a problem for the university, disability is now a problem that the university has. The solution? Medical and subsequent accessibility services' expertise. While disabled students share some of the same needs that their non-disabled counterparts have, 'disability needs' are different. All students are understood as representing a 'deficit' with regard to not possessing or lacking the knowledge that universities have. Closing this gap, however, is not the same for all students. The university is the means for closing this gap, but disabled students experience this 'means' as a barrier and not as a solution to the 'knowledge deficit.'

The needs of disabled students are conceived of as different from their non-disabled counter-parts or, in the vernacular of the day, they are 'special needs.' And, these 'special needs' are met with special measures – the provision of information and advice to students, university staff and faculty regarding accommodation strategies, the provision of alternative examination arrangements and note-taking, the provision of adaptive technology, the provision of assessment for learning disabilities, sign language interpreters, the provision of awareness training to university staff and faculty regarding the 'special needs' of disabled students. And finally, the provision of and, staying true to medicine – indicated in the penultimate point above – the 'referral.'

The spatial and educational organization of the university is not framed as a problem, instead, only disability is framed as such, and thus the problem of and with disability is conceived of as the problem of access. According to common sense reasoning, disabled people 'because' of our disabilities, do not typically have access to mainstream society and this problem is solved by society 'identifying and removing,' as the saying goes, barriers to such access. But, we have also demonstrated that this seemingly straightforward and simple conception of the disability problem/solution is much more complex than it initially seemed. We need only raise Titchkosky's (2011) question, 'Once we're in, what are we in for?' to provoke and reveal this complexity. On the heels of this question, we now conclude this chapter with an initial formulation of the problem to which the framework 'disability is a problem in need of a solution' is represented as a solution. We have also suggested that the university needs disability 'to be' a technical problem requiring a technical solution and we will reflect on what we understand a phenomenological approach needs disability 'to be.'

Needing disability... to be

Finding a home in the university as a disabled person, within the problem/solution frame, means 'getting in' as an individual understood as having a personal problem. This problem finds its solution through the invocation of expert and technical intervention meted onto the life of the person with the problem who likewise is ordinarily expected to deal with their problem thereby gaining some distance from the status of 'being' a problem for self or for others. Disability thus becomes a stage or social space over and against which individuals achieve a sense of their individuality; it is that space where we can show each other we are oriented to the doing of ourselves as individuals but only so long as we conform to the normative sense that no life is to be found or forged 'in' disability. Hence, we need to stage our life as one 'with' disability rather than 'in' disability (Michalko, 1999: 172).

Individuals deal (or not) with disability since disability is only a problem. Thus – the relatively recent identity category 'person with a disability.' In this way, a sense of obtaining the identity of person is achieved by containing disability within the frame of problem and letting nothing of disability slip into alternative relations between self and other which could potentially change the exclusionary prowess of everyday life. Disability is thus conceived of as the problem-background against which the figure of individuality is achieved; it is not, however, imagined as that scene where we might re-think and re-cast the normative order of individuality and thereby of everyday life.

The figure of individuality is framed as our normative task and duty creating disability as a problem and as a way to achieve our task of producing the startling reasonableness of a taken-for-granted sense of individuality. Disability now serves as the key scene for the re-achievement of the primacy of personhood understood as the development of an individual identity. In his work on the modern 'identity,' Zgmunt Bauman (2004: 21, 32) says,

> Identity could only enter the *Lebenswelt* [life-world] as a task, as an *as-yet-unfulfilled, unfinished task*, a clarion call, a duty and an urge to act – and the nascent modern state did whatever it took to make such a duty obligatory for all people inside its territorial sovereignty… In the liquid modern setting of life, identities are perhaps the most common, most acute, most deeply felt and troublesome incarnations of *ambivalence*.

Within modernity, disability is framed as a space where the 'duty and urge to act' as an individual is expertly announced, technically organized, and bureaucratically arranged as a duty for all. Always constituted as a problem, and as one imagined as marginal to mainstream existence, disability becomes, ironically, central to the question of belonging and thus akin to a sacrificial space where all that disability could be is submerged, even annihilated, for the good of demonstrating the common ubiquity of an urge toward individuality. Insofar as disability is the problem over and against which we can demonstrate that we are worthy of belonging within modernity's structures of individuality, it is of paramount importance to conform to the sense that disability is merely and only a problem in need of a solution.

The structure of education, for example, has incorporated disability as a disembodied project of individual identity and the expertly identified 'person with a disability' becomes not only expected but also accepted within the modern organization of belonging. In more general terms, Bauman (2004: 22) puts it this way, '[W]hoever else you might have been or have aspired to become, it was the '"appropriate institutions" of the state that had the final word. An uncertified identity was [is] a fraud…' As we showed, it is neither reasonable, nor natural, let alone good, to aspire to find life, that is 'real' embodied limits and possibilities, and thus identity in disability. Instead life is forged only and simply against it (adjusting) and as background (overcoming).

But herein lies a radical ambiguity, if not paradox. We come to the scene of embodied existence as people who, first and foremost, can act as though any bodily difference that could make a difference to being-in-the-world is merely the occasion to show each other the 'normal' achievement of a 'normative' sense of individualized identity as persons. Framed as people with a disability, individuals become those who do not live through their bodies, minds, senses, or emotions, but with them and with them assert claims to personhood. This is the socio-political consequence of understanding disability as problem in need of a solution that we now witness in almost all traces of disability conceptions today. In short, the problem to which 'disability is a problem in need of a solution' points is *individuality* – the problem of individuality generates the solution of 'disability is a problem in need of a solution.'

Now, what of phenomenology – what sort of problem has *it* made of disability and what does it need disability to be? Our chapter has demonstrated that whatever else disability might be it is lived as a problem in need of solution and it is made present as a space to think about everyday life that makes disability present in this singular and unified fashion. It is both over-determined by culture and, ironically, it is also thus an ideal place to reflect on how we make and organize devalued and excluded people in routine and ordinary ways. Disability is, in this sense, ambiguity incarnate, a rupture in the clarity and unquestioned flow of daily life, and thus almost a 'natural' starting place for thinking about the workings of culture.

From the perspective of a phenomenologically informed disability studies approach, the question is not one of asserting a better, more correct, or more socially just definition of the situation called 'disability.' Instead, phenomenology asks 'What is the phenomenon called disability?' It does not do so by asserting a definition, but by addressing how disability makes an appearance in the world and is lived. If disability is lived primarily as a problem in need of a solution, as we claim it is, then this is what phenomenology needs disability to be in order to pursue its commitment to question and theorize. Phenomenology needs disability to be a *life* lived in the natural attitude. This allows us to ask – What sorts of people are understood as living in the singularity of 'problem' and what sorts of cultures need to have so many of their people understood, managed and expertly controlled in regular and predictable ways? Disability, for phenomenology, becomes a place where such questions thrive.

By not taking disability for granted, it is possible to show how disability comes to appear as a problem and thus to reveal the frames, or what Husserl (1970: 104) refers to as the 'ruling concealment' that generates the 'need' to understand disability as a problem in the first place. The phenomenological urge is to find a way to hold in tension any of the ways that disability makes an appearance in everyday life as always already part of what disability has been made to be so as to reveal how cultures make the problems they need. The need of a phenomenological approach in disability studies, then, is to understand disability as constituted as a space for critical cultural inquiry regarding the normative order that makes disability always already a problem. And, herein lies the political potential of a phenomenological approach to disability and disability studies – the experience of disability, our own or that of others, becomes the scene where we can frame how we experience embodied existence and, thus, disability becomes a place where culture can be examined anew, again and again.

8

DESIGNING COLLECTIVE ACCESS

A feminist disability theory of universal design

Aimi Hamraie (2013)

Excerpt from Disability Studies Quarterly
(DSQ) *(2013) 33: 4, http://dsq-sds.org/article/
view/3871/3411.*

In the [US] civil rights movement era, feminist and disability approaches to architectural design emerged to address the problems of spatial segregation. Activists argued that inaccessible built environments – such as segregated lunch counters, workplaces without childcare, suburban single-family homes, and buildings with stairs and without ramps – made oppressed people less visible and, therefore, less likely to receive legislative protections (Steinfeld and Maisel 2012, 13–15). Throughout the 1960s and 70s, disability activists physically occupied public buildings in order to demonstrate that law and society had failed to include them (Nielsen 2012, 168: see also Serlin, this volume). The efforts of these activists resulted in the passage of federal civil rights legislation that aspired to protect the access of people with disabilities to the built environment. The term *barrier-free design* emerged to describe the architectural strategies that underlie these legislative gains.

Barrier-free design was not merely a legislative trope or expedient; rather, the theory of barrier-free design supported efforts in the architectural profession to design environments according to the spatial needs and demands of women, people of color, and people with disabilities (Matrix 1984; Steinfeld 1979; Mace 1985; Weisman 1989; Welch and Jones 2002, 193). As architect Ray Lifchez wrote (1987, 1) in his groundbreaking *Rethinking Architecture: Design Students and Physically Disabled People*:

> Building forms reflect how a society feels about itself and the world it inhabits. … Valuable resources are given over to what is cherished – education, religion, commerce, family life, recreation – and tolerable symbols mask what is intolerable – illness, deviance, poverty, disability, old age. Although architects do not create these social categories, they play a key role in providing the physical framework in which

the socially acceptable is celebrated and the unacceptable is confined and contained. Thus when any group that has been physically segregated or excluded protests its second-class status, its members are in effect challenging how architects practice their profession.

A key contribution of late twentieth-century social movements to theories of architectural design is crystallized in the connections that these movements drew between physical environments and the social realities that they create. These movements and their professional counterparts showed that the design of buildings is not a value-neutral and passive act; rather, the design of the built environment actively conditions and shapes the assumptions that the designers, architects, and planners of these value-laden contexts hold with respect to who will (and should) inhabit the world. In short, built environments serve as litmus tests of broader social exclusions.

Universal Design (UD) is an approach to access to the built environment that goes beyond barrier-free design (Mace 1985). UD seeks to design built environments to be as accessible as possible from the outset, to as many people as possible. That is, UD seeks to design built environments that will not require future retrofitting or alteration. Furthermore, UD goes beyond legal accessibility requirements (for example, what is required to comply with the Americans with Disabilities Act) to integrate into disability-access strategies the specific requirements that accrue when designers take into account aging, gender, size, and health (among other variables) (Steinfeld and Maisel 2012; Welch and Jones 2002). In the critical disability studies literature of the humanities and social sciences, UD has gained theoretical attention under the banner of "universal access." As feminist geographer Isabel Dyck notes, "conceptualizing the environment has been crucial to the politics of disability research in delineating issues of access, a crucial dimension of a *socio-spatial model* of disability" (Dyck 2010, 254; emphasis added). Feminist philosophy of disability and other disability theories cite UD to prove that disability is a product of the built and social environments, rather than a medical state that is intrinsic to the body of a given individual (Wendell 1996, 46; Silvers 1998, 74–75). In the terms of these philosophies and theories, the idea of a universally accessible environment is synonymous with the best, most inclusive, approach to design and defines the ideal outcome of disability politics. Disabled feminist philosopher Susan Wendell inaugurates this position when she calls for a "universal recognition that all structures have to be built and all activities have to be organized for the widest practical range of human abilities" (Wendell 1996, 55).

Some feminist disability theorists have disagreed with Wendell, emphasizing that the physical environment alone is not enough to account for the exclusion of people with sensory, cognitive, or mental disabilities from social and public life (Corker 2001, 39–40). Parallel debates over the desirability and scope of UD occur within the design professions. These professional debates hinge on the very concept of a universal, one-size-fits-all approach to design (Hannson 2007, 17; Sandhu 2011; Steinfeld and Tauke 2002).

The implied tensions between these divergent approaches to access indicate that additional exploration of value-based justifications for UD is needed. In this paper, therefore, I parse out the potential meanings of the component terms of UD – namely, *universal* and *design* – rather than take for granted or dismiss what UD is or to what it aspires.

In order to engage in this inquiry, I perform what feminist theorist Karen Barad calls a "diffractive reading," which she describes as a method of "reading insights through one another in ways that help illuminate differences as they emerge." Such a reading illuminates "how different differences get made, what gets excluded, and how those exclusions matter" (Barad 2007, 30). This approach to UD responds to Rosemarie Garland-Thomson's call for feminist and disability studies to recognize their parallel development of theories in areas of overlapping interest (Garland-Thomson [2002] 2011a, 1). In addition, the approach responds to recent scholarly appeals for discussions of the "philosophical and theoretical basis" of UD (Imrie 2012, 876). Rather than limit my discussion to the ideological basis of UD, I explore how shifting its frame and emphasis can better address issues with respect to the body, environment, and interdependence that both feminist philosophy of disability and disability studies have articulated. In other words, I develop an idea of accessible design that construes it as a method of social justice activism, rather than as a marketing strategy. To do this, I draw upon four literatures, all of which address UD and have thus far had limited impact on UD thought: feminist philosophy of disability, feminist disability studies, feminist architectural theory, and disability geographies of access. By bringing these literatures together, I hope to introduce them to a design audience, as well as to create space for discussions about design within feminist philosophy of disability/feminist disability studies. I shall first explain what UD is, exploring its design methodology and addressing some of the problems that it raises. Then, I outline some of the issues and approaches that a theory of accessible design that is premised on interdependence can adopt to create broad and collective access to the built environment.

Introducing universal design

The architect Ronald Mace coined the term *universal design* in order to describe accessibility that goes beyond the scope of barrier-free design (Mace 1985). Mace, a designer who used a wheelchair, defined UD like this:

> [UD is] a way of designing a building or facility, at little or no extra cost, so it is both attractive and functional for all people, disabled or not. The idea is to remove that expensive, "special" label from products and designs for people with mobility problems, and at the same time, eliminate the institutional appearance of many current accessible designs.
>
> (Mace 1985, 147)

Mace's goal of making the environment "functional for all people" echoed activist demands for the integration of disability into broader conceptions of human community and citizenship. Mace's initial definition of UD reflected a desire to make the aesthetics and function of access more available and to focus less on disabilities as an additional, extra, and unusual consideration – that is, as a "special need." Because Mace's definition of UD did not specify methods with which to achieve these aims and goals, he and other experts recognized the need to further specify and elaborate what exactly *universal design* means and how it differs from legally-mandated accessibility under the Americans with Disabilities

Act (ADA). In the mid-1990s, therefore, Mace convened access experts at North Carolina State University's Center for Universal Design to craft a new definition. These experts defined UD as "the design of products and environments to be usable by all people, to the greatest extent possible, without the need for adaption or specialized design" (Center for Universal Design 1997). This definition retained Mace's initial notion of a broad user group ("everyone" or "all") and added to it the idea that buildings and products must *already* account for the diversity within this group in the way that these buildings and products are designed. The authors of this new definition also wrote the "Seven Principles of Universal Design," a document that continues to be cited as the basis of UD (ibid.). The Seven Principles that accompanied the new definition were: (1) Equitable use; (2) Flexibility in use; (3) Simple and intuitive; (4) Perceptible information; (5) Tolerance for error; (6) Low physical effort; and (7) Size and space for approach and use. Notwithstanding the appeal to equity in the first two principles, these guidelines do not appear to make an overarching ideological or value-based claim. Nor do any of the Principles mention disability, leaving unanswered the question of whom equity and flexibility are meant to benefit.

In addition to the architectural strategies that have been developed to expand the work of barrier-free design and improve rehabilitation (Steinfeld, Paquet, D'Souza, Joseph, and Maisel 2010; Sanford 2012), several approaches to UD have emerged that address the scope of inclusion and the strategies that can achieve it. Social justice approaches to UD build on disability, feminist, and environmental justice movement work in order to educate architects and designers about human diversity (Ostroff, Limont, and Hunter 2002; Steinfeld and Tauke 2002; Weisman 1999). Industrial design (consumer-oriented) approaches take UD beyond architecture to the design of consumer products and fixtures (Mueller 1997). Each approach brings a different value, object, or methodology to UD.

Theorizing value-explicit design

Feminist and disability theories of access argue that supposedly value-neutral built environments are material-discursive phenomena that mask the dominance of perceived majority identities and bodies. Leslie Kanes Weisman, a feminist architectural theorist and UD educator, exemplifies this position in her "Women's Environmental Rights: A Manifesto," declaring:

> The built environment is largely the creation of white, masculine subjectivity. *It is neither value-free nor inclusively human.* Feminism implies that we fully recognize this environmental inadequacy and proceed to think and act out of that recognition. ... These are feminist concerns which have critical dimensions that are both societal and spatial. They will require feminist activism as well as architectural expertise to insure a solution.
>
> (Weisman [1981] 1999, 5, emphasis added)

In other words, the epistemic positions of designers matter for the material-discursive qualities of value-explicit design. Supposedly neutral design often privileges the most common bodies through (what I have called) the "normate template" for architectural design

(Hamraie 2012). Garland-Thomson's term *normate* represents the unmarked privilege of majority embodiments – white, male, cisgender, heterosexual, able-bodied, and middle-class bodies – that appear neutral when their social location is in fact highly specific (Garland-Thomson 1996, 8–10). When the normate serves as a neutral template for design, what emerges is a built environment that is accessible only to certain bodies. The normate template produces the illusion of what disability geographer Rob Imrie characterizes as disembodied environments that "deny the presence or possibility of bodily impairment" (Imrie 2010, 40, see also this volume). Since marginalized and minority bodies must necessarily use space, they often experience what Garland-Thomson calls "misfit." She writes:

> Like the dominant subject positions such as male, white, or heterosexual, fitting is a comfortable and unremarkable majority experience of material anonymity, an unmarked subject position that most of us occupy at some points in life and that often goes unnoticed. When we fit harmoniously and properly into the world, we forget the truth of contingency because the world sustains us. When we experience misfitting and recognize that disjuncture for its political potential, we expose the relational component and the fragility of fitting. Any of us can fit here today and misfit there tomorrow.
>
> (2011b, 597)

Fitting and misfitting are material-discursive, relational, and interdependent categories. In order to sustain itself, the normate template relies upon the impression that normates are normal, average, and majority bodies. Misfitting shatters this illusion, marking the failure of the normate template to accommodate human diversity. As disability sociologist Tanya Titchkosky explains, epistemic claims about disability as unknowable and therefore excludable sustain misfitting. Titchkosky puts it this way:

> The apparent and obvious ease of a statement like "things just weren't built with people with disabilities in mind" is a way to make inaccessibility sensible under contemporary conditions. This ordinary "truth claim" is a type of say-able thing in relation to disability. …The say-able is where cultural understandings reside.
>
> (Titchkosky 2011, 74)

In addition to revealing the cultural devaluation of misfit, keeping bodies and people "in mind" is an epistemic and material-discursive position (Imrie 2002, 55). Designers produce misfit when they make claims such as: "You can't accommodate everybody. You've got to draw the line somewhere" (Titchkosky 2011, 31). As Barad explains in her theory of "agential cuts" (Barad 2007, 176), acts of line-drawing are material-discursive practices that actually shape what kinds of bodies appear to be possible and likely to live in the world. Following Lifchez, inaccessible environments make the argument that disabled bodies are unworthy of inclusion and quite possibly do not even exist as potential spatial inhabitants. The delineation of normate bodies as likely spatial inhabitants and misfits as "justifiably excludable" is not merely an act of omission, but rather, is also a material-discursive act that solidifies normate privilege (Titchkosky 2011, 78).

Garland-Thomson's notion that environmental fit makes nondisabled people less aware of their own embodied privilege ("we forget the truth of contingency because the world sustains them") echoes moral philosopher Charles Mills's (1997, 97) argument that racism makes white people less likely to acknowledge and understand structural racism. Insofar as normate architects and lawmakers claim that there are too many disabilities to "keep in mind," or that they do not have the requisite information to design for minority embodiments, they do not merely lack available information. On the contrary, these declarations reflect what critical race and feminist epistemologists call "epistemologies of ignorance" (Mills 1997; Tuana and Sullivan 2007). According to these theorists,

> ignorance is not the result of a benign gap in our knowledge, but deliberate choices to pursue certain kinds of knowledge while ignoring others. We must therefore concern ourselves with our choices of knowledge production and who we take ourselves to be accountable to through these choices.
>
> (Grasswick 2011, xvii)

In other words, epistemologies of ignorance show that misfit is an active construction of what appears to be a lack of information about the range of human diversity. Knowledge and ideologies privileging the normate are always present in built environments. The point, following Garland-Thomson, Grosz, and Lifchez, is to affirm the normate template as a produced *parti* – that is, the basic starting concept – of ignorance, rather than simply an effect of designerly business as usual.

Privileging the embodied user experience of misfit through accessibility can also assist in the conceptualization of alternatives to epistemologies of ignorance. Value-explicit design can challenge the epistemic subject-object relationship between designers and spatial inhabitants. For instance, participatory design methodologies that feminist and disability-focused designers have developed offer a way in which to use designerly knowledge to critique the normate template's epistemology of ignorance. Lifchez famously invited people with disabilities into the design studio at the University of California-Berkeley School of Architecture in order to train students in accessible-design strategies (Lifchez 1987). In doing so, he centered disability and made design students accountable to the needs of disabled users. He also decentered the designer as the authoritative knower or expert, training students to take on partnership roles with their intended clients and to value their authority and expertise about their experiences of the built environment. The translation of experience into design is hardly straightforward; it is not surprising, therefore, that participants in the process noted the difficulties that students had with shifting expertise to clients with disabilities (Sarkissian 1987). Nevertheless, Lifchez's methods privileged users, brought them into much closer proximity with designers, and made disability intelligible to design students. Other architectural educators, like Weisman, have educated new generations of design students in UD methodologies and research through work like the Universal Design Education Project (Welch 1995) and user-centered community partnerships (Weisman 2012). This work provides alternatives to value-neutral design in order to productively engage with epistemologies of ignorance.

User involvement is, nonetheless, only one piece of the UD puzzle; that is, UD requires *more than* additional knowledge about disabled people and bodies (in which case designers may come to treat misfitting bodies as *no more than* objects of knowledge for designers). UD must also address the structural conditions that prevent marginalized people from becoming professional designers or having access to decision-making in design processes. As I explain in the next section, a UD politics of interdependence can privilege disabled people and others who experience misfitting in order to address intersectional inequalities through design.

Body-environment interdependence

The task of a feminist disability theory of UD is to make the normate template's *parti* explicit, hold designers accountable for what appears to be disability-neutral design, and show that this neutrality is a constructed form of ignorance. Making UD's values and ideologies explicit requires consideration of excluded bodies and full acknowledgement of the range of interactions between bodies and environments. In recent years, disability geographers have argued for attention to the embodied experiences of users in consideration of questions of access, rather than an exclusive focus on physical structures (Chouinard, Hall, and Wilton, 2010; Imrie 2010; Gleeson 1999). In this work, bodies push back against inaccessible environments and "overturn some of the problems relating to poorly designed environments" (Imrie 2002, 64; Imrie 2012, 876). Refusing to take inaccessible design for granted as deterministic of exclusion, recent qualitative research in disability geography has documented embodied experiences as evidence of spatial use and agency. Indeed, disability geographies have set an important new agenda for research on access and have provided user perspectives that should be applied as part of the knowledge base of accessible design. Philosophical and theoretical explorations of the values, ideologies, and methodologies underlying physical environments are, nevertheless, still necessary, particularly in the context of UD. Building upon the concepts of material-discursive, *parti*, and normate template laid out above, I maintain that a feminist disability theory of UD demands attention to how physical environments produce symbolic and material access or exclusion through their interactions with and knowledge about bodies. As feminist geographers and architects have pointed out, the notion that there is a physical environment that exists regardless of, or prior to, embodied knowledge and experience fails to acknowledge the implicit reliance of design processes on normate bodies (Brown 2011; Rose 1993; Weisman 1992).

Because design is a value-laden material-discursive practice, a feminist disability theory of UD must consider how body-environment interactions can be sites of a politics of interdependence. Such a theory must begin with intersectionality, understanding environmental misfit as both an epistemic position and a material-discursive axis of oppression (Code 2006; Garland-Thomson 2011b). As feminist disability scholarship has shown, the lack of access to physical environments is often due to the stigmatization of dependencies and the interdependencies that they entail (Garland-Thomson 2005; Eiseland 1994). In a liberal democratic understanding of access, disability, aging, femininity, non-normate size, and lack of resources all characterize dependencies to overcome or eliminate. This refusal to acknowledge dependency ignores the fundamental interdependence of all bodies for sustenance, community, and care (Wendell 1996, 145–148).

Intersectionality must consider how the normate template for the built environment is a system of exclusion that segregates spaces and people along the axes of disability, race, class, and gender (among others). Recent disability justice work from activists such as Mia Mingus on the notion of "collective access" promotes the interdependence of disability, anti-racist, and gender justice (Mingus 2010b). In addition to guiding disability justice organizing, collective access can be a material-discursive design goal that emphasizes the relationality of built environments with social and structural conditions. A collective access understanding of intersectionality can produce a theory of body-environment relations focused on social justice. For instance, collective access recalls the work of feminist materialist architects who designed built environments to challenge inaccessibility through the politics of interdependence. Dolores Hayden, famously asking, "What would a non-sexist city be like?" imagined the feminist re-appropriation of suburban homes to fit the needs of non-traditional families who would live in collective housing (Hayden 2000). She tied this work to an anti-capitalist critique of consumer culture and the spatial divisions between "the household and the market economy" (Hayden 2000, 270). Redesigning existing spaces allowed Hayden and other feminist architects to address broader economic structures, the existence of which depended upon suburban household design and urban planning. Hayden's work shows why a theory of access must continue to think about the built environment. Her analysis of the construction of the suburbs, for example, is not about marginalized people as "passive victims of insensitive design" (Imrie 2010, 35). Rather, her analysis shows how feminists have targeted the culture of suburban home life to simultaneously address capitalism and patriarchy through attention to unpaid labor, lack of safe housing and green space, and the spatial needs of non-traditional familial arrangements. UD's approach to collective access by design can proceed with a similar orientation. That is, UD can understand design to be a value-based activity that generates material-discursive conditions of inclusion or misfit depending on what kinds of bodies are included within the scope of the "universal." [...]

When feminist and disability studies scholars claim that UD is a form of inclusive design that keeps a range of human variation in mind, they invoke the notion of broad accessibility, that is, the notion of "design for all people, to the greatest extent possible" (Center for Universal Design 1997). Broad accessibility assumes that the normate template creates misfits beyond categories typically considered to be disabilities. As recent work in disability geography has shown, misfit is as much about age, size, weight, emotional, cognitive, and gender diversity as it is about physical and sensory disabilities (Chouinard, Hall, and Wilton 2010). Broad accessibility recognizes that intersectionality compounds environmental misfit and requires a more collective notion of access than barrier-free approaches and individualized accommodations can afford (Mingus 2010a). For instance, for reasons related to structure, design, heavy doors, lack of space, signage, and social policing, public restrooms are often inaccessible to people who use wheelchairs, children, elderly people, and transgender people alike. Broad accessibility understands that all of these types of people and bodies have a stake in accessible built environments.

Because design is a value-based activity, however, not all human variations straightforwardly count as part of the universal. When the content of the universal is unspecified, UD can slip into vague notions of "all" or "everyone" that assume normate users and de-center disability. For example, a common claim about curb cuts is that they are usable to a broad group of people, including users of wheelchairs, strollers, or bicycles. However, this claim indicates that there are multiple potential uses for these features of the built environment, not all of these uses were intentionally incorporated into the design. The values and knowledges through which wheelchair users, bicyclists, and people pushing strollers come to count as part of "all" and "everyone" remain unexamined. Very easily, curb cuts or ramps can be constructed too steeply or narrowly for a manual wheelchair user, though they may be usable to a walking person who pushes a stroller. Broad accessibility serves as a more complex notion of inclusion, showing that UD must still center disability access in order to avoid lapsing into the normate template.

★★★

Added value is exemplified by claims that accessible designs have (usually economic) value for "other people" beyond the benefits of disability access. Considerable attention within the UD literature has been paid to demonstrating that a market demographic exists for broadly accessible designs (Hannson 2007, 23; Steinfeld and Maisel 2012, 45–48). UD proponents argue that design with broad consumer appeal has the "added value" of *destigmatizing* disability access by taking it out of the context of a "special needs accommodation" (Steinfeld and Maisel 2012, 23). This framing is in response to the preponderance of assistive technologies that are only usable by individual people with specific types of disabilities, have a medical aesthetic, and are excessively costly (Mace 1985; Mueller 1997). Accessibility requires de-stigmatizing, however, only if disability is *taken for granted as* a stigmatizing quality. Positioning UD as benefitting "other people," in addition to disabled people, contributes to the impression that valuable design requires utility for nondisabled people in order for its creation to be justified. In turn, the concept of added value itself becomes stigmatizing toward disability as a category deemed to have not enough value. Unlike broad accessibility, which expands the category of "all" to include multiple stigmatized minority embodiments, within added value, it seems, disabled people themselves are never enough to comprise the category of "all," regardless of how demographically pervasive they may be.

Conclusion: toward collective access

What would it mean for designers committed to universal access and social sustainability to take up interdependence and collective access? In addition to the recognition of design as a value-laden activity that produces material-discursive effects, and beyond the adoption of a goal of broad accessibility, further work on a feminist disability theory of UD must address the neutralizations, omissions, and ignorance that extant approaches to access perpetuate. In particular, this work should attend to how racism and economic injustice are structural conditions that both create a lack of access and are perpetuated by consumerist and added value positions. Who has benefitted from value-added UD products? Who has been left out? How can UD address the structural conditions that prevent disabled people, people of color, and poor people (by no means mutually-exclusive groups) from training in the design professions? How can the UD concept of social sustainability become a collective access strategy for anti-racist urban planning, rather than a buzzword for the promotion of gentrification or "smart growth?" These questions underscore the necessity of a social justice orientation that does not take UD for granted as the best, most inclusive, form of design.

The application of U.S.-based UD principles to transnational contexts is another area that could benefit from the exploration of interdependence, broad accessibility and added value framings, and the economics and politics of design. To address these issues, a feminist disability theory of UD work should build upon existing work on international UD efforts (Mullick, Agarwal, Kumar, and Swarnkar 2011; Sandhu 2011). That is, a feminist disability theory of UD should consider what collective access and interdependence mean in the context of international movements for disability justice. For instance, what is the status of designer expertise in international UD projects? What kinds of knowledge are privileged? What broader ideologies and values does the promotion of U.S. UD principles serve internationally? How has the enforcement of disability access become contingent on neoliberal economic reforms justified according to added value? How have users and designers pushed back against these values and ideologies?

A feminist disability theory of UD based on disability justice, collective access, and interdependence can understand value-explicit design as a form of activism within the design professions. UD practitioners and theorists, building upon the theory outlined here, could continue to develop strategies for participatory design, shifting from value-explicit design *for* disability to design *with* and *by* misfitting bodies more generally. These subtle differences in framing could shift both the role and work of designers, as well as render UD as a more capacious and social justice-oriented material-discursive practice.

9

MORE THAN ACCESS

Overcoming limits in architectural and disability discourse

J. Kent Fitzsimons (2016)

In recent decades, regulations and guidance aimed at making architectural environments less disabling have improved daily life for those with mobility and sensory disabilities. This approach to accessibility clearly produces social progress. However, it also has the unfortunate side effect of casting architecture as a prosthetic device that normalizes lived experience based on an able-bodied paradigm. Rather than generate architecture whose qualities draw from the specificities of a great variety of physical conditions, it tends to reinforce what may be called the "eyes on legs" benchmark, where architectural experience is understood as a function of a body that associates the ability to walk with fully operational vision. I will argue that approaching accessibility as a compensatory measure can distract from other aspects of the complex relationships between space design and the experiences of disability. This requires challenging assumptions that imagine and interpret architectural space predominantly through a seeing and mobile body, to the detriment of other senses and of other ways of appropriating the built environment. In this chapter, I will therefore forefront disabled spatial practices that involve "more than access." I will discuss two cases in which an architectural work provides the opportunity to conceptualize disabled experiences in ways that challenge limits in accessibility theory and practice as well as in architectural thought. Through architectural analyses of these works, I will argue that the full spectrum of bodily capacities could benefit if both architectural discourse and disability guidance and advocacy conceptualized the specificities of disabled architectural experience beyond the habitual terms of access.

Both cases studies consist of architectural environments that are open to the public. In the first work, Peter Eisenman's Memorial to the Murdered Jews of Europe in Berlin (2005), I explore how access can consist of more than just functional ease of movement to a destination; rather it can be integral to our meaning-making around, and experiences of, material space. This is because the Memorial's formal and spatial organization creates the potential for an infinite number of meaning-making experiences, without pre-judging their nature and by favouring the activation of all the senses. As a result, it challenges the notion that accessibility consists of compensating impairments that hinder ostensibly 'normal' building occupation, and suggests rather that built space can enable encounters of architectural and experiential significance, whatever one's unique physical relationship to the world.

The second work, Sejima and Nishazawa and Associates' Rolex Learning Center at the Polytechnic University in Lausanne, Switzerland (2005–2010), provides the opportunity to examine how architecture might redefine the boundaries that normally divide ability and disability into separate categories. Because it includes a significant amount of floor area that neither complies with accessibility regulations nor corresponds with conventional expectations for usefulness, this educational facility creates an unprecedented environment that constantly draws its users' attention to the way they move through space. As a result, it disables some able bodies and enables others with disabilities, and thus redraws the contours that gather individuals together into different "types" of building occupants.

Both the Berlin Memorial and the Learning Center in Lausanne were discussed in an article entitled "L'art d'une architecture discriminatoire" ("The Art of Discriminatory Architecture") in the November 2005 newsletter of the Zurich-based Swiss Center for Disability-adapted Construction (Centre Suisse pour la construction adaptée aux handicapés). That article rightly critiques both works for their lack of consideration of disabled peoples' rights, pointing out that the initial design proposals demonstrate a great divergence between the needs of inclusive design and what it calls the "aesthetic and formal qualities" of "artistic or architectural interventions." While that article provides a convenient backdrop and useful information for this chapter, my argument here will be of a very different nature. For while the struggle for architectural accessibility remains justified and necessary, there is also room to claim that disabled experience is a legitimate architectural experience in its own right, because of its specificity and through its difference from supposedly normal experience. That claim, which echoes a certain tension within disability criticism, also makes it possible to question the conceptual framework of architectural discourse where the body is concerned, and to speculate on a broader agenda for corporal experience in the built environment beyond the language of access or of current disability advocacy and guidance.

Accessibility trouble: the Memorial to the Murdered Jews of Europe

In the heart of Berlin, a large plaza-like architectural work constitutes the Memorial to the Murdered Jews of Europe (Figure 9.1). Designed by American architect Peter Eisenman for a competition in 1997, the Memorial was inaugurated in May of 2005. It occupies a whole urban block on the street that links the Brandenburg Gate with Potsdamer Platz, which also corresponds to the line followed by the Berlin Wall between 1961 and 1989.

Eisenman's project consists of over 2700 stelae or slabs made of concrete, each one measuring 95 cm x 2,38 m, with heights varying between zero and four metres. The resulting proportions of many of these concrete monoliths makes them resemble unadorned sarcophagi. They are organized on an orthogonal grid, with lines running north–south and east–west. Each line is a path or alley, 95 cm wide, the same dimension as the short side of each stele. There are 130 such paths cutting straight through the site (Eisenman 2006: 152). The ground plane that these paths traverse is a rolling relief of hills and valleys. The tops of the stelae also create a changing topography. However, it is different from that

FIGURE 9.1   View of a path through Memorial to the Murdered Jews of Europe, Stelenfeld, Berlin, Germany

Photo by Stephan Czuratis (Jazz-face) – Own work, CC BY-SA 2.5, https://commons.wikimedia.org/w/index.php?curid=1288384

of the ground, neither mimicking nor mirroring it, but rather creating a field of random interference between two formal systems. The result is that each path through the site sinks and rises along continuous slopes, while the slabs surrounding it change heights in a more staccato manner. These interfering topographies are generated through a savvy calculation that includes parameters taken from different grids and lines meeting on the site.

As often happens, the result of this particular design process was not a model of accessibility. The paths in the memorial project possessed slopes that were often more steep than permitted by regulations. Furthermore, the undulating landscape did not provide the level landings at required intervals that offer a moment of rest. Finally, the narrowness of the paths, while technically sufficient, was not hospitable to people in wheelchairs, being on the "tight'" side. In the article "L'art d'une architecture discriminatoire," the Swiss Center for Disability-adapted Construction targeted Eisenman's project, claiming that "the Berlin memorial illustrates, in a particularly acute manner, discrimination against people with disabilities for purely formal reasons" (2005: 2). The article recounts that it was only after disability activists took legal action that the memorial design was adapted to be partially accessible in terms of German law. Historical and geographical conditions made the project's disregard for what by then were considered standard accessibility requirements all the more shocking for disability activists. It is just steps away, at number four on the Tiergartenstrasse, that the Nazi regime's euthanasia programme (1939–41), "Operation T4," had its headquarters. This programme was responsible for the deaths of over one hundred thousand Germans with various types of physical and mental impairments. Disability rights organizations judged it distasteful that a memorial dedicated to one group of Nazi Germany's victims be inaccessible to those who share the physical traits of other victims.

Of interest here is *how* activist advocacy was able to affect changes to the design, based on compromising between architectural intention and disabled access requirements. The Berlin Tribunal decided that at least thirteen of the one hundred thirty paths traversing the site would have to meet the accessibility code. Why not more, or all? The Tribunal argued that too much modification would harm the work's "artistic concept." The court thus understood that the paths are not simply functional elements that provide access to the memorial, but constitute an essential element of the "artistic work" itself. The impression of tightly spaced stelae sitting on a moving ground – through which Eisenman sought to evoke a sense of insecurity and constraint – presumably depends, at least in part, on the slopes' otherwise prohibitive steepness. The Swiss Center's article ironically deduces that the negative effects of depriving the "general public" of this concept were deemed greater than the negative effects of excluding those with mobility disabilities from full access.

Looking at the Tribunal's argument more closely, we find that it creates a logical conundrum. If the paths do not function as access to the memorial, they do not fall under the provisions of the law. But it is precisely because of their narrow and undulating nature that they *are* the work, rather than merely its access route. In other words, it is by *not meeting* accessibility norms that the paths are excused from their application; not respecting the law justifies them being outlaws. This strange bit of reasoning betrays some interesting aspects of design thinking in architecture. In particular, it creates a distinction between a path as access, and path as substance, as a meaning-making experience. Eisenman's memorial constitutes a limit condition where there seems to be full coincidence between circulation and sense, between movement and meaning. But the Court's statement implies precisely that, normally, there *is* a distinction. It opposes two sets of terms: on the one hand, access–circulation–functionality; and on the other hand, experience–substance–meaning. In this reading, the means of getting from one place to another is 'normally' purely functional, devoid of experiential interest. In contrast, the destinations – for example the rooms of a building – would constitute the substance of the architectural work. They would be where the architect's intention is realized through bodily experience, and is thus not expressed as an "access" issue at all. For the Tribunal, when it comes to thinking about disabled people, circulation and programme – access and experience – are valued differently with regards to their architectural significance.

Re-assessing access

Interestingly, the Tribunal's distinction is constantly challenged by real architectural proposals. Many projects from the last twenty years – museums, theatres, transit hubs, libraries – incorporate large ramps or sloping ground as an integral part of the architectural experience. In these cases, we might be tempted to argue that, because the bit of tilted ground is part of the architectural concept, and is therefore not simply an access element leading from one space to another, it need not meet accessibility standards. In cases where the circulation is a meaningful part of the work – where access is the experience – is it acceptable that the very form of paths and passageways prevent easy movement? Rather than take sides in this inherently contradictory debate, we might consider its underpinning assumptions. The first question might be: what is being accessed, and how is it ostensibly accessed? Regarding the Berlin case, recall that for the Tribunal, the paths are not on the way to something, but rather *are* that something. It is by experiencing the paths themselves that one accesses the sense of this particularly difficult subject of remembering, that is, memorializing the Holocaust. Eisenman explains how the contrast between the ground plane and the stelae tops achieves this effect:

> A perceptual and conceptual divergence between the topography of the ground and the top plane of the stelae is thus created. This divergence denotes a difference in time, between what Henri Bergson called chronological, narrative time and time as duration. The monument's registration of this difference makes for a place of loss and contemplation, elements of memory.
>
> (2006: 152)

We might ask if any one path best produces this divergence between perception and concept, or if, on the contrary, any path makes it manifest as well as any other. If we push this question to its logical conclusion, we could ask if one must pass by each of the two thousand stelae, on all four sides, from every possible arriving itinerary, to every possible departing itinerary, in order to realize the work's meaning, its potential, to experience it in an appropriate way for it to be the memorial that it is. Since it is practically impossible for any one person to exhaust the possibilities, the meanders, the turning in circles, the disorientation, we would then ask: is the Berlin Memorial really fully accessible to anyone?

As far as architectural meaning is concerned, the Memorial's specific configuration brings the conventional way of thinking about access to a critical limit. It reveals another possibility: architecture need not define singular experiences revealed by a unique path. It could rather create a great potential for making paths. The stelae make perceptible the prospect of seemingly infinite pathways, just as there are infinite routes through a large city's grid. It is unlikely that visitors try a dozen paths, let alone the one hundred thirty straight paths through the Memorial. Rather than choreographing one particular experience, Eisenman's architectural intervention in Berlin is the armature for countless individual experiences. Architecturally these engage directly with mobility itself as a sense: as something that is directed or disoriented, slowed down, or speeded up (even if the underlying assumption is of a body that starts out able). This line of reasoning admittedly runs the risk of downplaying the right to choose one's path from all the variations. But the memorial's specific form makes the claim for choice seem less urgent by asking us to reconsider what architectural experience is, how one may have access to it, and the extent to which access is assumed to mean ease of movement and way-finding.

In his 1886 dissertation Prolegomena to a Psychology of Architecture, architectural historian and theorist Heinrich Wölfflin noted that:

> [W]hen Goethe once remarked that we ought to sense the effect of a beautiful room, even if we were led through it blindfolded, he was expressing the [...] idea [...] that

the architectural impression, far from being some kind of "reckoning by the eye," is essentially based on a direct bodily feeling.

(1886: 155)

Since the Berlin Memorial's paths are not access but are rather the work's very substance, in other words the source of architectural experience, we might ask what it would be like to "be led through it blindfolded." Eisenman hints at the prospect of non-visual perception in his comparison between his Memorial and traditional monuments:

> The traditional monument is understood by its symbolic imagery, by what it represents. It is not understood in time, but in an instant in space; it is *seen* and understood simultaneously. [...]
>
> In this monument there is no goal, no end, no working one's way in or out. The duration of an individual's experience of it grants no further understanding, since understanding is impossible. The time of the monument, its duration from top surface to ground, is disjoined from the time of experience.

(2006: 154, author's italics)

The contrast is meant to oppose chronological time with what Henri Bergson called duration. This passage also associates vision with a particular sort of architectural experience, with the assumed immediacy of understanding through looking. Eisenman thus opens the way to consider the experience of his project not through vision and representation, but through the body and its many senses' duration in space.

When vision impairments are addressed in architectural regulations, it is as a disability affecting ease of movement and way-finding. The regulations do not ask that architects convey the beauty, the surprise, or even discomfort of an architectural space to blind and visually impaired people. Instead, they settle for grooves in the floor to give cues to the white stick, and discourage disorienting curving walls in favour of clear orthogonal spatial distribution. None of this is ostensibly so that those who cannot see can appreciate the architecture. It is rather so that they can get from one place to another without trouble. The Berlin Memorial expands on such a limited interpretation of accessibility. Whilst taking motion for granted, the grooves for walking sticks found along some of the Memorial's paths do not only ensure that one can navigate to a given destination (Figure 9.2). Like the groove on a vinyl record, they draw a sensitive instrument along a channel whose rhythmic structure and changing amplitudes unfold in time. As one moves between stelae and through intersections, there are variations in air pressure caused by compression and release. Heat and coolness alternate on skin as the sun peaks out from behind a stele and disappears again. The air temperature drops in the descent into the sunken areas, akin to the incremental changes in a repetitive Philip Glass composition, drifting almost imperceptibly from one scale to another. The resonance between rhythms in space and those in the body may be related to functions such as the heartbeat, digestion and respiration (McNeill 1995: 6). In these ways, the Berlin Memorial draws attention to the possibility that meaning-making and experience come through *changes* in perception rather than from *instances* of perception; not from what something looks like but through the very multiplicity of its sense experiences, layered through time. It puts brackets on vision as a privileged vehicle for architecture and unleashes all the senses as fully legitimate forms of architectural experience. It thus challenges the habit whereby one associates the sensorial experience of a spatial configuration with a specific representational and visual meaning, a shortcut that too often considers some experiences to be more true to an architectural work than others. In contrast, the Memorial makes it possible to hypothesize a design process in which modifying architectural form for the eye would be the last step after it has been designed to work with the other senses; that is, as an extra gesture for those who see.

FIGURE 9.2 View across Memorial to the Murdered Jews of Europe, Stelenfeld, Berlin, Germany

This last point underscores how much the Memorial departs from the conventional question that is raised when addressing disability considerations in architecture: in other words, can everyone, including those with mobility or sensory impairments, access this building? In Berlin, we must formulate a different question: to what modes of experience does this architecture lend itself? Or, to paraphrase Julia Kristeva (2003), what ways of being does it anticipate and realize? The difference between these two concerns may have a great impact on design practice. A design process nourished by the ways that bodies with different sensory and mobility capabilities develop impressions of architecture could result in environments where we see otherwise through touch, feel otherwise through sound, hear otherwise through vision. It would imagine the differentials and collusions of one sense with another in the space of perception. Updating Wölfflin's invitation, it would consider how we might hear our way through a room with skin tingling. While this process need not be only a detour by which we return to the ostensible normal body that walks and enjoys five functioning senses, that body, too, has much to gain from architecture designed in this way.

(Dis)ability trouble: the Rolex Learning Center in Lausanne

The Berlin Memorial disturbs a common understanding of circulation and sense in architectural thought, and by the same token questions the notion of accessibility in disability guidance and advocacy. The second case studied in this chapter also entertains an atypical relationship to concepts of mobility in architectural space. However, the consequences of its particular architecture involve the very definition of physical disability. The Rolex Learning Center for the Ecole Polytechnique Fédérale de Lausanne (EPFL) in Switzerland was designed by the Japanese firm Sejima and Nishizawa Architects and Associates (SANAA). SANAA won the competition in 2005, and building construction was completed in 2010. This university building is a large rectangle measuring about 120 metres by 170 metres, or three football fields side by side. It is ostensibly a one-storey structure, as it consists of a single rectangular layer of space held between a floor and a roof (while there is also a large basement area, its architectural characteristics do not warrant discussion here). However, it is in fact an unprecedented type of space: a single, continuous interior that is subdivided thanks to the ingenious combination of an incessantly sloping floor and a series of oval-shaped external patios. The result is an indoor landscape of rolling hills, wrapping around outdoor voids that bring natural light and air into the heart of the building. The topographic quality is underscored by the contour lines that figure in the plan (Figure 9.3).

The Learning Center's 14,000 square metres include a library and scientific information areas, teaching areas, living areas (cafés, restaurant, offices, boutique), cultural areas (exhibition space, university press offices, conference room), and service areas. The Polytechnic's idea is that the Learning Center complements existing facilities on campus as a hothouse for intellectual and social exchanges. For the university's head librarian, as the "point of entry to the EPFL, the Learning Center will be a place to learn, to obtain information, and to live. It will become a place where virtual and physical components combine to provide facilitated *access* to knowledge" (author's italics). The architects present the Learning Center as "a center for exchange and exploration of ideas for everyone"

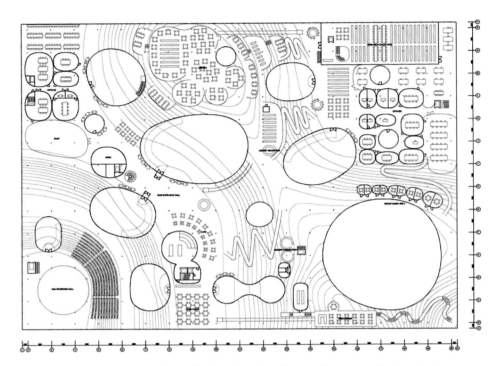

FIGURE 9.3 SANAA (2010) Plan of Rolex Learning Center, Lausanne, Switzerland

Reprinted by permission from SANAA

(Aymonin 2008). The use of sloping floors for changing elevation within the building, along with the near absence of doorways, might lead one to think that it would be barrier-free for users with mobility disabilities. Indeed, while all the other competition entries distributed the programme in multi-floor buildings, this building ostensibly eliminated the need for stairs, ramps and elevators: what could be more universally accessible than an entire building contained in a single room?

However, like Eisenman's Memorial, the project for the Learning Center – as presented for the competition and ultimately to the public – lent itself to critique from an accessibility perspective. The ramping ground plane that ran throughout the building did not respect local accessibility regulations: its slope varied constantly and could be downright steep in some places, and there were no resting landings. Moreover, orientation for people with vision disabilities would be particularly difficult, as there was no regular geometry for reference, and almost no walls to serve as guides. Despite the Center being a single-storey building, consisting entirely of that hallmark of architecture rendered accessible – the sloping ground – the project was in fact very inaccessible from a regulatory standpoint. In this context, the aim to provide "access to knowledge" expressed by the project's client and architects could seem rather ironic. One can understand that disability rights activists reacted negatively when such language was used to present a building that would be very difficult to inhabit for those with mobility or vision disabilities. All the more if one considers the high profile of the undertaking, reflected not only in the budget, but also in the design competition held to select the architects: in total, ten architecture firms competed, drawn from the roster of international star architects, including many Pritzker Prize winners. As the Swiss Center for Disability-adapted Construction pointed out in "L'art d'une architecture discriminatoire" "rendering people disabled with a new ninety million [Swiss] franc building intended to house a study centre is particularly shocking" (2005: 4).

As a result, the design development phase – as the project moved from the competition version through building permits and then to construction – required changes so that the building would comply with accessibility regulations. The revised plan looks as though elements were traced from a snakes-and-ladders game board. To ameliorate the level changes that sometimes amount to 4.5 metres (almost two storeys), the designers used switchback and S-shaped ramps, and straight-shot funicular-like lifts, to complement the usual vertical elevators. The result is surprising at points, for example where the relatively small restaurant dining room is served on one side by a multi-stop inclined lift (for mid-climb access, for kitchen access, and finally for dining access), and on the other by a rather original winding ramp broken up with steps: this kind of circulation redundancy would be a luxury in almost any other project. This latter stair-ramp suggests that even able-bodied building users would have trouble with the Learning Center's unusual floor plane in some places. In any case, the matter was apparently settled from a regulatory perspective. But as with the Berlin Memorial, the Rolex Learning Center calls for closer attention to what it has to say about how the body and its experiences are conceptualized in architectural thought.

Blurring the difference?

One characteristic of particular note is that there are two types of floor area in the Center. Some spaces are accessible according to conventional interpretations of accessibility codes. These are areas of level ground, whether open or enclosed in glass partition walls, and are joined to each other and to the building exterior by uninterrupted surfaces whose slope never exceeds the maximum allowed by law, with resting landings at specified intervals, and a vertical or inclined lift intervening where ramps are not possible. In the final project plan, these areas are identifiable by the tables, chairs, desks and bookshelves that populate them. This furnished landscape is a continuum of code-abiding architectural space.

In contrast, the remaining ground floor area in the building consists for the most part of relatively steeply sloped ground, as the dense contour lines in the plan reveal. This interior space has a strange status. It is clearly not considered important enough by Lausanne's building commission to require that it be accessible. But at the same time, the Polytechnic obviously considers it important enough to spend great amounts of additional money for its construction and maintenance: indeed, it represents a good third of the built floor area. Snaking around the prudent, law-abiding parts of the building, this other kind of space raises interesting questions about how architectural thought conceptualizes inhabitation and, by extension, the assumed bodies of its various inhabitants.

To start, we could contrast the unusual binary opposition between accessible and inaccessible space at Lausanne with the radical distinction between circulation space and meaningful space discussed in the Berlin Memorial. In Eisenman's project, the problem was that meaning and inaccessibility coincide. In contrast, the spaces that are arguably the most significant (because useful) in the Learning Center are fully accessible, yet they coexist with large swathes of floor area that are apt to cause accessibility trouble. On the one hand, there are areas with familiar programmes such as library, offices, multifunction room, or cafeteria, whilst on the other, the remaining space – that is, the sloping ground of the interior landscape – is supplemental, bonus floor area whose nature is not expressible in conventional design terms, neither for regulatory purposes not from a simply practical point of view. It is neither clearly circulation space, as there is so much of it, so much of it is uncomfortably steep, and access to all other spaces is handled otherwise; nor is it easily usable space, at least in terms of conventional building programmes: aside from the perfunctory solution of graded seating – which is already included in an auditorium space (in the lower left part of the plan), it is very difficult to furnish such spaces for any usual occupation, as may be observed in outdoor areas with similar relief. It is interesting to note that the contrast between furniture-friendly spaces and areas with excessively inclined planes is much more pronounced in the revised plan than in the original competition scheme. It is as though practical considerations – including but not limited to those related to disabled building users – exacerbated the differentiation between space that may be occupied "normally" and that other, indefinable space.

As we will see, this new space may be understood as a challenge to the usual distinction between mobility ability and disability. It disrupts the clear-cut border between barrier-free sequences through a building and paths that are interrupted by impediments to smooth, easy movement. In conventional buildings, the limits to the continuity of accessible space are clearly defined by steps or more significant breaks in floor levels. Indeed, the presence of such breaks cues one to look for a ramp or lift nearby. Furthermore, the ramps that compensate for such obstacles virtually always have a constant pitch. In contrast, the unconventional space in the Learning Center in Lausanne is composed of floor areas with constantly changing slopes, making it more akin to a natural landscape than to an architectural environment. Whereas conventional architecture exhibits a clear distinction between discontinuous paths on the one hand (where steps are involved) and smooth, barrier-free routes on the other, the Learning Center repeatedly solicits occupants to evaluate at what point the ground's incline might become too steep for them to use (Figure 9.4).

A first consequence of this architectural quality is that the need to judge whether or not one should use a slope is as true for those not normally associated with mobility disabilities as for those who are. While this may be a common situation outdoors (especially in Switzerland), it is not often encountered indoors. A second consequence is that, in the Learning Center, some users who would be obliged to use a stigma-inducing ramp when changing levels in other buildings might fall in with the users who would usually use the stairs. A flight of eight steps in a conventional public building deters even the most athletic wheelchair user: the steps create a clear distinction along rolling lines. In the Learning Center, this distinction is blurred. The breaking point between an acceptable incline and one that is too steep is much more subjective, more situational or contextual. Some hills are clearly too steep for safe use by wheelchair users or people with difficulty walking, for whatever reason. But many parts of this "other" space, including some that are adjacent to

FIGURE 9.4 Interior views of Rolex Learning Center showing constantly changing slopes

Reprinted by permission of SANAA.

code-respecting ramps, may be easily practicable by building users who would normally be characterized as disabled. This architectural work thus upsets a distinction that arises in other buildings where level changes occasion the juxtaposition of steps and ramps, and by extension a differentiation between normal and "non-normal" occupants based on how they move around. In short, the Learning Center blurs the line between able- and disabled people twice. First, it presents slopes that are a challenge for all: parts of the building "disable" those not normally affected by the few steps that inconvenience wheelchair users and others with mobility difficulties. The Learning Center's specific form, in particular its steeper slopes, prevent full, unlimited use for many bodies. Then, it blurs the line a second time by making it possible for some users to eschew regulatory ramps in favour of more challenging slopes. The steeper slopes "enable" certain individuals to do things not usually possible in a building. One can slalom up a slope to lessen the strain, or take a straight line to test muscle strength and respiratory control – or simply to show off. The descent could also be an opportunity for a thrill. Daring the same slopes as people walking on two legs, some wheelchair users may revel in the opportunity to exercise on something other than the usual six per cent pitch. Combined, these disabling and enabling moments redistribute bodies in space according to parameters that differ greatly from those that normally hold sway in architectural environments. This other space in the Learning Center could therefore be qualified as a very specific kind of circulation, one that reconfigures the usual distinction between mobility ability and disability.

Echoing this idea of (dis)ability trouble, here is John Hockenberry, an American wheelchair-bound war reporter, describing his daily Chicago commute between his apartment at the bottom of Michigan Avenue and his office at the top: "Rolling to work every morning was a character-building, hand-over-hand, rope climb. Coming home in the evenings was flat-out, downhill, and effortless" (1995: 209).

While Hockenberry would probably not agree to allowing steeper access ramps in general, he writes from the experience of his disability; something that tends to be suppressed by the ability/disability binaries within architectural discourse and built into access guidance. He further raises important questions about how his particular way of being is perceived by others:

> Though I rolled in rhythm and wove my way with precision, the presence of a wheelchair in the crowd never seemed as natural to the crowd as it did to me. Where I saw beauty and grace gliding down, others, particularly those walking toward me, saw terror, collisions and serious injury. Going up, where I saw a bracing physical challenge, others saw pain and suffering.
>
> (1995: 209)

Based on this testimony, we might speculate that if Hockenberry were to visit the Learning Center, he would challenge assumptions of an obvious dividing line between ability and disability. In Lausanne, those who enjoy some muscle strain, or who are in a rush, or who are trying to impress someone, can identify with each other, whether they walk on two legs or roll on four wheels. Meanwhile, some individuals normally counted amongst the able population may be discouraged by the slopes, and feel solidarity with others with certain physical impairments. Such new channels of identification are possible because of this strange, new space in the Learning Center, space that is neither official programme nor functional circulation. Conventional accessibility regulations attempt to erase the distinction between physical ability and disability by providing ramps and lifts to complement steps and stairs. The Learning Center blurs the line, or redraws it day by day, depending on how each building user feels.

This different way of imagining architecture's relationship to the body could benefit ostensibly non-impaired individuals as much as those whose particular physical or sensory conditions become disabilities when encountering an unaccommodating built environment. In the Berlin Memorial, we saw that the significance of an architectural space may come from changes in perception and experience, rather than from instances in which symbolic messages are conveyed through representation. This both reduces discrimination by opening up the legitimacy of multitude, embodied experiences in all their diversity, and broadens the palette of senses that may be called upon by designers. For different reasons, the Learning Center in Lausanne also compels us to ask how considering the complexity of disabled individuals' different ways of being can enhance architectural thought and, by extension, architecture in general. As Carol Breckenridge and Candace Vogler have pointed out, "the disabled are 'good to think'" (2001: 353). The wager here is that everyone can benefit from innovations if architects start from the variety of lived experience to generate architectural form.

Another quote from John Hockenberry can serve as a conclusion. Regarding his downhill commute, he observed that, on good days,

> The spaces between pedestrians were made for wheelchairs, and I belonged there. Pedestrians saw it as well. On their faces was: "That looks like fun." When had they ever yearned to be in a wheelchair before? […] The promise of art and revolution is that people might discard their preconceptions and truly understand what is in the mind of another. What would a world look like in which people dare to wish to know what it is like not to walk?"
>
> (1995: 214)

Whether or not its architects intended it, the Rolex Learning Center may give us a glimpse of that world.

10

FROM STEEP STEPS TO RETROFIT TO UNIVERSAL DESIGN, FROM COLLAPSE TO AUSTERITY

Neo-liberal spaces of disability

Jay Dolmage (2016)

"[D]isabled people in Western societies have been oppressed by the production of space," writes Brendan Gleeson (1999: 2). As I will show, disability is a reality – but disability is also produced, sometimes most powerfully through our design of space. In this chapter I will examine three central spatial metaphors from the field of disability studies: the *steep steps*, the *retrofit*, and *universal design*. The *steep steps* reflect social structures wherein hierarchies of privilege are reflected in conventional architecture. The *retrofit* refers to the mandate to redesign spaces for access, albeit often under temporary, backdoor and overly legalistic parameters. *Universal design* refers to the movement to design spaces for the broadest possible access, anticipating diversity. All three metaphors have physical as well as symbolic entailments.

I will map these spatial metaphors across the history of the disability rights movement, but I will also connect them with what I see to be "new" spatial logics, connected to industrial capitalism, late or fast capitalism, and neo-liberalism. My examples will connect to the architectures of higher education, spaces that we should feel invited and compelled to critique as embodying social (re)productions: the buildings in which students learn can and should also be seen as carrying and conveying lessons about societal values for the bodies and minds within (and without) those spaces. The goal in this chapter is to give readers some metaphorical tools for analyzing built spaces from a disability rights perspective, acknowledging the stories and the histories and the attitudes and prejudices built into these spaces and also built against bodily diversity and mobility.

In this chapter, I return to some previous research to create some new ideas (2006). In doing this, I am returning to old places to map new ones. In past work, I have examined and used the aforementioned three spatial metaphors to explore and explain the ways that disability is positioned in culture and society, and in particular in social institutions like the university. The first premise has always been that we need to care about space. To begin with, we do "think" spatially – we readily see the world in terms of physical space and spatial relations. Thus, spaces already convey information, and reconstructing or re-imagining these spaces is a mode of argument. As David Harvey and others have argued, "places have material consequences insofar as fantasies, desires, fears and longings are expressed in actual behavior" (1993: 22). Spaces, and how we write about them, think about them and move through them, suggest and delimit attitudes. As Brendan Gleeson wrote, the production of space can oppress disabled people "due in part to their exclusion from the discourses and practices that shape the physical layout of societies" (1999: 2). Disability is also *produced*, sometimes most powerfully by our uses of space. For this reason, I've argued that we must see the *steep steps* all around us in the academy; we must see our work as constructing alternative modes of access – *retrofitting* – whilst recognizing the critical dangers of this mode of mapping; but we must also conceptualize new ways to more broadly conceive of what we do, and therefore we should consider *universal design* (UD). In the past, I have pretty robustly challenged the steep steps and the retrofit, while in a way situating UD as the "just right" alternative (2006), like in the children's fairy tale of *Goldilocks and the Three Bears*. But in this chapter I will challenge Universal Design as well, particularly as it is invoked through times and spaces of late capitalism and neo-liberalism.

Steep steps

The *steep steps* metaphor puts forward the idea that access to privilege is a movement upwards – only the truly "fit" survive this climb. At the university, these steep steps, physically and figuratively, lead to the ivory tower. The steep steps metaphor sums up the ways the university constructs spaces that exclude. It seems as though, regardless of the architectural style(s) of a campus, steep steps are integral, whether these are the wide marble staircases of Greek-revival administration buildings or the brutalist concrete stairs and terraces like those constructed on my own campus at the University of Waterloo in Canada or at Brunel University in Britain. The most "traditional" of campuses, many of them built around churches, or in classical Ionic style, similarly rely on steps not just as architectural details, but as symbolic social center-pieces of university life. *Traditional* university life. For example, think of Amory Blaine in Fitzgerald's *This Side of Paradise*. He develops a "deep and reverent devotion to the gray walls and Gothic peaks [of Princeton] and all they symbolized as warehouses of dead ages [...] he liked knowing that Gothic architecture, with its upward trend, was peculiarly appropriate" to his elite university (1996: 62). This same upward trend builds stairs, as well as some peculiar attitudes about who can come within the walls, and who can ascend the heights. Unsurprisingly, when Disney/Pixar animators wanted to create a realistically forbidding setting for the film *Monster's University,* they studied several Ivy League schools: the MU School of Scaring has broad, high marble stairs just like those you'd find at Harvard or Stanford. In reality, and in the public imagination, higher education is about steep steps.

The university allows some people up these stairs, and it throws others down the same steep incline. Historically, steps were also closely associated, eugenically, with cognitive levels and forms of work. Thus these steps also classed citizens and linked their value to labor-output. In this way, the steep steps are an apt metaphor for industrial capitalism, just as they are created by capitalism and its values of bootstrapping, autonomy, winner-takes-all competition, progress as upward mobility, and so on.

Indeed, one way to map the spaces of academia and disability would be to look at the ways land – land already stolen from indigenous peoples – was parceled out in the U.S. in the early to mid-1800s. While land-grant universities were popping up in rural spaces, asylums and "idiot schools" were popping up in other adjacent settings – on old farms and abandoned land. From within one privileged space, academics were deciding the fate of others in similar, yet somehow now pathological, other and impure spaces.

In the architectures of both these developing institutions, stairs made powerful ideological statements. As Trent (1994) and others have pointed out, American academics, through the flawed science of eugenics, systematically developed the means to segregate society based upon often arbitrary ideas of ability – the university was the place for the most able, the mental institution the space for the "least." Not only have people with disabilities been traditionally seen as objects of study in higher education, rather than as teachers or students; not only has disability been a rhetorically-produced stigma which could be applied to other marginalized groups to keep them out of the university; but the university has always had a mutually-reinforcing and polarized relationship with societal institutions like asylums and asylum-schools (and even immigration stations, reservations, and prisons). In short, the privileged status of the university is an argument for other spaces of incarceration, sterilization, and deportation.

As Craig Steven Wilder has shown, in America, "European powers deployed colleges to help defend and regulate their colonial possessions and they turned to [the slave trade] to fund these efforts [....] College founders and officers used enslaved people to raise buildings, maintain campuses, and enhance their institutional wealth" while they also "trained the personnel and cultivated the ideas that accelerated and legitimated the dispossession of Native Americans and the enslavement of Africans" (2013: 9–10). In Canada, with a different but similarly devastating history of enslavement and dispossession (nonetheless) university founders relied on what Mosby (2013) calls "colonial science." Let's define that as: experimentation on aboriginal peoples, immigrants, and people with disabilities that was thoroughly institutionalized and reinforced by government policy, at the same time establishing the knowledge and power of universities. These eugenic practices, and in fact eugenics itself, can be seen as the invention of the North American university and, as I have written elsewhere, we can read this history through university buildings built in large part by and upon the exploitation of people with disabilities (Dolmage 2015b).

Take for example three "asylum schools" or schools for the "feeble-minded" in the Boston area in America. Wrentham School for the Feeble-Minded was opened in 1906. In the 1950s, "residents" at this and the Fernald School (founded 1854) were fed radioactive isotopes in a scientific experiment. Young boys at these schools signed up to be part of the "science club," a club name invented by the Massachusetts Institute of Technology (M.I.T.) faculty club, and they were given Mickey Mouse watches and armbands, and taken on special outings, in return for taking part in a "nutritional study." Seventy-four boys were fed oatmeal injected with radioactive iron or calcium (Welsome 1999: 231, 235). Welsome suggests there was "nothing unique" about this study, as the school had become a "veritable laboratory" with a "captive population" for academics from Boston (231, 233).

Thus, the asylum schools were built in the long shadow of the universities, also as their perverse mirror-image, also as the foundation and source of the research that built the academic reputation of North America's "finest" schools.

Another example: in Canada, the Children's Psychiatric Research Institute, a residential "school" in London, Ontario, was in part established because researchers from the University of Western Ontario were tired of having to travel all the way to Orillia, Ontario, to access patients/research subjects at the Hospital School there (Zarfas 1963).

And another: recently a construction crew at the University of Mississippi discovered a graveyard on land it was clearing to build a medical center. News coverage of the discovery registered shock that this would halt the building (Mitchell 2014). In clearing the land, they found over 1000 unmarked graves, believed to be those of patients at the former Mississippi State Lunatic Asylum. But nowhere in this coverage is there any outrage or horror about the fact that these graves were unmarked, that these patients weren't deemed deserving of a proper burial, that these lives were so demeaned.

These examples, and the many others I could have included here if space allowed, establish several important facts. First of all, there is a steady pattern of setting up such sites in close proximity to universities, where one group of humans could be held and studied by another. Yet we also can comprehend what the binary relationship has always been between universities and asylums, hospital schools, and other institutions. This violent exploitation, this structural connection, has underpinned the expansion of the North American university. What a statement to the future doctors and other medical professionals who were trained in these places. At these universities, because of the absence of awareness of this history, learning now literally unfolds upon an ignorance of the eugenic past. This, then, is perhaps the most perverse instantiation of the logic of the steep steps we might hope to find: we continue to actually *build* universities in service of eugenics, lifting some bodies upwards towards privilege upon the footings of segregation and oppression.

The retrofit

So how do we address this eugenic past, laid out up and down all of these steep steps? Maybe we come around the back. To retrofit is to add a component or accessory to something that has been already manufactured or built. This retrofit does not necessarily *make* the product function better, does not necessarily fix a faulty product, but it acts as a sort of correction – it adds a modernized part in place of, or in addition to, an older part. Often, the retrofit allows a product to measure up to new regulations. Retrofits may be seen as mechanical, or as a matter of maintenance; thus they aren't seen as creative. Retrofitting is also often forced or mandated. Another entailment of the retrofit is that it is a stop-gap measure – this leads to the idea that a retrofit can, in fact should, be given low priority. Thus, as a building is retrofitted to accommodate disability, as per the "specs" of the Americans with Disabilities Act (ADA) or the UK Disability Discrimination Act (DDA), ramps are added onto the side of a building, or around back, instead of at the main entrance. Both the ADA and the DDA call for *reasonable accommodation*. Common reason then seems to dictate that disability is supplemental to society, that it is an afterthought or an imposition.

The construction of elevators or ramps instead of steep steps, these are well-intentioned ideas; they speak to our desire for equality. Yet the retrofit is a sort of cure, but half-hearted, thus leaving many people with disabilities in difficult positions. In the university the retrofit is also a part of curriculum and pedagogy, particularly in relation to issues of difference. Too often, we *react* to diversity instead of planning for it. We acknowledge that students come from different places, and that they are headed in different directions, yet this does little to alter the vectors of pedagogy. Most often, the only time disability is spoken or written about in a college class is in the final line of the syllabus, when students are referred to disability services should they desire assistance. The message to all students is that disability is a supplementary concern – and then that it is not the teachers' concern, not really a part of the course; it's at the back door of the syllabus. Teachers "deal with" disability via the ideological equivalent of a ramp – disability as an identity category can come in the side or the back entrance if it is to be included at all. If a student does seek accommodations, teachers treat them according to the cliché about Las Vegas: what accommodations happen for this student, stay with this student; what accommodations happen in this class, stay in this class. The nature of the "retrofitted" accommodation requires that teachers make no lasting changes to pedagogy or to the culture of the university. Of course, this same sort of retrofitting happens across all of society, and across all of architecture.

I want to cautiously suggest that, in some cases, a retrofit can be useful, can aid students in their navigation of this space – just as an elevator or a ramp might enable mobility to a building. It is important, however, to recognize that the retrofit is often only an "after-the-fact" move because "the facts" refuse to recognize disability as part of normality rather than separate and additional to it, or "the factors" cast disability as a strategy, or "the benefactors" claim accessibility not as everyone's right, but as their opportunity to provide charity, or as an opportunity to construct these students as drains or threats. Of course, the intellectual implications of the retrofit are many. When we look at the buildings and spaces of our universities and cities, we see how thought about disability has almost always been a side-thought or an *after*-thought: count the appended ramps, the painted-in parking spots, the stair-lifts. As a building gains its extra accoutrements to meet these requirements it creates a sort of comical and hazardous obstacle course for people with disabilities. Moreover, even to *use* these retrofits frames the user as deficient, as a "drain" or "threat." Retrofits might be seen as huge concrete sorting mechanisms for ableism. En route, the retrofit sends a very clear message about its values for bodily diversity.

For instance, consider the meme of "curb-cuts to nowhere" – images, posted online, of ramps and curb-cuts that literally lead nowhere, or lead to inaccessible spaces or features, thus negating their purpose. These images have commonly been posted as a form of backlash *against* accommodations, yet they more accurately reflect an absurd critique of the late capitalist industry of retrofitting. One excellent example comes from the aforementioned Brunel University in London, a school that, like my own University of Waterloo, has many examples of brutalist staircases – expansive cast-concrete sets of steps used not just as stairs, but also as potential outdoor seating, even as social or communal gathering space (Figure 10.1). These staircases can also be seen aesthetically, ostensibly, as key players in the rhythm and continuity of the university space. A key feature of such steps is that these staircases often connect perpendicularly, or in seeming waves, with other similar banks of concrete steps. In the image in Figure 10.1, taken of the outside of the (in)famous brutalist Lecture Centre at Brunel, we see one set of these stairs as wide at the building itself leading up to the entrance, and another perpendicular set connected and leading to the building from another direction, creating a concrete plateau at the entry level and a kind of small pyramid of stairs. Because these staircases are so wide, a pedestrian can access them from any place, and thus can use the stairs in a wide variety of ways. The largest bank of stairs leads down to a green space, for instance. But when a ramp is retrofitted onto these stairs and down to this green space, instead of leading directly up to the entrance it climbs only up a single set of stairs at the forefront of the picture, thus ensuring that if one wanted to travel from the building to the green space, you'd need to use two ramps. Further, the ramp itself is made of steel and "feels" temporary against the cast concrete steps. Further still, the ramp does not lead down to a pathway in the green space, but instead leads down to the base of a tree, seemingly difficult to navigate around. Even further, the ramp is arranged crossways and directly in front of the broad set of concrete steps, thus making about twenty feet worth of the concrete steps unusable for anyone.

The building itself is essentially a giant concrete box, held up on the stairs-side by a series of thin concrete columns. Tiered staircases with small balconies appear at the front of the building, with each balcony a different color and with bright arrangements

FIGURE 10.1 Stairs at Brunel University, UK

Photo by Ken MacLeod.

of flowers (each balcony being a central design feature and at the same time inaccessible). The entry level is entirely glass. Another small ramp leads up to the entry level from the far left of Figure 10.1 – the second ramp you'd need to use to get from the green space to the entry, and located basically as far from the first ramp as possible. In this one example, we can come to understand just how retrofits function aesthetically and architecturally: positioned as temporary, as so often in opposition to the rest of the space, sending a message that disability is an unforeseen and uninvited presence. These "curb-cuts to nowhere" and accessibility-gone-wrong examples reveal the half-heartedness of retrofitting, or they show how most accessible design is facile, or so long as it *begins* addressing an inequity, or looks as though it is addressing an inequity, that is considered enough. In the Brunel example, the accessibility "fix" is unsatisfactory, clashes with the other architectural messages of the space, and in fact ruins or invalidates the architectural character or message. Disability itself is clearly "misfit" by the ableist or "normate template" that the campus was built upon (Hamraie 2013). This said, curb-cuts to nowhere, and other memes of accessibility-gone-wrong, themselves can become a way to circulate anti-ableist critique. Thus, the curb-cuts and the absurd ramps could be added into other recent online movements intended to call out colleges and universities for their inaccessibility or for the ways that their existing accommodation processes are insufficient or absurd retrofits (Dolmage 2015b; Price 2011; Titchkosky 2011).

I have been suggesting that steep steps are an apt metaphor for capitalism – well, let me suggest that the retrofit is a logic of *late* capitalism. That is, the retrofit points up the inadequacy of capitalism's ability to deal with various crises of its own making and other long-term structural problems. The retrofit is also a logic of *fast* capitalism – fast capitalism is the tendency of capitalism to extract surplus value with as little investment as possible for the greatest possible return, while adding as little to the real economy as possible, often by means of financial speculation and the quickening of production to the point of making next-to-nothing. This fast capitalism can be seen as the necessary consequence of capitalism. Like philanthropy, which gets marketized as a consequence of late capitalism, the retrofit is something that is seen as charitable.

. Yet at the same time, the industry of temporarily correcting or normalizing disability is massive, one of the largest and fastest growing industries in our modern world, encompassing global pharmaceutical and biotechnology corporations, as well as architects, access consultants, lawyers, and even educational specialists. Retrofits – be they architectural or biomedical – are a huge part of these industries, and the temporariness and contingency of every retrofit simply speeds up the cycle – and the capitalism. Filtered through fast capitalism, the retrofit offers only a quick and temporary fix to critical socio-political and economic conditions, and it does so with solutions that, as we know, often offer next-to-nothing of practical use.

In terms of rights and access for those other bodies that our society has deemed marginal, the retrofit as a logic of late capitalism might actually ensure what Lauren Berlant calls "slow death": "a zone of temporality [...] of ongoingness, getting by, and living on, where the structural inequalities are dispersed, the pacing of their experience intermittent" (2011: 759). Slow death through "accommodation" and the supplemental logic of the retrofit would not be a way of "defining a group of individuals merely afflicted with the same ailment, [rather] slow death describes populations *marked out for wearing out*" (2011: 760).

"Slow death" might seem a bit maudlin or dramatic, but that shouldn't deter us from investigating exactly what it means and how it applies. Slow death, to me, seems to be the chronology of accommodations such as those made to the steep steps at Brunel – it means having to take two ramps, located as far as part from one another as possible, and it entails similar processes of wearing out across non-physical spaces. And, perversely, the faster the capitalism, the more difficult it becomes to recognize the pace and impact of the wearing out, as it gets spread across space. For students in the UK, for instance, it's not just the ridiculous ramps, it's also that a government austerity budget has led to huge cuts to the Disabled Student Allowance, meaning there is no certainty of where those ramps will lead (and you'll find those ramps, and those cuts, across North America as well).

Universal design

The retrofit can hold us captive in a logic of fairness: it apportions out access and accommodation in minimal ways, governed by legalistic and medicalized rhetorics that disempower, but also defended by liberal values that seem unimpeachable, even admirable. The "playing field" isn't even! Of course we need ramps! But then we also need ways to understand what has made the field uneven. We also need ways to understand academia as something much more than a "playing field." With all of this in mind, then, from the beginning, we should import lots of skepticism into our discussion of my final spatial metaphor and way to move: universal design. UD also can very effectively camouflage other forms of administrative discrimination.

In looking at the steep steps and the retrofit, one thing becomes clear – we can recognize these metaphors as physical structures. Yet we also need to recognize these as temporal metaphors. The steps are steep, and they are also "steeped" in tradition. Steps become symbolic center-pieces of university life. *Traditional* university life. My point is that students with disabilities are excluded not just from campus space, but from the entirety of collegiate history and philosophy. Likewise, the steep steps of government buildings, art galleries, monuments, and other cultural and public spaces make the same temporal arguments. And the retrofit is, as I said, an after-the-fact construction, an after-thought. It is always *supplemental* – always not-originary. The retrofit is additional. But as a supplement, to retrofit is to *fix* in some way. Unfortunately, this "fixing" provides little opportunity for continued refitting, for a developmental and progressive process. In developing my third metaphor, I want to emphasize the importance of the *priority* of universal design – universal design as a process and mode of becoming.

As Ronald Mace wrote, "universal design is the design of products and environments to be usable by all people, to the greatest extent possible, without the need for adaptation or specialized design" (1985: 147). The UD movement was first an architectural movement that worked against the exclusion of people with disabilities, and argued that instead of temporarily accommodating difference, physical structures should be designed with a wide range of citizens in mind, planning for the active involvement of all. To do so, disability and diversity needed to be central and not marginal in the design process. As Mace and his team discovered, "many of the environmental changes needed to accommodate people with disabilities actually benefited everyone. Recognition that many such features could be

FIGURE 10.2   Ed Roberts Campus Ramp. Image used with permission of Ed Roberts Campus Photograph courtesy of Will Henderson-Nold.

commonly provided and thus less expensive, unlabeled, attractive, and even marketable, laid the foundation for the universal design movement" (1985: 148).

In practice, a universally designed building can make accessibility the central message of its design. Take for instance the Ed Roberts campus in Berkeley, California. Named after a disability rights pioneer, instead of making steps its central argument, a huge curving ramp is the center and the focus of this building. As you see in Figure 10.2, when you enter the building at a level entrance, a large, red, cantilevered "helical" ramp is in front of you and it curves around within the central mezzanine to take visitors to all three floors of the building. In contrast to the Brunel steps and ramp, here the accessibility feature is also the central architectural and aesthetic feature.

Universal design offers us a way to locate ourselves not in response to changing, hostile geographies, but as proactive architects of future possibilities. UD, registered as action, is a way to move. In some ways, it is also a world-view. Universal design is not a tailoring of the environment to marginal groups; it is a patterning of engagement and effort. The push towards the "universal" is a push towards seeing spaces as multiple and in-process. The emphasis on "design" allows us to recognize that we are all involved in the continued production of space. As Aimi Hamraie has powerfully shown, UD is a form of "value explicit" design, a design that "provides a framework within which designers can be held accountable for the types of environments that they produce. UD is an approach to value-explicit design that critiques the false value-neutrality of inaccessible environments" (2013: n.p.). With this focus on value, as I turn to this spatial metaphor, then, I want to connect UD to an economic logic as well.

Of course, you'll remember that I defined the steep steps as a logic of industrial capitalism, and the retrofit as a logic of late capitalism and/or fast capitalism. I am not going to let universal design off easily here. Thinking of UD as a logic of specifically *neo-liberal* late capitalism can be an important way to interrogate its meanings, possible uses and misuses. Neo-liberalism takes the values of free choice, flexibility, and deregulation and translates them into market reforms and policies designed to maximize profits, privatize industry, and exploit all available resources. But much more importantly, neo-liberalism should be seen as a system that powerfully masks inequalities and readily co-opts concepts like autonomy, diversity, tolerance and democracy. Not only this, but neo-liberalism has been shown to interpellate its logics and grammars into our everyday lives – so that we all become middle-managers, so that we run our classrooms and cultural institutions like corporations while allowing corporations to take over the discourses we used to control and sell them back to us (Dolmage 2015b). It is highly possible that a concept such as universal design could simply become a proxy system for demanding the flexibility of bodies, increasing the tenuousness of social and physical structures, rebranding our intellectual work, constantly moving the target for technological innovation as flows of information are made ever more proprietary, and placing the privilege of "design" in the hands of a narrowing and exponentially profiting few. Potentially worse, a cheap and easy mention of universal design might, as Stephanie Kerschbaum reveals happens with other discourses of diversity, "enhance pedigree" while "obscur[ing] differences" and "reinforc[ing] the status quo" (2014: 36–37). For instance, very much *unlike* the Ed Roberts campus depicted in Figure 10.2, many buildings that claim to be universally designed, or that have even won UD awards from agencies like the Royal Institute of the Architects of Ireland, just have elegant retrofits. See for example the restoration of St. Mel's Cathedral in Ireland, which retained all exterior and interior stairs and simply added ramps off to the side of the main ideological and architectural pathways through the space. I urge you to similarly interrogate other buildings that tout UD, to discern whether what is being featured is in fact anything more than retrofitting.

UD as a metaphor also seems especially prone to the false promise of expanding – neo-liberalism promises an expanding world, more jobs, greater access to more and more technology and information. But what expands is truly just the market; this expansion is often false, supplemental, derivative; the benefits of this expansion are only ever financial, they flow upwards rapidly, and the benefits that do trickle down do so ever more slowly if they trickle down at all, while risk is transferred downward by the truckload. The inclusive design (UK terminology for UD) of something like the London Paralympics offers a powerful example. As Robert McRuer shows, the

> politics of affect that has accompanied this [inclusive] agenda has been multivalent – a limited but spectacular celebration of disability and disability identity [...] around the London 2012 Olympic and Paralympic Games [...] has coexisted with a concerted campaign to cast recipients of disability benefits as "scroungers" or "spongers" or "shirkers."
>
> (2015: n.p.)

In the end, what good are a few accessible stadiums and public pathways when one of the key sponsors of the games (Atos) is also the company comprehensively downgrading and rejecting disability Work Capability Assessment claims? Isn't it possible that one limited celebration or one accessible park creates the vacuum into which a thousand cuts can slide, and can hide?

Collapse and austerity

Of course, now is the moment in the chapter when I am supposed to offer a much more hopeful message. Now, I am supposed to land on a final metaphor that solves all of the social, spatial, and even economic problems my other metaphors have posed. But instead I want to identify a few further spatial, architectural connections that we need to be increasingly wary of, and that might in fact oppose the goals of universal design, and instead create what Margaret Price calls "conflicts of access" (2012: n.p.).

I offer only first thoughts on these metaphors here, and encourage you to think them through as we continue to move through them spatially, temporally, and economically. First, I think we are called upon to re-conceptualize the ways that, even though universes, societies, and structures might expand, they also collapse – and this metaphor – the collapse – might be an interesting one to reclaim and re-inhabit, given global financial crises, but also given the fact that this is a disability metaphor: canes and wheelchairs and portable ramps collapse so that we can move them, hide them, store them, put them back together again later. Collapsing is a way to fall apart as we come together, and connects to invigorating, powerful rhetorical acts of refusal and delay. I would suggest that the idea of "collapse," which has come to powerfully inflect all of our discussions of capitalism, must be thought *from* disability, and this will save it from purely pejorative readings: what is beautiful, useful, inevitable about collapse? What about the collapse of an inequitable economic and social system can and should be celebrated, and what space gets created for a more just and inclusive set of structures? What is design for collapse, how does it differ from UD? How do we avoid rebuilding steep steps or simply continuing to offer temporary retrofits? Generally, architects are taught to think through collapse very carefully: materials and processes must be tested for collapse. But what about testing built environments for the collapse of intentions and the conflicts of economic and aesthetic, or academic and embodied concerns? Of course, we have generally responded to collapse with other temporal, architectural, and economic metaphors – like austerity. So the concept needs further thinking. But a place to begin a "value explicit" design would be to map where and how the designs' intentions might break down or overlap with other needs and concerns.

Austerity is also – like collapse – a form of design-thinking and an architectural *value*. Some of the power of austerity comes from the misleading aesthetic character of the word itself, something that we see as smart, simple, intuitive, a virtue. A Zen principle. Synonymous with simplicity. Indeed, many see economic recession as being, eventually, good for architecture. As Adam Mayer and others have suggested, this might herald the end of "starchitecture" and instead a "new commitment to build an environment that is both sustainable and affordable" (2008: n.p.). Yet this assumes that the current "strapped fiscal environment" will look anything like the environment that may have produced more simplistic and civic-minded design in past eras.

In *The Body Economic: Why Austerity Kills*, David Stuckler and Sanjay Basu write that "austerity is medicine intended to reduce symptoms of debt and deficits, and to cure recessions. It cuts government spending on healthcare coverage, assistance to the unemployed, and housing support" and yet "the real danger to public health is not recession, per se, but austerity" (2013: ix, xiv). Their data persuasively and repeatedly shows that austerity "does great harm, punishing the most vulnerable" (140). They ask "what good is an increased growth rate...if it is hazardous to our health?" (145). This has become the type of question that disability studies must repeatedly answer. In Mark Blyth's book *Austerity: The History of a Dangerous Idea*, he suggests that "partly because it enables conservatives to try (once again) to run the detested welfare state out of town, [austerity] never seems to die" (2013: 10). Then, what if something like universal design as it is being argued for and implemented (at universities and elsewhere) just camouflages clawbacks to other essential support systems? How will design be impacted by austerity politics and economics? How can something like accessibility, inclusive design or UD be foregrounded in an era of intensive privatization?

Lisa Duggan (2003) suggests that neo-liberalism is characterized by the shrinking of the public sphere as the government renounces responsibility for social welfare. This connects to a key concept underlying austerity: that cuts to public programs can lead to private growth. David Harvey has also suggested that the neo-liberal state attempts to "reconstruct social solidarities, albeit along different lines [...] in new forms of associationism" (2005: 81). In *The House of Difference* (1999) Eva Mackey famously studied discourses that invoke liberal multicultural practices, but do so in order to protect existing economic and cultural power structures. It is easy to see how a celebration of universal design could be a way to actually shrink the safety net and widen structural inequalities, as seemingly happened in the UK around the Paralympics. So this is where we have ended up, but also where we must begin to build something new. My hope is that all of these metaphors – their physical existence, their arguments, their places and times and economies, give us new ways to understand and encounter architecture – as we refuse to forget the eugenic past and as we refuse to build a future that recreates exclusion.

PART III
Education

Whilst there has been a long history of concern with universal and inclusive design in architectural and built environment education, it continues to remain marginalised and fragmented. Many reports on this situation have proposed reasons why this is the case, demonstrated examples of good teaching practices, and suggested strategies for better embedding dis/ability into learning and teaching architecture and urban design (Lifchez 1986; Morrow 2001a, 2001b; CEBE 2002; Kennig and Ryhl 2002; Afacan 2006; De Cauwer et al. 2009; Centre for Universal Design 2010; Heylighen and Bianchin 2013; Tauke, Steinfeld and Basnak 2014; Basnak, Tauke and Weidemann 2015). Rather than just reiterate the arguments in these important studies, the collection of articles here instead focus on thinking differently about how dis/ability might be included as normal – or even avant-garde – within architectural and built environment education (Boys 2014). As with other contributions to the *Disability, Space, Architecture* reader, this approach starts from opening up 'ordinary bodies' to critical and creative investigation, and explores in a variety of ways what happens when 'unruly bodies' (Mintz 2007) are prioritised instead.

Stefan White aims to teach design by questioning (via Spinoza and Deleuze) 'what a body can do', to go beyond stereotypes about, and fixed categories of, able-bodied and disabled people – where one is unthinkingly the design 'norm' and the other requires 'retrofitting' additions (see Dolmage, this volume). But this is also about the *kinds* of knowledge that design students learn, and how that knowledge is applied. Through an example of a studio project related to ageing, White illustrates the implications of developing design strategies that go beyond simplistic categorisations, that accept and productively engage with difference, and that are inherently critical and reflective of the nature of architectural as a discipline.

Jos Boys also explores some examples of the knowledge and skills that are inculcated through design education, to unravel how these come to embed particular ways of thinking about bodies rather than others. She suggests here, as elsewhere (Boys 2014, 2016), that it is the *underlying* conceptual frameworks of building design approaches and methods that can act to close down and exclude more critical and creative thinking and doing about dis/ability and architecture. In this chapter Boys looks at aspects of diagramming as a design method – through the work respectively of Peter Eisenman and UN Studio – to illustrate how disabled bodies consistently disappear down the cracks in the architects' arguments about *how* to design. And she suggests that 'by inserting dis/ability (that is, disability *and* ability) as both concepts, and diverse lived experiences into this space-of-diagrams between originating ideas and built product, we can simultaneously open up contemporary practices to critique, and find alternative ways of thinking and doing dis/ability *within* the architectural design process.'

The next essay in this section – Margaret Price's 'Un/shared space: The dilemma of inclusive architecture' – powerfully illustrates current directions in disability studies that examine the conceptual, social and material spaces of the university. If feminism has often looked to the spaces of domesticity to investigate gender relationships, and critical race and queer studies have explored public and social domains, disability scholarship has returned again and again to academic space and life. This work has emerged strongly from the fields of literature, rhetoric and composition – particularly in Canada and the US – as these have increasingly examined what happens when writing and reading are framed as deeply situated and embodied (Titchkosky 2003, 2007; Dolmage 2013). Such research is interested in how the talking, writing and doing of everyday social, spatial and material practices act to constitute higher education as a *place*. It looks at how such a place is made and remade differentially across ability and disability. And it understands inclusion and accessibility as simultaneously entangled across ideas, assumptions, actions and practicalities, and as needing both critical and creative engagements that can work towards improvement (see for example, Dolmage 2005, 2008, 2009, 2015; Newall 2008; Price 2009, 2011; Goggin 2010; Yergeau et al. 2013; Kerschbaum et al. 2013). As Price writes in her piece for this volume, intersections between disability and built space – as these are enacted on a daily and ordinary basis in academic life – are inherently complex and fraught. This leads her to ask 'how might architecture take into account the radical unpredictability and ambient emergence of disability when we gather together?' As with Dolmage's essay in the previous part, Price's work is about unravelling the ways in which academic life includes disabled faculty as excludable (Titchkosky 2008: 41) and about exploring what kinds of approaches and analysis could enable us to work towards real inclusion, even whilst recognising that it is never fully achievable.

Aaron Williamson also comes from a position of creative critique about the academy, but as an artist, his forms of practice operate differently to expose the hidden contradictions, contestations and absurdities of its everyday social, spatial and material practices. 'The Collapsing Lecture' is a description of a series of performances from an ongoing live art project. The work grows out of Williamson's experiences as a deaf student (for whom no 'accommodations' were made) and teacher, as well as his long-standing interest in slapstick and burlesque. As with much of Williamson's work, this project deliberately troubles what is usually (that is, for able-bodied people) the self-evident ordinariness of daily routines and artefacts. It thus reveals the often ridiculous nature of the spaces of unnoticed normality.

Each of these readings, then, suggests a substantial challenge for architectural and built environment students and educators. Doing dis/ability differently is not just about 'including' consideration of disabled people at some stage in architectural and built environment education. Rather it demands a much deeper, more critical and richly creative examination of how attitudes to, and assumptions about, disability shape which bodies *matter* in architecture, and of the everyday ways through which some bodies are noticed at the expense of others. This requires engaged study of dis/ability as a concept and disability as a diverse lived experience. But is also means more. It means paying close analytical attention to how dis/ability is constituted through the very methods of thinking and doing that are embodied in architecture as a discipline, and in the university as a particular type of place for learning. And it means exploring innovative ways for architecture and urban design to resist and redesign everyday, normal, practices that exclude some bodies, but not others.

Recommended further reading

Ahmed, S. (2012) *On being Included: Racism and Diversity in Institutional Life*, Durham, NC: Duke University Press.

Boys, J. (2014) *Doing Disability Differently: An alternative handbook on dis/ability, architecture and designing for everyday life*, London and New York: Routledge.

Boys, J. (2016) 'Architecture, Place and the "Care-full" Design of Everyday Life', in C. Bates, R. Imrie and K. Kullman (eds) *Care and Design: Bodies, Buildings, Cities*, London and New York: John Wiley & Sons, Ltd, 153–179.

Dolmage, J. (2013) *Disability Rhetoric*, Syracuse, NY: Syracuse University Press.

Dolmage, J. (2015) 'Universal Design: Places to Start', *Disability Studies Quarterly* 35(2). Available at: http://dsq-sds.org/article/view/4632/3946

Fox, A. and Macpherson, H. (2015) *Inclusive Arts Practices and Research: A Critical Manifesto*, London and New York: Routledge.

Hamraie, A. (2016) "Beyond Accommodation: Disability, Feminist Philosophy, and the Design of Everyday Academic life', *Philosophia* 6.2 November

Hickey-Moody, A. C. (2009) *Unimaginable Bodies: Intellectual Disability, Performance and Becomings*, Rotterdam: Sense Publishers.

Kerschbaum, S. L. (2014) *Towards a New Rhetoric of Difference*, Urbana, IL: National Council of Teachers of English.

Kuppers, P. (2014) *Studying Disability Arts and Culture: An Introduction*, London: Palgrave MacMillan.

Price, M. (2011) *Mad At School: Rhetorics of Mental Disability and Academic Life*, Ann Arbor, MI: University Of Michigan Press.

Titchkosky, T. (2008) '"To pee or not to pee?" Ordinary Talk about Extraordinary Exclusions in a University Environment', *Canadian Journal of Sociology/Cahiers canadiens de sociologie* 33(1): 37–60

Titchkosky, T. (2010) 'The Not-Yet-Time of Disability in the Bureaucratization of University Life', *Disability Studies Quarterly* 30(3/4). Available at: http://dsq-sds.org/article/view/1295/1331

Titchkosky, T. (2011) *The Question of Access: Disability, Space, Meaning*, Toronto: University of Toronto Press.

11

INCLUDING ARCHITECTURE

What difference can we make?

Stefan White (2016)

> We do not know what the body can do...
>
> (Spinoza quoted in Deleuze 1988: 18)

Key contemporary accounts of the relationship between individual human action and global issues such as economic prosperity (Sen 1999), environmental protection (Arne Naess 1989) and human rights (Nussbaum 2011) explore conceptual approaches using philosophical frameworks which prioritise 'difference' over identities. That is, rather than focus on identified categories of disability, race or gender, they engage with the potential for creativity and inclusion created in the relationships between *different* people, places and practices. This essay contributes to similarly inspired attempts to construct design philosophies that can describe the 'ethical' or 'ecological' role of architecture in enabling, ameliorating or challenging economic, environmental and social ambitions (Rawes 2013). Here I sketch connections between Gilles Deleuze's contemporary re-reading of Spinoza's *Ethics* (1677) and a selection of architectural and educational practices implicated in attempts to create more inclusive urban environments (focused here on neighbourhood planning and design). To explore these ideas in an architectural context I discuss correlations between Deleuze's critique of 'representation' and the ideas of architectural theorist, Robin Evans, using Evans' concept of 'projection' as a non-representational way of thinking through the role of architectural practice, processes and products in creating inclusive urban environments.

On ethics

> Ethics [...] replaces Morality which always refers existence to transcendent values. Morality is the judgement of God, *the system of judgement*. But ethics overthrows the system of judgement. The opposition of values (good-evil) is supplanted by the qualitative difference of Modes of existence (good-bad).
>
> (Deleuze 1988: 23)

Spinoza begins *Ethics* by distinguishing between the *understanding* of God (or Nature) and Human kind (Deleuze 1992: 218). Unlike many of his contemporaries, he sees God as encompassing the whole of the natural world without being separate from it. His God-as-Nature is a whole body composed of parts, which are themselves, whole bodies. Thus, Nature as a whole is absolutely adequate and necessary, because it is a totality composed of an unlimited and infinite number of wholes or parts. Nature is completely adequate because its actions are always a necessary result of its entire composition of parts. However, the individual wholes (and their parts) of which it is composed are less adequate or necessary, because such modes of existence – for example human – are created in relation to the actions or influences of bodies outside themselves. We can only be reactive when we interact with bodies or parts with which we are not already actively composed. Thus, individual modes of existence tend to be inadequate, passionate consequences of greater wholes *but* remain simultaneously part of the composition of the active whole of nature. For Spinoza the project of improving both our collective and individual quality of life is a pursuit of increasing the proportion of ourselves which is *active* and by which we can become more 'adequate' – a composed part of a greater whole.

In Spinoza's time, this was a heretical point of departure because it placed human nature on a continuum with the nature of God. Deleuze reinvigorates its potential by exploring how making 'the body' into a relational composition *with* Nature prioritises the reality of the *differences* between these bodies in composition. This remains rather a radical idea because it insists on differentiating between bodies and beings on the basis of *their actual relationships with other bodies* rather than according to characteristics *attributed to them* by the 'common sense' of other (more powerful) bodies. Rather than follow the predominant tendency of reducing or eradicating difference in order to imply clarity through simplification (such as the 'norm' or average), the relational differences between different bodies are instead seen to be the actual, creative and productive substance of Nature. '[...] difference becomes an object of representation always in relation to a conceived identity, a judged analogy, an imagined opposition or a perceived similitude' (Deleuze 1994: 138).

Deleuze argues that using our imaginations to reduce complex compositions to identities or categories with fixed meanings and representations is a process which systematically eradicates difference in order to imply clarity through simplification. It produces reductive 'norms' or stereotypes. It does so through a process of common sense analysis, which tests the value of things or 'bodies' in terms of whether they are conceived 'the same', perceived 'similar', judged 'analogous' or imagined to be 'in opposition' – relative to an *identity* we already have *in mind*. His alternative approach does not rely on such 'representations', averages, pictures or stereotypes (held in the *imagination*) to decide or categorise bodies as stable entities (as particular 'subjects' or identities in terms of disability, gender or race). It instead insists on accounting for the intellectual *and* physical compositions of bodies with their environment which necessarily change over time and whose power or potential is actually produced through the differentials between composing bodies. Here the bodies which are constituting Nature include everything – from humans and their individual cells and possessions to architectural drawings and built environments and all the way over to mountains and galaxies. *Imagination* (and conception) are not then simply put in opposition with *experience* (and perception) but both are seen as parallel and embodied features of composed Being. Deleuze uses Spinoza to show how *both* bodies of thought *and* material can be creatively composed to increase our capacity as part of Nature.

> Spinoza offers philosophers a new model: the body. [...] What does Spinoza mean when he invites us to take the body as a model? It is the matter of showing that the body surpasses the knowledge we have of it *and that thought likewise surpasses the consciousness we have of it.* [...] it is by one and the same movement that we shall manage, if possible, to capture the power of the body beyond the given conditions of our knowledge and to capture the power of the mind beyond the given conditions of our consciousness.
>
> (Deleuze 1988: 18)

Rather than the mind being the sole or primary source for the understanding of our Being, the expressions of both mind and body – that is to say, both imagined (and conceived) forms and experienced (and perceived) functions – are seen as 'merely particular cases' (Deleuze 1992: 333–335) of the expressions of nature. This means that the way we decide what is good or bad in particular situations should recognise the positive differences between bodies, which are manifested through the capabilities of *both* thought *and* action rather than decided by judging our erroneous deviation from pre-identified norms. In this approach, we understand our bodies (which include our minds) as a kinetic and dynamic set of capabilities produced through active composition with *other* (and by definition different) *bodies*. These material and pragmatic judgements are made on an empirical basis of what are good and bad compositions, not only in relation to what is commonly agreed as good or its moral opposite (evil/error). What or who we are in this context is not a category we fit into or an identity we most resemble (an identity necessarily decided by the 'common sense' of the majority or the most powerful) but is instead what we can do, what we are capable of. In this approach, we make our identity through exploring and extending our capabilities with others. It is a positive and creative exploration of what we are capable of through attempting to do it, through actively performing new compositions.

Three kinds of knowledge

So here, the differences between bodies is a positive and creative starting point rather than an unfortunate remainder, left over once identification or agreement is complete and fixed. Beginning with difference is, however, not straightforward. Deleuze argues that it is not just our basic tendency (a first kind of knowledge) to seek easy answers and form convenient categories as a matter of habit which makes our current ways of thinking obstructive to understanding the differences between people, things and cultures (reducing the affects of external bodies upon us to representations, signs or pictures). For him is it also how we implicitly limit our much more careful attempts at rationally understanding the world (a second kind of knowledge) through the persistence and insidious power of 'common sense' which claims access to universal reason and dispassionate objectivity but continues to rely on stereotypes and readymade 'pictures'. Whilst clearly we do use shared or more thoughtful reasoning to achieve more adequate knowledge of the causes of the affects of external bodies on us, Deleuze says that there is an additional third kind of knowledge which we routinely deny ourselves access to when we are satisfied with common sense rationality alone. His third kind of knowledge sees us produce a much more adequate understanding of relationships to external causes when we are actually creating or changing them. The intuitive production of knowledge when we produce particular causes or 'affects' through actively composing in specific ways transcends our conscious 'rational' knowledge and at the same time is completely adequate because it is empirically tested (Deleuze 2003).

1. Representations, signs or pictures

For Deleuze the first and least adequate model of knowledge is *representational* – it greatly prioritises intellectual objects and their physical identifiers as the only relevant indications of reality, presupposing an overly deterministic causal relationship to actual objects, which, in fact, these intellectual conceptions and visual perceptions only contingently *represent*. Models of disability or difference which focus on the physical dimensions of the environment or quantitative understandings of the capabilities of individuals are often employed in medical contexts because they appear to provide the basis for definitive judgements of action against averages or 'norms'. In these cases the complexity of the relationships of capability which enable specific individuals to live their particular lives successfully are reduced to sets of parameters in order to provide general guidance on responses to measurable determinants like specific illnesses and in design terms, purely physical accessibility such as benches or entrance thresholds. For example, this is seen in the World Health Organization's (WHO) Age Friendly Cities and Communities (AFCC) guidance as a focus on physical aspects of the environment and the abilities of older people to navigate it – describing the role of design in terms of lowering 'disability thresholds' in the environment (WHO 2007: see Figure 11–4).

2. Shared or involved reason

> The word 'active' [ageing] refers to continuing participation in social economic, cultural, spiritual, and civic affairs, not just the ability to be physically active or to participate in the labour force.
>
> (World Health Organization 2002: 12)

The second state of knowledge produces reasons for action through experience and imagination, allowing us to positively repeat our encounters with the world outside. This second model of knowledge is characterised by being a development of agreement between a variety of understandings – 'a ratio of common notions or reason' where the views of our different 'faculties' (meaning our perceptions, imaginations, judgements and conceptions of a situation) are internally (through seeing, thinking and feeling) and externally (through drawing, discussion, reading) compared to generate an adequate account of causes (Deleuze 2003). It can be likened to more holistic accounts sometimes referred to as 'social models' such as for 'disability'. Social approaches problematise purely physical or medical understandings by – for example – suggesting that disability is not absolute but relative and at least partially socially constructed. For Deleuze this second kind can go beyond the formalisations of the first kind of knowledge to include individual experiences as well as the relationships between individuals and wider society as determinates of those experiences. However, social approaches broadly retain or reinforce 'representational' limitations by continuing to construct (new) categories and identities rather than prioritising the differences they discover. The specific definition in the WHO AFCC guidance of the nature of 'activity' in their concept of 'active ageing' is an example of this, as it attempts to prevent recuperation as a quantitative valuation of an older person's economic contribution, but in so doing makes clear that this is what is at stake.

3. Intuition – citizen

> [Age-friendliness is the experience of ...] factors (social, economic, environmental, personal, physical) and the interaction between them [which ...] play an important role in affecting how well individuals age.
>
> (WHO 2002: 1)

For Deleuze both the first and second kind of knowledge *are essential* for the development of a third kind of knowledge which goes beyond more 'passive' knowledges which *inform* action to instead create knowledge *through* action. This third kind of knowledge aims to account for the creativity and creation of individuals, environments and societies – which is why it is of interest for designers and social activists. Deleuze argues that we need such an understanding in order to better account for the interlocking relationship between our environments, ourselves and our societies. I summarise these three kinds of knowledge, using the WHO guidance as an example in Figure 11.1.

So for example, rather than seeing active ageing in terms of the first model of difference where the contribution of older people is measured with respect to their productive outputs as paid or unpaid work, or in the second kind, acknowledging that there are interlocking social components to the activity of older people in a community such as friendship, belonging and pride, a third more relational approach to active ageing seeks to directly account for how individual actions, voices and positions lead to particular constitutions of the city and neighbourhoods – through producing them. To reiterate however, all three models are essential because the third kind of knowledge is enabled by the first two; they are not in opposition. To explore all three levels of knowledge clearly requires an (inter- or transdisciplinary) architectural and educational approach that actively attempts to produce more age-friendly environments as an essential step in understanding how to do so. Such a Deleuzian approach seeks to connect the city and individual levels together through the constitution of neighbourhoods (and other places) to enable a more adequate discussion of how the actions and existences of individual citizens constitute the city and how that city in turn determines some of the qualities of their existence. I will return to examples of this kind of exploratory practice later; but will first briefly explore how Deleuze's work connects to related ideas within architectural theory and practice itself, through the work of Robin Evans.

Kinds of knowledge	Models of difference	WHO guidance
Intuition	**Citizen or capability** Relation between city and individual seen as constituting the nature of the city as it is experienced and its capacity as a body	**Age-friendly city** The WHO Age-friendly city topic areas which are determinants of how well an individual age are represented as eight petals making up a flower at the centre of which is the individual experience of an Age-friendly city (WHO 2002: Fig 6)
Common notions or reason	**Social or relational** Individual is seen as part of a network or community where multiple kinds of relations to others are seen to interact to influence an individual's ability to perform both social and physical functions (it is not just the relationship between their body and the physical environment)	**Active ageing** The WHO Age-friendly city diagram of the determinants of active ageing list social, economic, behavioural, personal and physical factors within a wider context of culture and gender (WHO 2002: Fig 3)
Signs or representations	**Medical / Environmental** The relationship between the physical dimensions of a body and the physical environment are seen as primary factors for deciding on or locating 'interventions' designed to improve the experience of the general population of people understood to belong in specific, assigned categories	**Disability threshold** The WHO guidance explains how changes to the physical environment can lower the threshold at which it becomes inaccessible, especially as people grow older (WHO 2002: Fig 4)

FIGURE 11.1   Summary table of correlation between kinds of knowledge, models of difference and WHO Age-friendly City and Communities guidance

Source: Author.

Evans and the problem of representation in architecture

[pictures are…] fixations within a metamorphic flux of possible experiences. A picture is something that has to be arrested before it can be mobilised. That is why pictures play so ambivalent a role in architecture.

(Evans 1995: 359)

Evans uses the concept of *projection* to describe the relationship between architect and architectural drawing and between those drawings and the objects they describe. He argues that projection is an embodied distinction made simultaneously in the imagination *and* the perception, which is then manifested in the architect's production. This is in contrast to the representational assumption of an instantaneous and seamless *translation* between a drawing and its object, made with the aim of removing all 'errors' of dissimilarity between them. He argues that predominant accounts of architectural knowledge operate according to what he calls 'picture theory' (1995: 358). He shows that whilst architecture tends to begin and end with pictures, these are in fact limited and artificially fixed. He identifies the inadequacies of a representational account of architecture which both formalist and functionalist approaches suffer.

His 'picture theory' critique mirrors Deleuze's analysis of the failings of representational thought, as he finds architectural accounts tend to be constructed from *either* the perspective of imagined and conceived forms *or* perceived and experienced functions – both of which, for Evans are merely particular cases of *projection*. Evans also echoes Deleuze in identifying positive potential in these embodied 'transitions between objects' (Evans 1995: 367), arguing that it is in fact the 'dissimilarities' or differences between 'representations' and 'what is represented' that are central to 'the drawing's power as a medium' (Evans 1997: 154). He describes ten such differential moments of projection, which occur between an architect and architectural products in the process of drawing and building (Figure 11.2).

Evans prefers 'projections' to translations because he demonstrates that creative – drawing – processes literally 'project' a particular set of contents into a new – expressive – form (e.g. when a plan and section are used to create a perspective using lines of projection). However, he also applies it less literally (e.g. when a sketch model is 'drawn' into an axonometric) *and* more broadly, to explain how design techniques and abilities progressively and differentially inform each other. Evans' 'projection' is an intuitive and embodied capability of the architect that enables them to actively iterate compositions from the content of one formal product (a drawing or model) to a new one through a particular drawing or modelling process over time or in series.

This concept of projection has the potential to value architectural design as a serially projective or expressive process between *embodied* expressions (the process or content, e.g. a drawing or multiple drawings in series) *and* what these express (the product or form, e.g. what is understood by the drawing and actually built). The expressions of an expressive process – the drawings produced by the intuitive capability of an architect – have their actual existence as a power produced in the differences between what the architect imagines and what they perceive in relation to it. Similarly, when the drawing becomes a product it is embodied in forms external to the architect or the architectural process, ultimately being built through a set of interpretations and realisations, which will all involve embodied projections of

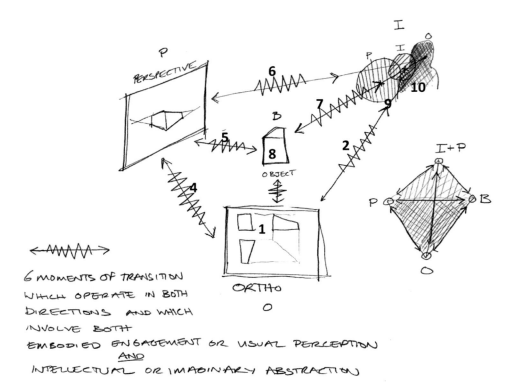

FIGURE 11.2   Adaptation of Robin Evans's 10 relationships of projection from "Projection and its analogues: The Arrested Image" in Evans, R. (1995) *The Projective Cast: Architecture and its Three Geometries.* MIT Press p367

Source: Adapted by Stefan White.

those involved. Evans demonstrates through numerous case studies that it is fundamentally impossible to reduce this process to a direct translation. He also shows that it is undesirable, precisely because these embodied moments of projection are how creative acts are stimulated.

In this non-representational paradigm, the creative – projective – act always involves an active, intuitive engagement outside both Deleuze's first and second kinds of knowledge within architecture. Making such projective relations explicit is the first step to critically valuing the embodied creative labour that moves our intellectual and physical bodies from one form of content to another via the expressive affect of drawings, models and buildings during the design process. This valuation of embodied and creative differential relations articulates a positive role for the architect. This kind of 'architecture' is in the explicit business of creating critical (affective) relations between discipline and society to increase the capacity of both. This is a radical move away from common sense, representational accounts of architectural practice (of either formalist or functionalist flavour), which claim we have to resist social pressure or contact in order to protect our creative 'autonomy'. A non-representational approach does not seek to 'close down' problems or conflicts but instead to reveal the differences that create them so that they can be productively composed with. It is such compositions of difference (between drawings, disciplines, cultures and individuals) that are themselves composed into *projects*, and which can then exist through and within architecture but always as capacities moving beyond it. While Evans predominantly seeks an adequate explanation of architectural knowledge from within the discipline, Deleuze precipitates a desire for a more adequate explanation of the composition of *architecture itself*.

Redefining the project of architecture

This Deleuzian shift to a third – projective – kind of knowledge generated through action or capability must then also recognise and engage with the composition of architecture as a discipline. Evans saw that the power of the drawing is produced in the differential relationships between the architect and the production process, and between the drawing and the process of construction. He understood the critical creative impulse as an explicit opening of the architects' compositions to the outside of their habit. However, such compositions are conventionally restricted to formal expressions from within the discipline and its 'culture'. The predominant 'diagrams' of 'professional' and 'critical' creative practice require that we defend an authorial position through restricting the extent of our 'criticality' (also understood as a breaking of norms or habits) as relating to the historical constitution of the discipline and/or the interior processes of architectural design (see Ghirardo 1994, Eisenman 1995 and White 2014). The habitual architectural body defines its boundaries by setting limits on its ability to engage beyond its existing characteristic relations.

Unfortunately, this is an increasingly ineffective attempt to ensure disciplinary survival in the face of commercial pressures that only serves to limit our powers of creation and our capacity to evolve new selves, practices and societies. Returning to Spinoza, via Deleuze, active composition is understood as an increase in capacity produced between bodies composing in relation to their outside. Compositions which increase the capacity of a body are considered affirmative and ethical and are speculative by their creative and emergent nature. The aim of this account is to show that the architectural body can no longer exist within the categories 'architect' or 'architectural drawing' nor the categories 'architectural discipline' or 'architecture' because the creative impulse of the individual architect is at once determined *by* the discipline *and* serves as its constitution. It is the active compositions of the architect that constitute an architectural *project* (through their agency and movement) and in turn theirs and others' multitudinous architectural projects that actively constitute 'the discipline' within and through society.

In Figure 11.3 a *project* is understood as the construction of relationships which extend the set of all social capabilities and which by definition already include the existing capabilities of the discipline of architecture. Particular expressions, products or processes (individual drawings or representations, including the actual building) are now valued in terms of the *project* they constitute rather than the *product* they delineate. Questions normally excluded from architectural discourse begin to re-enter as a personal *and* structural imperative: How does architecture contribute to social progress? How can architecture create inclusive environments? What difference can the actions of an architect, *this* architect, make? Here

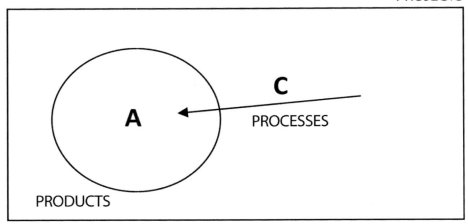

A = set of existing disciplinary capabilities

B = set of all social capabilities

C = Agency of individual architects

FIGURE 11.3   Diagram of relationship between architectural discipline and society

Source: Author.

architecture must differentiate itself from within society rather than create, presume or pretend an exclusive identity separate from it. Some of the implications for an inclusive urban design method are shown in Figure 11.4.

Designing for spatial inclusion

In this approach, the 'architect' is just a particular case of the expression of citizen. Citizens are understood as embodied subjects distinguished and produced through changes in characteristic relations and affective capacities. Cities are understood as bodies described by a set of social and physical capabilities, constituted by the expressive forms and content of their citizens in relation and over time in the formula Cities = Architecture + Citizens. Creative and active engagements are the production of real distinctions of affect between bodies, necessarily external to the subject, and necessarily distinctions in both expression and content.

From experiences undertaken in both a professional and pedagogic capacity working in Manchester, we have found that exploring the nature of the embodied knowledge of a particular community can appear to reveal the affective relations that make a city liveable or loved.

However, by definition, the projective relations of a particular context are without form until they are *made explicit* through attempting to construct new relations outside habitual characters or abilities (new, real distinctions). Architectures' *real* – social – autonomy or expertise is expressed in circumstances when architects act to make or enable projective relations to be made explicit – because to do so redirects or changes implicit and exclusive paradigms of action and their associated processes of identification or representation. Conversely, if the architectural project does not make its own relations explicit it acts to passively comply with the representational repressions of the professionalisation of the discipline. In order to avoid the representational tendencies of reducing our understanding to either simple experiences and perceptions or isolated imaginations and conceptions we must always seek to both articulate our processes *and* visualise our products. Making explicit the serial projective relationships between our processes and products (economies, clients, architects, drawings, contractors, constructions and citizens) attempts to prevent representations from keeping implicit the labours of their creation.

In the example in Figure 11.5, Katherine Timmins (as a post-graduate student in the Manchester School of Architecture projects group) developed her product (a building design) as a process involving the development of a range of other products (which included running a choir working with women's groups who would be end users for a building if it were to exist) and these processes and products were part of a project with the intention of actually increasing the access of women in Manchester to support services.

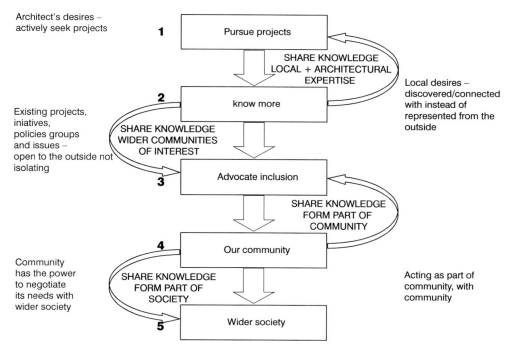

FIGURE 11.4   MSA projects inclusive urban design method from presentation to the Belgian Ageing Studies programme, 2010

FIGURE 11.5   The Pankettes Choir, 2012

Photograph: Kat Timmins / MSA

The project of the Manchester School of Architecture (MSA) post-graduate teaching and learning atelier has emerged as a positive and creative response to dissatisfaction with the current ability of the architectural discipline to impact on social inequality and intended also to begin a recuperation of critical aesthetic techniques. The MSA projects studio is hosted by the centre for Spatial Inclusion Design research (cSIDr), a community-engaged research and design partnership between Manchester's City Council, architecture school and universities. Over the past decade we have developed a number of cross-sector projects working to make cities and neighbourhoods more inclusive. In this time architecture students from the studio have engaged with a large number of members of the public and developed a wide range of collaborative social and physical architectural projects. These include building an age-friendly allotment designed with the children of an adjacent primary school to instigating a campaign to save a derelict town hall, enabling over £1 million pounds to be allocated to prevent its demolition, subsequently enabling successful redevelopment. The professional, funded research of the group focuses on multiple excluded populations with an emphasis on experiences across the life-course, developing an approach to delivering age-friendly city policy in local contexts recognised as exemplars by, for example, the Organisation for Economic Co-operation and Development (OECD 2015). In our professional inclusive urban design-research

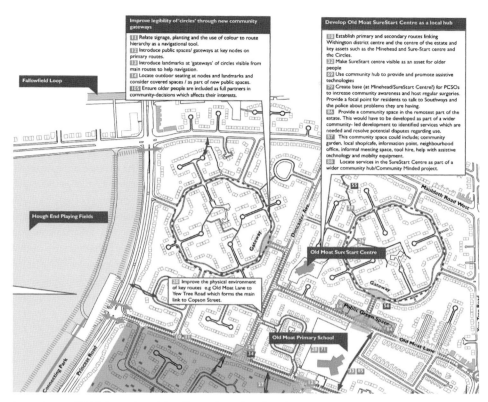

Improve legibility of 'circles' through new community gateways

11 Relate signage, planting and the use of colour to route hierarchy as a navigational tool.
12 Introduce public spaces/ gateways at key nodes on primary routes.
13 Introduce landmarks at 'gateways' of circles visible from main routes to help navigation.
14 Locate outdoor seating at nodes and landmarks and consider covered spaces / as part of new public spaces.
105 Ensure older people are included as full partners in community-decisions which affects their interests.

Develop Old Moat SureStart Centre as a local hub

10 Establish primary and secondary routes linking Withington district centre and the centre of the estate and key assets such as the Minehead and Sure-Start centre and the Circles.
32 Make SureStart centre visible as an asset for older people
69 Use community hub to provide and promote assistive technologies
79 Create base (at Minehead/SureStart Centre?) for PCSOs to increase community awareness and host regular surgeries. Provide a focal point for residents to talk to Southways and the police about problems they are having.
86 Provide a community space in the remotest part of the estate. This would have to be developed as part of a wider community-led development to identified services which are needed and resolve potential disputes regarding use.
87 This community space could include; community garden, local shop/cafe, information point, neighbourhood office, informal meeting space, tool hire, help with assistive technology and mobilty equipment.
88 Locate services in the SureStart Centre as part of a wider community hub/Community Minded project.

Fallowfield Loop

Hough End Playing Fields

20 Improve the physical environment of key routes e.g Old Moat Lane to Yew Tree Road which forms the main link to Copson Street.

Old Moat Sure Start Centre

Gateway

Public Green Space

Old Moat Primary School

FIGURE 11.6   Old Moat: Age-friendly action plan detail, 2012

Regeneration officer

Public Health Officer

RSL executive

Policeman

Student

Transport executive

Older person / local resident

FIGURE 11.7   Old Moat: Age-friendly action plan workshop, 2012

Photo by author

practices we attempt to positively speculate by providing a propositional focus around a specific spatially located set of social and physical relations. In the Old Moat in an Age-friendly Manchester research project we brought architectural and urban design skills and knowledge to the analysis and production of the social relations necessary to construct an urban design in the context of a economically, socially and physically excluded older population of a particular area of the city (White, Phillipson and Hammond 2012). We created collaborative 'action plans' which were literally spatial *plans* as an important part of the explicit manner in which the research was 'presented' – keeping the research information live and accessible to an audience of non-scientists and non-architects (Figures 11.6 and 11.7). In practice, therefore, revealing the specificity of the embodied knowledge of a particular community in a particular environmental setting involves the personal and active – projective or propositional – involvement of the urban design-researcher. This active pursuit is the first step in a continual process of the construction of a situated and collaborative *project*. 'Inclusive' architectural practices that operate using a representational paradigm will remain constrained within deliberately exclusive disciplinary habits, however much they seek to grant the power of inclusion to excluded groups. We can only make a real difference in society when we are an actively composed part of that whole – we will only begin to find out what it is architects are actually capable of when architecture itself is considered included rather than exclusive.

12

DIAGRAMMING FOR A DIS/ORDINARY ARCHITECTURE

Jos Boys (2016)

In this essay I want to consider how starting from dis/ability might help us critically and creatively interrogate some 'normal' design methods in architectural education. I want to explore how learning to design is inculcated into students in particular ways rather than others, and as requiring certain types of thinking and doing rather than others, that act to literally build exclusionary practices into what it is to be an architectural professional. I ask how it happens that we (within the discipline) simultaneously believe architecture to be a socially engaged practice whilst thoughtlessly centring design on only the most independent, mobile and fully abled members of humanity. And I will suggest that, following the seminal work of Titchkosky and others, it is architecture's own justificatory and deeply embedded narratives that normalize and perpetuate a continuing forgetfulness about other kinds of bodies – those that do not fit the norm, but are instead unruly in a multitude of ways (Michalko 2002; Titchkosky 2008, 2011). By justificatory narratives I mean the competing and compelling stories architecture tells to and about itself, thereby framing what comes to be sayable and doable in order to be an architect (Garfinkel 1967). The problem lies, then, not just in particular design approaches and methods – that is, with some better than others at being 'inclusive' – but in how *the whole subject of architecture* is debated and contested. What we have to unravel is not an inability to include human occupancy in design – because students, educators and practitioners do think about people intensely and often – but the flawed and problematic *framings* within which we are taught to think about occupancy (that is, what kinds of bodies matter, and how these become translated into actual designs).

At the same time, I want to draw out the critical and creative potential of architecture's justificatory narratives. Such stories are not inherently problematic. In architecture as in other disciplines, they are a central means through which ideas and practices are generated, challenged, adapted and rethought. So, the other aim of this chapter is to see how we might begin to enjoy subverting such stories, to creatively explore how contemporary design methods might be 'done differently' so as to include dis/ability as both a radical and a normal part of what students (and tutors and practitioners) already do.

I have been attempting such explorations of different aspects of architectural approaches and methods for several years with varying degrees of success (Boys 2014, 2016). Here I will concentrate on diagramming, a design method that was important during the modernist period and then fell out of favour, before being reinvigorated within architectural education and practice from the 1990s. This was first at a theoretical level, particularly through the writings and work of Peter Eisenman, and then more recently as a central design approach – exemplified here by the work of UN Studio (led by Ben Van Berkel and Caroline Bos). Of course, these examples just represent moments in a much larger, more complex array of multiple, connected and competing design methods, so such an analysis can only be partial and exploratory. The central aim is to draw alternative creative trajectories out of the critique, not to provide a comprehensive overview of diagramming. So I will look at each of these moments in turn, aiming to unravel how the underlying justificatory narratives come to be framed, to see what is left out in the process, and how these methods might be productively subverted by the insertion of dis/ability into the picture.

Finally – and crucially – it should be noted that the alternative versions of diagramming played with here are *not* intended to be 'better' than those used by Eisenman or UN Studio, and are *not* a 'solution' to incorporating diverse bodies in design methods. Rather, the aim is to build on absurdist crip traditions in order to open up the specific peculiarities of architectural diagramming as a means of interrogating the world, so as to critically investigate what become normal, even radical, designerly types of operation.

Learning to design: diagramming as a method of translation

To design built spaces requires a projection into the future of a realizable physical 'thing', via two-dimensional representations of our three-dimensional world:

> Architectural drawings are projections, which means that organized arrays of imaginary straight lines pass through the drawing to corresponding parts of the thing represented by the drawing. [...] We are surrounded by these flat images of embodied events to such an extent that they have long since ceased, in themselves, to be a matter of any amazement, or even of mild curiosity.
>
> (Evans 2000: 19)

Design drawing, then, is an act of selection and translation. It is also, of course, a means of communication both between and across those within architecture, and those beyond it. I will return to these wider intersections later; here I will just focus on drawing as a central element in the designer's own processes.

As Evans goes on to make clear, it is in the spaces *in-between* the drawing and its built version that many – often unnoticed and not discussed – actions occur. Here lie the conceptual stories (both deliberate and 'common sense') that justify particular ways of interpreting the world, representing it, and (re)designing it. Here is the space where these stories come to require a designer's engagement with a particular selection of 'reality' rather than others. And, through the resulting representations another space is made. That is, the drawn images themselves come to seem transparently obvious and sensible. Because they exist as 'finished' and complete, we believe in the correctness of their represented reality. We do not question the peculiarity of their underlying logic. So how can we begin to prise apart some of what Evans called the 'eddies and circuits' (2000: 20) between building design as a process and its finished artefacts?

First, I will look at the seminal work *Diagram Diaries* by Peter Eisenman (1999) to explore how he located himself and his proposed method (at that time) within and against existing architectural disciplinary narratives, particularly modernism. I will suggest that he sets up a deliberately perverse 'anti-humanist' argument in support of formalist composition, by unexpectedly articulating this as a radical and creative 'opening up' of design. This also suggests investigating what such an approach closes down, and what kinds of alternative conceptual and formal disruptions might be just as (or even more) interesting to pursue. Second I will look at more recent diagramming techniques using an analysis of patterns and flow – enabled by access to large datasets – based on a UN Studio project in Arhem, the Netherlands. Here what starting from dis/ability reveals is how particular representation methods can act to assume the human body as an 'unimpeded line', that is as an already mobile, autonomous and fully competent subject. Again, it then becomes possible to consider what happens when that line is acknowledged instead to be inherently unruly.

Peter Eisenman: justifying the formalist diagram

In the 2000s, architectural writers increasingly saw the re-emergence of diagramming in the work of contemporary architects such as Herzog and de Meuron, Sejima and Nishizawa and Associates (SANAA), Frank Gehry and Greg Lynn (Vidler 2000). Crucially this was seen not so much as one analytical method among others but as becoming *the* central generative approach for design – a way 'to find unexpected relationships between diverse elements in the design process and to re-imagine what architecture could be' (arq 2012). In this view, diagrams were not just analytic, but 'both constitutive and projective, performative rather than representational' (Vidler 2000: 6). At the same time, diagramming already had its own – problematic – history within architectural practice and education. Through the later twentieth century modernist architects were seen to have used diagrams to codify and rationalize building types, with the explicit intention of enabling universal, objective solutions. In the process however, it came to be recognized that 'the diagram, these experiments suggested, might as readily close down possibilities as open them up' (arq 2012). Modernist buildings seemed even to end up looking like over-simplified diagrams: 'Architecture … looked too much like the geometry with which it was designed and depicted. Geometry is thus seen as the underlying cause of architectural alienation, the degradation of humanism, and the split between architecture and its "public".' (Vidler 2000: 8)

By the 1970s and 80s then, using diagrams had a bad name. (When I was an architectural student in this period, our tutors would say a design project looked like a diagram as an insult.) It was in this context that the revival of diagramming as a potentially avant-garde method – particularly in Peter Eisenman's *Diagram Diaries* published in 1999 – seemed so radical. In this period he was creating drawn sequences of abstract and gridded three-dimensional cubic forms (Figure 12.1). Here, an initial simple 'box' is first sketched, and then repetitively cut through in multiple, and often increasingly complex, ways, but always

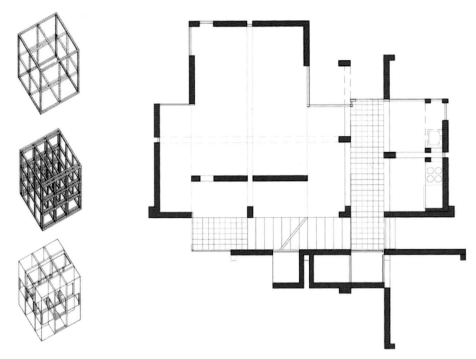

FIGURE 12.1 Examples of diagramming development process and effects on design

Source: Adapted from House VI floor plan (1975) and Eisenman (1999).

based on a rectilinear grid. Out of these mutations, a final form is produced. Eisenman had already created controversy through building just such a 'polemical' house – House VI – based on these formal abstractions rather than function or 'livability'; in this building a geometric 'slot' across the bedroom forced the occupants to have two single beds (Eisenman 1987; Frank 1994) (for later work, see Fitzsimons, this volume).

In opposition to many of his contemporaries, Eisenman argued for a focus on formal composition as a design generator of buildings. He revisited some of the influential sources for modernist ideas about form, based on the grid, such as the historian Rudolph Wittkower, whose systematized diagrams of Palladian villas were published in 1949, and the architect-critic Colin Rowe whose essay 'The Mathematics of the Ideal Villa: Palladio and Le Corbusier compared' originally came out in 1947. He thus aimed to positively reclaim how the 'postwar generation of modernists look[ed] for a geometrical and stable authority for form in the demonstrated absence of any single functional determinants' (Vidler 2000: 14). At the same time, his proposed method for engaging with, and manipulating, formal composition was offered up as radically different to these earlier versions. This was informed by contemporary interests in linguistics and semiotics:

> Shifting architecture from a formal to a structuralist base, or from an iconic or semantic to an indexical or syntactic one, would enable architecture to finally

register the insights of modernist avant-gardes, an account which suspends classical-humanism's centrality of the subject and proposes architecture as the abstract mediation between pre-existent sign systems.

(Somol 1999, 17)

Eisenman's central narrative was that three-dimensional form-making could reclaim its own autonomy, operating in a space *before* the arrival of the subject. In this understanding architectural composition is a kind of non-verbal language that exists *before* meanings have been applied. Using the formal notation of orthographic drawing, multiplied through iterative repetition and difference, enables 'the diagram [to] act like a surface that receives inscriptions from the memory of that what does not yet exist' (Eisenman 1999: 100). By repetitively diagramming formal characteristics – what Eisenman calls the interiority of architecture – rather than starting from a socialized or historicized exteriority (that is, context, or client for example) the designer creates new, unexpected forms and relationships. The act of diagramming comes to 'exceed' the architect's intentions and knowledge; it becomes its own design generator. This, then, is about opening up formal diagramming to its own creative potential.

It is important to understand that this *was* a radical move within architectural practice in the post-modernist period, as the discipline struggled to dis-entangle what continued to be relevant about architectural modernist thought, what should be challenged, and how that challenge should be articulated. Theorists and critics tended to want to reintroduce a more explicit engagement with the social (through the 'meaning' of building, for example, or through more direct and participatory relationships with clients and users). To perversely explore abstracted formal composition put Eisenman simultaneously in the forefront and at the fringes of radical architectural practice. He could be touted as one of the 'titans of architecture' (Artemel 2013) and condemned as 'bogus', pretentious and deeply irrelevant (Ghirardo 1994). By putting himself in conscious opposition to more socially minded architects and critics as an out-and-out anti-humanist, he claims the territory of the intellectual – against the more (and currently more fashionable) 'experiential' and sensually immediate work of architects like Peter Zumthor (Artemel 2013).

Here, though, rather than get caught up in the ongoing binary opposition between formalist and experiential approaches to architecture – with disability always assumed to fall in the second camp – I want instead to unpick a little how Eisenman justifies his approach, both as a means to explore its limitations and as a way into possible creative interruptions. To do that I will visualize what happens when disability is treated conceptually and formally, as a generator of compositions and proportional relationships. This might be considered a perverse move: the obvious 'common sense' about disability in architecture is to align it with humanist approaches and with 'caring' designers, not with those who start from form and aesthetics. But, following Alison Kafer, I want to deliberately queer some of our assumptions about what are obvious and 'appropriate' design approaches to disability (2013).

Cripping the grid? Inserting disability into architecture as form

As the editors of a special issue of *Architectural Research Quarterly* (arq) write, diagramming is: 'a powerful rhetorical device, a way of establishing a logical basis for a project, of justifying design intentions and of drawing attention to particular aspects of context while excluding others' (2012: 4).

What, then, is Eisenman's justificatory narrative and how does it work to make certain things central and others marginal? Well, as will be obvious to non-architects, his story-telling takes place entirely within architecture's own discourses, and particularly within its modernist/after-modernism Anglo-American confines. This location is emphasized through the focus on the designer's own authorial and intellectual intentions (even where this is opened up to non-conscious understandings), with all external influences removed. By explicitly only using the coded architectural language of the axonometric, Eisenman also reclaims the designer's autonomy and special power:

> The diagram acts as an agency between an authorial subject, an architectural object and a receiving subject: it is the strata that exist between them. ... The diagram enables an author to overcome and access the history of the discourse whilst simultaneously overcoming his or her own psychic resistance to such an act.
>
> (Eisenman 2007: 94)

Diagramming, then, acts to maintain both the designer's objectivity and rights of authorship, whilst enabling his creativity to be released. This is a clever, and I suggest, masculinist, trick (Boys 1996, 1998). By offering the possibility of returning to a place *before* human intervention in architecture – with all the messy needs and desires that implies – the architect is freed from the modernist taint of making inaccurate assumptions about what people are like, or should be like; his intentions are pure. People instead become 'receiving subjects' – that get what they are given, justifiable because of the intellectual clarity and creativity of the designer. Of course, this is an artificial, polemic and even 'tongue-in-cheek' argument. Eisenman seems to revel in the artificiality – his is deliberately a conceptual game. His design decisions may be argued as based entirely on formal and 'pre-human' grounds, but are in fact enacted in specific ways in his buildings and spaces, often as a deliberately anti-humanist – some might say nihilist – commentary on everyday life, whereby what is 'common sense' and meaningful becomes expressed as conceptual and meaningless. In the process the author both stamps his intellectual authority on the design project, and appears to stand back and let the diagramming do the work of 'uncaring' social commentary.

In the overall structuring of his argument Eisenman justifies this position through the simple technique of a binary opposition – between (bad) modernist typologies with their closing down of possibilities, and the (good) opening-up of multiple compositional repetitions. This central binary then resonates throughout, and is rhetorically supported by, a series of other similarly constructed associations – formalism/functionalism, modernism/contemporary, radical/normative, objectivity/subjectivity – that act in unison to create the idea that this design method is progressive and avant-garde. As Ghirardo notes (1994), such an approach has led to worldwide success for Eisenman, as he seems to have touched a resonant chord within architectural education and practice.

Precisely because of this predominant framing within the discipline, via binary oppositions and in a voice aimed only at other architects and architectural students, it should be noted that Eisenman's arguments do as much closing down of what diagramming is, as opening up its potential. He closes down on other alternatives, or on more nuanced or juxtaposed intersections between his method and others. He closes down on anything other than designers' intentions. And he closes down any 'difficult' discussions about the interrelationships between such a method and the built spaces that result (see for example Goldberger (1989) over the Wexner Center for the Arts at Ohio State University).

So, what if instead of making arguments for one form of diagramming over another as the most 'progressive', we treated all design methods as always uneven, partial and problematic – and explore what kinds of criticality and creativity can be produced by taking notice of/playing with the differences and gaps? Rather than following Eisenman and restricting unexpected and creative design developments to the generation of multiple iterations *within* formal composition and the interiority of architecture, we could look for exactly this creative potential in the spaces *in-between and across* various design methods and their resulting built spaces. We could intersect (rather than merely make oppositional) the various theoretical narratives that justify particular ways of interpreting the world, representing it, and (re)designing it. We could open up – for inspection and creative interruption – the particular selections of 'reality' rather than others that different kinds of diagramming enable. And, through the resulting representations themselves (both drawn and built), we can investigate how particular choices rather than others become normalized as transparently obvious and sensible.

As an example: rather than refuse to have anything to do with a diagramming method that appears to leave bodies out completely, let alone disabled bodies, I will explore how to generate built compositions from an equal abstract and artificial figure – the wheelchair user. The supporting justificatory narrative goes as follows: the most mechanist and utilitarian diagram in Western modernist architecture was not the grid or the universal building type but the averaging out of diverse human bodies into the 'norms' of ergonomic and anthropometric data such as produced by, for example, Henry Dreyfuss and the Neuferts, that are still in use today (Dreyfuss Associates 1974; Neufert and Neufert 2012; but see also Lambert 2012; Lambert and Pham 2015). Within this process of overall statistical simplification, the wheelchair user becomes the most supremely anti-humanist icon of all. The disabled person becomes only the chair and the chair becomes the symbol of disability, enabling it to be reduced to a pure, abstract and meaningless trope.

This should be music to Eisenman's ears. The cubic space of the wheelchair and its 'average' occupant can offer us an alternative compositional element from which to generate a three-dimensional grid, and then generate multiple repetitions and iterations on that grid as it is extruded through the spaces of motion. Using his explicit logic, this becomes an objective set of procedures that can open up unexpected design potential (Figure 12.2). The unspoken 'human' logic – usually of course that of an upright and differently mobile body – is refused, just as personal and social norms are ignored in House VI. Enjoyably, such diagramming also produces a similar frisson of discomfort to Eisenman's own; it too treats a body (a disabled body!) as merely a formal compositional component.

What would such diagramming involve and what does it reveal? Most immediately, the ideal 'wheelchair user' can be turned into a nine-squared diagram with ease, by including the arc of arms above the body, as with the Vitruvian Man (Da Vinci 1490) or Le Corbusier's Modulor (2004 [1954 and 1958]). I have based my sketch on a 60 in. or 1524 mm bounded frame, itself taken from the dimensions of a 'normal' wheelchair turning circle. Within that

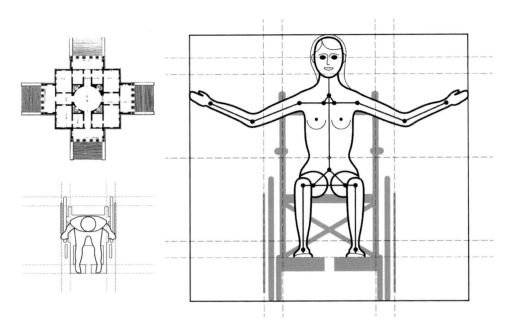

FIGURE 12.2 'Cripping the Grid - 1', Generating architectural proportions based on a wheelchair user

Source: Sketch by Thomas Carpentier.

cubic frame, by taking horizontal lines through eyes and knees, and vertical lines aligning to each side of hands gripping wheels, we have a nine-square grid. Manipulating further elements of the body-chair for additional lines and planes (wheel hubs, footrests, pushing handles, ankles, shoulders) an increasing complex grid can be produced, that could be used to start building up a complexity of solids and voids, based on formal additions and subtractions, superimpositions and collusions, rotations and other interventions (Figure 12.2).

But what then? Such a logic could be used to generate architectural form; the 'box' could become the frame of a whole building. But, already what is most explicitly exposed is the artificial obsessiveness and *constriction* that imposes. Starting from bodies, however abstract (rather than dissecting an already 'whole' volume), demands a different sort of procedure, one that is inherently additive and generative. These alternative cubes need to be joined, intersected, made to dance with each other. To me they suggest generosity, spaciousness and dynamism (Figure 12.3), very different to the obsessive retentiveness shown in *Diagram Diaries*. In this version, the outstretched hands of each wheelchair figure can be imagined to touch, clasp and spin around each other. Space, volume and movement takes on the potential spaciousness of a different kind of proportion. Groups of two and four make maybe circles and spheres within the dimensions of the grid frame, expanding spaces outwards. Just as Eisenman proposed, using the formal notation of orthographic drawing, multiplied through iterative repetition and difference, can generate new, unexpected forms and relationships. Just as with his work, these can help to *exceed*

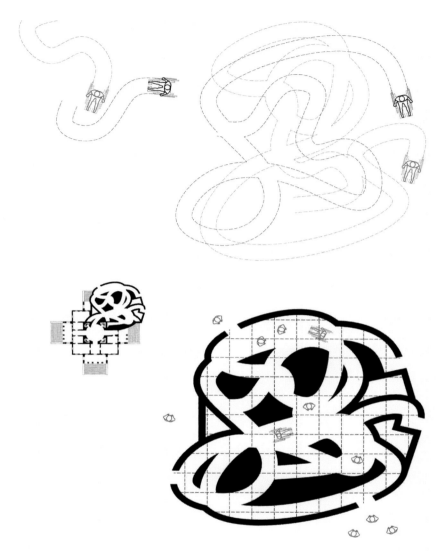

FIGURE 12.3 'Cripping the Grid - 2', Absurdist attempt to generate architectural form from the movements of a wheelchair user

Source: Sketches by Thomas Carpentier.

common sense assumptions embedding in anthropometric descriptions about wheelchair users. The resulting exploratory quick sketches here are not about determining a particular form; only hinting at how such alternative diagramming might be taken forward.

There is much work in disability studies and related disciplines that has begun to engage with diverse bodies and space in this way, by aiming to disrupt assumptions of a normal user who is unproblematically the 'receiving subject' of architectural designing. Whether through Rosemary Garland-Thompson's concept of misfitting (2011) or Sara Hendren's unexpected overlap between a wheelchair user and a skateboarder (see this volume), or Thomas Carpentier's alternative The Measure(s) of Man project (Figure 12.7) these approaches all refuse to start by assuming the 'norm' of the able-bodied. This is both about critiquing what is left out when design starts from an unnoticed and unconsidered fully autonomous, mobile and component body-in-space, and about opening up the creative potential of disability as a concept and as a diversity of lived perceptions and experiences.

Diagramming in a world of flows

More recently, with the impact of both digital forms of representation in architecture, and the ability to manipulate huge datasets, what constitutes diagramming has again been explored and debated within the discipline. Here the conceptual underpinning looks more to contemporary philosophies, rather than back to modernist architectural history or linguistic theory – particularly to the work of Gilles Deleuze and Felix Guattari (2013) in *A Thousand Plateaus: Capitalism and Schizophrenia*: 'Most common is their notion of the diagram as an 'abstract machine' that is conceptually abstract, yet fully functional as a concrete device for assemblage and deployment of spatial and social effects' (Fedorchenko 2008: 293).

If Eisenman focused on diagramming architectural form, these more recent approaches use diagrams to capture dynamic processes such as circulation flows, spatial relationships and patterns of intensity. Form is no longer a separate, artificially composed or even 'representational' entity, designed to express meanings. It is generated entirely from the accumulated actions of its occupants, layered up through time, and therefore becomes whatever it 'needs' to be. This means that the architectural composition is something that is neither designed first, nor added on after, once the analysis has been done. Instead it grows out of that analysis, as a process rather than a 'shape'. In the *Atlas of Novel Tectonics* (2006) Reiser and Umemoto give an example to explain what is meant by this. They first suggest that architectural modernism was very influenced by the streamlined shape of machines such as aeroplanes and cars, and the rational appearance of industrialized processes ('a house is a machine for living in'). They then propose that more recent design is less interested in looking like a machine, and much more in generating designs by understanding how the engine of that machine works.

Working from an investigation of underlying processes also helps to enable the appearance of a smooth, transparent and direct transition from design method to finished built result. This is because vector-based and animated digital techniques have now almost completely taken over from hand-drawn sketches or orthographic drawing in architectural education and practice. This means that there is an increasingly easy equivalency of 'diagrams' between the two- and three-dimensional mapping and visualization of occupancy and other data flows and the two- and three-dimensional form-making that uses parametric design (also know as 'blob' architecture). Parametric design involves the generation through algorithms of multiple and dynamic iterations of form, based on playing with the various design parameters involved, such as site conditions, usage patterns and functional requirements. This is

> the excitement of digital aesthetics; the potential of mapping, finally, space, time, and movement in formal terms; the possibilities inherent in direct milling from

design to finished object, all these too might be understood, if not as directly postmodern in affect, certainly as smoothing the transition from an old industrial to a new digital world.

(Vidler 2000: 17)

Like Eisenman these more recent practices also emphasis the diagram as a mode of opening up to unexpected possibilities. In 'Beautiful Apparatus: Diagrammatic Balance of Forms and Flows' (2008), for example, Maria Fedorchenko argues that a project by UN Studio (Arhem Central Station in the Netherlands) exemplifies a design method where diagramming not only analyses movement through space and time, but intersects this creatively with form-making. For her, architectural design can no longer be conceived of as making singular buildings, but must create built space within much larger, often urban, patterns of dynamic exchange:

> Processes of flow, change and integration take priority over compositions of static objects and staged appearances. Faced with the need to negotiate the instability of their project sites, designers redefine the conceptual treatment of the production of space. … Converting a static project into a dynamic system of collection and distribution is a way to achieve maximum effect with minimum intervention. Thus, most infrastructural designs are configured primarily as operative scaffolds for a complex series of programs and events.

(Fedorchenko 2008: 288–289)

Architecture in this understanding is articulated as a kind of framework that fixes organizational and occupational patterns, while letting the formal structure emerge out of these 'field conditions' (p289). To repeat, architecture becomes about what it can do, rather than what it looks like. This, in turn, challenges previous 'standard' representational and diagrammatic techniques of architectural practice. This is because new diagrammatic design tools can simultaneously model and mediate across both operational and visual diagrams – do more, that is, than organizational 'bubble diagrams' and other conventional methods. The resulting analyses of datasets not only intersect with more traditional – and inherently static – orthographic plans, sections and elevations, but change these for new kinds of dynamic three-dimensional modelling. This is not simply a back-and-forth between form and function, it is an:

> emerging consistency between architecture as a background support for fluid performance and as a foreground tool that alters and concretizes flow dynamics. Such a consistency can serve as the foundation for a prototypical design methodology that reconciles two seemingly contradictory pressures: how to use the instability of program for social effects and how to employ the precision of form for visual impact.

(2008: 290)

In this process, diagrams become both distilling and generative devices, 'multiplying programmatic and spatial options' (p293) (Figure 12.4).

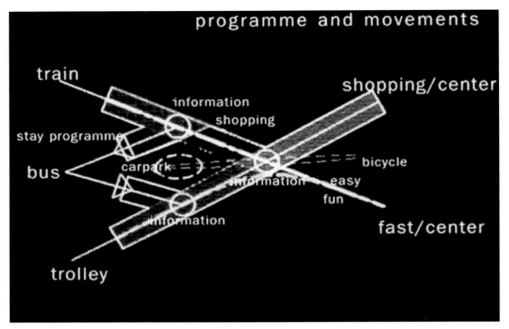

FIGURE 12.4 UN Studio (1999) 'Program and Movement' diagram for Arhem Station, Netherlands

Reprinted by permission of UN Studio

UN Studio: the problem of the unimpeded line

Most crucially for Fedorchenko, the ability to move between and across functional and formal diagrams avoids their potential opposition as modes of design thought:

> With the diagrammatic approach, beauty can be reconciled with practical necessity. Diagrams allow the designer to handle infrastructural logistics while retaining the freedom to construct powerful imagery, akin to artists or filmmakers. The resulting 'beautiful apparatus' reclaims the status of the architectural project as not only an efficient mechanism but also as a work of art.
>
> (2008: 301)

The justificatory narrative that Federchenko employs here on behalf of UN Studio, and perhaps parametric design more generally, then, is that form and function no longer need to be separate – as in the famous 'form follows function' tagline for modernist architecture – and thus functional and practical requirements do not need to act as a 'drag' on creativity or beauty (that is, on the formal and compositional aspect of designing). This version of parametric design sets itself in opposition to, and better than, any other design method that artificially divides the practicalities from form-making, or prioritizes one over the other. In fact, such an argument is in direct continuity with modernist approaches, in offering up a specific diagramming method as a smooth, comprehensive, transparent and logical generator of – and thus justification for – particular types of form-making, in this case 'blob' rather than 'grid' architecture. Precisely because the building's shape seems to grow directly out of design analysis, it is beautiful (that is, through the elegance of the method itself). We are invited to admire the beauty of the apparatus, not make judgments on the aesthetics or compositional qualities of the building itself. Similarly the architects' engagement with function and programme – their systematic description and evaluation of the complex intertwined facts, aims, values and needs that form the basis of any design – is naturalized as obvious and appropriate, because it seems to lock so seamlessly with the ensuing architectural form.

At the same time, parametric design is set in opposition to, and better than, modernist approaches, because its development of programme incorporates multiple and dynamic variations of occupancy and 'social effects'. Rather than starting, for example, from a universal Modulor man (Le Corbusier 2004 [1954 and 1958]) in order to delineate compositional form out of a singular 'ideal' (and normalized) human, parametric design generates data from the 'mass' of humanity and our accumulated and various actions through space. Such an approach does not pretend to objectivity as modernist architecture did, but its justification remains solidly located in demonstrating an ability to combine rationality with creativity.

Inserting unruly bodies into the world of flows

How, then, might we critically intersect dis/ability with this second project? Perhaps we could start by investigating exactly what kinds of bodies are acknowledged and mapped through the analysis of flow and pattern. What gaps and invisibilities exist within and behind an argument for creative rationality? Unlike Eisenman who refuses to 'bow down' to the social, UN Studio are a progressive practice who are concerned with the social effects of design, and incorporate inclusion and accessibility into their work. But, in diagramming for the Arhem Station scheme only particular types of difference are recognized. These are differences of direction, distance and destination. The already-existing variations between diverse bodies disappear; mapping of multiple patterns of movement and circulation occur *after* a fully capable, mobile and autonomous subject has been assumed. All these multiple journeys are mapped as the *unimpeded line* of the 'normal' body that, as Titchkosky so memorably writes:

> just comes along 'naturally' as people go about their daily existence. People just jump into the shower, run to the store, see what others mean while keeping an eye on the kids, or skipping from office to office and, having run through the day whilst managing to keep their noses clean, hop into bed. All of this glosses the body that comes along while, at the same time, brings it along metaphorically. Speaking of 'normal bodies' as movement and metaphor maps them as if they are a natural possession, as if they are not mapped at all
>
> (2002: 103)

Other authors (see Dolmage and Price this volume) have shown how architectural design generally tends to work from a 'normal' body, with disability only added on afterwards, through a retrofitting of the resulting environment. Here, I want to examine explore in more detail how we might use diagramming to make explicit some of the complexities of diverse human occupation of built space. and that can I want to explore how an alternative diagramming can act to comment on and disrupt some of the disciplinary assumptions in contemporary uses. architectural diagramming, at the same time And I want to illustrate how diagramming can also offer creative potential for thinking about disability differently.

This raises the question of what kinds of work are going on as humans differently (and differentially) occupy spaces and buildings. There are also already a multitude of ways in which architects diagram human occupation. For example, this may be through mapping personal and organizational needs, through articulating our sensory and experiential relationships to built space, and/or through analysing and extrapolating from the patterns of events and flow that we create en masse. Yet in almost every case bodies are assumed mobile, autonomous and with fully working senses. To critique this ablest assumption is simple. It just means making explicit what work it is bodies do as they occupy built space and – just as importantly – what bodies matter, that is, are designed for, and what bodies don't. What happens when we start from what *impedes the line*?

Most immediately, this means that rather than assume a clear and obvious separation between disabled and non-disabled people, we should look to a form of diagramming that can embody the complexities and fragilities of *all* our bodies. It needs to enable a mapping of dis/ability as ambiguous, relational and variable. This begins with individual bodymind (Price 2015) perceptions and experiences, but it is also completely entangled in the everyday social and material practices that frame what counts as normal (human) and as abnormal (less than human) in a society and specific moment (Boys 2014). Figure 12.5 sketches out a possible list of what it is to be human and occupy space.

The embodied and situated actions listed are not fixed (either to a particular body or place). Where and how we locate ourselves – and are located within and by different contexts – will have many diverse enabling and disabling effects through time on each of us. Embodiment is not simplistically being 'disabled' or 'non-disabled'; it is relational, dynamic and varied. But each heading also recognizes that fit and healthy bodies need pay little heed, whilst those with impairments are – or quickly become – increasingly expert at taking notice, at planning ahead, at negotiating difficulties. This is not about the 'strangely familiar', a well-known architectural strategy concerned to make us all take more notice of our surroundings by increasing the unexpected (Borden et al. 1996) but which *start from* a body that can just 'nip about' without thinking. Nor it is about the deeply experiential, as so well developed by architects like Peter Zumthor (2006, 2010). These architects also emphasize the senses – but again assume that these reside in a completely adroit and capable body; a body that can also be a *flâneur*, deliberately able to drift through the city, without any impediment (see Serlin this volume). Instead the table here tries, albeit in a limited way, to make visible the very everydayness of our bodies, and how it might begin to be described in all its variations and differentiations. Figure 12.6 then explores how such a set of criteria might be inserted into a diagram of circulation flows and patterns of use, as a means of taking into account the differential experience of moving through space. This is a procedure that attempts to map patterns of slowing down, of dis/orientation, of energy, of differential intensities, and that refuses to only diagram with lines that are unimpeded, identical and interchangeable.

Having a body	Examples of personal, social, material and spatial intersections	Some social norms about space
Keeping your balance	Gravity. Slippery and uneven surfaces. Confusing reflections. Carrying or pushing loads. Scanning for things to hold onto. Dealing with exhaustion and weakness.	Assumption of uninterrupted and fast motion, autonomous, independent and unimpeded by others or by built surroundings.
Negotiating obstacles and hazards	Heights, widths, steps. Judging distances and gaps Planning accessible and doable routes. Needing help. Watching out for others.	Assumption of continuous visual, physical and mental agility; with high-speed, instinctive and independent processing of, and responses to, immediate experiences and changing circumstances.
Maintaining energy	Deciding journey length and time. Looking for places to rest. Slowness and unevenness of progress.	Assumption of own unnoticed and boundless fatigue-free energy. Imperviousness to others and/or frustration as others' perceived slowness.
Thinking ahead	Pre-planning. Scanning spaces for needed resources and facilities. Navigating via environmental clues. Managing orientation and disorientation.	Assumption of lack of external need, based on self-containment and adequate personal resources. No need of recourse to support.
Dealing with sensory overload	Negotiating crowds, noise, bright or flashing lights. Managing complex and multiple data inputs.	Assumption of ability to retrieve required data seamlessly and to be able to block out non-relevant data.
Managing encounters with others	Staring, or unwanted interactions. Not matching communication norms. Social policing such as 'gaslighting' and micro-aggressions. 'Out-of-placeness' and misfitting. Feelings of exposure.	Assumption that face-to-face encounters are non-problematic. Ability to handle unspoken and neuro-typical social rules as obvious, unnoticed and straightforward.

FIGURE 12.5 'Having a Body': table outlining some of the characteristics of everyday materials and spatial embodiments

Source: Author.

As with the Effortless City project for San Francisco (http://www.effortlesscity.com/) this requires the development of multiple notations. The sketch here uses a variety of lines – dotted and dashed, wobbly, stopped in their tracks – and also some icons that represent potentially fraught encounters, such as sensory overload (from noise, crowds, data), balance-affecting moments (slippery surfaces, steep and unmarked steps, shadows and glare) and hazards and obstacles. Using big data diagramming to map and then analyse

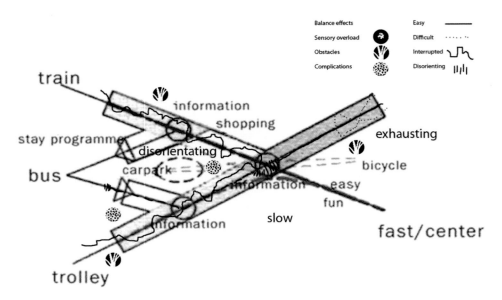

FIGURE 12.6 Adapted diagram for Arhem Station, as example of mapping differential perceptions and experiences of space

Source: Sketch by author.

statistics on the likely proportions of population experiencing these potentially disabling effects, and showing where in built space these are most likely to appear, has the creative potential to embed accessibility into the very centre of the design process itself.

Importantly though, working this way would also need to challenge the implied comprehensiveness and rationality of such a diagramming approach. This is in two ways. First, starting from disability aims to refuse ableist assumptions about what bodies can do, and which bodies matter. Expanding the creative potential of alternative diagramming therefore needs to incorporate critical reflection of the very grounds from which the design of built space begins, that is, an ongoing critique of what it enables and disables. Second, recognizing that disability and ability are a series of unstable and overlapping concepts and experiences, with varying and differential effects that are ambiguous and relational, means also acknowledging that gaps, tensions and contestations will always be produced. No amount of big data analysis will resolve this; it is design decision making that selects and prioritizes. Starting from disability does not lead to universal or simple design solutions. It does not provide any easy answers and will certainly not result in a built environment that is perfectly accessible to everyone, everywhere. But this is not a good reason not to try and move towards improvements.

Conclusion: diagramming the dis/ordinary

In this essay I have outlined some of the arguments made about diagramming within architecture, as a means of critically revealing gaps, avoidances and slippages. I have briefly examined two examples of how diagramming operates, both to delineate architecture as a discipline and designing as a method, in particular ways rather than others. Like Robin Evans, we cannot assume the spaces between design idea and built result are transparent or obvious, but need to prise these apart for critical and creative investigation. By inserting dis/ability (that is, disability *and* ability) as both concepts and diverse lived experiences into this space-of-diagrams between originating ideas and built product, we can simultaneously open up contemporary practices to critique, and find alternative ways of thinking and doing dis/ability *within* the architectural design process.

Of course, this aspect of design is only one small part of the procurement, design, construction and management process of buildings and spaces – a process that architectural students are not yet engaged in, and architects in practice do not have much control over. This, though, is what makes it such an interesting space for examination. The *multiple sequences of translation* that make up the design process – with diagramming often at its centre – is where architectural practitioners and students can operate most intensely as creative beings. If disability can find a place here, it has some chance of becoming a more ordinary part of what learning and doing the discipline of architecture involves.

However, this is not merely about 'making a space' for disability, or designing 'for' disability by just adding it to existing diagramming methods. Much more profoundly, as Lambert and Pham put it, it is about shifting our focus

> from what a body is to what a body can do, [so] we can begin to explore the political – sometimes violent – relations of bodies, objects, and environments that are produced and maintained through standard design practices and knowledge. How might a collaborative relation of body and environment create the potential for a more non-hierarchical architecture? How might it build one that frees all bodies from the abstract concept of a 'normal' body?
>
> (2015)

I have already noted that there are some design practices which work in this direction, by explicitly challenging the normal body through architecture, that is, by creating designs that force normal bodies into an awareness of themselves in built space (Lambert 2012; Virilio and Parent 1996; Gins and Arakawa 2002). However, the argument in this essay intends to go further. The idea of diagramming for a dis/ordinary architecture – of which only very partial and unfinished examples are offered here – aims to explore not so much the buildings and spaces that make 'normal' people take more notice of their own bodies, but rather what kinds of design might be generated by *starting from* what I have called unruly bodies (see Introduction, this volume). This looks to alternative kinds of diagramming that begin with acknowledging disabled as well as abled bodies, and that recognizes the ambiguities and complexities of inter-relationships between them (Figure 12.7). It suggests using mapping and analytical processes that refuse to make invisible or reproduce thoughtless and inequitable hierarchies of inclusion and exclusion; and that are critically and creatively able to reflect on architecture's own disciplinary attitudes and practices.

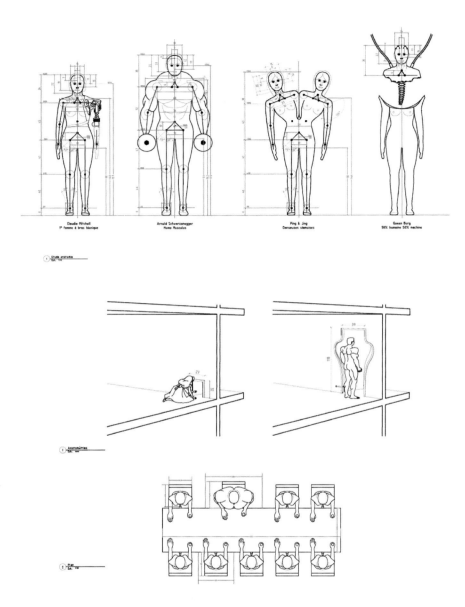

FIGURE 12.7 Thomas Carpentier (2011) *The Measure(s) of Man:* graduation design project from the Ecole Speciale d'Architecture, Paris. Reprinted by permission of Thomas Carpentier

This project questions the normatization of the human body proportions introduced by early Modernist Architectural manuals such as Neufert's Data and the anthropometric scale of proportion devised by Le Corbusier as the Modulor. Instead he designs products and spaces by starting from 'extraordinary' bodies such as a bodybuilder, an amputee, a pair of conjoined twins and Borg Queen, a character from Star Trek who has a biological head on a robotic body.

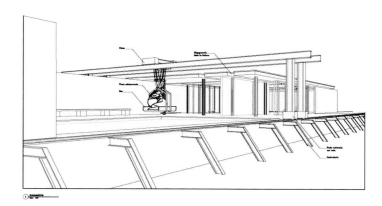

FIGURE 12.8 Thomas Carpentier (2011) Re-interpretation of the Modulor by Le Corbusier. Reprinted by permission of Fondation Le Corbusier

13

UN/SHARED SPACE

The dilemma of inclusive architecture

Margaret Price (2016)

Figure 13.1 shows a green sign poking up in front of a bank of evergreen shrubbery. On the sign is a stick figure in a wheelchair – this is the redesigned "Accessibility Icon" by Brian Glenney and Sara Hendren, with the figure leaning forward slightly and one arm poised over the wheel. Below the icon is the white-stenciled word "Entrance," accompanied by an arrow pointing to the right and slightly up. I'll say more about this image a bit later.

FIGURE 13.1 Accessible entrance sign on a university campus

Source: Photo by author.

In this three-part essay, I first review and re-define *inclusivity* through a disability-studies lens. Second, I turn to the concepts of "kairotic space" (Price, 2009, 2011) and "ambience" (Rickert, 2007, 2013) in order to suggest that inclusivity in architecture is better understood through a concept I call *crip spacetime*. Third, I support this argument by presenting evidence from an ongoing interview study of disabled faculty. In conclusion, I suggest new directions for architectural approaches to inclusivity in the future.

Part 1: excludable types

It would be hard to find a word of more interest on college campuses today than "inclusivity," unless it was "diversity," or possibly, "budget cuts." For example, a recent headline from the *New York Times* Education Life supplement is headlined, "Diversity is one thing, inclusion another" (Eligon, 2016). The article refers to the 2015 events at the University of Missouri involving an escalating series of racist attacks and student protests, which led eventually to the resignation of university president Tim Wolfe. As this series of events, and similar events that cascaded through U.S. campuses in 2014 and 2015 show, it's not possible to talk about inclusivity in higher education without also engaging the question of oppression. Yet, much too often, we use the term *inclusivity* as if we could take up its good parts without also confronting the historical and present-day practices of violent exclusion that make its emphasis necessary in the first place.

Often paired with the term *inclusivity* is *welcoming*, as in, "developing a welcoming classroom" or "safe and welcoming schools." But as Sara Ahmed (2012) points out in *On Being Included*, a study of diversity and racism in higher education, "To be welcomed is to be positioned as the one who is not at home" (p. 43). In this book, Ahmed conducts an investigation into the conditions attached to diversity for those whose presence produces that diversity. Diversity, she finds, is a commodity, a currency, sometimes an object: "Diversity can be celebrated, consumed, and eaten – as that which can be taken into the body of the university, as well as the bodies of individuals" (p. 69). This impulse is similar to one identified by Stephanie Kerschbaum, that of "fixing difference" (2014, p. 6). Difference and diversity are marked by certain metrics – brown skin, for example – and used as justification for an institution's measurably good intentions. This is, of course, a neoliberal logic, and also a "whitely" logic (Pratt, 1984; Fox, 2002). It's a logic assuming that intentions are equivalent to actions, that structural inequality is "no one's fault," and that representations of diversity (or inclusivity) can be folded into existing institutional norms without changing the institutions themselves.

If we take Ahmed's point about positioning a bit further, we might observe that the verbs *to welcome* and *to include* operate transitively. That is, there must be an object to the verb; someone or something must *be* welcomed, *be* included. And yet, in institutional rhetoric, these words are often made into other parts of speech (the adjective *inclusive*, the noun *inclusion*), in grammatical moves that specifically hide their objects. To say *welcoming school* or *inclusive classroom* places emphasis on the space itself – the school or classroom – thus eliding the question of who needs to be welcomed, who is positioned as doing the welcoming, or why that welcome has been deemed necessary in the first place. To say a school has the *goal of inclusion* similarly elides those who might be subjects in that goal: where will this goal be actualized, when will it occur, who will be shepherding the action, who will be subject to it?

Those questions – who, where, when – are drawn from Tanya Titchkosky's *The Question of Access* (2011), which approaches the problem of inclusivity from the point of view of disability studies. Like Ahmed, Titchkosky examines her own and other institutions as test sites to learn how attempts at inclusivity play out in material life. For example, having observed several instances in which discussions about access at her school focus on spatial issues such as ramps, doorways, and accessible bathrooms, Titchkosky draws the following conclusions from the justifications made during these conversations: "Wheelchair users are depicted as 'never showing up,' as an 'expense.' … Disability, in this instance, can be characterized as the abject underside of legitimated existence, included as an excludable type by signifying it as an always-absent-presence" (pp. 80, 90).

Both Ahmed and Titchkosky conduct intersectional analyses, with focus on different identity markers, but arriving at a similar point about the problem of trying to *make* inclusion happen. Regardless of how well-meant the efforts are, the very fact that gestures of inclusion are being made means that the distinction between those "in" and those "out" is reified; moreover, as the efforts and justifications play out, certain bodies are persistently marked as "excludable types" (Titchkosky, 2011, p. 90; see also Titchkosky, 2007).

It is important to recognize that the "excludable type" is excluded precisely because they are imagined out of existence, or imagined into a different space where they no longer present a concern. It would be relatively easy to point to instances of exclusion if the situation of exclusion were acknowledged as such; for example, if a wheelchair user were depicted sitting in front of a flight of stairs. (This is not to suggest that such exclusions are less violent or intractable, only that they may be more readily noticed.) However, exclusion often operates in such a way that its technologies – how it "sustains itself" (Titchkosky, 2011, p. 7) – are difficult to discern.

Justifications such as "Oh, this building was built before access standards were in place" or "But we did the best we could" or "There is an accessible bathroom, just not on this floor" shift the focus from the excluded disabled person and onto those who are "doing their best," or onto the semi- or non-accessible spaces themselves. Titchkosky offers a list of common justifications, each of which places the disabled bodymind either *elsewhere* (they can use that other bathroom; they can come in that other entrance; they can sit in this designated row in the back of the auditorium) or *elsewhen* (maybe they'll show up in the future; maybe they won't show up) (pp. 75–76). These rhetorical moves function to create a paradox of inclusion. Inclusion is approved and valued – just not right now, or not right here. This "paints the radical lack of access in an ordinary hue" (Titchkosky, 2011, p. 77). It also has the effect of shifting the issue of "the problem" from the inaccessible space to the "problemed" bodymind (Yergeau et al., 2013), and of compounding the pain of exclusion with the additional pain of being made to feel, well, crazy.

The socio-spatial process of identifying and separating "excludable types" can be observed in many architectural features. For example, let's return to Figure 13.1, shown and described at the beginning of this chapter. This time, we'll view it with a bit more spatial context (Figure 13.2).

First, here is the green-and-white sign itself, with the wheelchair logo, the word "Entrance," and the arrow pointing to the right and upward. This slightly more pulled-back perspective than the one at the beginning of this chapter shows that the sign is not

FIGURE 13.2 Accessible entrance sign on a university campus, showing inaccessibility

Source: Photo by author.

just posted in front of, but is nestled among, layers of shrubbery. In the background rise red-brick buildings, typical of many U.S. college campuses. This sign delivers a familiar message to wheelchair users and others who cannot use stairs: the accessible entrance is somewhere else, probably around back, and quite likely at the other end of a winding maze of pathways and passageways. Often, "accessible" entrances can be reached only by inaccessible pathways such as wood chips, or they may take the form of large, heavy doors (without automatic openers) which are ironically emblazoned with the accessibility symbol.

In this case, the sign pointing toward the accessible entrance is situated in a somewhat extraordinary context. The next image shows the front entrance of the building where the sign is posted.

Figure 13.3 is of the full building entrance. The building, a college library, is enormous and grand, built of stone in perpendicular Gothic style, with stained-glass windows, elaborate towers, and a flight of stone steps (slightly indented from the wear of many walking feet over the years) leading up to the large wood-and-glass front doors. A student wearing a backpack is climbing the front steps, and appears tiny in comparison to the imposing building. The "accessible entrance" sign is nearly impossible to make out; it's circled in white at the lower right-hand corner of the frame. From this perspective, it becomes evident that the sign is quite a long distance from the front entrance, and its small size and position snuggled within the shrubs indicate that it would probably not be noticed except by accident (which is how I happened to notice it).

FIGURE 13.3   Front entrance to university campus building

Source: Photo by author.

This sign, and its position, raise the question of *who it is for* – a question that both Ahmed and Titchkosky raise with respect to inclusivity. Is the audience for this sign a person using a wheelchair or cane, one who might approach this library eager to get inside, but be unable to navigate the steps? Or is it for the person who insisted that it appear in the first place – whoever they were, maybe a campus activist, maybe a member of the legal team? Is it for those of us who *could* walk up the steps, so that we don't have to think about those whom the steps exclude? What work are this sign, and the spatial arrangement of this entranceway, doing in the world?

In showing you this example, my intention is not to make fun of the school where this building is located, which in fact has made significant efforts toward accessibility. And that's my point. Even when best efforts are made, none of us is exempt from failure at inclusivity; none of us is fully able to make the leap beyond what Titchkosky calls "the unimagined type." The presence of this sign, its position vis-à-vis the building itself, the ways it was put in place, and the ways it *continues* to circulate meaning for those who pass by – these are all parts of the machinery that sustains a lack of access with a regretful look and a shrug of the shoulders. It's a shame; it's regrettable; it's no one's fault.

That impulse – to view the lack of inclusion as "no one's fault" – is unfortunately one that characterizes much architectural work. In the U.S., the Americans with Disabilities Act (ADA) has inadvertently encouraged a minimalist approach to access, to the extent that retrofits and exceptions have become the norm (see Newell, 2007; Dolmage, 2008, 2013 (also this volume); Yergeau et al., 2013; Keller, 2016). And even when aspects of physical access are carefully accounted for, other forms of access, including those that may be more difficult to discern, remain unexplored. These other forms of access may be more difficult to discern because we are accustomed to thinking of access barriers as recognizable, stable entities. But this misses the fact that many barriers – as well as forms of access – arise *in context*, shifting as the circumstances and bodyminds of/in a space shift (Boys, 2014, pp. 57, 85). Efforts for access must acknowledge the entanglement of social and material elements in the constitution of spaces. In the following two sections, I first offer a framework for thinking about these difficult-to-discern barriers by introducing the theory of crip spacetime, then flesh out that framework by describing the everyday experiences of disabled faculty in the higher-education workplace.

Part 2: kairotic space, ambient rhetoric, and gathering

Inclusivity is a topos in academic life. A topos, or commonplace topic (plural "topoi"), is a concept shared by a group as a starting place for communication. Some of the important topoi of academic life, as identified in my earlier work *Mad at School* (2011), include rationality, productivity, presence, security, and independence. Topoi function as a sort of shorthand for in-group communication; they are used as points of reference for ideas, phenomena, or people the group values or abhors. However, their meaning may not be agreed upon by *all* group members; rather, they tend to represent the *dominant* conceptions that govern the group. Thus, topoi not only enable communication, they also obscure certain assumptions; they are, as Sharon Crowley (2006) says, "part of the discursive machinery that hides the flow of difference" (p. 73).

The classical Greek word *topos* means "place," a point of etymology that emphasizes the importance of a socio-spatial analysis for inclusion. Spaces are, as Doreen Massey (1994) argues, "processes":

> Instead then, of thinking of places as areas with boundaries around, they can be imagined as articulated moments in networks of social relations and understandings, but where a large proportion of those relations, experiences and understandings are constructed on a far larger scale than what we happen to define for that moment as the place itself, whether that be a street, or a region or even a continent.
>
> (p. 154)

In other words, places (and spaces) both constitute and are constituted by the bodyminds, objects, practices, histories, and traces that inhabit them – and sometimes haunt them. This conception of space emerged in the 1970s and 1980s (see overview by Massey, 1994, p. 254) and has continued to develop through material feminist work such as Karen Barad's (2003, 2007). In this section, I begin from Massey's argument that space is a social process in order to revisit and update my theory of kairotic space.

When I initially conceived the idea of kairotic space (Price, 2009), I was preoccupied with academic conferences. Specifically, I was struggling to figure out why they were so hard for me to access. My access problems rarely occurred when I needed to ascend stairs, make my way through narrow aisles, hear speakers, view images projected onto screens, choose among narrow food options, or walk from session to session. Rather, I found that my difficulties manifested in puzzling, half-articulated concerns, which I didn't share with anyone else: *People are talking to me, but I can't make sense of their words. I can't remember what that person just said. People keep touching me. I'm exhausted. I have to go outside. I have to go home.* And there were also experiences not possible to articulate even in those not-very-articulate ways; for example, I can't think of a useful way to render the mingled horror and embarrassment of *I am having a panic attack during a meeting at a conference*, but it has happened (more than once), and it certainly meant the space was not accessible to me – though exactly where that inaccessibility might have been *located* is difficult to say. Initially, when I came up with the idea of kairotic space, I knew it would be incomplete, but I also felt that this strange and often painful form of spacetime needed to be named.

In *Mad at School* (2011), I wrote:

> *Kairotic space* draws upon the classical Greek notion of *kairos*, which refers to timing – that is, the good or opportune time to do or say something. Kairotic spaces are the less formal, often unnoticed, areas of academe where knowledge is produced and power is exchanged. A classroom discussion is a kairotic space, as is an individual conference with one's professor. Academic conferences are rife with kairotic spaces, including the question-and-answer sessions after panels, impromptu "elevator meetings," and gatherings at restaurants and bars on the periphery of formal conference events. Other examples from students' experiences might include peer-response workshops, study groups, interviews for on-campus jobs, or departmental parties or gatherings to which they are invited.

I define a kairotic space as one characterized by all or most of these criteria:

1. Events are synchronous; that is, they unfold in "real time."
2. Impromptu communication is required or encouraged.
3. Participants are tele/present. That is, they may be present in person, through a digital interface such as a video chat, or in hybrid form [see below for later changes to this criterion].
4. The situation involves a strong social element.
5. Stakes are high.

I specify "all or most of these criteria" to indicate that the boundaries of such spaces are neither rigid nor objectively determined. So, for instance, a meeting taking place either in person or via instant message between a graduate student and their academic mentor would probably qualify as a kairotic space. But an informal study session between two students who have been friends for years and who experience minimal risk in studying together probably would not.

The defining element of kairotic space is the pairing of spontaneity with high levels of academic impact. Attention to relations of power is of great importance in understanding kairotic space, as is recognition that different participants will perceive those relations differently. I don't claim the ability to define what is and is not a kairotic space if I am not directly involved; in fact, that's part of my point, that one person in a space may feel that it's entirely low-stakes and friendly (this is a common assumption on the part of academic mentors, for instance), while another may perceive a significant sense of risk.

Despite their importance, kairotic spaces in academia tend to be under-studied. One reason for this is that, because they are unscripted, it's difficult to collect data in them (Ventola, Shalom, & Thompson, 2002, p. 361). Another, more compelling reason is that their impact tends to be underestimated by those who move through them with relative ease. The importance of kairotic space will be more obvious to a person who – for example – can hear only scraps of a conversation held among a group sitting at a table, or who needs more than a few seconds to process a question asked during a one-on-one conference.

(2011, pp. 60–63)

In the years since I first developed the theory, I've revised my understanding of kairotic space. One revision is that I no longer assume the participants in kairotic spaces must be physically present; rather, I recognize that various hybrid forms of "presence," including presence via videoconferencing or other digital means, also come into play (Yergeau et al., 2013; see also Dadas, 2017). In addition, although I still think it can be valuable to think about "events unfolding in real time" when noting the inexorability and speed through which academic spaces are often constituted, I also acknowledge that there is no such thing as "real" time; or, as Lefebvre (1974) put it, "Time has more than one writing-system" (p. 110). Knowledge of "crip time" includes the understanding that crip time is not a simple speeding-up or slowing-down of normative time frames, but rather may represent radical forms of bending and folding, a quantum change – time "not just expanded but exploded"

(Kafer, 2013, p. 27). These changes reflect my developing awareness that kairotic spaces are constituted through the subject/objects that inhabit them and the emergent interactions of those subject/objects – an ever-unfolding process that Thomas Rickert (2013) calls "ambient rhetoric."

In *Ambient Rhetoric* (2013) and the earlier "Invention in the Wild" (2007), Rickert argues that kairos is not just a temporal, but also a spatial concept. In doing so, he draws on Debra Hawhee's (2002) work on kairos, which she argues manifests through "space-time" and enables "the emergence of a pro-visional 'subject,' one that works *on* – and is worked on by – the situation" (p. 18, qtd. in Rickert, 2007). This idea from Hawhee and others contributes to Rickert's theory of *ambient rhetoric*, through which our material, spatial, and environmental surroundings, or what Rickert calls ambience, "connotes the dispersal and diffusion of agency" (2013, p. 16). Not cited by Rickert, but also crucial in developing a theory of distributed and materially entangled agency, is work by material feminist Stacy Alaimo (2008), who argues that "material agency necessitates more capacious epistemologies" involving not only human will, but also "the often unpredictable and unwanted actions of human bodies, non-human creatures, ecological systems, chemical agents, and other actors" (p. 238). What this means for kairotic space is not just that its inhabitants are all having different experiences (which is still true), but also that their interactions, and the ways they are attuned to and responsive to each other, *constitute* their spacetime, just as that spacetime continues to constitute them. This understanding of spacetime overlaps with Karen Barad's (2003, 2007) theory of intra-activity and agency, a point I shall return to later.

Thinking about kairotic space invites further consideration/objects to *gather* in spacetime. Rickert, drawing on Heidegger, argues that the way people come together in ambient spaces, or "dwell," has an inevitably ethical charge (Rickett, 2013, p. 16). This resonates with my conviction that kairotic spaces cannot be meaningfully examined without attention to the relations of power that co-constitute them. For example, when I present at a gathering – say, a talk or workshop – I begin with an invocation that is specifically intended to call forth the socio-spatial nature of the venue, or what Rickert would call its ambience. A typical script for the invocation goes like this:

> I want to take a minute to observe the space we're in together. [At this point, I generally try to describe the space a bit. I remark on features such as the size of the space, the type of seating, whether there are steps, whether there are interpreters or captioners present, what sort of light illuminates the space, where the microphones are, and so forth.] I invite you to inhabit it in whatever way is most comfortable for you. You might wish to sit or lie on the floor rather than remain in a chair. You might want to stand up, move around, stretch, or go out and come back in. You might wish to stay in one seat, but engage in an activity such as stimming, typing, knitting, or drawing. All these forms of engagement are welcome.
>
> (See Price, 2016 for full invocation)

I didn't start making this invocation randomly. It was "born" in a specific moment, a conference gathering at which I witnessed a good friend, a fellow crip, being triggered – in her words, "being undone" (Kafer, 2016, p. 5). At that moment, I was thrown back in time to my own experiences of trauma; I too was undone; and later, I began to think hard about what it means to gather in spaces *together but radically not together.* The person experiencing trauma, sitting at a conference presentation (or in a meeting) (or anywhere), both *is and is not* in the same space as the non-traumatized person sitting next to them.

This is a quality of space that, I argue, architects need to think about more carefully. When imagining or rendering "bodies in space," how much do we know the space they may be inhabiting at any given moment? Are they in pain, are they experiencing a flashback, are they hard of hearing and thus using *all* their cognitive energy just to make out the flow of conversation? And without being overly deterministic about inhabitants' experiences or needs (for that would simply bring us back to an "accommodation" model), how might architecture take into account the radical unpredictability and ambient emergence of disability when we gather together?

Part 3: enfleshing the theory of crip spacetime

In this section, I share findings from an interview study of disabled faculty, carried out in collaboration with Dr. Stephanie Kerschbaum. As our interviews progressed, I realized that space was a key concept emerging in the faculty members' stories: how participants navigated their campuses, arranged their offices, entered and exited meeting rooms, interacted with colleagues in social encounters, and how they evaluated the "feeling" of the various spaces in which they worked. Through closer analysis of this broad theme of space, I developed a theory of crip spacetime, detailed in this section and "enfleshed" (McLaren, 1988) through analysis of interviewees' stories.

The interviewee pool, still growing, includes 34 disabled faculty members, whose positions vary widely with regard to race, gender, class, rank, type of institution, and discipline. During their interviews, participants self-identified with various disabilities, including autism, deafness (both signing and non-signing), Usher syndrome, bipolar disorder, spinal cord injury, multiple sclerosis, blindness, depression, chronic pain, chronic illness (both from-birth and later-emerging illnesses), physical impairment to face or hands, chronic fatigue, paralysis, electromagnetic hypersensitivity, and quadriplegia. Although analysis is ongoing, an initial process of open coding followed by category construction resulted in the following three themes:

- Exposure / vulnerability
- Fatigue / repetition
- Gaslighting.

The three themes, taken together, point to the necessity for co-design of academic space to foster inclusivity. However, as I emphasize in this essay's conclusion, "co-design" does not mean vaguely "including" disabled people in the design process, but rather a much deeper and more formative approach. Moreover, it means accepting that there is no such thing as "good" design for disability, at least not that can be definitively identified in advance. We are used to thinking of disability as something that can be accommodated through a series of predictable moves: Design the doorways like this, the walls like that, the lights like this. But instead, disability often must be accommodated *as it unfolds* through interactive spaces like classrooms and offices. That is more complicated than simply saying, "Allow time and a half for tests" or "Hire an interpreter" or even "Ensure the tables, chairs, and lights are adjustable." (And, as has been abundantly documented, accommodations that might initially seem straightforward, like adjustable tables or sign-language interpreters, are also complex and unpredictable; see Titchkosky, 2011, and Blankmeyer Burke and Nicodemus, 2013.) Disability as a critical analytic is compelling in part because it manifests human unpredictability. This is the challenge facing architecture.

Theme 1: Exposure / vulnerability

The term *exposure*, for a rock or mountain climber, refers to the steepness and openness of the terrain. It correlates with the level of risk one experiences when occupying a certain spot. For example, a steep area on a grassy hill with a long roll-out would probably be considered less exposed than a jagged rock face with similar steepness, because "exposure" is calculated not only by angle but also by consequences – that is, what will happen if you fall. Exposure, as a theme, describes a faculty member's awareness of vulnerability as they attempt to navigate access in their workplace. The contextual nature of exposure, in the rock-climbing sense, helps convey the way that risk, for disabled faculty members, is *spatial*: it emerges through the intra-activity of the spaces they move through at work. Importantly, it also includes the intersectional ways that disability is entangled with considerations of race, class, gender, nationality, sexuality, and so on, which are always present when a disabled faculty member is assessing their exposure in a given situation.

Many of our participants discussed feeling vulnerable at work, with some using that word directly, and some describing similar feelings and circumstances (for example, saying in relation to disclosing disability, "You know I've got sensitive information out there."). Just as with exposure in rock climbing, the level of risk for a disabled faculty member must be assessed by the person *in* the space, rather than being measured objectively or externally. This means that the disabled faculty member is carrying out extensive labor in remaining attuned to and guarding against that risk. Meanwhile, another participant in the same geometric space might perceive much less risk.

For example, consider the following account by Denise. In the interview, she had just stated that she has "my little blindness stump speech" that includes "canned answers that I give people" (for instance, a standard response to the question, "How long have you been blind?"). But in terms of addressing the actual day-to-day professional issues that may arise in relation to her blindness, Denise said, her sense of exposure is much higher.

D: I might have some of those conversations with my colleagues, but when I actually reveal true vulnerabilities that I feel as a disabled person, I am very careful about who I have those conversations with.
S: Right, right.
D: and I can give you an example about that. [pause]
S: Yes [please
D: [After my after my first semester, it was the first week of the spring semester, and we got our evaluations back from the previous semester.

S: Mh-hmm.

D: And in one of my classes in particular, two or three students wrote that it's very distracting that everyone is on their phones or on Facebook, and that people are falling asleep in class.

S: Mh-hmm.

D: This really paralyzed me, um, because I felt like I didn't have control over my classroom, and it makes me feel very vulnerable. Because on the one hand I know that is a problem that almost every teacher now faces.

S: Right.

D: So what that information can mean for other people is to say to sort of, it can almost give people the power to point me out and say, these are huge deficits she has as a teacher, and sort of not keep it in perspective that [pause] it probably has some unique challenges for me, but it is a problem that everyone faces. So I didn't talk to anyone for two days about it.

S: Right.

D: And I, I hid in my office and I just felt devastated. And because I couldn't think of an answ — a solution, because I just can't police students, I can't see what they're doing. So I decided to [actually=

S: [right

D: =bring it to my students, my new students, and I had them come up with rules together about how they were going to keep each other in check. So once I had that solution, and I felt that we had very good conversations in my classes, then I did tell two of my colleagues about the problem. [pause] I didn't tell two other colleagues, because I just didn't want that information, I don't want to say, to be used against me.

I have reprinted this section of Denise's interview in full because it demonstrates how her sense of exposure *emerges* through the intra-active features of her material situation. According to Karen Barad (2003, 2007), intra-activity demonstrates that agency is not a matter of an individual's will or intention. Rather, agency "is an enactment," something that arises through various "cuts" in matter and spacetime. Entities that intra-act (humans, objects, animals, etc.) are not helplessly thrown about in the process of intra-action; indeed, as Barad emphasizes, "our intra-actions contribute to the differential mattering of the world," and this fact carries with it a mandate for ethical action (2007, p. 178). But human will does not guide material encounters. Rather, the effects of those encounters arise through the intra-activity of all elements involved in a given moment. Putting this together with Rickert's contention that rhetorical situations are ambient, we are better able to understand the space that Denise found herself in.

If we think about the space of Denise's classroom in terms of intra-activity and ambiance, it offers a meaningful response to these common questions put to disabled (and all minority) faculty: "Well, why *not* ask your colleagues for assistance, if they've never shown any malice toward you? Why hide in your office? We've all gotten bad evaluations; isn't your reaction a little extreme?" The pain that Denise describes ("I hid in my office and I just felt devastated") occurs because *all* the elements of her work as a professor are intra-acting, including her lived experiences with ableism, dominant narratives about what "competent" instructors should be able to do, and the potential for catastrophic loss if she admits her vulnerability to the wrong person – in short, the *uncertainty* that surrounds disclosure. This is what I mean when I say that different subjects in a situation – for example, a blind professor and her sighted colleague – are actually inhabiting different spaces even if and when they are "together." The intra-activity that composes the spaces they inhabit is entirely different.

As Denise found out when she was finally able to talk to a colleague she trusted, not only did he not blame her, but he affirmed her concerns, and further noted that she had come up with a good solution. Despite this best-possible outcome, Denise still had to perform the labor of being attuned to her own vulnerability. That burden of being constantly on guard, of noticing and heading off potential problems, of protecting oneself from possible bad outcomes, not to mention managing the emotional stress involved, has also been remarked upon in other work by minority faculty (see discussion of intersectionality, below). The key thing I want to highlight is that it *does not matter* whether the intentions of the people surrounding the disabled faculty member are good, ill, or indifferent; the disabled faculty member must perform the labor of vulnerability regardless. This puts a markedly different spin on top-down campus efforts to become more "welcoming" or "inclusive." Those activating such initiatives are missing a salient fact: The space they inhabit is not the same space inhabited by those they are attempting to "welcome" (see Ahmed, 2012).

I've analyzed Denise's example in detail because it illustrates the point I want to make about exposure and how it changes academic space. But Denise's is not an isolated case: Many other faculty members interviewed expressed similar experiences about having to perform the labor of vulnerability, and how that affected the spaces in which they worked. Performing these constant calculations, remaining vigilant about potential risk, is exhausting.

Theme 2: Fatigue

The term "access fatigue" comes from Annika Konrad (2016), who defines it as "being plain sick of having to ask for access." Without conflating the situations of disabled and racially minoritized faculty, it is worth noting that a similar phenomenon has been documented for people of color: "racial battle fatigue" (Smith, 2004, qtd. in Wilson, 2012, p. 70). This repetitive labor is exhausting. Disabled faculty must meet the usual expectations of faculty work in the neoliberal university (growing class sizes, vanishing job security, shrinking job opportunities, increasing service duties), and also meet the constant demands of negotiating their disabilities at work. These demands range from arranging accommodations (if such are even available) to managing the ambient sense of exposure and vulnerability described in the previous section. As I analyzed faculty members' interviews, an important theme that emerged was the *constant* nature of the labor interviewees had to perform when negotiating being disabled at work. More than one interviewee, when asked "Do you talk about your disability at work?" responded, "All the time." The exact repetition of that phrase, from more than one interviewee, called my attention to the potential for this theme; when I analyzed the data further, it became clear that many of the faculty members we interviewed found "access fatigue" (Konrad, 2016) a salient component of their jobs.

One faculty member who said "All the time" was Trudy, a white non-tenure-track faculty member at a small private college. She had been in this job for more than 20 years at the time of the interview, a fact that makes her story about having to constantly recapitulate the issue of her disability and access needs even more striking:

T: I'm always asserting them [my access needs]. There are a handful of people who know me really well, who are good friends as well as colleagues, who always anticipate them. Most people forget.

S: Okay.

T: They don't—even though I'm very public, even though I'm always asserting them, even people I work with on a regular basis will say, "Oh let's have a breakfast meeting." You know. They already know that I can't do that.

S: Right, right.

T: But no, I have to do—It's continual, okay.

S: Okay.

T: Yeah, it is continual.

As Trudy's explanation indicates, the act of "coming out" as disabled is not a one-time event, but rather one that happens repeatedly. The barrier of having one's access needs forgotten, and having to re-assert those needs constantly, is one that must be surmounted regularly by disabled faculty. This barrier is further evidence that disabled faculty work in different spacetimes than their colleagues, even if they share the same geographic and geometric space. I might say the barrier is "invisible," but that is an inadequate metaphor; access fatigue is not just unseen, but *does not exist* for nondisabled faculty (although they may, of course, have to work for access for other reasons). Moreover, the nondisabled faculty member is unlikely to notice that a seemingly insignificant exchange they may have just witnessed ("I need this"; "I can't do that"; "I can do that only if the following conditions are in place") is sapping the energy and morale of their colleague, because the nondisabled observer probably witnesses only a few of the daily repetitions which can easily reach the dozens, or hundreds. Returning to the concept of kairotic space, this may help explain why architectural efforts to foster collegiality so often fail. A "relaxed, social" space for one person is, for another, simply yet another site in which they must carry out unpaid and unnoticed labor.

Many other interviewees described the toll taken by the need to constantly assert or adjust for their access needs. For example, Nicola, a working-class adjunct faculty member with multiple sclerosis, described the constant maneuvers she must perform, both internally and when communicating with colleagues, supervisors, or students, to match the demands of her job to the capabilities of her disabled bodymind. She explained that her daily routine "is basically a series of very clever strategies that I use to either conserve energy, to compensate for deficits [M: Mh-hm] or to mask what's going on with me." Marian, a deaf faculty member at a large university, said, "It's like disclosure over and over again, every single class that you stand in front of." Del, who is autistic, related that at a time in her career when it wasn't safe to reveal herself as autistic, she performed intense and constant labor to hide her usual mannerisms, which involve rocking and stimming:

"I carefully like kept my hands in my pockets all the time and my body tense and I didn't move … I made myself really sick." Some interviewees also described ways that structural changes in their workplaces helped mitigate the exhaustion of constant explanations. For example, Maya, a researcher with Usher Syndrome, is like most of her co-workers in that she is deaf and communicates mostly by signing; however, unlike most of her co-workers, she is also visually impaired and has epilepsy. After a number of individual exchanges with co-workers, her supervisor asked her to make two presentations to her research team to describe her access needs. Maya wrote, "That proved to be useful, and most colleagues were very understanding and appreciative of the information."

Although any faculty member could point to examples in which they've had to perform unpaid labor to accommodate their own needs, the difference between this experience and the ones described here is *scale*. For the disabled faculty we interviewed, these acts of unpaid labor often constitute an all-the-time, every-day series of calculations, moves, counter-moves, and corrections. When the burden of this sort of constant labor is scaled up, it leads to circumstances that are not just difficult but may be intolerable. Notably, our interview sample includes at least two faculty members who have left academia.

Theme 3: Gaslighting

The third theme, gaslighting, identifies the experience of being made to "feel crazy" when confronting inaccessible spaces in the workplace. *Gaslighting* is a term that originated with a 1930s stage play and was popularized through a 1944 film, *Gaslight*, in which a husband manipulates his wife's surroundings in such a way that she comes to doubt her perception of reality. The term traveled into psychiatric literature and has since been used colloquially, especially in minority communities, to describe the experience of being made to feel that one's perception of a situation is inaccurate – that one is remembering events wrong, or blowing things out of proportion, or interpreting events incorrectly. This theme appeared less frequently during interviews than exposure or fatigue; however, I am highlighting it because it was mentioned more frequently by multiply minoritized faculty, especially those who are queer and/or of color in addition to being disabled. Part of the purpose of our "maximum variation" sampling approach, in which we aimed to gather as wide a range of faculty experiences as possible, was to uncover such themes, which may be more salient for disabled faculty living with intersectional experiences of oppression.

Zoe, an assistant professor at a minority-serving institution, described a number of microaggressions she experienced on the job market; for example, at one campus interview, a search-committee member made a mocking comment about ADD (attention deficit disorder; one of Zoe's diagnoses), and later used the R-word. At her new workplace, issues continued, and Zoe described her sense of being pressed into a role as the "stereotypical crazy Latina":

> It's like, no matter how many degrees you have, you're always worried about being the stereotypical crazy Latina who just has to be a problem. [break] Who reads race into everything, who reads ableism into everything, or sexism. And it's like, how do I not do that? That's my life.

This comment also fits with the theme of exposure; however, it is further complicated because Zoe's sense of risk was heightened by the (micro)aggressions she encountered on the job. (I put "micro" in parentheses because Zoe commented at one point, "I don't wanna call them microaggressions because they're pretty blatant.") She described a process of gaslighting that unfolded after she met another professor at her school: when the two were discussing a topic their research had in common, this professor referred to medieval women mystics "as 'wild,' 'crazy,' and 'just plain nuts, which is why they're fun.' I [Zoe] was appalled." As Zoe continued the story, she indicated that this professor "maligned" her teaching, then described what happened when she tried to complain:

Z: When I complained about it, my concerns were dismissed.
S: My stomach is sinking reading this [break] I am honestly so shocked that this person wants to teach [topic of class].
Z: And I was asked if I might be reading into things or whether I might be blowing things out of proportion, and I know these questions come as a result of what people know about my disabilities. … So here's how I see it working: I have anxiety disorder and I worry about things a lot, and how they affect me or my students. I overthink things sometimes. As a result, when I have spoken to colleagues about my concerns with this person, no one has been able to offer any useful advice. One person said he hadn't heard anything negative, and the other person said I might just be taking things the wrong way and "reading into it." [break] One even asked if maybe I wasn't just being a little paranoid.

This example demonstrates why an intersectional analysis of factors leading to workplace discrimination is crucial: Zoe's story is not only about her disabilities, but also about the ways they intertwine with her race, gender, and the subjects she teaches. As with the earlier examples, Zoe's can be read as one in which elements intra-act to place her and her colleagues in entirely different spaces. There is an insidious additional factor at work here, however, which is that the reality of the space Zoe inhabits is *itself* called into question.

Stories of gaslighting did not come up as often as stories of fatigue or exposure. However, when they did come up, it was frequently by faculty who experienced intersectional pressures of disability, race, gender, sexuality, and/or class. Gaslighting overlaps with disability in complex ways, since not only may disability figure into the subjectivity of the person being gaslighted – as Zoe's story shows – but gaslighting itself *effects* disablement by forcing a subject to "feel crazy." In fact, the end stage of gaslighting, according to psychiatric research, is "severe, major, clinical depression" (Abramson, 2014, p. 23). Elena Flores Ruíz (2014) calls gaslighting "a kind of professionalized, ambient abuse" (p. 201) – using the term *ambient*, as Rickert (2013) does, to mark an emergent and spatial phenomenon. Much more work remains to be done on the intersectional pressures faced by multiply marginalized faculty, including those who are disabled and those who become disabled as a result of gaslighting. For the purposes of this chapter, I will point out that this is yet another way in which disabled faculty simultaneously *are* and *are not* in the same spaces as those they work alongside.

Part 4: conclusion

As I wrote this chapter, I found myself coming up against a difficult question: If architecture – at least the sort of architecture typically used to construct buildings in academe – is an essentially predictive endeavor, and I am arguing that disability should be recognized as essentially unpredictable, what does this mean for the future of accessible architecture? To put the question in somewhat less impossible terms, I am asking: If we accept that disability is an emergent phenomenon, one that materializes through the intra-actions of people, attitudes, histories, objects, that materialize as crip spacetime, how do we design for disabled bodyminds?

One approach that has proven *not* very successful is establishing a checklist and then adhering to it rigidly (see Wood, Dolmage, Price & Lewiecki-Wilson, 2014; Dolmage, 2015). This can be seen in "minimal compliance" applications of ADA standards (see Newell, 2007): too often, the law serves as a baseline for what designers can get away with rather than inspiring what new forms of access they might imagine. Other types of building standards may try for access, but in a hit-or-miss way that demonstrates an obvious failure to deeply consult disabled people. For example, the relatively new WELL building standard is explicitly centered upon health, and takes into account issues such as building occupants' mental health, need for physical/mental respite, and potential chemical sensitivities. However, WELL creates other problems, such as valorizing the use of stairs over elevators, on the assumption that this is a healthier choice, while apparently forgetting that some occupants are simply unable to use stairs (Keller, 2016). Even universal design, for all its revolutionary history, is often approached as nothing more than a checklist with seven items (see Dolmage, 2008; Hamraie, 2013). Still, at the end of the day, the standards themselves are not the main problem. Large-scale building would not be possible without some form of standard or guideline. The main problem is the failure to imagine access differently (Titchkosky, 2011; Boys, 2014).

Co-design, or participatory design, is an obvious remedy for poorly imagined architecture. This argument has been made within disability studies for decades, as the slogan "Nothing About Us Without Us" attests (Charlton, 1998). However, the problems of inclusion noted by Ahmed (2012) and Titchkosky (2011) characterize efforts at co-design as well. Many plans for accessible design state that disabled people must be "included" in the design process. But what does that really mean? When will we be included, and under what circumstances? To what extent will disabled people produce, rather than just comment on, the spaces where we work? For that matter, what sorts of disabilities will be "included" for consideration? As a disability activist working to foster accessible spaces in academe, I have learned over and over again that "inclusion" can mean almost anything when co-design is claimed. And, while disabled people in academe certainly do inhabit spaces in the way that Massey (1994) describes, that is, hacking and re-making them as we go, it's rare that disabled people are truly centered in the process of accessible design.

In *Speculative Everything*, Anthony Dunne and Fiona Raby (2013) propose an approach that moves away from realism and focuses instead on the question "What if?" (p. 141). They emphasize that, unlike most forms of social design, which continue to work within "the limits of reality as it is" (p. 12), speculative design attempts to work fictively, deliberately imagining worlds that *cannot* be in order to improve design in the world that is. In addition to centering disabled people as producers rather than bystanders or latecoming consultants (Yergeau et al., 2013), I call upon architects and those interested in accessible space to consider what it might mean to *identify with* disabled people – to enter our spaces rather than inviting us to enter yours. The process of identifying-with is described by Sami Schalk (2013):

> I use *identify with* to mean having acknowledged and prioritized political and personal connections to a group with which one does not identify as a member. … Identifying with is a careful, conscious joining – a standing/sitting among rather than by or behind a group – which seeks to reduce separation while acknowledging differences in privileges and oppression.

Schalk's definition of identifying-with is spatial: she notes that it involves "standing/sitting among rather than by or behind." This sort of action, this *among*, is different than calling disabled people in for a design charrette; it might mean visiting (with permission) the spaces disabled people *already* inhabit, learning about our hacks and our customs, learning where our barriers lie – with the understanding, once again, that no two disabled people will face just the same barriers. Dwelling in crip spacetime enables the development of what Mia Mingus (2011) calls "access intimacy" – that is, the ability to understand another's access needs viscerally, even intuitively at times.

There is no shortcut for this sort of visceral, ambient knowledge; like dwelling (Reynolds, 2004), it can only be effected through time and space, not willed or predicted. The "what-if?" of speculative design (Dunne & Raby, 2013), the possibilities of a "politics of wonder" advocated by Tanya Titchkosky (2011), mean that inclusion itself must be understood as fundamentally unstable. It means identifying with; accepting failure; trying, and trying again, through meaningful feedback loops. Today's academe is a prototype.

Note

The study reported on here was supported by a Research Initiative grant from the Conference on College Composition and Communication (Price and Kerschbaum, Principal Investigators). Our sampling method is "maximum variation sampling," sometimes called "diversity sampling," which aims to locate participants on as wide a range as possible. Our interest is not in asking, "Who is typical or representative?" but rather, "Who is unimagined?" In addition, we deliberately set up an "accessible interdependent research paradigm" (Price 2011; Price and Kerschbaum, 2016). Interviews took place in whichever medium participants identified as their preference, including face-to-face video-conference, telephone (with captioning), e-mail, or instant-message. Interviews were both oral and signed.

In the interview excerpts used here, "M" indicates Margaret Price; "S" indicates Stephanie Kerschbaum. Although our raw transcripts use line breaks to mark every breath, and omit all punctuation except to indicate linguistic features, the rendition of the interviews here is edited for readability, with some added punctuation, and fewer line breaks. Ellipses indicate omitted phrases or sections, rather than pauses. Pauses of two seconds or more are noted as [pause]. Open brackets and equal signs indicate overlapping and latched speech. For non-indented quotations, if speech overlaps, brackets are used to denote the overlap (for example, an interviewer saying "Mh-hm" while a participant is speaking).

For typed interviews, minor spelling errors have been corrected. [break] indicates a paragraph break in the typed instant-message conversation, i.e., when one of the interlocutors hits "return." In some cases, an interlocutor hits "return" and then adds something else; in that case, [break] will appear in the middle of their quote.

14

THE COLLAPSING LECTURE

Aaron Williamson (2010)

Reprinted from G. Butt (2010) (ed.) Performing/Knowing,
Birmingham: ARTicle Press.

It seems to me that the formally delivered academic lecture, dependent upon arguably precarious conventions (someone reads aloud off a page for no discernible aesthetic purpose: often the voice is flat, the delivery dull and the language of academic theory too dense for the hearer to grasp), is by and large predisposed towards collapse. As a deaf student I sat through much of my education without the provision of a sign interpreter and to counter boredom I would spend the hours observing peripheral distractions such as the lecturers' body language, attitudes and interactions with their lecturing apparatus. Above all, I watched closely for those moments when the objective of the lecture – to educate and inform – was disrupted or stymied by intrusions, technical breakdowns, or simply by a loss of nerve; since, quite often, assertion and bluffing appeared to be required. My opinion formed that this peculiar expression of cognisant propriety – the lecturers' performing of 'knowing' – was often predicated upon essentially transparent forms and methods of address that, sooner or later, like any over-inflated edifice, are inclined to fall apart. It was with some glee then, that over the past year I accepted several invitations to present a performance whose hidden objective was to reveal the dubious premise and scaffolding of the formal lecture, to deliberately 'collapse' it (Figure 14.1).

Performance theory

My area of expertise as a Lecturer on BA and MA Fine Art courses is in classic performance art of the 1960s and 70s – perhaps the single most subversive period of art making, constituting as it did, a concerted radical attack upon any and all artistic securities to that time. Since I am also an artist in the field of performance, I have always experienced a vague sense of unease and ambivalence towards the formal teaching of 'performance theory' via the lectern. Occasionally, I face a room of expectant faces and expound about performance presenting the artist with an 'expanding frame' that can stretch out from 'the work' to surround all of the conditions of art making and its presentation; to include or analyse them as part of its

FIGURE 14.1 Aaron Williamson (2011) 'Flannel' 'Parlour Principia' performance evening, Swedenborg House, London, May 13 (duration 1 hour). By permission of the artist. The word 'Flannel' has two meanings in English. Firstly it is a small cloth used for washing the hands and face with; but a lesser usage of the word means 'indirect or evasive talk'. It's impossible to estimate the average percentage of lecturing time that is filled with this kind of flannel.

effect. This imaginary, elastic frame, I aver, can be stretched to include – i.e. make apparent – all the processes of the art's manufacture, including the performative actions of the artist. In this specific way, performance is a useful medium through which to contest the transparent conventions through which most art traditionally comes into existence. I advise students interested in performance then, to methodically stage 'an observation of the periphery' – to look to the edges of a piece of art to grasp and deploy its wider impact and intent.

Sometimes I will be discussing this conceptual 'periphery' and describing examples of how it might be methodically observed, whilst being only too aware that the lecture itself is antithetical to this premise. It has struck me at various instances that the performative aspect of my lecture (which, according to my sweeping assertions, must necessarily circumscribe it) was entirely ignored since, following the conventions of formal lecturing, there were many aspects to it which, whilst observable in plain view, were not intended to be significant. As I negotiated the whiteboard, drawing diagrams and writing phrases, loading up the video projector, digressing from my notes and so on, I experienced some unease that in fact, the theory of performance art amounts to an argument precisely against the assumptions and actions that fortify the conventional lecture through which I was attempting to describe or impart them. I began to wonder what would happen if this 'fortification' (which became ever more perceptible, or less ignorable, as time went on), fell apart, began to collapse?

Quite aside from the larger question of whether performance art is in fact a teachable subject, this sensation of self-contradiction remained with me as students fell drowsy, fire drills were observed, late arrivals excused, I forgot my notes, the technician had to be fetched from afar; or as exciting moments of pedagogic discovery crashed into long periods of clock-watching. Over the years of teaching 'performance theory' this doubt – that I was presenting a warped inversion of the knowledge area – grew, largely because of the fact that I was acting from the decidedly non-performative, valorised role of a 'Lecturer', attempting to describe a philosophy that seemed intrinsically antithetical to that position.

'Collapsing lecture 1' – Byam Shaw School of Art (9th October 2008)

As a Cocheme Fellow at the Byam Shaw School of art in October 2008 I was invited to give an inaugural lecture to describe my work and artistic concerns. This was to be only 20 minutes long but the convenor, Anna Hart, suggested that I approach it as a performance as well as a lecture – a hybrid presentation. Wondering how that could be done, I was reminded of two events that seemed relevant: the first was the infamous lecture/poetry recital by Antonin Artaud at the Vieux-Colombier theatre, Paris in January 1947. Artaud had recently been released after spending the years of the Second World War in a harrowing mental hospital at Rodez and his artistic reputation and character had reached legendary status in artistic circles during his absence. The event was billed – somewhat exploitatively – as 'The Story of Artaud the Momo' [Momo' is Marseillais pejorative slang that roughly translates as 'loony' or 'idiot'] and Parisian society was out in force (a capacity audience of 900) to observe the spectacle.

Witness accounts describe Artaud's initial nervousness as he read stiltedly from his pages at the lectern for the first hour. Returning to the stage after an interval he started again but accidentally scattered his large pile of notes all over the stage floor. Rather than collect them up, Artaud simply began screaming and tearing at his face and hair – he spent the next hour improvising a wild performance of exclamations, chanting, vocal eruptions, crude gestures and curses that appalled the astonished audience (Barber 2003 136–138).

The second example that I'd recalled – of a lecture that surpassed or deliberately sabotaged its formal premise – was by William Pope.L which I'd attended at the Tate Modern as part of the Live Culture event in 2003. As Pope.L leant on the plinth, peering over his spectacles in time-honoured professorial manner, he spouted a stream of gibberish for 30 minutes to a baffled audience. An American artist who subverts white/racist perceptions of black people, Pope.L, it later transpired, had been speaking in a bastardised version of 'Klingon' – a dialect borrowed from Star Trek movies. Most of the audience (along with the sign interpreters) appeared to believe that he was an artist of obscure nationality, who unfortunately had not warned the curators that he would be speaking in his 'native' language.

So, for my 'inaugural lecture' at Byam Shaw, inspired by Artaud and Pope.L, I devised a short repertoire of setbacks or 'collapses'. These included the inevitable crashing computer and malfunctioning projector; dramatising being unable to find my reading glasses; dropping my notes à la Artaud; suffering from a pronounced coughing fit; stammering through a sentence and repeating it ponderously for a minute or more; drinking copious amounts of water. . . . each time approaching the lectern again as if now, having finally surmounted these insufferable setbacks, the lecture could begin. Until, finally, after 15 minutes, it was announced by the Convenor that the lecture was in fact over.

'Collapsing lecture 2' – Goldsmiths College (4th December 2008)

Invited by Jenny Doussan and Gavin Butt to present a formal lecture to Goldsmiths College's MA Visual Cultures Department, I decided that I wanted to continue developing 'The Collapsing Lecture' and expand it to a full-length, 1 hour-long performance. I could see how this might in fact serve to illustrate my concerns with performance art much more effectively than a conventional, illustrated lecture ever could.

By now, I had become methodical in gathering material. I canvassed friends who lecture in Universities and on the conference circuit for anecdotal accounts of mishaps and misfortunes at the lectern and thus amassed a stockpile of wryly amusing tales. By far the commonest were those involving computer incompatibilities and the ever-elusive link to the digital projector. But also, there were tales such as the one about the cocky Don who had slapped his disc on the desk of the school secretary instructing her to print his conference paper in time for its delivery an hour hence. At the lectern, in front of a packed audience, he opened the envelope containing his paper and was mortified to discover that it had been printed at 8 point-type which he was unable to read.

Another story had a Conference Lecturer taking the lectern almost immediately upon arrival from the airport – so acutely jetlagged, he literally fell asleep on his feet midway through and had to be startled awake. Many accounts made it sound as if the material world had reared up and refused to submit to the speaker's will: whiteboard pens ran out of ink, lights dimmed down and flickered on, microphones squealed and chairs collapsed. Several of those I spoke to mentioned the curious button on the remote controls of digital projectors which, when pressed, rather than firing up the light, closes the machine down after which it then takes an excruciating 10 minutes wait to come back on (or to 'warm up') again. Many of my lecturing friends told of reading their pages out of sequence, having forgotten to insert page numbers, and one recounted how he had misplaced the crucial page that spelt out the central formula in his thesis after he had spent half an hour building the audience's expectation towards it. Perhaps the most bizarre example of all though, was the ballistics expert in Orlando, USA who, during a lecture on 'Methods of Gun Safety', accidentally managed to shoot himself in the thigh.

By now then, I was armed with a collection of mishaps that I intended to string together in order to form an hour's 'Lecture'. It was agreed with Gavin and Jenny that I would arrive 15 minutes late: a novelty in these days of University lecturers' 'customer accountability' to students. Gavin gamely took on the task of filling the 15 minutes waiting for my entrance by laboriously itemising my biography and CV to the students, all the while nervously checking his watch and mobile phone.

Dragging a huge suitcase and with a copy of 'The Racing Times' poking rakishly from my tweed jacket (with elbow patches), I finally made an entrance by nervously poking my head around the door to the packed Theatre, querying in a mumble whether anyone was expecting a 'Dr. Williamson'? My regular sign interpreter, Chloe Edwards was present and

– in on the ruse – spent the first few minutes laboriously and repetitively introducing me via finger-spelling, after which I proceeded to work through the following 'script':

Collapsing lecture Goldsmiths College, 4th December 2008

Turning up at the lecture theatre in a fluster, fifteen minutes late, rolled-up 'Racing Post' in pocket.

The laptop slowly starts up before crashing, (pull plug lead).

The projector won't respond to the handset, request replacement batteries (Jenny).

The replacement batteries don›t fit.

The dry marker is out of ink, (tape secretly covers the nib).

Cause alarm by attempting to marker pen the expensive-looking projection screen.

Remain oblivious to mobile phone ringing in my pocket (I'd arranged with a friend for him to call me at some point during the performance).

Request a jug of water – the plastic cup springs a leak.

Request that floor is mopped.

I can't find my spectacles, unable to read.

I drop the thick pile of notes.

Find glasses but drop and tread on specs.

An extended, violent coughing fit, much chest beating etc.

The technician finally arrives to help.

Gets the projector working.

But my desk top files will not open – 'corrupted' notice.

Try to recall password, audibly mouth A-N-A-R-C-H-Y-I-N-T-H-E-U-K.

Nervously remove jacket and jumper, before replacing them again.

Discourse obscurely on the pink forms that I was told everyone was supposed to collect from the Dean's office – does anyone know about this?

Further improvised slapstick business with interchangeable use of water, newspaper, the pile of notes, batteries, handset, crashing computer, broken specs, ink-less pen and so on.

Threaten formal complaint to college about the parlous state of their technical services.

Become irate.

Conduct conversation with Chloe in sign language about last night's television. (Unless there are other deafies present!)

Become very sad, withdrawn/defeated.

Start laughing/giggling/crying.

Draw meaningless diagrams on whiteboard: 'vernacular vs perfunctory modes of action'.

After 45 minutes: Any questions?

When I reached the request for 'any questions' after an excruciating, seemingly endless 45 minutes I asked the students whether they knew what I'd been doing? They had been remarkably patient throughout, chatting while something was supposedly being fixed but focusing back on me immediately when requested. After the 30 minutes mark I noticed some students were becoming amused and were trying to stifle giggles, but the majority seemed to take the 'lecture's' sequence of collapses at face value.

Most of the students seemed unsure as to the implication of my question but someone eventually asked tentatively whether it had in fact been (gulp) a performance? So at that point I switched to 'normal' mode and a discussion ensued about the essential performative aspect to even the most familiar, habitual activities. It was agreed that a conscious acknowledgement of the performed dimension of any given situation was a condition of performance art per se and that attempting to lecture on the subject without deploying this consciousness was intrinsically a contradiction.

The subject was also raised about the inert objects/paraphernalia of the lecturing trade and that they seemed to take on a 'life' of their own during the performance-lecture. Someone pointed out this was reminiscent of silent cinema comedy and indeed, preparing the 'Collapsing Lecture', I was influenced by an article titled 'Slapstick Theory' (2007; 19), by Brian Dillon in which he proposed: 'just as humans are rendered thing-like, so by the logic of slapstick things themselves start to rebel, to take on a life of their own'.

While we were discussing these and other ideas in the 'question and answer' session I experienced the very curious sensation of being unable to return to the 'normal' discursive mode upon which lecturing is premised and I kept lapsing back – compulsively – into the 'collapsing' state. Brian Dillon, in the same essay cited above, mentions the slapstician's 'tragic impossibility of escaping oneself', describing how the subject of the pratfall or collapse experiences a curious split (which I had throughout the 'Collapsing Lecture') into 'the falling self and the observing self'. This split is at the core of performance art generally, and so it was with some vindication, (I was alert to the 'career suicide' element to the 'Collapsing Lecture') that I felt sure I had hit the mark precisely midway between performance and lecturing in a visceral as well as theoretical way.

'Collapsing lecture 3' – The Whitechapel Gallery (19th June 2009)

Gavin Butt was to curate a conference day titled 'Performing Knowing' at the Whitechapel Gallery and invited me to continue developing the 'Collapsing Lecture' as part of it. I felt it was worth taking the piece further since I'd been rumbled by a significant section of the student audience at Goldsmiths, and thought that it could be done more schematically and with greater subtlety. Gavin's précis seemed appropriate:

> 'It (ie: the day) raises issues about the efficacy of performance as 'convincing' scholarly argument; about the ethics and politics of performance presentation'.

By agreement again the audience would not be forewarned of my 'real' intention and I decided to explore this version of the performance more as an extended put-on than as a sequence of slapstick actions as in the Goldsmiths version. I also wanted to work closely with the technical staff at the Whitechapel's lecture theatre and so I arranged to visit Richard Johnson and Nicola Sim the week before. They were enthusiastic about the concept of the 'Collapsing Lecture', and had their own horror-stories of technical mishaps to share.

Admirably, they were undaunted by whether the piece might cast aspersion upon their professional efficiency and so we spent an hour together exploring the Theatre's technical facilities to devise a repertoire of collapses and mishaps.

Additionally, to heighten the Collapsing Lecture's veracity to that of a conventional one, I provided Gavin [Butt] with an 'abstract' for him to circulate in advance [he has characterized this mannered style of academic writing as 'sclerotic theory' (2005)]. This 'abstract' was stylistically similar to the type of thing I wrote whilst developing and presenting parts of my Doctoral thesis at conferences in the mid-1990s. It is worth reproducing here since in fact it is a disguised description of my lecture's actual concerns, but expressed in a wildly abstruse, 'academic' prose (5) that was an equivalent 'put-on' to the eventual performance-lecture itself:

'Performance: The Unwalled Laboratory', or: 'A Language in Search of its Metalanguage'

ABSTRACT:

For the artist, performance provides a medium to make statements about the physical language of everyday living; through which, that is, to experiment and then formally present a metalanguage of gestures, interaction, object-deployment, utterances and so on.

But performance also occurs apart from this 'laboratory' of controlled experiment that proposedly produces a designed impartation of meaning and its reception. Beyond the 'walls' of this lab, at the intangible periphery of a staged event, there will always exist supposedly surplus occurrences that in themselves invite interest and observation. Here, unaccountable, (yet equally valid), autonomous accidents, disruptions or alimentary spasms of intent arise to defer the willed direction of meaning (ie: on the part of both the artist and the audience).

My question is: how can this phenomenon be represented? Can there be a language that does not have a metalanguage? In this presentation I will explore how perfunctory, habitual acts – subjected to the laboratory of performance – can unexpectedly, perhaps unwelcomely, become alien, confusing or awkward. I will attempt to demonstrate how an unanticipated 'turn of events' can rear up, intractable to will, to ultimately surpass intent.

This excess (to requirement), I will argue, is in fact an ungovernable vernacular issuing from the metalanguage circulating around any given performance. Thus, in a schematic, perhaps fanciful model, performance is an 'unwalled laboratory' that can always reward observation beyond its proposed frame.

This time, at the Whitechapel, I delivered the performance in a more deadpan way but with the added, helpful factor that the theatre technicians, Richard and Nicola, distracted much of the attention as they fussed about, seemingly in the throes of a nightmare technical meltdown. This diversion allowed me to explore another aspect of formal lecturing that is incompatible with performance art: its dependence on the lecturer's air of authority and control over the situation. Often, performance requires the artist to relinquish precisely these aspects in order to open the work out to unpredictable responses and occurrences (such as unexpected malfunction or collapse).

And so, I performed more 'realistically' as a haughty, authoritative figure constantly undermined by the repeated flickering on and off of the auditorium lights, extreme microphone feedback and a shivering light projection. Having unpadded the doors just outside the theatre, they would bang loudly when people passed through, whilst Nicola and Richard climbed onto the stage pretending to assist me for lengthy periods, thereby adding further plausibility to the ruse. Chloe Edwards was again present as my interpreter and during the lengthy periods of repairing the fake technical breakdowns we conducted banal conversations in sign language once again. Part of Chloe's 'character' was to play a truculent, unhelpful jobsworth and so, when asking her verbally for even minor assistance on stage she would chastise me with a response to the effect that she was there only to sign-interpret.

I had made two video works which I introduced at length titled 'Stick 1' and 'Stick 2'. These were made to be stylistically reminiscent of video art identified with 'structuralist' minimalism of the 1970s: in the first a handheld stick cautiously enters the frame but as it reaches the front of the camera, the video is edited to 'stick' in a visually equivalent way to a vinyl record. Maintaining that this 'sticking' was down to malfunctioning equipment, another bout of wiring and knob-twiddling ensued in the control booth (visible through a window onto the theatre). Abandoning 'Stick 1', I requested we play 'Stick 2': another banal piece in which a hand in close-up attempts to open a pot of glue until, once again, the DVD disc apparently becomes stuck.

And so it went on, the audience becoming fidgety during the excruciatingly dull and stuttering 'Lecture', which, while being painful to watch, somehow managed to kill 45 minutes. Resolving to end this 'Collapsing Lecture' in a different way to the one at Goldsmiths, I wanted to avoid the gradual slide back into the 'normality' of the 'question and answer' session. However, I did want the audience to realise that the whole 'lecture-performance' had been a put-on. The solution was satisfyingly simple: having achieved the 45 minutes, I collected my notes and stood dramatically poised as if about to attempt another restart, but instead froze in place, holding the pose for 5 very long minutes. This 'freeze' effectively served notice to the audience that all had not been what it seemed and, as I looked out at them, I could see the audience's dawn of realisation as they started to laugh and debate what on earth had just happened.

Postscript

Not long after the Collapsing Lecture at the Whitechapel Gallery, I was brushing up on my knowledge of mid-20th century existentialism and came across the following text in one of those philosophy 'Introduction' books rendered through cartoons:

'In Kean (1953), Sartre comes close to saying that since we have no choice but to play a role, we should do so with a conscious enthusiasm that may even give us a degree of authenticity' (Thody and Read 1998:107). For the introduction to my book in 2008, *Performance / Video / Collaboration*' (p15) I had been interviewed by Marquard Smith to whom I described my performance works as a series of 'mock-authentic' portrayals of ' sham-shamans, cod-feral children, charlatan Saints, bogus hermits and dubious monsters. . .' To this list could now be added 'the Collapsing Lecturer' who (following Sartre) whilst being a 'played role', had also managed to give audiences interested in performance art 'a degree of authenticity'.

FIGURE 14.2 Aaron Williamson (2015) *Demonstrating the World*. Performances at Rainham Sheds and Experimentica Festival, Chapter, Cardiff

Williamson enacts everyday tasks such as opening a cupboard, removing a jacket, or sitting on a chair, with detailed step-by-step instructions – both reinforcing and destabilising their apparent familiarity. 'Demonstrating the World' is presented on a purpose-built mobile performance platform that houses a radically displaced domestic interior. Designed in collaboration with architect Ida Martin and built by Studio LW, this unique series of household objects provides an opportunity to demonstrate the sculptural qualities of ergonomic design. For more about this on-going project go to: http://demonstratingtheworld.tumblr.com/ Reprinted by permission of Aaron Williamson. Performance at Rainham Sheds: Photo by Manuel Vanson. Performance at Experimentica Festival, Chapter, Cardiff: Photo by Warren Orchard. Supported by Unlimited; celebrating the work of disabled artists, using public funding by the National Lottery through Arts Council England, Arts Council of Wales, Creative Scotland and Spirit of 2012.

PART IV
Technologies/materialities

Over 20 years ago, Lennard Davis looked at contemporary cultural theory, with its new interests in embodiment, otherness, transgression and hybridity, and had this to say:

> The disabled body is a nightmare for the fashionable discourse of theory, because that discourse has been limited by the very predilection of the dominant, ableist culture. The body is seen as a site of *jouissance*, a native ground of pleasure, the scene of an excess that defies reason, that takes dominant culture and its rigid power-laden version of the body to task. The body of the left is an unruly body; a bad child thumbing its nose at the parent's bourgeois decorum; a rebellious daughter transgressing against the phallocentric patriarch. The nightmare of that body is one that is deformed, maimed mutilated, broken, diseased. … Rather than face this ragged image, the critic turns to the fluids of sexuality, the gloss of lubrication, the glossary of the body as text, the heteroglossia of the intertext, the glossolalia of the schizophrenic. But almost never to the body of the differently abled.
>
> (1995: 5 italics in original)

Cyborgs, robotics, bodily augmentation, technological innovations in prosthetics, digital technologies and responsive materials can all suggest seductive, gorgeous and unexpectedly novel forms of engagement with corporeality. But scholars writing from the standpoint of disability persistently ask – what kinds of bodies are assumed here, and which technologies are noticed, which ignored? Vivien Sobchack, for example, in her seminal writing on prosthetics (2006), unpicks the problematic romanticisation of disability-as-metaphor that is predominantly concerned with rethinking normal bodies, *not* with better understanding the complex intersections of ability and disability. She contrasts this to her own experiences of living with an artificial limb. Whilst prosthetics and other forms of bodily augmentation are often written about as excitingly disruptive, this is only because they disrupt the *abled* body. This is not reflected in the experience of disabled people, where technologies play different and various roles – both practically useful and complicatedly reinforcing a 'publically perceived normalcy' (2006: 23).

Technologies, then, (both old and new) cannot be separated out from their embodied use in particular situations – both materially in everyday life and conceptually in theory and critique. In 'Where does the person end and the technology begin?' Peter Anderberg illustrates this very directly. He describes how his wheelchair naturally augments his own body, and then considers why technologies that support disabled people are named and imagined differently to those used that support 'normal' bodies, as well as the anxieties and discomfort such 'assistive devices' produce in non-disabled people.

In 'The prosthetic imagination: enabling and disabling the prosthesis trope' S. Lochlann Jain also explores the tendency to mythologise prostheses, and the contradictions between an imagery of 'superhumanity' and the actualities of technologies that both enable and disable, dependent on the social, spatial and material practices through which they are enacted. By considering the writing of Mark Wigley on prosthetics and architecture (1991) as an example, she shows how actual bodies come to disappear in conceptual framings of body–technology interactions; and how technologies become generalised, naturalised and de-politicised as 'obviously' enabling and improving.

This leads Jain to ask the question 'how do body-prosthesis relays transform individual bodies as well as entire social notions about what a properly "functioning" physical body might be?' The next two contributors to this section investigate this in relation to the often ignored and more mundane technologies of everyday life – disability aids and public toilets. Bess Williamson in her article 'Electric moms and quad drivers: People with disabilities buying, making, and using technology in postwar America' explores the aftermath of the US polio epidemic from the 1930s to the 1950s, and how it generated a 'tinkering' culture and network amongst survivors and their families and friends. She explores the sharing of inventive homemade devices for making everyday life easier for disabled people, but also how these operated as strategies for negotiating ' being disabled' in and against the medical and social practices of the period. Here, then, the adaptation of existing technologies is revealed as one of the means through which disadvantaged groups attempt to make sense of, and survive, in the world. Williamson argues that in this case survivors groups focused on becoming more integrated and normalised as a 'form of self-preservation in a society that presented few options for people with disabilities to live independently'.

In 'Pissing without pity: Disability, gender, and the public toilet' David Serlin shows how – ten or so years later – disability rights activism in the US was increasingly refusing such a model, instead challenging discriminatory social notions of disability, particularly around access to public spaces and buildings. As he writes:

> for many disability rights activists in the 1960s and 1970s, the built environment served as an immediate conduit to social tolerance and inclusive citizenship. Accommodations – physical and social, symbolic and material – such as curb cuts, wheelchair ramps, and teletypewriter devices, and transportation options such as kneeling buses were envisioned as technologies of empowerment that would inspire a more fully democratic society.

Here, demands for accessible public toilets were not just about functional provision, but also concerned more complex, often competing claims for dignity and equity.

By tracing the history of the disabled toilet as 'a technology that ostensibly neutralizes social difference', Serlin is able to unravel some of these problematic relationships across disability, gender and sexuality. He explores the effects on toilet design and usage of an assumption of individuality and independence, rather than of collective care and interdependencies; and of the erasure of gender and sexuality in provision for disabled people. He argues that we need to recognise the extent to which the categorisation and design of public toilets continue to be delimited by the framings of heterosexual male privilege, whilst at the same time 'harnessing the power of gender non-normative critiques of the public toilet' to explore alternatives.

Finally in this section, Ingunn Moser examines the interrelationships between disability and contemporary technologies, particularly environmental control systems. 'Disability and the promises of technology: Technology, subjectivity and embodiment within an order of the normal' explores in detail how one severely physically disabled man (who she calls Jarle) engages both practically and subjectively with the technologies that give him some control over his living situation. For Moser, Jarle both subscribes to, and enacts, a particular mode of masculinity as independent, controlling and fully competent, enabled through a complex array of supporting equipment. This is underpinned, in turn, by the privilege of individual wealth that (usually) obscures how close he is to potentially 'returning' to dependency on others and on wider social policies and services.

Moser takes this as an example of how individual agency is assumed to be located in normal bodies, and can thus be adapted to disabled bodies through the merely functional process of 'making normal' such bodies via technologies. Yet, what being disabled reveals is that agency is *not* located *in* bodies but mediated *between* them, and between bodies, artefacts, spaces and social structures. With abled bodies, the distributed and differential nature of agency tends to fade into the background and not be noticed. With disabled bodies, though, such assumptions of individual embodied agency become visible and immediate, thus present as problematic, because disability 'does not fit with the standardized environments that allow agency to flow without constant interruption'.

The process of using technologies as 'compensation' for having a disability thus exposes the underlying inadequacy of assumptions about independent subject-centred agency. Whilst new technologies are important in enabling disabled people to be 'competent normal subjects', this is gained at the expense of critically challenging individualist, masculinist and privileged definitions of what constitutes ability. And it perpetuates the simplistic division between ability and disability, normal and deviant, which constitute some people as disabled in the first place.

How then can we get beyond the two tendencies critiqued in a variety of ways by the contributors in this section: either treating particular bodily enhancements as abstracted, mythologized and weighted with a figurative potential disassociated from real bodies, or seeing technologies as neutral, unproblematic and practical improvements that can help to 'normalise' disabled people? After all, both of these tendencies have resonances within architectural theories and practices. To return to Sobchack: this is about how to integrate conceptual and discursive engagements with everyday, and material practices, rather than to keep them apart (or even oppositional). Theoretical frameworks are not separate from, but completely entangled with, practicalities. Ideas about technologies – and the enactments through which these are constituted – are in fact simultaneously 'in and out of focus' dependent on the specific, embodied context:

> …in most situations, the prosthetic as lived in use is usually *transparent*; that is, it is 'absent' as in the rest of our body when we're focused outward to the world and successfully engaged in the various projects of our daily life. Ideally incorporated not 'into' or 'on' but 'as' the subject, the prosthetic becomes an object only when a mechanical or social problem pushes it obtrusively into the foreground of the user's consciousness – much in the manner in which a blister on the heel takes on an objective presence that is something other even though the body's own bodily fluid and stretched skin constitute it.
>
> (Sobchack 2006: 22–23, italics in original)

In this understanding, technologies *do not* take on a life of their own. Prosthetic and other technological devices – including those that take their shape through buildings and spaces – are an integral part of our more general lived perceptions and experiences, and thus of our assumptions about what is normal and what not. It is therefore important to critically engage with how different technologies come to be imagined, articulated, implemented, enacted, adapted and contested; how they can act to enable rather than disable in different contexts; and how they can be used to reinforce and perpetuate, or challenge and transform, existing inequalities in everyday social, spatial and material practices. As all the writers here acknowledge, analysing and then intervening in this sphere is not an easy or straightforward task. It is fraught with complexities and tensions. But that is not a reason not to try.

Recommended further reading

Cachia, A. (2015) 'The (Narrative) Prosthesis Re-Fitted. Finding New Support for Embodied and Imagined Differences in Contemporary Art', *Journal of Literary & Cultural Disability Studies* 9(3): 247–264.

Davis, L. J. (1995) *Enforcing Normalcy: Disability, Deafness, and the Body*, London: Verso.

Goggin, G. and Newall, C. (2002) *Digital Disability: The Social Construction of Disability in New Media*, Washington, DC: Rowman & Littlefield.

Kafer, A. (2013) *Feminist Queer, Crip*, Bloomington, IN: Indiana University Press.

Mol, A. (2002) *The Body Multiple: Ontology in Medical Practice*, Durham, NC: Duke University Press.

Mol, A., Moser, I. and Pols, J. (eds) (2010) *Care in Practice: On Tinkering in Clinics, Homes and Farms*, Bielefeld: Verlag.

Ott, K., Serlin. D. and Mihm, S. (2002) *Artificial Parts, Practical Lives: Modern Histories of Prosthetics*, New York: NYU Press.

Roulstone, A. (2016) *Disability and Technology: An Interdisciplinary and International Approach*, London: Palgrave Macmillan.

Serlin, D. (2004) *Replaceable You: Engineering the Body in Postwar America*, Chicago, IL: University of Chicago Press.

15

WHERE DOES THE PERSON END AND THE TECHNOLOGY BEGIN?

Peter Anderberg (2006)

Excerpt from doctoral thesis, 'FACE: Disabled People, Technology and the Internet' (2006) CERTEC, Division of Rehabilitation Engineering Research, Department of Design Services, Lund University Sweden pp 40–47, http://www.arkiv.certec.lth.se/ doc/face/Anderberg_Peter_FACE-doctoral_thesis.pdf.

It is difficult, often meaningless to try to figure out where the person ends and the technology starts. You touch the ground and feel the pavement with your wheelchair and when you turn around, your wheelchair turns with you. You are part of a functional system consisting of your body, your wheelchair and the ground beneath you. The boundaries you have for experiencing the world go beyond the physical limitations of your skin and are determined by the system for experiencing the world in which you exist.

In his book, *Steps to an Ecology of Mind* (1972), the cybernetics pioneer Gregory Bateson illustrates this point with the example of a blind man with a walking stick.

> Where do I start? Is my mental system bounded at the handle of the stick? Is it bounded by my skin? Does it start halfway up the stick? Does it start at the tip of the stick? But these are nonsense questions. The stick is a pathway along which transforms of difference are being transmitted. The way to delineate the system is to draw the limiting line in such a way that you do not cut any of these pathways in ways which leave things inexplicable.
>
> (Bateson., p. 459)

Bateson's view is that the information received through the cane is directly relayed to the person's mental system and processed as any other information received, for example, by the eye or the finger: "There are lots of message pathways outside the skin, and these and the messages which they carry must be included as a part of the mental system whenever they are relevant" (ibid., p. 458).

The image of the prosthesis as an extension of the body, and an enhancement of the bodily functions evokes many connotations and thoughts. In her book, *The War of Desire and Technology at the Close of the Mechanical Age*, Allucquere Roseanne Stone (1995) describes her feelings after attending a lecture given by the physicist, Stephen Hawking. Stone starts off listening to Hawking outside the overcrowded auditorium through the Public Audio system (PA), but decides she wants to go in and see and listen to him in person.

> Sitting, as he always does, in his wheelchair, utterly motionless, except for his fingers on the joystick of the laptop; and on the floor to one side of him is the PA system microphone, nuzzling into the Votrax's tiny loudspeaker...Exactly where, I say to myself, is Hawking?...In an important sense, Hawking doesn't stop being Hawking at the edge of his visible body. There is the obvious physical Hawking, vividly outlined by the way our social conditioning teaches us to see a person as a person. But a serious part of Hawking extends into the box in his lap. In mirror image, a serious part of that silicon and plastic assemblage in his lap extends into him as well... No box, no discourse...On the other hand, with the box his voice is auditory and simultaneously electric, in a radically different way from that of a person speaking into a microphone. Where does he stop? Where are his edges?
>
> (ibid., p. 4–5)

Stone sees the prosthesis in the shape of a speech synthesizer. Her fascination with how Hawking "extends" into a piece of technology and her thoughts on his vocal presence and displacement in time and space, could in one way be seen as typical for the time, at the beginning of the era of information technology. This "extension" of Hawking into the speech synthesizer is not fundamentally different from how people can be seen as extending into a computer or an email or a chat room, when using that kind of text-based conversation. The limitations of the prosthesis of written communication, as well as the habit of answering email without too much time for reflection, are limiting factors that are taken for granted today. One could easily argue that it is the format of an IRL (In Real Life) lecture that creates a discrepancy between how the prosthesis in the form of an external speech synthesizer is experienced, relative to using the voice from one's vocal cords (internal speech synthesizer). Sarah S. Jain puts it as follows:

> Questions of human-prosthesis or human-machine interfaces are central to one's active agency in a community embedded in prefigured modes of technological praxis that always already privilege certain body configurations.
>
> (Jain, 1999: 41)

It is easier for the person using the prosthesis. It is first and foremost about function, and the desire to perform and control this function. But secondly, the function is inscribed in a system of internal and external perceptions of this technology, and the integration of technology into the self is not unproblematic (Sobchack, 1995).

Hernwall uses the concept "cyborg" when considering a human being with his or her technology as a functional unit. He sees the cyborg as a "human who incorporates technology and its affordances into her own essence to the extent that the technology becomes a self-evident prosthesis" (Hernwall, 2001; translated from Swedish by the author). Hernwall views the cyborg concept as a chance to move beyond technology's limitations and focus on the individual's opportunities and terms in the utilization of technology. He argues, with support of Haraway (1991) and Landow (1992), not to separate the human from her technology and not to evaluate the individual based on norms of technology and its limitations, but to focus on the potential gain for the individual.

The concepts of cyborg and prosthesis as metaphors with unnecessary or undesirable connotations are not unproblematic when used to describe a person's usage of technology. For the modern person, different products and artefacts as functional aids have become so natural that they already represent an extension of the human. For disabled people where technology is often necessary to perform a function, it should also be seen as a natural element. Technology can be individual and accompany the person, such as a wheelchair, hearing aid or glasses. Or it can be built into the surroundings such as ramps, door openers, hearing loops, contrastive signage, etc. This does not make the question of where the borders between man and technology are drawn uninteresting. But based on the expanded technological perspective applied in this thesis, the focus on the desired function means the person is central and that the technology used is problematized from the individual's wishes concerning the function.

The influence of artefacts and technology on disabled people

In 1985, you could receive a mobile telephone as a disability aid in Sweden, but today it is an obvious functional aid for almost all people. What is considered to be assistive technology versus standard technology is determined by the culture, location and point in time. Progress often lags behind. In an interview for *Time Magazine*, the Independent Living Institute Director, Adolf Ratzka, posed the rhetorical question about the situation in Stockholm: "I cannot go by ordinary bus," he says. "Is that because I had polio 37 years ago, or because the transport authority doesn't buy buses that will work for everybody?" (*Time Magazine*, 1998–1999). Technology for adapting buses has existed for quite a while, and the only reason why so few buses are adapted are political and financial.

Science and technology studies examine how commercial, political, cultural and social values and interests steer scientific and technological developments and vice versa. One subject in the field is Actor-Network Theory (ANT) (Akrich & Latour, 1992; Callon, 1986; Law, 1987). In ANT all actors, human or non-human, are considered equally important for the analysis and are referred to in the same vocabulary. An example: The mobility of a wheelchair-user is dependent on a large number of factors, among them, the design of the wheelchair, the funding to buy a suitable wheelchair, the user's ability to manage and control the wheelchair, the organization and accessibility of the environment in which the wheelchair is used, etc. It is up to the person doing the analysis to find the relevant factors for the action under analysis.

It may seem radical and somewhat ethically shaky to grant objects and artefacts the same explanatory status as human beings in an actor network. But for the ANT analysis, the border between humans and machines is not the issue, and their equity in the analysis "does not mean that we have to treat the people in our lives as machines. We don't have to deny them the rights, duties, or responsibilities that we usually accord to people. Indeed, we might use it to sharpen ethical questions about the special character of the human effect – as, for instance, in difficult cases such as life maintained by virtue of the technologies of intensive care" (Law, 1992). Ingunn Moser and John Law (1999) have used ANT to elaborate on disability and ability in a series of stories about Liv, a wheelchair and personal assistance user. They find that the "links between dis/ability and subjectivity are close – which means that any study of the materialities of dis/ability is incomplete unless it also attends to the continuities and discontinuities of subjectivity" (ibid.). Liv is inscribed in an enabling network, with technological aids and personal assistants, giving her a considerable amount of agency in some of the environment she exists in, less in others.

Moser and Law see Liv as a cyborg, "in the sense, that she is irreducible to a unity, even though 'she' is also a unity" (ibid.). They make a convincing argument in showing how dis/abilities are created in networks made up of heterogeneous, material, and specific entities as described from this particular ANT perspective.

Myriam Winance (2006) has studied how persons with neuromuscular problems test their wheelchairs. With Actor-Network Theory as a starting point, and also leaning towards phenomenology, she analyses the network made up of the wheelchair user, wheelchair, technical personnel, etc. The negotiation of various compromises and improvements during the trial period gradually transforms the entities involved, including the person's identity, and the relations between them. [...]

About the need to define assistive technology

The US National Council on Disability has summarized the focus on the qualitative and quantitative difference in the use of technology as follows: "For Americans without disabilities, technology makes things *easier*. For Americans with disabilities, technology makes things *possible*" (Radabaugh, 1988). Among all the definitions of assistive technology, I want to cite two. First, the US law text:

> Any item, piece of equipment, or product system, whether acquired commercially off the shelf, modified, or customized, that is used to increase, maintain, or improve functional capabilities of individuals with disabilities.
> (The US technology-related Assistance for Individuals with Disabilities Act of 1988, Section 3.1. Public Law 100–407, August 9, 1988)

Second, the international standard, ISO 9999, which defines a technical aid for disabled persons as:

> Any product, instrument, equipment or technical system used by a disabled person, especially produced or generally available, preventing, compensating, monitoring, relieving or neutralizing the impairment, disability or handicap.
> (International Standardization Organization, 2002)

The only absolute reason to define assistive technology is the funding people with disability can receive to obtain assistive devices. If I drive my three-wheeled powered wheelchair scooter to work, is it an assistive technology device or is it a vehicle with which I go to work? When my personal assistant drives it home, because I have to go somewhere else with a car, is it still an assistive technology device? When my sons borrow the scooter to drive around the park outside the house because it is fun, does it cease to be an assistive device and become a toy?

I cannot get off it and walk if I wanted to, but my personal assistants and my sons can. I, my scooter and the surrounding environment make up a functional system that is necessary for me to get to work. That is what makes it an assistive technology device for me. But if I try to go down to the beach, in the fine-grained sand, or go up two stairs, it ceases to assist me and to be assistive technology, because it does not provide any function in those settings. But does the actual wheelchair cease to be an assistive device at that moment?

Some of my assistants refuse to sit on my powered scooter when they need to take it home or anywhere else. Sitting in a wheelchair makes them feel uncomfortable, although not in a physical sense. Some of them would rather take on the complicated and risky task of walking next to it, trying to manoeuvre it from the side. One assistant who was driving it home said that he felt that everyone was staring at him, and he felt so uncomfortable that he had to stop and get off the scooter and walk around for a while so that everyone would see that he did not have an impairment. He felt that people's attitudes towards him changed considerably when he was driving the scooter. The actual device signals the disability. That is not inherent in the technology per se, however, but an aspect of the attitudes towards disabled people is transferred to the technology associated with them.

16

THE PROSTHETIC IMAGINATION

Enabling and disabling the prosthesis trope

S. Lochlann Jain (1999)

Excerpt reprinted from Science, Technology and Human Values *(1999) Winter, 24: 1, 31–33, 38–40.*

Freud ([1930] 1962) echoed a common teleological fantasy of the promises of prostheses by pronouncing:

> With every tool man is perfecting his own organs, whether motor or sensory, or is removing the limits to their functioning. ... Man has, as it were, become a prosthetic god. When he puts on all his auxiliary organs he is truly magnificent: but those organs have not grown on him and they still give him much trouble at times.
>
> (p. 42)

Freud's hesitant caveat surely referred to his own prosthesis, a palate replacing an original that was removed as a result of throat cancer in 1923. His prosthesis, without which he could neither speak nor eat, caused him immense pain. Yet, if he went without it for more than two hours, the tissue circumscribing the chasm between the mouth and nasal cavity would shrink – necessitating yet another agonizing fitting session and prosthesis (Wills 1995). Freud's speculations on godlike magnificence stem, perhaps, from his own all too mortal experience with a technology that simultaneously enabled and wounded him. Freud's simultaneous embodiment of faulty technology and extreme optimism about technology's promise illustrates the contradiction that I explore in this article.

First introduced into English in 1553 as a term of rhetoric meaning "attached to" or "setting forth" or, literally, "adding a syllable to the beginning of a word," prosthesis did not come to bear the medical sense of the "replacement of a missing part of the body with an artificial one" until 1704 (Wills 1995, 215). As a trope that has flourished in a recent and varied literature concerned with interrogating human-technology interfaces, "technology as prosthesis" attempts to describe the joining of materials, naturalizations, excorporations, and semiotic transfer that also go far beyond the medical definition of "replacement of a missing part" (Bateson 1971; Brahm and Driscoll 1995; Gray 1995; Grosz 1994; Scarry 1994; Seltzer 1992; Sobchack 1995; Stone 1995; Wiener 1985; Wigley 1991; Virilio 1995).

There can be no question that one is constituted by interaction with one's physical surroundings. Hegel argued that the object takes the person from abstract to actual, and Marx claimed that one's humanity is contingent on working with the world. As a number of recent theorists point out, the use of tools and artifacts requires a degree of incorporation into the body; Elaine Scarry (1994, 97) calls this process the "labor of animation." Yet, surprisingly little work has been done on the everyday social, economic, and semiotic mediations that occur between persons and objects in the technologically infused spaces of life in the United States. Perhaps this is the fascination held out by "prosthesis" as a potential theoretical tool with which to account for the ways in which technologies are always and never constituent of the body. On the other hand, the proliferation of its use has overburdened it; theories themselves can be, after all, both enabling and wounding.

My stakes in the trope of the prosthesis are twofold. First, I believe that the ways in which human bodies are marked, maimed, constituted, conjured, extended, and wounded by both the physical and the auratic properties of commodities is an imperative concern that arises in areas as diverse as tort law, product design, health insurance, and marketing. My second concern is how a promising trope that might in some measure account for the technological extension of bodies can also take into account the variety of bodies and the social construction of abilities. Certain bodies – raced, aged, gendered, classed – are often already dubbed as not fully whole. This article, then, cavorts along three overlapping, richly intertwined (and ultimately inseparable) axes of identity: social (race, gender), physical ability and disability, and another category that considers identity as a correlate to technology. "Prostheses" are discursive frameworks, as well as material artifacts. Thus, the concept of prosthesis gives rise to a set of key questions: Which bodies are enabled and which are disabled by specific technologies? How is the "normative" configured? How does the use of the term prosthesis assume a disabled body in need of supplementation? How might the prosthesis produce the disability as a retroactive effect? Where and how is the disability located, and in whose interests are "prostheses" adopted?

With these questions in mind, […] I examine the rhetorical ways in which prosthesis encodes disability and the notion that the prosthesis compensates for some sort of physical disability – although this disability may be in relation only to the realm of the possible rather than a handicap in the way in which it is classically conceived. […]

Mark Wigley (1991), in his influential article "Prosthetic Theory: The Disciplining of Architecture," provides a […] set of assumptions about the enabling functions of prosthesis, situated more closely in the body and intimate spaces of everyday life. (He) takes the departure point as the body, although his larger thesis integrates architectural theory into the figurative body of the university: the architectural discipline itself figures a "prosthesis." His article is interesting first of all because it has provided a model for other arguments about prosthesis that similarly rely on metaphors rooted in the (disabled) body, and also because of the specific assumptions about the body that underpin the theory. Wigley writes that the prosthesis is "always structural, *establishing the place* [to which] it appears to be added" (p. 9; emphasis added).

A blurring of identity is produced by all prostheses. They do more than simply extend the body. Rather, they are introduced because the body is in some way "deficient" or "defective," in Freud's terms, or "insufficient," in Le Corbusier's terms. In a strange way, the body depends on the foreign elements that transform it. It is reconstituted and propped up on the "supporting limbs" that extend it. Indeed, it becomes a side effect of its extensions. The prosthesis reconstructs the body, transforming its limits, at once extending and convoluting its borders. The body itself becomes artifice.

(Wigley 1991, 8)

The significance of this argument lies in its testimony to the difficulty of delineating the physical and psychic boundary of the body in the circuits produced through bodies and their relationships to material and social structures. I take Wigley's comments to be emblematic of a particular reading of prosthesis within a conventional mind-body dualism that directly follows his own quotation of Lou Andreas Salome's claim that the body is always a prosthesis of consciousness, and Freud's contention that consciousness itself is a prosthetic attachment. In this version of the body and its prosthesis, the body is always already a prosthesis of the mind, the mind of the drives; and the semantic content of mind, body, and prosthesis is evacuated. Indeed, the body undergoes complete erasure as it takes on the nuances of the superbeing, as in Freud's ideal of the "prosthetic god."

Wigley's (1991) notion of the defective and insufficient "body" depends on the transformative capacity of supportive limbs that reconstitute the entire collaboration as "artifice." But the unspecified deficiency, the generalized defect or absence, seems to naturalize the general form of the prosthesis and the body alike. If the prosthesis presumes an enhancement to the "natural" body in this account, then bodies and prostheses are already naturalized rather than being understood as socially constructed. In asserting that the interface of body and prosthesis is not a one-way intervention and that boundaries are easily blurred, analyses such as Wigley's are useful. However, Wigley stops short of genuinely considering how interfaces between the body and prosthesis operate in dynamic tension with the body, and he (perhaps unwittingly) takes for granted a politics that considers the body, as a general category, to be a "side effect" of technologies of production. This version of prosthesis naturalizes the enabling facets of technology such that a microscope becomes just more vision, or a printing press just faster, permanent speech. Furthermore, the metaphors of prosthetic extension are presented as if they are equivalent in someway, from typewriters to automobiles, hearing aids to silicone implants, allowing each of us to extend ourselves into the world on the liberal premise of free choice. The disabled body appears here again as a generalized form in need of "propping up." The metaphorical model for this general theory gets lost in "the body" and the "supporting limbs" in a simultaneous apotheosis (the article is illustrated with all sorts of quaintly dated pictures of prostheses, not of amputees) and disavowal (no real discussion of bodies and the multiplicity of "disabilities"). Both the prosthesis and the body are generalized in a form that denies how bodies can and do "take up" technologies of all kinds. However, the specificities demand to be read faithfully. How do body-prosthesis relays transform individual bodies as well as entire social notions about what a properly "functioning" physical body might be?

Not calibrating the differences in disability, ability, and godlike ability leads to the obliteration of issues of bodily expectations; that is, what it means to be a productive and consumptive agent at the turn of twenty-first-century capitalism. I emphatically do not mean that distinct boundaries can or should be drawn and maintained between some naturalized and organic "body" and various forms of prosthetic attachments; rather, I mean to bring into relief the material differences of absences. For example, both artificial legs and automobiles are media of mobility that also can be the cause of multiple sites of wounding (from blistering and cutting in the first, to pollution and road kill in the second). Both require and assume certain political, biological, and semiotic conditions of possibility that are enabling in certain capacities for certain people and disabling for overlapping sets of bodies and interests. But the differences in social constructions of "needs" remain unaccounted for by Wigley's (1991) theorization – the material differences of the deficiencies, or defects, that "need" supplementing or correcting are not specified.

17

ELECTRIC MOMS AND QUAD DRIVERS

People with disabilities buying, making and using technology in postwar America

Bess Williamson (2012)

Excerpt from American Studies *(2012) 52: 1, 5–29.*

In 1958, a young mother named Ida Brinkman reflected on her life after contracting polio. Five years had passed, she told the readers of the *Toomeyville Junior Gazette* – a magazine for polio survivors – since she had become paralyzed in her arms, legs, and abdomen. After a two-year stay at the Toomey Pavilion, a rehabilitation center in Ohio, she admitted she was "secretly frightened" about how her home life would be, using an iron lung at night, a "chest shell" respirator during the day, and a wheelchair to get around (Brinkman 1958). "This is beginning to sound pretty grim," she wrote, admitting concern about resuming her life as a wife and mother; still, she continued, it really hadn't been so bad. At home, her husband Johnny had taken up shopping duties, while her three children helped keep house and prepared their own breakfasts. A cartoon accompanying the article showed Ida in a wheelchair, a tube at the center of her chest connecting her to an electric respirator, as her little daughter gazed at her quizzically. "Bonnie gets acquainted with her Electric Mom," read the caption. "To my glee," Ida reported, "she accepted me."

Ida Brinkman's life as an "Electric Mom" extended beyond the plug-in chest respirator that drew her chest muscles up and down. She ticked off a number of tools she and her husband selected and, in many cases, altered to support a busy and active life at home. Johnny constructed a flat aluminum connector for the hose of her respirator, making the breathing apparatus less bulky. The electric Hoyer lift that Ida used to get into and out of bed included "a new wrinkle added to it ala hubby [sic]": a shorter hook that could be used to help her into the car, effectively making two lifts out of one. Ida's father built a portable wooden ramp that was "especially practical for steep declines"; she used an extended cord and headset for the telephone; and, in case of "urgent s.o.s." while alone with her children, she had an "alarm box which can be set off by a kick of a foot" (ibid. 15).

In a photograph in a later issue of the *Toomey J Gazette* (as the magazine came to be known), Ida appeared propped up in bed, reaching past the customized respirator tube to type with a "mouthstick" – probably a simple dowel with a sharpened tip – clenched between her teeth. Surrounded by her collection of medical, homemade, and standard consumer technologies – the chest shell and "mouthstick," the hospital bed, an over-the-bed desk, and the typewriter – Ida showed herself in action as a writer and editor.

Ida Brinkman was one of a growing number of people with significant physical impairments who lived at home in mid-century America. Given innovations such as the "iron lung" respirator and advancements in spinal surgery, people who survived disabling diseases and accidents were more likely to live long, relatively healthy lives after the 1940s. The new medical specialty of "rehabilitation" emphasized a return to home, rather than long periods of convalescence, as the end goal of treatment. Despite these improved prospects, however, individuals with paralysis, missing limbs, weakened joints or restricted breathing left the hospital for home lives full of physical obstacles. Accommodations now familiar in the United States, such as wheelchair ramps, automatic doors, accessible toilets, and "kneeling" public buses were not widely extant until the late 1970s and 1980s (Percy 1989, 110). The American National Standards Institute published "Specifications for Making Buildings and Facilities Accessible to and Usable by Handicapped People" in 1961. While these standards were officially adopted for new construction in many states and municipalities, few accessible buildings and streetscapes were actually built in the 1960s. Features such as curb cuts, wheelchair ramps to public buildings, and accessible restrooms were not common sights in American cities until the mid-1970s, and in many locales were not widespread until new federal regulations were adopted in 1977, following nationwide protests by disability rights groups. Before that period, people with disabilities could expect minimal assistance in navigating public spaces, let alone the built-in obstacles of the postwar home.

In the *Toomey J Gazette*, Ida Brinkman and dozens of other people with disabilities documented their work as tinkerers, taking a "do-it-yourself" approach to available consumer and technological products. Adapting specialized medical and assistive equipment, altering their own houses and everyday household tools, and using forms of transportation – especially customized automobiles – to move beyond the home, these individuals used technology to fill a gap left by postwar medical treatment of disability. The growing rehabilitation movement in American medicine presented an optimistic view of disability, trumpeting the individual's ability to "overcome" given proper care and training. The message that new specialists delivered was equal parts encouragement and pressure, particularly when it came to physical mobility and access. Prodding people with even severe paralysis to learn to walk, eat, and care for themselves without outside assistance, specialists found the solution to accessibility in individual effort, not physical accommodation. For people with disabilities and their families, technological tinkering could alleviate some of the burden of everyday access.

People with disabilities documented their technological experiments in community periodicals of the time and in retrospective memoirs and oral histories. The *Toomey J Gazette* provides a remarkable source of first-person accounts of technological adaptation in the 1950s and 1960s. The sometimes-annual, sometimes-quarterly magazine began with

125 mimeographed copies compiled by "three horizontal and two vertical editors" – three women paralyzed by polio and two volunteers they had met undergoing rehabilitation at the Toomey Pavilion (one of whom, Gini Laurie, remained at the editorial helm throughout the magazine's run). Circulation grew to 2,000 in one year and exceeded 10,000 by 1967. The *Gazette* focused with great detail on the logistics of everyday life for those with significant physical impairments. The editors defined their audience as primarily "respos," or those who had had respiratory cases of polio, but eventually included people with spinal cord injuries and other "quads" and "paras," medical shorthand for quadriplegics and paraplegics. As many as three quarters of the articles in a given issue addressed technological issues, from user reports on assistive devices in the regular "Equipment" column, to an eclectic mix of do-it-yourself and imagined products under the headings of "Oddments and Endments" and "Brainstorms."

Although this publication provides the most extensive store of amateur technological reports, other periodicals targeted towards physically disabled readers also addressed these activities. In the Paralyzed Veterans of America's *Paraplegia News*, which began publication in 1951, a different population shared suggestions on such things as new automatic and remote-control appliances, preferred commercial and homemade solutions for wheelchair ramps, and customized, hand-controlled cars. Personal documents and oral histories gathered from the generation who survived the peak epidemic of polio fill out the picture of a population who managed daily activities through technological adaptation.

These accounts reflect the demographics of people with disabilities who were able to live at home, create their own forms of access, and share them through community publications during this era. The polio survivors and veterans featured in the *Toomey J Gazette* and *Paraplegia News* represented two small slices of the population of people with disabilities who garnered disproportionate public attention and resources. In the years following World War II, the U.S. government funneled significant resources into helping disabled veterans transition into civilian life, promising that they, like their non-disabled fellow service-members, would share in the prosperity of postwar life. Likewise, during and after the peak polio epidemic of 1937–1955 – a period when more than 415,000 cases of the mysterious and terrifying virus were reported (declining only after Jonas Salk's discovery of a vaccine) – polio became central to a new public discourse on charity and public health. In the 1940s and 1950s, organizations such as the National Foundation for Infantile Paralysis (NFIP, also known as the March of Dimes) launched campaigns including mailings, advertisements, television shows, and public events, cementing disability – and specifically polio – as a key target for private philanthropy (Oshinsky 2005, Wilson 2005, Brandt and MacPherson Pope 1997).

In addition to these attributes of relative privilege among the disabled population, the writers for disability-community periodicals narrated a version of adaptation within the relatively limited arena of middle-class, largely white America. In the twelve-year run of the *Gazette*, there were only three photographs of identifiably non-white Americans: two of them, of apparently African American men, appeared in an article about activities at a residential institution, reflecting the disproportionate representation of poor and nonwhite persons among the institutionalized population. The majority of photographs and articles presented adults who were young and white, and lived with parents or spouses. The technological work they did also reflected these demographics, with mentions of single-family houses, cars, and a variety of consumer gadgets at the ready. The format of these community magazines also echoed the mass media of their time, with reports on home renovation and consumption delivered in the bright, optimistic tone of magazines such as *Ladies' Home Journal* or *Popular Mechanics*, with their respective gendered associations.

Emerging from the rigidly regulated world of postwar domestic life, these accounts present a view of technological work as both a triumph and a defense. On the one hand, the buoyant tone of many of the accounts related the joy of finding tools and arrangements that improved everyday routines. On the other, these writings depicted a population highly conscious of the stakes of rehabilitation. As disability historian Henri-Francois Stiker has observed, the modern concept of "rehabilitation" hewed to existing categories of respectability and acceptance (1999). For each group considered viable for rehabilitation, there remained those considered incapable or unworthy of "return" to mainstream society. Adapting to the physical spaces and tools of white, middle-class life was crucial to maintaining status among the "acceptable." The enthusiasm of innovation and discovery in these narratives often shields an underlying fear about the possibilities of failure.

Technology from hospital to home

For many people learning to live with new disabilities, the trials of finding useful and usable technologies began in the hospital. As patients moved from surgery or emergency medical care to rehabilitation, their doctors, insurance companies, and medical administrators exerted control over choices of medical equipment and physical treatment. Members of the medical establishment often ignored or dismissed patient input, assuming that whatever medical supply companies or research programs produced would be good enough. The difficulties encountered by people with disabilities in acquiring, fitting, and using assistive technologies introduced them to life on the margins of American culture. For many, experiences negotiating with and circumventing the medical equipment system instilled a sense that consumer products and technologies provided useful raw materials, not end products. Suitable, comfortable, and appealing tools for everyday life would require further intervention.

Rehabilitation treatment, whether in long-term residential facilities or outpatient clinics, involved a panoply of "adaptive" or "assistive" technologies. When acute cases of polio caused paralysis in the chest cavity, patients battled the peak of symptoms in an "iron lung" respirator, a full-body-sized tube with bellows-like air pressure mechanisms that forced the lungs to expand and contract. Rehabilitation doctors and therapists encouraged "weaning" from the iron lung, but many severely paralyzed patients continued to rely on the iron lung either full-time or for limited periods each day, particularly while sleeping. Respiratory polio came with a variety of other accoutrements, including "chest shell" respirators that were less powerful than the iron lung but wearable in a sitting position; rocking beds, which used a see-saw motion to force air in and out of the lungs through gravity; and standing beds, to which patients were strapped in order to come to a vertical position and stretch their legs (Wilson 2005: 154). Patients with partial or even complete lower-body paralysis wore steel braces to support and straighten their legs and corsets to make their spines straight. The expense of this equipment was offset by support from charitable groups such as the NFIP, private insurance, or veterans' subsidies for many, but the tasks of selecting, fitting, and adapting these tools were battles of their own (Wilson, 2005: 134).

The equipment that people with disabilities obtained through hospitals often fell short of ideal fit and function. Choices of equipment were limited: wheelchairs came in three sizes (adult, junior, and child, with the occasional addition of "adult narrow"), and braces in just small and large versions. Moreover, equipment was assigned based on a doctor's prescription, so the type of device might reflect an overly aggressive rehabilitation plan. Polio survivors remembered painful hours of trying to walk in steel braces and balancing precariously on crutches. Throughout the mid-twentieth century, doctors insisted that all but the most severely paralyzed patients should be able to walk, so long as they had, in the words of orthopedist Dr. Philip Lewin, "one good arm and an arm good enough to hold a crutch, [and] at least fair intelligence" (Wilson 2005: 154). Patients often dreaded fittings of whatever medical "appliances" they used, as well as follow-up appointments with doctors and therapists who might assign new, stringent exercise routines and brush aside complaints about discomfort. Mary Grimley Mason wrote in her memoir of polio that a tight new brace "felt as if a hundred little fingers were pinching me up and down my legs," and that the brace-maker adjusted it only reluctantly, mumbling that she "was probably just not used to them" (2000: 23).

At a time when Americans had access to an ever-widening array of consumer goods in hardware, grocery, and department stores, the market for medical equipment remained firmly separate from mainstream consumer culture. Though the number of Americans who used assistive technologies was significant – one survey conducted in the late 1950s counted just under a million Americans who used wheelchairs, arm or leg braces, or artificial limbs (Brandt and MacPherson Pope 1997: 2–3) – manufacturers made few direct appeals to users, opting instead to target marketing to medical providers and hospitals. Medical professionals and equipment suppliers asserted that patients needed their help and guidance. Mid-century practitioners would likely agree with the doctors, prosthetists and orthotists interviewed for a survey in 1976: they all agreed that "consumers [should] avoid the risks of shopping on their own in all instances" (Bruck 1978: 147).

Even when patients did order their own equipment, they encountered an industry not organized to serve the individual buyer. Many wheelchair companies produced a variety of metal goods, of which hospital supplies were just one category: for example, the Colson Corporation, one of the largest wheelchair makers of the mid-century, manufactured carts and casters, and, as an offshoot, wheelchairs. Their catalogs devoted dozens of pages of wheels and carts before one or two with wheelchairs. Descriptions were brief, with listings simply declaring "sturdy construction" or touting easily replaceable, smooth-running "ball-bearing wheels" (Colson-Cleveland Co. n.d.). The images in Colson's catalog showed wheelchairs in hospital settings, not in homes or in public. In these trade materials, wheelchair companies affirmed the message that these were products for medical, not consumer use, and that people who used wheelchairs did not fit easily into home or public environments.

In addition to prescribing assistive equipment to help patients "overcome" disability, rehabilitation specialists acknowledged the difficulty many people with disabilities would still have operating everyday products and navigating standard environments. At the New York Institute for Physical Medicine and Rehabilitation, leading rehabilitation expert Dr. Howard Rusk included a "Self-Help Aids" workshop where staff showed patients simple tools for daily activities. For example, eating utensils could be altered with metal loops or foam padding, or razors and combs given extended handles for easier manipulation (Lowman and Rusk 1962). Few of these devices were manufactured products, but instead were devised over the years by staff and patients themselves. Rusk and his New York Institute colleague, Edward Lowman, wrote in articles and books of the lack of mass-market products for everyday lives of people with disabilities. They suggested, however, that many solutions could be found among the "gadgets" of mid-century consumer culture. "The 'gadget era' has particular implications for the person with a physical limitation," they wrote in a 1953 volume entitled *Living with a Disability*, urging readers to look beyond medical supplies. They encouraged patients to "try the hardware department, and other stores, or seek help from your classified telephone directory for further assistance on what's available or new," and noted that the do-it-yourself magazine *Popular Mechanics* was "full of useful suggestions" (Rusk and Taylor 1953).

"Self-Help Aids" of the postwar era are artifacts of Rusk's and other rehabilitation specialists' assumptions and expectations about disability. Disability historians have traced the many ways in which cultural values influence medical prescriptions. For example, the ever-present goal of "walking again" was a relatively new development in the mid-twentieth century. In earlier periods, when one's gait was socially paramount, this goal was not a primary interest since walking imperfectly was seen as worse than not walking at all (Ott 2002). The "independence" that doctors and therapists, and even patients, envisioned for life outside the hospital entailed adjusting oneself – "helping" oneself – to fit into a society with virtually no accommodations for disability. Traces of the "Self-Help" approach to rehabilitation remained as people with disabilities and their families sought to address the realities of life in the houses, on the streets, and among the products of 1950s and 1960s America. The so-called "gadget era" did present many potentially useful objects for people with disabilities, though few of these were manufactured with that intention. As chronicled in the *Toomey J Gazette* and *Paraplegia News*, people with disabilities made creative use of available products and materials to improve their own comfort and pursue their own interests. As they renovated and rearranged their houses, selected useful products from the mainstream marketplace, and altered others to make them useful, people with disabilities found ways to use technology to their own advantage. In doing so, they asserted their own presence in a world that largely ignored them.

Constructing a life at home

In his memoir of polio, Charles Mee remembered stumbling home the night the virus set in. Out on a high school double date at a friend's house, the ache in his belly and weakness in his legs became too much to ignore. Mee described making his way home on rubbery legs, a trek of "maybe fifteen blocks… these were small-town suburban blocks, brick and wood frame houses from the twenties and thirties mostly, some new ranch houses with big lawns both front and back; I knew just which back yards I could cut through" (Mee 1999).

This was the neighborhood he would leave that night to go to the hospital, and the same one to which he would return after treatment for acute polio and rehabilitation for paralysis in his legs. The particular setting of Mee's upbringing was common to many polio patients. The disease disproportionately affected white, Western and Northern communities of the United States, areas in which rigorous use of modern sanitation reduced the chances that children would develop immunities through exposure in infancy, and where geographic mobility increased the spread of the virus. People of all regional and class backgrounds who became disabled in the postwar decades returned from hospital care to a world that was not built for them. Details in architecture and landscape they may never have noticed before – the slope of a driveway, the height of a countertop, a tricky doorknob – now had new significance.

The worlds that polio survivors described in the *Toomey J Gazette* would have been familiar to Mee. Many of the magazine's correspondents depicted lives in single-family houses in the suburbs or small towns, surrounded by consumer technologies and accompanied by a nuclear family. The work they described, too, echoed familiar activities of middle-class, mid-century domestic life. Whether sewing their own slipcovers and curtains, installing cabinets in their kitchens, or soldering and welding in their garages, middle-class homeowners performed a variety of creative and skilled work to maintain and improve their homes, furnishings, and automobiles (Goldstein 1998). Do-it-yourself activities allowed men and women of the 1950s and 1960s to express individual taste and style in the mass-produced consumer culture of postwar America. These projects carried high stakes for people with disabilities. Eating, dressing, bathing, and getting around the house provided a sense of personal independence, particularly for those who, like Ida Brinkman and her fellow "respos," required family or attendant help in many basic activities. If suburbanites who built additions to their subdivision houses and accessorized their cars did so to distinguish themselves as tasteful or creative, people with disabilities did the same work to fit in, to prove their worthiness of inclusion in a society where many considered the severely disabled to be incapable or unworthy of rehabilitation.

For households with a physically disabled family member, the house itself often presented a technical challenge. Small, single-family houses were common in many American communities, from urban neighborhoods built in the 1920s and 1930s for a new industrial working class to the rapidly expanding suburban "Levittowns" constructed in the post-World War II years (Clark 1986). The efficient, modestly scaled Levittown Cape Cod houses that were first built in 1947 on Long Island included doorways 28 to 29 inches across and hallways not much wider. Standard-sized wheelchairs, which typically measured 25 to 29 inches in width, not to mention iron lungs and rocking beds, fit awkwardly into these spaces.

Contributors to the *Toomey J Gazette* wrote of small and large home renovations to accommodate wheelchairs and other equipment. One "Brainstorms" column included the suggestion of cutting a hidden swinging door into the existing wall adjacent to a doorway, providing space to move equipment when needed. With the hidden door "papered to match," the house's décor could remain complete even with the new presence of unwieldy equipment. Other suggestions hinted at the same problem. Readers wrote in with descriptions of improvised "wheelchair narrowers," contraptions that consisted of wire hangers or a belt looped around the handles to draw a chair inward by an inch or two to fit through these passageways. Commercial versions were also available, promising to squeeze a wheelchair in by as much as four inches using a hand crank mechanism.

As they conducted patchwork renovations on their houses, families sought to balance practical concerns of disabled and non-disabled inhabitants. One couple sent the *Toomey J Gazette* photographs of the clever ramp built by the husband for his wife. The long ramp, calibrated to keep a gentle slope, hugged the side of the house, leading to a side door. Since this addition blocked the front stoop, the man added a trap door for the ramp that could be raised off of the stoop to give access to the steps below. Inside houses, barriers built into the layout were even more difficult to remedy. In some cases, families had to move or conduct extensive renovations to accommodate a disabled relative.

Ed Roberts, a prominent participant in the Disability Rights Movement, was almost completely paralyzed from the neck down after his teenage case of polio. His family moved to a new house after he returned from the hospital so his hospital-style bed could fit in the dining room (Roberts 2000). The family organized activities together around Ed's bed rather than transfer him to a wheelchair and strap him into a corset for everyday activities. His wheelchair was of limited use beyond the threshold of the house, given poor street-level accessibility during his adolescence in the late 1950s.

Over the weeks and years following rehabilitation, families continued making adjustments to their everyday environments. Women who took on homemaking roles after polio or other paralyzing conditions became consumer product testers, vetting new gadgets and materials from the standpoint of their own physical needs. The 1968 issue of the *Gazette* featured an eleven-page section on "Homemaking" with forty readers' suggestions on arranging kitchens, doing laundry and cleaning, and cooking from wheelchairs or with limited manual strength or dexterity (*TJG* 1968, 16–27). Their notes describe everyday life within households where floor plans, furniture, and appliances posed obstacles. Readers wrote of such practices as filling a pot on a stove one cup at a time, as the height of the standard stove made it awkward for a wheelchair user to lift a full pot from sink to stovetop. To use outlets at the back of countertops – hard to reach from a wheelchair or with limited mobility – they connected extension cords, while mirrors hung over stoves to provide a view over back burners. Some contributors described the challenge of using small drawer handles and stiff faucet heads with shaky or paralyzed hands. "I walk my fingers around the sink to the water faucet," wrote one; another used "a long wooden spoon with four nails in the bowl section" to twist the small handles (Figure 17.1). Some wrapped rubber bands around "small slick knobs," while one contributor, perhaps frustrated with various experiments, suggested that "if you are unable to use the hardware on drawers and cabinets, just skip it and fasten on inexpensive towel racks for easy pulling."

People with disabilities balanced the frustration of contending with the design of mass-market products and furnishings with pride and delight in finding the right tools for a given job. Contributors advised careful selection, suggesting that fellow readers "[t]hink about weight as opposed to ease of handling… Handles are quite different on knives. Very individual decision is needed here." This kind of individual decision-making, based on one's relative strength and coordination, as well as personal taste, engaged people with disabilities in an intensive form of shopping. The women homemakers – as well as some

- "I use a long wooden spoon (A) with four nails in the bowl section. Wrap nails with electrician's friction tape."
- English booklets list both homemade and commercial models of tap turners:
  (B) For a single bar tap, a groove whittled out of a cylindrical piece of wood.
  (C) A tap turner made of a length of wood, a drilled hole, and two cup hooks.

FIGURE 17.1   Faucet turners in "Homemaking," *Toomey J Gazette* 1968, 18

Reprinted by permission of Post-Polio Health International.

bachelors and husbands – who wrote to the *Gazette* took careful note of brand names, noting specific models of automatic can openers, electric knives, and mixers they found most promising for persons with limited hand strength. For those who fumbled with glass and ceramic dishware, new plastics offered more than just colorful or airtight storage: "Bless Tupper Ware [sic]" wrote one contributor, "you can drop it and it doesn't fly open and spill contents."

The *Gazette*'s special "Homemaking" section echoed the tone and look of mainstream domestic literature. The section featured a two-page drawing of ways to arrange kitchen equipment, with crisp outlines of pegboard storage, lazy Susans, and pull-out shelves to hold efficient, organized rows of pots and pans, dishes, jars, and bottles. The outlines of dishware and familiar appliances recall the geometry of mid-century consumer magazine layouts, which showed products floating in space or tidily arranged in ideal kitchens. [...]

Although their needs were more specific than those of homemakers concerned about storage space or matching belts, contributors to the *Toomey J Gazette* showed some of the same creative excitement over the world of consumer products conveyed by [mainstream magazines]. A page from a Spring 1960 *Toomey J Gazette* featured sixteen different designs for homemade "mouthsticks" – tools used in writing, typing, and other actions in replacement of hand movement – in a cheery, sunburst layout (Figure 17.2). People with limited use of their arms and hands used these sticks, assembled from various available materials, to type, write, dial the telephone, and do other small tasks using their mouths for leverage.

In the mouthsticks illustration, the simple implements radiated out from a sweetly outlined mouth. One stick with a paintbrush attachment pointed inward, completing the illustration and suggesting the action of "mouthstick" painting, a common hobby taught in rehabilitation centers and often celebrated in the *Gazette*. The materials used in the "mouthsticks" were of the moment, incorporating the novelties and synthetics that were newly available for affordable consumption in postwar America (Meikle 1995). Most were made of simple dowels or pens, with rubber erasers or eye-dropper tips to provide a soft surface to be gripped between the teeth. Some incorporated more novel materials, such as

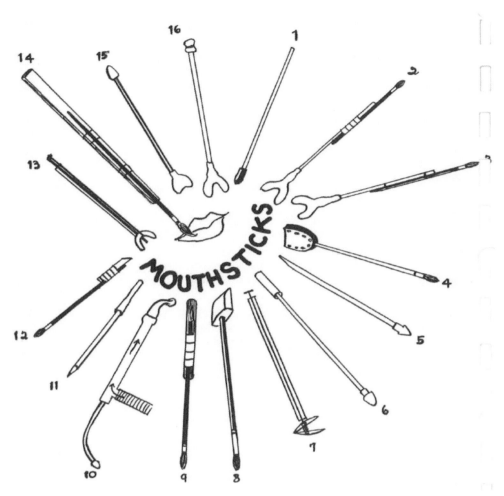

FIGURE 17.2   "Mouthsticks," *Toomey J. Gazette* Spring 1960, 8

Reprinted by permission of Post-Polio Health International.

the rubber heel of a doll's shoe, a cigarette holder, and a spring-loaded clamp that could be operated with the tongue. The illustration of these different options and the cheery mouth at the center takes a cue from the visual culture of the 1950s: we can almost imagine a similar layout in an advertisement or magazine editorial showing kitchen utensils or lipsticks. In these collections of readers' inventions, the *Gazette* translated some of the light, joyous appeal of mid-century consumer culture into the world of highly specific and personal assistive equipment.

The upbeat, optimistic tone in which *Toomey J Gazette* contributors described finding the right drawer-pull or the best page-turner suggests a distinctive role for consumption in the lives of people with disabilities living at home in this era. Disabled people's interactions with the world of products and spaces reinforced their difference from the mainstream. In these intra-community documents, they presented technical adaptation as part of familiar, expected activities of household life, akin to the housework or home decoration discussed in women's home magazines of the time. Layouts such as the "Homemaking" article depicted the tasks of finding and customizing consumer goods as components of class- and gender-specific roles of the postwar household. In a final category of adaptation – the use of automobiles – people with disabilities took a creative approach to technology to take part in public life as well.

Access on the road

Although people with disabilities could create a modicum of access within their own houses, they could do little to change the abundance of street-level barriers in American cities and towns. Accessible architectural features in public buildings such as curb cuts, widened doorways, and public toilets with spaces for wheelchairs were virtually unknown until the 1960s, when the American National Standards Institute first provided a guide to these measures. Even as local and state governments adopted this standard, compliance was uneven. As one polio survivor described his life after returning from rehabilitation in the 1950s, his family's alterations to their house to facilitate wheelchair use were "enough to help, but not enough to get me accustomed to living in any sort of specially constructed world" given pervasive barriers beyond the household (Wilson 2005: 137).

In this era before ramps and curb cuts, people with disabilities found ways to move about in their communities, albeit with great difficulty and unpredictability. Some wheelchair users told of riding in the street to avoid curbs, entering traffic until they found driveways or other breaks in the sidewalk. They relied on friends, family, or passing strangers to help them get over curbs and up steps, an uncomfortable and often frightening experience. Portable ramps – both commercially manufactured and homemade – could be used to traverse a small number of steps, but required the help of a companion to set up and take down these cumbersome devices (Brinkman 1958: 15). Some industrious inventors devised more complicated devices, such as the "outdoor elevator" described by Vince La Michle in a 1959 article in the *Toomey J Gazette*. Powered by a 1/6 horsepower motor, the elevator raised or lowered at one inch per second and was, according to La Michle, "certainly easier than a ramp." Whether rudimentary or complex, these devices were attempts to bridge the gap between desires to enter the public world and physical barriers in the American landscape.

One of the most-discussed tools in the *Toomey J Gazette* and the *Paraplegia News* was not a piece of "assistive" equipment, but an iconic technology of the twentieth century: the automobile. Historians of American car culture have used the term "automobility" to describe the way in which the personally driven motor vehicle became linked with a sense of freedom and independence (Wajda and Shuemaker 2008, Flink 1988, Hounshell 1984). For drivers and passengers with disabilities, automobility had an extra layer of meaning, as it offered a chance to move freely past street-level barriers such as steps and curbs. In pursuit of what the *Toomey J Gazette* called "quad driving," people with disabilities became auto enthusiasts of a very distinctive kind. They took advantage of new technological devices in the mainstream automobile market, including the automatic transmission and various add-on accessories. Others enlisted the help of family members and independent mechanics to assemble and accessorize cars that could be driven by hand or with one leg. "Quad drivers" operated on the fringes of an existing technological culture, deploying car technologies to achieve their own form of automobility.

The first devices that allowed people to drive with limited or no use of their legs targeted an elite audience. De Soto developed a custom hand-operated model for President Franklin Delano Roosevelt in 1933, which he test-drove at Warm Springs, the polio rehabilitation center in Georgia that he founded and visited throughout his presidency. In the following year, Warm Springs' in-house magazine, the *Polio Chronicle*, extolled the promise of several new, patented hand controls to let "the President and other polios become their own chauffeurs." Self-driving was not a necessity for many Warm Springs patients, since they came from social circles where employing drivers was the norm, yet hands-on experience had its own appeal. Despite Roosevelt's enthusiasm, the hand controls of the 1930s and 1940s were difficult and dangerous to operate. Driving a manual-transmission car entirely by hand meant juggling levers for brake, clutch and accelerator pedals, all the while operating the steering wheel. Inventors tried several approaches to dual clutch-brake hand control, including buttons and switches allowing the driver to use the same handle to depress the clutch alone, or the clutch and brake pedal at the same time. Still, these left the driver with no option for using the clutch and brake pedals independently: for example, to ease the brakes off slowly when starting on a hill.

The greatest technological improvement for drivers with disabilities was not a new hand control, but the automatic transmission. Automakers introduced a few models with automatic transmissions in the early 1930s; they became widely available in the 1940s. This new technology coincided with a new demand for cars for people with disabilities, particularly disabled veterans, who could receive a government benefit of up to $1,600 towards the cost of a hand-controlled or otherwise adapted vehicle. This subsidy made cars and driving a distinct component of veterans' culture, with models and accessories discussed in a special "Hand Controlled" column in the *Paraplegia News*. The column's author, Joe Jordan, wrote of the special connection veterans had to cars, noting that "there is very little controversy and possibly near unanimous agreement that 'mobility,' our effort to get around once again, rates a high and very special place among [veterans'] problems"(Jordan 1951, 7). As Jordan noted, however, not all available vehicles worked well for the needs of disabled drivers. Even with an automatic transmission, drivers had to vet the specific configurations available, since many name-brand "drives" still required some clutch-shifting by foot. The Oldsmobile Hydramatic, for example, which had a clutchless shift mounted on the steering column, was "widely used" among veterans, according to Jordan.

In the pages of the *Toomey J Gazette*, people with disabilities and their families showed off a broad variety of customized cars that went far beyond commercially available models with hand controls and automatic transmissions. Fred Taberlet's "Para-car," described in a 1968 *Gazette* article, was a Citroen 2 with the top and back completely cut off to make room for an elevating floor. Accompanying photos featured Taberlet lifting himself, wheelchair and all, into the driver's position, eliminating the need for help in climbing in or stowing a wheelchair (Figure 17.3). The customized vehicle had not one, but two sets of hand controls, so that Fred

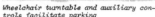

Wheelchair turntable and auxiliary controls facilitate parking   *Two positive sets of driver-operated locks secure wheelchair*   *To this prototype will be added rear door, enclosed top and windows*

FIGURE 17.3   Para-Car, in "Equipment," *Toomey J Gazette*, 1968, 54

Reprinted by permission of Post-Polio Health International.

could rotate himself completely and drive the car forward or backwards, keeping him from having to crane his neck to see while driving in reverse. Fellow *Gazette* contributors showed off other creative approaches to driving. One British reader displayed a pair of leather "mitts" that helped him grip his hand controls. For those with more coordination in their legs and feet than upper extremities, an American entrepreneur developed "a kind of ski boot attachment" that could be used to operate the steering wheel by foot.

"Quad driving" was for passengers as well. For people whose impairments meant that they would never drive themselves, riding in a car was a way to participate in public without being strapped into a wheelchair, let alone contending with steps, curbs, and the stares of other people. Ida Brinkman named drive-in movies as a favorite activity of her family and showed off a special head rest she used in the family car. Other families went to dramatic lengths to include their disabled relatives in car travel. More modest than Fred Taberlet's Citroen convertible, but no less inventive, were the alterations the Ray family made to their family car so they could travel with their daughter Susan and her reclining wheelchair and respirator. Susan's father Cecil, a Baptist minister (and "mechanical whiz," according to his wife), removed both front and back seats on the passenger side of their 1955 Ford station wagon and installed a smooth platform for her recliner. He moved the post between doors and re-hinged the rear door, making a double-wide entrance for Susan in her chair. The Rays traveled with a small homemade trailer with compartments for extra respiratory equipment and doors on both sides for easy access. The family reported traveling in this car from their home in San Antonio, Texas, to the Southern Baptist Convention in Miami, Florida, and national parks in the Smoky Mountains, Yellowstone, Mesa Verde, Arches National Monument, and the Grand Tetons (*Toomey J Gazette* 1961, 18–19).

The customized cars driven by people with disabilities and their families likely turned heads in town, but they were not alone on the road. Local mechanics who installed specialty equipment had experience customizing cars for other uses, such as hot-rodding or camping. They might even come across familiar equipment. For example, many catalogs and articles on adapting cars for use by people with disabilities suggested installing a knob for the steering wheel to aid driving with a prosthetic or a single hand. These knobs were not exclusive to the community of disabled drivers, but were available as options from major car manufacturers throughout the 1940s and 1950s. Though they ostensibly offered a more secure grip for any driver, they were known colloquially as "necker's knobs" for one-handed drivers who kept one arm around their dates. Disabled drivers had most in common with fellow tinkerers who altered sedans, station wagons, and buses for long travel. As the auto historian Roger White has explored, in the days before the commercial introduction of "Recreational Vehicles," car owners made motor homes by removing back seats to make room for beds, hanging curtains for privacy, and installing shelves to hold amenities like camp stoves and washtubs. One driver described the joy of a "carefree Gypsy life" to be found in extended trips in his custom motor home (White 2000).

People who altered familiar technologies to work for their own disabled bodies shared much with their nondisabled counterparts. As with household technologies, these tools took on different meaning for a population for whom everyday mobility could be difficult or impossible. "Quad driving" provided a version of access that people with disabilities could not experience on the sidewalks of their hometowns, but it also allowed disabled drivers to participate in the American hobbies of picking out, tinkering with, and finding adventure in automobiles.

Technology and rights in the twentieth century

These disabled tinkerers and inventors join a long history of consumers who reconfigured products of the mass consumer culture for their own needs. Historians have traced examples of consumers who altered mass-market technologies for their own distinctive uses, from rural farmers who used early automobile motors to power appliances in their houses, to indigenous groups who appropriated tourists' video cameras to tell their own stories of cultural endangerment (Kline and Pinch 1996, Eglash 2004). For those on the fringes of society, appropriation can be the only means of finding tools to operate for one's own needs – be they mechanical, personal, or cultural – when manufacturers and advertisers target other populations. In claiming consumer citizenship in these ways, people with disabilities acted from a position of marginality, but did not seek to resist or subvert mainstream culture. Their technological efforts were acts of integration, not resistance, into the normative roles for men and women of their class and race.

These technological efforts to "fit in" to the spaces of postwar life were a form of self-preservation in a society that presented few options for people with disabilities to live independently. When "Electric Mom" Ida Brinkman confessed to *Toomey J Gazette* readers that she had been "secretly frightened" about her return home, she voiced a feeling many readers and writers of the *Gazette* surely felt. The insecurity with which people with disabilities lived during this time should not be underestimated, particularly for those whose injuries or impairments necessitated daily assistance. The specter of being locked away in an institution hovered over many, especially those who were poor or whose disabilities resulted from injuries or diseases not supported by the March of Dimes or other charities. Those who returned home from rehabilitation were hardly exempt from these worries. In less optimistic narratives than those of the *Toomey J Gazette*, some polio memoirists reported isolation and mistreatment in their home lives, with their parents or spouses who left them in bed for days, withheld help in bathing or eating, or, worse, took out their frustrations in emotional and physical abuse. Even people with severe disabilities who, like Brinkman, had families willing and able to support them had to wonder what would happen if family members died or could no longer assist them. Starting with the "daily life" training they received in hospitals, people with disabilities got a strong message that they needed to show continual progress and a good attitude, lest they be labeled "bitter" or "uncooperative" (Wilson 2005: 154–155, Longmore 2003, 233). While they experienced some excitement from creative work on their kitchens, cars, and houses, these technical tasks were also a constant reminder that the burden was on them to adapt, not on the society at large to provide accommodations. Whether they performed this technological work themselves, or with the help of handy family members, adapting to the inaccessible built environment remained a private affair.

In the eleven-year run of the *Toomey J Gazette*, there were only small hints at a sense of political identity emerging from this community network. In a 1959 editorial, Sue Williams, who took on a primary editorial role alongside "vertical" editor Gini Laurie, warned readers of the *Gazette* of the need to turn the attention directed towards polio cases into long-term, sustained support. "The 'iron lung story' that has been told about each of us was a heart-wringer and a purse-opener," she wrote, referring to the pitying gaze of the mainstream media. "Now that we cease to be a sensation in this way, there is quiet un-newsworthy work for us to do," she continued, including insisting on long-term home care funds to alleviate readers' dependence on their families for care. Four years after the discovery of the Salk vaccine, these "polios" were aware that their time in the spotlight was coming to an end. Others who lived during this period later reflected on their experiences of pressure and condescension. Mary Lou Breslin, who grew up with a polio-related disability in the 1950s and 1960s and later became active in the Disability Rights Movement, remembered feeling pressured to present an image of flexibility and positivity, despite the everyday strains of operating as a wheelchair user in public. She described this false front of confidence and ease as "shucking and jiving," drawing a parallel between this behavior and African American minstrelsy (Breslin 2000).

The comparison Mary Lou Breslin made between herself as a successful rehabilitant in postwar America and African Americans who performed to white expectations reflects the perspective of one looking back, after an awakening to disability rights, at the "bad old days" of the 1950s. Like many who participated in social movements of the later twentieth century, Breslin saw the optimism and homogeneity of postwar culture as a false veneer hiding tensions that would later become apparent in the upheavals of the late 1960s and 1970s. The *Toomey J Gazette* and other disability-community periodicals conveyed a more positive tone as individuals shared their stories of returning to family and home. Searching for accessible tools in the "gadget era" – as Howard Rusk and Edward Lowman dubbed it – was a practical approach to the problem of outsider status in postwar society. In an era before civil rights laws required some measure of physical access in the built environment, people with disabilities used and adapted technologies of everyday life to close the gap between the promise of inclusion and the reality of the world in which they lived.

18

PISSING WITHOUT PITY

Disability, gender and the public toilet

David Serlin (2010)

Reprinted from Harvey Molotch and Laura Norén (eds)
(2010) Toilet: Public Restrooms and the Politics of
Sharing, *New York: New York University Press pp 167–185.*

In April 1977, a coordinated group of disability rights activists staged protest actions at the Department of Housing, Education, and Welfare in Washington, D.C. and in eight of its regional offices across the country. These demonstrators, many of whom used wheelchairs or mechanical ventilators, were fighting for the full-scale implementation of the Rehabilitation Act of 1973 and its significant Section 504, which was established to extend civil rights legislation of the 1960s by prohibiting programs that received federal funding from discriminating against people with disabilities. Historically, people with disabilities had been either segregated within or isolated from the social world for so long that their public presence typically solicited pity rather than registering recognition. In San Francisco, disabled activists deliberately defied that history by occupying the Health, Education, and Welfare offices for twenty-five days, fed and cared for by their friends and attendants as well as by local unions, Bay Area countercultural groups, and Oakland's Black Panthers that recognized in their struggle much of what other civil rights organizations, both radical and mainstream, had tried to achieve in the 1960s and early 1970s (Johnson 1983, Shapiro 1993).

Section 504 was an heir to the anti-discrimination laws that emerged from the Civil Rights Act of 1964 and from under Lyndon Johnson's "Great Society" programs of the mid-1960s that were used to redress social, structural, and architectural manifestations of a segregated society. As articulated by activist Judy Heumann, "[w]hen you erect buildings that are not accessible to the handicapped, you enforce segregation" (Zames Fleischer and Zames 2001: 68). For many disability rights activists in the 1960s and 1970s, the built environment served as an immediate conduit to social tolerance and inclusive citizenship. Accommodations – physical and social, symbolic and material – such as curb cuts, wheelchair ramps, and teletypewriter devices, and transportation options such as kneeling buses were envisioned as technologies of empowerment that would inspire a more fully democratic society. Such accommodations were also intended to challenge the legacies of "separate but equal" treatment, which for the disabled was manifest as separate vehicles and spaces rather than vehicles and spaces that were integrated (Zames Fleischer and Zames 2001: 93–102)

The lack of available toilet facilities during the occupation of federal offices in San Francisco did not prevent disabled activists from sustaining their protest but in fact may have shifted its terms, since their inability to use the toilet was both symbolic of and material evidence for their exclusion from the public sphere. As historian Joseph Shapiro has written, "[s]ome of the most severely disabled protesters were literally putting their lives on the line, since they risked their health to be without catheters, back-up ventilators, and the attendants who would move them every few hours to prevent bedsores, or who, with their hands, would cleanse impacted bowels every few days" (1993: 67). One could argue that the decision to tolerate unpleasant and potentially lethal personal circumstances in order to promote democratic goals suggests that in those difficult days of protest the human need to eliminate was more than a courageous act of civil disobedience.

By lifting the veil on their most intimate bodily functions, protesters demanded recognition that the piss and shit of the disabled were produced not by androgynous bodies or amorphously asexual bodies but by bodies shaped by the same kinds of material and experiential needs as the able-bodied. Providing public provision for disabled people thus raises broader issues of what it means to recognize "special needs" in the context of claims, sometimes competing and complex, for dignity and equity. This runs counter to the idea that providing, in minimal material terms, a place for the disabled to go to the toilet solves the problem.

How then do we begin to understand the disabled toilet as a technology that ostensibly neutralizes social difference if it exists within a public sphere that privileges able-bodied status—and a gender-normative able-bodied status at that? The premise behind the disabled toilet, after all, is that it transforms the public restroom into a level playing field; and once this field is so made, no one gets – or deserves – any further special privileges or consideration. Once there is compliance with the legislation, such as the US Americans with Disability Act (hereafter ADA), or some other regime of physical accommodation, the architectural and political deed is done. Yet this presumption of equality obscures the complex logic of the situation, at least in part because equality before the law is a paradigm that has been organized historically around white male able-bodied privilege. As anthropologist Carol A. Breckenridge and philosopher Candace Vogler have written, "The 'person' at the center of traditional liberal theory is not simply an individual locus of subjectivity (however psychologically fragmented, incoherent, or troubled). *He* is an able-bodied locus of subjectivity…who can imagine himself largely self-sufficient because almost everything conspires to help him take his enabling body for granted (even when he is scrambling for the means of subsistence)" (2001: 350 emphasis added).

The discourse of equality, then, is not always a sophisticated mechanism designed to generate respectful difference between parties with shared access to social or political power. Given what we know about the pressure toward assimilation experienced by many ethnic and sexual minorities in the United States, the discourse of equality also can be a blunt instrument used to flatten difference. As disability historian Henri-Jacques Stiker has argued, the discourse of equality for the disabled can be as oppressive as it is liberating, marking "the appearance of a culture that attempts to complete the act of identification, of making identical. This act will cause the disabled to disappear and with them all that is lacking, in order to assimilate them, drown them, dissolve them in the greater and single social whole" (2000: 128).

Much anxiety still remains at the core of contemporary encounters with difference, especially as the able-bodied must continue to grapple with tolerating the Other while valiantly struggling to defend its status as the default position of public culture. And few sites, it seems, are as fraught with encountering the terms of difference and navigating the conditions of equality as that of the disabled toilet, as evidenced by the arcane rules of social etiquette and awkward confrontations that take place at the borders of tolerance and patronizing gesture. A dam of unintended consequences can break through the discomfited silence, as the "normal" person seeks ways to not notice, avoid looking like they are trying not to notice, all the while busily defending their own capacity for privileged accomplishment.

The disabled toilet in the US emerged genealogically in parallel to other dilemmas of liberalism that continue to haunt discussions of difference. In the nineteenth and early twentieth centuries, the emergence of gender-segregated public and commercial spaces such as schools, gymnasiums, and bathhouses were closely linked to the influx of immigrants from Eastern Europe, Scandinavia, and the Middle East to large and medium-sized American cities. The example of the gender-segregated bathhouse did not by itself establish any legal or architectural precedents for disabled toilets, but it did make material the presumption among civic leaders that there was a demonstrable link between creating accessible public and commercial spaces and facilitating the hygienic and economic uplift of those at the margins (Bérubé 1984, Serlin 2004). Following the establishment of a public bath by the New York Association for the Improvement of the Condition of the Poor in 1852, free municipal baths, swimming pools, and showers for the residents of cities such as Boston, Chicago, Detroit, New York, Philadelphia, and San Francisco were considered politically and morally necessary by social reformers concerned about problems of poverty, overcrowding, sanitation, and hygiene among the immigrant groups.

While public toilets became increasingly common throughout much of the nineteenth and twentieth centuries in commercial spaces, public parks, government buildings, train stations, and transportation terminals, people with disabilities were not among those populations around which the design and functionality of public toilets were organized. By contrast, able-bodied individuals were able to meet and exceed conformity to moral and bacteriological expectations of good health in the public sphere. Even today, people with disabilities, who carry the stigma of dependence and lack of control over their bodies, have often been perniciously associated with failures, deliberate or otherwise, of personal hygiene.

As the various social and political movements of the 1960s bore their fruit, authorities responded with national design standards for updating existing facilities or building new ones (Figure 18.1). In the US, the federal Architectural Barriers Act of 1968 implemented the now-familiar curb cuts and ramps for wheelchair users. Along with the Act came a host of proposals to make resources such as public toilets accessible, though the first innovations in toilet design such as grab bars, lowered sinks, and so forth were initially developed in the 1960s for private homes and institutions specifically established for the disabled rather than for public spaces. Only later did their installation in public toilets become reality, with the rules finalized in 1980. The new stalls, known as A117.1 [in the US], were built at an increased depth of 66 inches, ten inches larger than the previous standards, and were to be built on a very slight incline from the floor so that wheelchair users could navigate and position themselves more easily within the stall and ambulant but visually impaired disabled people could "feel" a slight step up that physically distinguished the stall area from the rest of the public toilet. The A117.1 also required metal grab bars behind and to the left side of the commode that could be used by the toilet patron or his or her assistant in order to help set the body in the appropriate eliminating position (Goldsmith 2001: 79). There were analogous modifications to existing sink designs to incorporate levers with large, wide paddles that can be moved easily rather than faucets that demand greater muscle coordination and strength. These related standards of accessibility became law, in the form of the 1990 ADA, which brought with it a host of other legal mandates for equal access. It was not uncommon even in the 1970s and 1980s for disabled people traveling on public transportation, such as trains or airplanes, to have to wear adult diapers or use catheters and collection bags for the length of their journey due to inappropriate or non-existent facilities (Serlin 2006).

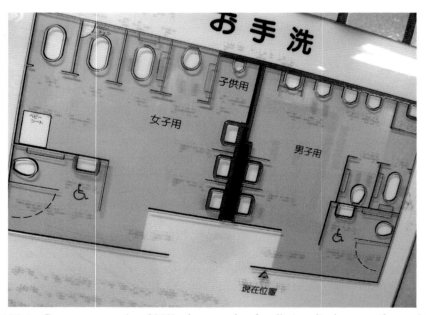

FIGURE 18.1 Contemporary (ca. 2010) photograph of wall-size display map for multi-user public restrooms, Kyoto, Japan. The map is tinted in conventional pastel colours (pink on the left, blue on the right) to indicate intended users, but it also deploys Braille lettering as well as universal access icons to indicate separate wheelchair-accessible stalls near entrances as well as the locations of sinks, urinals, and both Western and traditional (squat) toilets

To a large degree, the exclusion of people with disabilities from the composition of the public, which went largely unchallenged until the disability rights movement of the early 1970s reached critical mass, grew from the stigma historically attached to numerous forms of visible disabilities in the public sphere (Charlton 2000). It is true that veterans and survivors of at least some types of catastrophe had their injuries exhibited as examples of patriotic sacrifice. Their bodies, in the late eighteenth century and beyond, were usefully deployed rhetorically to promote national ideologies in times of crisis and war (Serlin 2006); in the US, the federal government acknowledged the specific needs of its paraplegic and amputee veterans from the Civil War onward. By contrast, many cities in the United States expanded nineteenth-century municipal vagrancy codes to prohibit people with physical disabilities from appearing on city streets. As literary historian Susan Schweik has argued in her recent monograph *The Ugly Laws*, many of these laws were not lifted until well after World War Two (2009). Those individuals who were not institutionalized or cared for at home or through local institutions or federally mandated resources such as the Veterans Administration were left to fend for themselves. Able-bodied personhood remained the default position, and the goal of rehabilitation was to integrate the disabled person back into society, but often with only primitive ideas and techniques for making it happen. So even wealthy disabled people who otherwise could design their own large and elegant bathrooms were forced to use chamber pots and other makeshift receptacles before the evolution of toilet designs dedicated to non-standard or non-normative body types, something that did not begin until the 1960s.

For much of the twentieth century, manufacturers of commodes, urinals, sinks, and faucets as well as the walls, doors, and floors that comprised standardized public bathroom fixtures were oblivious to the body with special needs (Ogle 2000). Innovations in toilet design lagged for a number of reasons—the social exclusion and disaffection of the disabled from all corners of public life, for one. But a second factor, perhaps ironic, was the ascent of mid-twentieth-century research sciences such as ergonomics, industrial design, and anthropometry that adopted a rather rigid and uncompromising sense of the "normal" physical body as the basis for design. This may have run parallel with the zeal for a generally conforming landscape with normative assumptions of physical ability as part of the iconic vision of an American nation. Any sort of distinctive body type perceived to be deviant was considered repugnant. The deployment of scientific authority and legislative barriers in the social control of difference is a testament to the power of putatively objective discourses that increasingly helped shape understandings of those who constituted the public, and those who did not, for much of the twentieth century (Carter 2007, Igo 2008, Terry 1999).

Disability itself comes in wide variations and it pays close attention to those variations to anticipate the range of potential needs. For people who use canes and crutches, for example, grab bars or roomier stalls may be a pleasing feature but ultimately an irrelevant one. On the other hand, grab bars on or near urinals may be a useful accommodation for an ambulant disabled man who is visually impaired or who uses a walker (Goldsmith 2001: 180–183). And blind people have very different sets of needs. It is important that things be maintained in standard locations, something that can conflict with innovations designed to help those with other types of disabilities as well as the general public's desires for stylistic novelty and functional design improvement.

This raises the question, as can often come up in such discussions, are: to what degree should those with disabilities strive to accommodate the world as it is, and to what degree should that other world change because there are disabled people in it? Put in a more positive way, what are the benefits to others of taking into strong consideration those with non-conforming traits? Many types of people, disabled or otherwise, have benefited from ADA and accommodations that exceed them. Clara Greed, in particular, has emphasized how many of the design principles employed in disabled toilets – doors without handles, roomier stalls, lowered sinks, and interior spaces that allow one to move around other patrons – help those who do not identify as disabled, including the elderly, the temporarily disabled, large-sized people, and parents pushing strollers. Ramps and more commodious spaces help those traveling with suitcases or making a temporary pit stop while delivering goods.

On a more profound analytic front, the disabled toilet and its attendant controversies shows us something more about the nature of "dependency"; it flags the possibility that autonomy may not, in itself, be without limits as a desirable social goal—not just for the disabled, but for people in general. Autonomy often rests on a culture of deference without intimacy, granting others the "right of way" without having the patience for empathy. The people who encounter each other in public toilets, men especially, act as independent agents tied together through little more than an ethos of benign neglect. At the same time, the homosocial space of the public toilet is, by its very nature, an intimate one that creates numerous opportunities for bonding and that also holds the potential to be erotically charged. The combination devolves to the disadvantage of those who might need help that would take the form of conversation or touching. Able-bodied culture disdains any kind of mutually supportive activity in public toilets beyond small talk and, perhaps among women, the daring move of passing a toilet roll beneath the stall door. For the disabled, the accommodative technologies available are psychic compensations for their dependence; they render invisible, at least temporarily, the vulnerability and need for "help" that dare not speak its name. This happens conjointly with the desire by authorities to lower costs by dispensing with human care personnel – nurses, social workers, domestic caregivers, and so forth – whose role is not sufficiently valued to encourage their retention. Better to replace them with architectural supports or mechanical devices. Indeed, for some disability rights activists, the person who offers toilet assistance – a set of skills largely associated with hospital care or rehabilitation medicine – is regarded as a residual effect of the medicalization of the disabled body and thus anathema.

Ultimately, however, what is accomplished by technologies in the public toilet is the loss of the exchange that otherwise might occur between human beings working with each other (Figure 18.2). Not only does the relationship between the disabled individual and the technology undergo a shift, but then so does the social connection. That is, the privileging of independence may underestimate the social and ethical values that accompany dependence: reciprocity, caring, and cooperation. This has profound implications not only for how we understand the disabled toilet user, but also for how we understand the social networks in which both the disabled and able-bodied are embedded.

In her brilliant collection of essays on the theme of interdependence as a form of political organization, *Love's Labor* (1999) philosopher Eva Feder Kittay offers a feminist critique of political philosopher John Rawls's influential work on the transformative

FIGURE 18.2 Contemporary (ca. 2010) photograph of the interior of single-user accessible toilet stall, Hamburg, Germany. While the flexible armature and flush buttons (both in hygienic stainless steel) surrounding the commode are familiar amenities of Western toilet design, the rope rigging and horizontal hold bars, which allow a wheelchair user to manoeuvre him- or herself comfortably onto and off of the toilet, are unusual for a public toilet

possibilities of cooperation and mutual obligation in a democratic society. Kittay argues that Rawls imagines a democratic ethos in which all citizens share in dividing labor equally among all "fully functional" members of the society but fails to recognize that within any social system there invariably will be individuals designated as dependents – children, the elderly, the temporarily infirm, and chronically disabled – as well as those who are designated as caregivers, those on whom dependents rely for basic human needs. At the core of such a critique, Kittay argues, is the recognition that the lack of gender specificity in Rawls's model presumptively positions a heterosexually masculine and able-bodied figure at the core of democratic discourse since women do the disproportionate amount of caregiving in our culture and have been, historically speaking, positioned more often than not as dependents themselves. "To model the representative party on a norm of a fully functioning person," Kittay writes, "is to skew the choices of principles in favor of those who can function independently and who are not responsible for assuming the care of those who cannot" (p93).

Kittay's critique of Rawls's work has much to do with how we interpret the privilege given to the body that is "fully functioning" as well as the body that eschews dependence as a marker of weakness, vulnerability, and disempowerment. Dependence, especially as it relates to the care of the self, is characteristically regarded as an obstacle to masculine self-realization and therefore a badge of emasculation. Manuals written by physicians and orthopedists for the care of disabled veterans during and after World War Two, for example, traditionally emphasized male self-reliance as part of the recuperation process in order to restore and maintain heterosexual masculinity (Serlin 2004: 39–48). And because of the freedom traditionally accorded to the male, heterosexual body in the public sphere, any body that requires some form of special accommodation or has particular needs is often regarded as feminized, as dependent. As a result, those who are recipients and/or facilitators of caregiving fight social stigmas on multiple fronts.

Although Kittay recognizes the potential for the dependent to challenge expectations of both a gendered and able-bodied public body, the greater hurdle to mutual respect and cooperation, it seems, is the way in which independence is valorized unproblematically as the ideological commitment to which the disability rights activist must pay unwavering loyalty. As Kittay writes,

> It is a source of great inspiration and insight in the disability community that independent living, as well as inclusion within one's community, should be the goal of education and habilitation of the disabled. But this ideal can also be a source of great disempowerment…[The] focus on independence, and perhaps even on the goal of inclusion when inclusion is understood as the incorporation of the disabled into the "normal" life of the community, yields too much to a conception of the citizen as "independent and fully functioning"

(1999: 171–2)

Kittay repudiates the value placed on the linkage between "independent and fully functioning" and what can be socially productive and socially valuable citizenship. In so doing, she is in effect contesting the classical demarcation of a gendered female private sphere versus the male public sphere. Privileged access to a public toilet fuses with privilege, male and able-bodied, more generally. The disabled toilet, then, is that which collapses the private – that which is gendered as female, domestic, and altogether dependent – into the public sphere, so that the disabled toilet becomes a type of *non*-male space that is conspicuously neither publicly male nor privately female. Although the disabled toilet was perhaps envisioned as a material embodiment of equal access and democratic equality, it also expresses, by its nature, the masculine principle that slippage of gendered difference risks display of weakness and dependence.

One aspect of male performativity is the use of urinals, themselves totems of masculinity. But for certain types of disability, use of the urinal becomes problematic and this poses gender-identity difficulties as they turn to toilets as urination receptacles. Hence a manual for health professionals and rehabilitation specialists published in the early 1980s counsels on the need to teach disabled men to sit on the commode for "both bowel movements and urination," ensuring that it "avoids the difficulty that some handicapped men and boys have in aiming urine while standing so that it does not splash on the seat, floor, or clothing" (Bettison 1982: 24). The task here, it seems, is on how to give disabled men, and boys as well, the repertoire for performing bodily control, overcoming avoidance of a characteristically female toilet posture. Failing to build up men's inner reserves would efface their distinction with women, destabilizing the historic male compulsion to demarcate and maintain the feminine private sphere as entirely separate from the masculine public sphere.

For all newly disabled people there are challenges in acquiring and mastering toilet skills. Men bring special baggage of not only their own immediate pragmatic goals but also gender-based dependency anxieties. These come into play in dealing with, as an adult, the most intimate bodily functions: how to raise and lower one's self from a wheelchair to a toilet seat, for instance, or how to wipe one's self while balancing on grab bars – and maintaining dignity. On a routine basis, an ambulant person who is visually impaired must negotiate the space of a public toilet alone and deal with problems, like paper towel holders placed well outside of one's ordinary reach or toilet paper that has somehow gone missing from its usual place. There may be a slippery puddle, perhaps due to a missed maintenance call, that involves danger. In his biographical analysis of the life of Leonard Kriegel, a polio survivor who grew up in the 1940s, the historian Daniel Wilson has written, "[w]hat had changed [for Kriegel] was not the masculine values he embraced but the locale in which they operated[:]…not on the athletic field or on the field of battle but in the rehabilitation hospital and on the streets of Brooklyn as he struggled to rebuild his body and to confront the barriers of an unaccommodating society" (2004: 122).

Among the challenges to dealing with the anxieties at hand, are the (literal) disabled signs that announce and confirm one's bodily separateness and, at times, re-group gender identities. Such a recalibration is evident in a photograph (Figure 18.3) taken in May 2004 at the London Chelsea Flower Show, held annually since 1913 (now on the grounds of the Royal Hospital) – the "world's greatest flower show" as proclaimed on their web site. In the photograph, one can observe the banner reading "Ladies and Disabled Toilets." Event planners know that crowd management is an organic part of any toilet landscape, manicured or otherwise, but, as those who have waited in the ladies' line know all too well, it is not always done right. In this case, the disabled share designation with the gender that is dependent and charged with caring for the dependent – children, the elderly, and the infirm. Under the prominent banner, toilets for disabled users are not only spatially linked to those of women but also are conceptually linked to that classic category of dependency, while the other population – men – maintain their unproblematic identity as separate creatures. Men share lines, let alone toilet stalls, with no one. Such a spatial polarization

FIGURE 18.3 Bathroom queue for ladies and disabled, London Chelsea Flower Show, May 2004

Source: Photo by the author.

of facilities and choreographies becomes still more significant when one realizes the deliberate planning and attendant expenses involved in laying out the facilities, designating these as demarcated social spaces, and creating the actual signs. This is a gendering of public toilets by design as well as the gendering of disabled toilets by default.

In her memoir *Waist-High in the World*, writer Nancy Mairs observes that "[m]any of us with disabilities require some assistance, but with the right facilities we can maintain dignity for ourselves and those who care for us" (1996: 96). Such an insight suggests that Mairs understands that the technology of the disabled toilet does not necessarily eliminate the dependent relationship between the disabled person and his or her caregiver in the vaunted name of independence for its own sake. Instead, it transforms the relationship so that disabled people maintain some level of privacy and self-esteem while acknowledging the mutually beneficial dynamic inherent in the caregiver/cared for relationship. Yet how does one provide the disabled toilet user with an environment in which he or she can use a facility that is both specially marked for accommodation and yet unmarked in terms of categorizations that stigmatize?

In the US the Rehabilitation Act of 1973's Section 504 and the Americans with Disabilities Act of 1990 remain cornerstones of federal legislation for people with disabilities: those who benefit from these rights, as well as the people who give them care. It is worth recognizing, however, that federal guidelines for enforcing or invoking the ADA deliberately presume a disabled body that is unmarked or unaffected by differentials of gender, race, ethnicity, class, or sexuality, let alone differentials of bodily difference and bodily normativity. As Jennifer Levi and Bennett Klein have shown, the ADA as well as the federal Rehabilitation Act explicitly exclude from protection any persons who claim to have been discriminated against on the basis of "transvestism," "transsexualism," or "gender identity disorders not resulting from physical impairments" (Levi and Klein 2006: 77) The last of these exclusions is a reference to the controversial strategy by some trans people to attain an "official" medical diagnosis that confirms that their gender dysphoria constitutes a disability. Using gender dysphoria as a medical diagnosis conflicts with many disability rights activists' disavowal of the medical model of disability, which claims that non-normative bodies should be rehabilitated and "fixed" through technology to meet the expectations of a society deeply invested in the concept of physical and psychic wholeness.

The insistence on homogenizing the experiences of disabled toilet users is reminiscent of a process that disability scholar Patrick White has described as the heterosexualizing of the blind, in which he shows how institutions and textbooks for the visually impaired have deliberately controlled and encouraged particular kinds of sexual intimacy and gender performance in situations where young blind people will interact with one another (2003). Perhaps it is precisely this fear of sexual and gender nonconformity that surrounds ADA rules against protection for trans people and that, furthermore, has permitted the ADA to flatten out or erase outright the specific and often irreconcilable elements of one's private (and therefore gendered) bodily experience that constitute the terms of one's public (and therefore gendered) disabled identity. This misrecognition of the importance of gendered and sexual difference in the experiences of people with disabilities reinforces the impression that disabled citizens are interchangeable with one another. Disability is their assigned master status, with no other social or cultural identifications appropriate or necessary. Those identifications, in other words, are meaningless within the language of tolerance and formal equality and, insofar as they are recognized at all, they are gender-neutral. But as we have seen, the discourse around public toilets has never been gender- or sex neutral but is inflected through and through with gendered prescriptions for autonomy and self-reliance as well as, of course, with rights and privilege.

The sociologist Erving Goffman, in his 1977 essay "The Arrangement Between the Sexes," argued that toilets were spaces in which the socially constructed expectations of gender equality, the hard-won efforts of the sexual liberation movements of the 1960s and 1970s, did not hold sway. Segregation would remain. As Goffman asserts, "The *functioning* of sex-differentiated organs…[does not] *biologically* recommen[d] segregation; *that* arrangement is totally a cultural matter….[Yet] toilet segregation is presented as a natural consequence of the difference between the sex-classes, when in fact it is rather a means of honoring, if not producing, this difference" (1997: 316 emphasis in the original). While Goffman may have regarded the gendered toilet as a retreat from or an alternative to the androgynous sexual politics of the mid-1970s, disability rights advocates in the main accepted gender segregation. For them, accessing the women's or men's room was a way of *entering* the social, not retreating from it. Many were surely willing to take on and accept the terms of a deliberately delineated sexual difference if it meant being able to use a public toilet in the first place.

Yet even with its problematic and inherently homophobic and transphobic language regarding gender and sexual difference, we cannot in good conscience dismiss or dismantle the ADA's policies without recognizing the enormous achievement that the bulk of its legislation represents for human rights in the United States and for disabled people around the world (Figure 18.4). The work of contemporary transgender and genderqueer activists who are taking on the public toilet as a site of gender liberation borrows liberally from disability rights activism (Chess et al. 2004). Perhaps a more effective challenge to the ADA's policies regarding trans and gender non-normative populations might be: how might a non-gendered toilet policy transform the way that we talk about gender and disability, recognizing that the use value of public toilets is too often defined and delimited by the historical legacies of heterosexual male privileges within public space? In other words, in what ways can we harness the awesome power of the ADA to enact effective

FIGURE 18.4 Contemporary (ca. 2015) photograph of signage for a single-user "All Gender" toilet at San Diego International Airport, USA. Although the sign itself does not announce wheelchair accessibility, the Braille lettering works in tandem with icons representing a variety of gendered positions, including that of infant caregiver, to suggest the accommodation of diverse bodily and social needs. The single-user toilet is in fact wheelchair-accessible

Source: Photograph courtesy of the author.

spatial accommodations for people with disabilities while also harnessing the power of gender non-normative critiques of the public toilet?

There have indeed been some practical solutions offered up. Since the 1960s, a growing group of architects, urban planners, and education specialists as well as those in the fields of rehabilitation medicine and palliative care have been actively thinking about disability and the built environment, including the status of public toilets (Goldsmith 2001). One response, coming primarily from the practitioners of architecture and planning, is the call for "universal design" – that is, the concept of user-centered design for all ages and body types that eschews uniform notions of a single, able-bodied, ergonomically-normative subject – or a single user. Single-occupancy unisex facilities provide an example. Space otherwise given over to the separate men's and women's rooms (and perhaps more space as well) is re-articulated as a series of small walled-in enclosures, each large enough for wheelchair access and that of a helper. Each has a sink as well as toilet. People who identify as transgender would not have to make a choice, and those observing them would not be in a position to remark or reject. The stand-alone outdoor pay toilets now common in Europe and appearing in a few US cities such as New York and San Francisco are a variant, with the New York versions at least of sufficient size to accommodate wheelchair users.

But there are drawbacks, both in terms of ecological and financial costs. Use of urinals requires less space and less money for installation and maintenance than does toilet use. Current urinal models are waterless, resulting in ecological benefit. A plausible answer is to install urinals in a single unisex facility where men who wished to do so could use them for urination and both men and women could use toilet stalls as desired. Those with physical disabilities would use whatever appliance they preferred. This is a radical solution because it requires both men and women to share the intimate space of the rest room. It also, of course, eliminates the efficiency of restricting the disabled to one or two "special" spaces; every stall must be large. In the case of stand-alone pay toilets, provision of wheelchair access decreases the number of street locations large enough to accommodate them.

Numbers of architect-scholars treat all this as a design as well as a political and moral issue. Some have recognized public bathrooms, as in the words of Raymond Lifchez and Barbara Winslow, "a focal point of the drive to create a barrier-free community" (1980: 90). Lifchez and Winslow were involved in the formation of the Center for Independent Living, Inc., founded in Berkeley, California, in 1972 by disabled students at the University of California, which became a paradigm for disabled community activists around the world and remains an active model for developing services and initiating anti-discrimination legislation. Indeed, the Center for Independent Living was among those Bay Area-based organizations that dispatched its activists to occupy the offices of the Department of Health, Education, and Welfare during the April 1977 protest actions. From its inception, the goal of organizations like the Center of Independent Living has been to work simultaneously on developing legal strategies for protecting the disabled individual alongside those for transforming the built environment. Activists collaborate directly with urban planners, architects, technology specialists, and civic leaders to conceptualize urban landscapes with the toilet playing a central role.

The disabled toilet exemplifies the tension between autonomy and equality at the core of classical liberalism: how far do we go to reconcile the protection of individual freedoms with the need to satisfy the majority's needs and preferences? How much expense and inconvenience must the majority "suffer" to provide not only adequate numbers of rest rooms for the disabled, but equipped for their diverse needs and respecting their own sense of dignity, gender-based and otherwise? Disabled people's use of public toilets focuses attention on the issue in particular ways. As historian Patrick Joyce has written, urban public space has long been the site of negotiation of this tension. It was in large cosmopolitan cities like Manchester and Vienna during the eighteenth and nineteenth centuries where European citizens learned how and where to exercise both civic autonomy but also civic restraint in their direct physical engagement with urban thoroughfares, public squares, and municipal parks. Public spaces thus became political theaters where the productive strains of liberalism were not only exhibited but were materially manifest. While liberating individuals from the typical constraints of social life, the new urbanity restrained particular kinds of behaviors in an ongoing need to perpetually negotiate power relations that remain both dynamic and unresolved. As Joyce writes, "If forms of power and human agency, and of bodily competence and of knowledge, are carried in the material world, and in the *use* of objects," then one might characterize the history of modern liberalism as a narrative of a "strange and complex history of objects and material processes" (2004: 98 emphasis in the original).

Disabled people's use of the public toilet has indeed its own "strange and complex" history, part of which is the naturalization of the able and gendered body. Variations from this human model have, in countries like the US, enlisted an attitude of tolerance but not a fulsome embrace of the opportunities for celebrating and learning from difference. As always, more is eminently possible.

With a stance perhaps appropriate for a pioneer composer and performer, the British musician and disability activist Alan Holdsworth (a/k/a Johnny Crescendo) coined the slogan "Piss on Pity" in 1992 (Ervin 2002). It describes the attitude felt by many disability activists toward the patronizing compassion of the non-disabled, exemplified by the Annual Labor Day Telethon for the Muscular Dystrophy Association hosted by Jerry Lewis, that promotes maudlin sentimentality instead of self-empowerment (Longmore 1997). Combining the image of pissing as a natural biological function with the image of pissing as an aggressive act of individual and group disobedience, the "Piss on Pity" movement forces a recalibration of the stigma attached to disability, as propagated shamelessly by the medical-industrial-entertainment complex. Pity is not good enough and, indeed, it is destructive. Toilets remain contested terrain with the question remaining of how, truly, to make all toilets, and all toilet users, equal before the law of the commode.

19

DISABILITY AND THE PROMISES OF TECHNOLOGY

Technology, subjectivity and embodiment within an order of the normal

Ingunn Moser (2006)

Excerpt from Information, Communication & Society
(2006) 9: 3, 373–395.

The topic of this article is the promises of technology for disabled people. Technologies, and especially new information and communication technologies, are thought by many to hold the power to bridge and even undo disability. But how to interrogate such promises? The objective here is to provide a set of tools and resources for such an inquiry, and offer analyses and discussion of the generative and transformative power of technologies in the lives of disabled people. For this endeavour I draw on recent work in disability studies as well as social studies of science and technology (STS). The point of departure is that 'disabled' is not something one is but something one becomes, and, further, that disability is ordered and enacted in situated and quite specific ways. A set of questions follows from this. First, there are questions about how people become, and are made, disabled in practice, and, in particular, what role technologies and other material arrangements play in enabling and or disabling interactions. Second, there are questions about what is made of disability (and ability), what is made of the disabled subject and body, and, even more specifically, what positions, capacities and competences are enabled through the mobilization of technologies. What are the normativities enacted, what does one seek to achieve, and what specific configuration of subjectivity, embodiment and disability can we see emerging? And last, but not least, there are questions about the limits to the power and productivity of technologies and the way of becoming abled and/or disabled they contribute to, and what they exclude and suppress.

To explore these questions, I work through a set of excerpts from two interviews with a man I call Jarle, ethnographic notes from these visits, and a videotaped television interview given by him in another context. The data were collected as part of a study of the uses of new technologies in the lives of disabled people in Norway. I start by addressing the question of what it is actors seek to achieve in their interactions with technologies. I draw out the normativities at work, ask what positions and capacities they establish, and how they are made possible and achieved in practice. […]

The argument I develop is, first, that in this context of the Norwegian welfare state and its extensive apparatus of public services and measures, the mobilization of new technologies works in a powerful way to build an order of the normal and turn disabled people into competent normal subjects. However, such a strategy based on compensation achieves its goals only at a very high price: by continuing to reproduce boundaries between abled and disabled, normal and deviant, which constitute some people as disabled in the first place. There are thus limits to normalization. And so, notwithstanding their generative power, technologies working within an order of the normal are implicated in the (re)production of the asymmetries that they and it seek to undo. In this sense, the strategy cannot succeed. It continues to produce disability along with ability.

The productivity of technologies for the subject

In the following, then, my interest and concern is with what subjects are enabled and enacted in interactions with technologies and other material arrangements, as well as how they are enabled in practice. For this I adopt the notion of 'subjectivity' in its semiotic and poststructuralist usage, as referring to a location of consciousness, knowing, thinking or feeling. This is a very open definition that makes very few assumptions about where or what kind of location this is, and so provides me with an undetermined framework for tracing the making, shaping, embodying and delineating of subjectivities empirically. I use the term 'subjectivities' in the plural to emphasize that a subject position is not something one has, occupies or is structured into, once and for all, but rather a set of differently structured positions one moves between and is moved through, more or less fluidly. Whenever I refer to 'the subject' in the singular, this refers to a position that draws together, unifies and hides a more complex set of subjective capacities.

I also make an analytical distinction between capacities for action and capacities for consciousness, thinking and feeling. This must, however, not be understood as an argument about what a subject is, or how the subject should be conceptualized, a priori. The theory and ordering of the subject proposed here is more local: it comes from the materials and is based on what I have found to be crucial component parts that go into making subjects in the specific context and interactions I have studied. In this normalizing mode of ordering disability, becoming a subject also involves agency. It is distinguished and separated out from subjectivity as the external and embodied expression of an inner subjectivity. These capacities can, however, be broken down further into their component parts, and in the following I do this in order to explore more carefully what it takes to become a subject, and what kind of configuration this builds or seeks to achieve.

Making active and independent agents

So agents express and demonstrate a capacity to act in the world, to initiate and cause things to happen. Two components of this capacity turn up repeatedly in my materials: activity and independence.

One example is a video I got from Jarle. Before his accident, he used to be team captain of the national team in 8-way formation skydiving. On the tape he sent me, he had collected his own appearances on television. It starts with a report on TV2 news on the national team training for the upcoming World Championships. The next cut is made one year later, also by TV2 news. It recalls how the hope of a medal snapped as the team captain was struck down by an accident and broke his neck. But now, the news presenter tells us, Jarle is on his way back to life. Then we see Jarle driving around in an electric wheelchair in the garden outside the rehabilitation hospital. He drives down to look out on the fjord, and then returns. He drives up towards the reporter and the wheelchair comes to a halt. Jarle explains that he is paralyzed from the fourth cervical vertebra and down – which is exactly the critical limit for the ability to breathe on one's own. 'I am dependent on a ventilator, 24 hours a day', he says, 'but I can do without it for twenty or twenty-five minutes if I have to.' The first question the reporter directs at Jarle is: 'Has your life become totally inactive?' Jarle's answer is prompt:

> No, in no way. At the moment life is just beginning to take shape again. Now I finally do many things that abled people do, too: I go to the movies, I go out socializing, and I have mates. I am just starting to build my own house, and I will have my own car. Actually a lot of very normal things.

It almost goes without saying that the normativity enacted in the interactions in this television report is active agency. This is clearly what Jarle seeks to establish. But it is obvious that the TV2 reporter also values active lives. The crucial thing, however, is that this is taken to apply to disabled as well as abled people. The reporter's question about whether Jarle's life has become totally inactive first takes up the medical voice that Jarle himself introduced when he gave a description of his situation – locating the disability within his body, as a condition in and of the body. But it takes up this medical voice only in order to reject it: the question asks to be refused and to be displaced into another discourse. It firmly establishes that inactivity is not a good, but it does not relegate disabled people to lack, and to passivity. The moral lesson of this report is that disability can and should be bridged. It establishes active agency as norm for the disabled as well as for the abled.

But, returning to the video, it is striking that even more important than the reporter and Jarle's words is what the television report shows about how Jarle practices active agency. After the introductory presentation, the report starts with a camera following him and his electric wheelchair around in the garden. Without further commentary, this demonstrates how Jarle steers and controls the movements and functions of his wheelchair by way of chin control. What we learn is that he can start and set the wheelchair running, move and steer it in different directions, make it go faster or slower, bring it to a halt, regulate the sitting position etc. – simply by pushing a stick with a switch mounted on a rack that goes from the back of the wheelchair to the front and up to his chin. It allows him to move within a tree-like menu of opportunities, through which the system scans automatically. By triggering the switch, Jarle can initiate action and so practise active agency. The form he demonstrates it in here is mobility.

So this is how it works: the electric wheelchair enables Jarle to move around as he wishes – at least as far as the environment is accessible to his wheelchair. It was granted to him by the social security authorities – and so indirectly by Norwegian policy on disability – which guarantees everyone the right to free technical aids, provided it can be convincingly argued that they contribute to better functioning and/or the capacity for self-support. And in a quite straightforward manner, this is what the electric wheelchair does for Jarle: it works like a prosthesis to compensate for bodily functions such as walking on legs and having the use of one's arms and hands to control the wheelchair.

But there is more to it. By attaching himself to the electric wheelchair, Jarle gets an opportunity to be mobile, but also to practise active agency in ways that surpass simple function: he can be spontaneous and make unexpected moves. Acting on the spur of the moment, he can visit a friend or go to the cinema. And these are also manifestations of a capacity for independence. Independence, here, is a practical and material matter. It means to manage on one's own, without having to ask for help from family, friends, carers or assistants. But it also means to be free – or sufficiently disentangled and self-sufficient – to be able to do things that were not planned. And spontaneous action, it seems, is particularly effective as a demonstration of active and independent agency: it is one thing to be enabled to act, as in the way the wheelchair enables mobility, but quite another thing to be able to act spontaneously. The attribution of spontaneous action to a disabled person like Jarle emphasizes his capacity to initiate and cause things to happen independently rather than being moved by others.

What becomes clear here, then, is that independence may require a lot of technologies and/or other material objects and arrangements to which one becomes attached. Independence is not simply about disconnection, but also about the shifting out and replacement of some attachments (or dependencies) by others. It is also about the distribution and delegation of tasks: moving for instance from attachments in the form of delegating tasks to people to delegating, instead, to things, technical aids in the widest possible sense, or even parts of the physical environment. Becoming independent thus turns out to involve discrimination, a process where you find out what kinds of attachments and dependencies are necessary, optional, good, not so good, better or worse than others.

Building positions of centred control

I now turn to subjective capacities and competences and how these are made possible. At this point, I also turn 'inwards', to what is taken to be inside the human and inside the human mind or brain in particular. Another story: I first met Jarle in a seminar where he gave a presentation on the possibilities smart house technologies offer to disabled people. Using his own situation as example, he described how his new voice-based environmental control system finally allowed him to live at home and control his own life. He invited me to come and visit him in his new house. When I arrived, however, Jarle could not work the environmental control system as he normally would with a microphone, headset and a transmitter at the back of the electric wheelchair. He had been given a new electric wheelchair and the system was not mounted on it yet. But he could still show me around and demonstrate his house, he said, because he could also control it from his bed. He worked this by way of a suck-and-blow-system, a switch that is activated by sucking or blowing in a pipe, almost like a straw, in front of his mouth. Turning the system on, the computer started scanning through and reading all the alternatives aloud. When it got to where Jarle wanted, he blew the pipe: the television turned on, it switched to another channel, the sound was turned off, and the television was turned off again. He could also call for assistance, adjust the bed, open doors and windows, regulate the light, control the blinds or turn down the heating. We moved from the bedroom to Jarle's office. He worked the computer in the same way by sucking and blowing, with a digital keyboard on the screen, a small box on top of the computer sending out infrared beams, and a small reflector tag between his eyes to control the marker on the screen. Using this computer, he told me, he had organized the plan for the step-by-step achievement of his goal – to build himself a house and move back to live in his own home. He made budgets, calculated costs, set up schedules and deadlines, wrote applications and appeals, negotiated with architects, building authorities, banks, local authorities and the social security authorities – and kept track of everything that needed to be done. He concluded:

> I can work the computer exactly the same way as 'a normal' (person) … Indeed, this is a big step in the right direction of raising my quality of life. In principle, I control my whole life via my voice, microphone, chin, sucking and blowing, and the environmental control system.

What Jarle demonstrates here is centred control. This is a normativity that was repeatedly enacted in stories I got in interviews. To get control over your everyday life is seen as a good, and as an obvious right. It means that disabled people should be informed and be making the plans and decisions concerning their own situation, and that they should have the initiative and be taking action in matters concerning themselves.

So centred control is a competence that implies that the person knows, has an overview of the situation, can control it, and is in a position to act upon it. As such it is a capability that is linked with and goes into other related capacities such as discretionary choice, autonomy and strategic planning and management, as well as active and independent agency. When Jarle claims control, all of these capacities, and positions, are involved. Different combinations of these components of subjectivity are important in different situations, but they all contribute to – and rest upon – a centring of the subject.

And this, I want to argue, is also what the environmental control system and the computer do for Jarle. They bring together and make available tasks and functions that would otherwise have been distributed in time and space. The environmental control system also arranges these tasks and functions in the order of a menu, a hierarchically structured, tree-like menu, so that they can be distinguished, overviewed and acted upon. In this way, it builds a centre of control and action, a position raised above the matter of the practices itself, and places Jarle in the middle – the centre – of it. It is structured in the same way as a command and control centre in a railway or air traffic control system. Using technology, paths are built that direct and collect information and control at certain defined locations that become centres of knowledge and action.

But Jarle is not only above and outside the action and the mundane realities he has knowledge and control of. Even if he is strongly centred and placed in a position where he can control important parts of his everyday life, this is only possible as long as he is linked to his environmental control system. That is, he – his body – must remain attached to a set of ordered relations between elements such as cables, infrared beams and apparatuses, transmitters and receivers, the electricity network and its cables, a computer, a software program in which the many possibilities are programmed, a fuse box the size of a wardrobe, switches, remote controls. What this shows is that subjectivities, such as centred control, are made possible by and emerge in such embodied relations and arrangements. They include, but are not limited to, Jarle's body or, say, his mind.

Jarle both subscribes to and enacts this norm of centred control as he mobilizes technical aids. He describes it as a big step forward, raising the quality of his life. In principle, he says, he controls his whole life via his environmental control system. In practice, as my visit demonstrated, it is a bit more complicated. For instance, the system does not always work. And Jarle needs people looking after him every hour of the day, in case mucus needs to be sucked out of his lungs, to change the ventilator tube, to turn him in bed, to feed him, and so on. It is the local authorities that are responsible for providing him with the necessary healthcare services. But if they say no, we cannot afford it, or we don't have the necessary personnel – then Jarle has no control whatsoever.

This was the case when Jarle was released from hospital, and the local council had simply reserved a room for him in the local nursing home. But this was out of the question for Jarle, and teaming up with a nursing officer on the one hand and a computer and telephone on the other, together they made a plan that was going to make it possible for him to move home.

Moving to his new house was a move from a sociotechnical order premised on hospitals and large institutions, to one treating the home as private sphere and the (ex-)patient or resident as citizen. This move was made possible in part by earmarked grants from the state to the local councils to build residences where disabled people could live in their own way, like abled people. At the same time caring services were reorganized to develop more flexible home services and in particular a new care scheme called 'personal assistance managed by users'. This means that while Jarle is still dependent on care and assistance, he has escaped the most dreary routines of the nursing home and the caregivers are turned from professional experts into personal assistants. Living in his own place, Jarle is also allowed – and required – to take care of his finances. A series of new social security rights is also attributed to him: he is granted the right to an individual rehabilitation plan, to technical aids and to a car.

What Jarle's story suggests, and what I want to argue, is that centred control, and the autonomy, discretion, strategic planning and management that go into it and also contribute to it, is not only a question of rationality and ability to speak for oneself – a competence of the mind that just needs assistance (technically or otherwise) in order to be expressed. Rather, these are capacities that are made possible in and produced by specific ordered and ordering socio-material arrangements. It is the layout of and distributions in the current arrangements, including computer and environmental control systems but, crucially, also a place of one's own and the 'personal assistance' that together allow (and require) Jarle to choose and decide for himself.

The subject of technology: the competent normal subject

What the above analyses suggest is that Jarle's agencies, subjectivities and embodiments, together with the relations, practices, materials, technologies, and collectives they are enacted in, all tend to become ordered in specific ways. They become ordered, and also contribute to ordering. Further, the analyses also suggest that the enactments are related, and often implied in each other. The questions that follow here, then, are how these different enactments go together to make a particular kind of subject, and what kind of ordering this subject is involved in.

My argument is that the mode of ordering disability at work here is geared towards normalization. It works by way of compensation to build and fix in place an order of the normal, and to turn disabled people into competent normal subjects. This order is enacted, and enacts itself, in and through subjects and bodies, technologies and physical environments, healthcare practices and relations, policy documents and social services, rehabilitation methods and grants for the manufacturers of technical aids, the media and even more distant locations and practices. The links between enactments of this order – for instance in everyday life on the one hand and policy documents and discourse on the other – go through an extensive apparatus of social services and other compensatory measures and means that include for instance the adaptation of physical environments and provision of technical aids. Indeed, it is the collection, articulation and translation of the normalizing mode of ordering into a welfare state ideology and public policy on disability that has become embedded in an extensive apparatus of public services and measures that lends it its strength in the ordering of disability in Norway.

But what specifically is it that normalization strives to enact and establish? How can we describe the specific composition, form and character of this competent normal subject and how does it arise from interaction with technologies? And, finally, what does it make of disability, as well as of ability? I will start with agency. What my data and analyses show is that the normal competent actor is discontinuous, bounded and detached. Normally, and ideally, agency is seen as a capability given in the individualized subject and in the naturally ordered and bounded body – as a sort of disposition or available functionality. Disability, however, is constituted as a breakdown of this normal order of the body, undermining the capability to act. As such disability is seen to constitute dependency, and the disabled body to be unbounded and continuous, at best relying on a network of relations that enables one to act.

The strategy for compensating for disability within normalization also builds upon this image of agency as distributed in relations: one approaches normality, here in the form of a capability for action, by putting in place a functional network of relations. This set of material arrangements may include both people and technologies. However, it is only the disabled body and person who is seen to be an actor produced in a network, with shifting boundaries, and to be dependent on agency that is distributed and delegated. The normal competent actor is seen to have natural, inherent and bodily bounded agency.

This is also apparent in how technologies used by disabled people are described in ways unlike those used by abled people. Technologies used by disabled people are conceived of as 'assistive technologies' or 'technical aids', and disabled people are constituted as dependent upon these. It is not usually suggested that abled users depend on aids or need them in the same way. So here is a paradox, and a contradiction, within normalization: on the one hand the norm is a bounded, and a naturally bounded actor. On the other hand, normalization proceeds by way of a theory of agency as a network effect.

But my argument is that agency is not a capability or property that belongs inherently in particular and bounded human bodies. Agency is always mediated. People are not actors, they are enabled to act in and by the practices and relations in which they are located, and they become actors because agency is distributed and attributed. The difference is that with standardized abled actors, this distribution, the arrangements and even the bodies tend to move into the background and become invisible. With disabled actors, however, the heterogeneous materiality and embodiment is much more present and visible. And the reason it does not disappear into the background is that it is constantly problematic. It does not fit with the standardized environments that allow agency to flow without constant interruption.

I think that this situation (with one theory of agency for the presumptively normal actor and another for the abnormally disabled) is one reason why active and independent agency is so important to many disabled people. One may very well be enabled to act, but then one might find that agency is not attributed to the enabled actor but to an other that acts by enabling. In this situation, active and independent agency, as in the form of spontaneous action, are capabilities that contribute to the creation of a bounded actor. Despite the networks and relations they rest upon in practice, demonstrations of these capabilities help make boundaries and discontinuities. The enactment of active agency attributes – and centres – agency in the body and the subject. Independent agency works to produce a bounded and discontinuous actor. When it comes to the ordering of the subject, the data and analyses show that the competent normal subject is composed of a set of subjectivities including autonomy, discretionary choice, centred control, and strategic planning and management. As noted, they all contribute to – and rest upon – a centring of the subject. In this way, these subjectivities contribute to building a distinction between body and mind.

Again the mode of ordering geared towards normalization operates with two theories of subjectivity, one for the subject that is taken to be normal, and another for the potential subject-to-be. And again my argument is that just as agency is always mediated and emerges in relations, so subjective capacities and competences such as autonomy, discretionary choice, centred control and strategic planning and management are also always the distributed effects of relations. Subjectivities are locations or positions that are made possible in relations, practices and collectives that reach far beyond the individualized human mind – and body. And yet what the above demonstrations also show is that the competent normal subject is centred. The norm is that it is centred. But how does this work? How can things be distributed and centred at the same time? My suggestion is that, within the distributed relations, paths are built that work to centre the subject, to build centres of knowledge, reasoning, thinking, consciousness – and agency. The point, then, is that centredness, autonomy, discretion, and also independence and active agency, are achievements which rest upon distribution – but where the distribution usually, and ideally, disappears into the background. And also, in the same way as the environmental control system that works to centre Jarle rests upon distributions and networks of relations, so too do other centred locations of knowing and consciousness.

The remaining difference however is, again, that whereas the standardized environments and forms of embodiment of abled normal subjects seem to become invisible, and have the ability to perform 'disembodied mind', non-standard, disabling, and even normalizing and so enabling networks usually do not. With disabled subjects materiality resists: there are always bad passages, missing links and problematic bodies which mean that the distributions remain visible and present in the situation.

PART V
Projects and practices

Professional practice guidance on disability, accessibility and inclusion has been available for many years, underpinned by legislation in many different countries (Mace 1985; Goldsmith 2001, 2012). There are also many other published resources aimed at enabling architects and other built environment professionals to think about disability, diversity and design more generally (Anthony 2001; Pullin, 2011; Tauke et al. 2015).

As with other sections of this Reader, contributions have been selected that build on, but also engage critically with, these resources. This is particularly by thinking about disability differently – as something that helps us engage with what constitutes normality; as diverse lived experiences which designers can learn from; and as a way of generating alternative ways of 'doing' architecture.

This perspective is important because disability within architecture and urban design practice is often assumed as a loss and a lack, something to be both 'accommodated by' and 'ameliorated through' the design of built space. Whilst movements for inclusive and universal design and accessibility have been of crucial importance, informed both by disability activism and by generations of committed designers and policymakers, such approaches can also be critiqued and rethought. As already noted, designing a 'normal' environment and then 'retrofitting' it for people with disabilities is argued by many disability studies scholars as 'enforcing normalcy' (Davis 1995) instead of critically and creatively challenging the grounds on which those environments are made in the first place (in particular see Hamraie, Dolmage and Price, this volume).

In recent years, for example, many disability activists have been campaigning for a shift from interpreting disability as a loss or tragedy, and towards valuing the richness of bio- and neuro-diversity. Rather than aiming to enable disabled people to become 'more normal' such approaches emphasise the gains that corporeal and intellectual differences can bring (see Silberman 2015, for example, on autism). In Deaf culture, the concept of Deaf Gain is defined as a reframing of 'deaf' as a form of sensory and cognitive diversity that has the potential to contribute to the greater good of humanity (Bauman and Murray 2013, 2014). The first piece in this part, on the development of Deaf Space, demonstrates what Deaf Gain might look like in practice. It originated at Gallaudet University, the only higher education institution in which all programmes and services are specifically designed to accommodate deaf and hard of hearing students, and was undertaken as a participatory process through a series of courses offered within the university syllabus, thus enabling students to research and co-design principles and spaces that start from Deafness. As Hansel Bauman, who led on the creation of DeafSpace principles, has said, 'The clarity with which a deaf person communicates relates to the clarity and clutter of what's around them. Space becomes an essential part of how you communicate' (O'Connell 2012). In 'Deaf Space', reproduced here, Todd Byrd graphically – and poetically – describes the spatial and design implications.

In 'Along disabled lines: Claiming spatial agency through installation art', Amanda Cachia also forefronts the unique qualities of disabled bodies. She explores the work of two artists – Wendy Jacob and Corban Walker – who have worked with lines to map out what Cachia calls 'a new geometry of space', informed by the respective experiences of autism and dwarfism. These installation projects thus act as a commentary on, and disruption of, normative embodiment and its associated assumptions both about artistic practice and about what constitutes 'proper' gallery space.

Cachia is deeply interested in shifting normal assumptions about disabled subjectivity and agency through art, opening up for critique how rarely it is addressed in art theory (see Siebers, this volume), and also explores how 'the disabled body offers new perspectives on architecture itself: on its simultaneous limits and possibilities, and how it might be disrupted and transformed to account for a wider variety of body types and movements'.

Thinking about what can be learned from diverse disabilities is not to ignore the very real (and various) effects of living with impairment. But it is to recognise that disabled people are *already* experts in engaging with the built environment, as they negotiate its complexities on a daily basis. Disabled people are not just passive users of services and buildings, but can offer something powerful back to architects and other built environment professionals. In 'The Ramp House: Building inclusivity', Thea McMillan and Katie Lloyd Thomas write about one particular design process where a foundational aim was to involve the whole family, including daughter Greta who is severely disabled. This, then, is not a story of 'special needs' and accessibility requirements but of what the writers call an 'ongoing process of inclusivity' where the new building has grown to embody a resonant set of relationships between the people in the house, and the many others who have been, and/or are involved. As they put it, 'for support workers, carers, friends and visitors, the Ramp House can alter perceptions of what a disabled person can do, replacing limitations and practicalities with possibilities and dreams'.

In the next piece, 'Resistant seating', Sophie Handler also works within a participatory process, in this case with older people in East London, UK. The project not only engaged with the diverse experiences of ageing, but also started from an examination of how sitting down in public comes to be 'normally' enacted in particular forms rather than others (see also Liz Crow, this volume). From this point of view, the necessary but often impromptu need to sit down for older people becomes a 'mis-use of space'; can even be re-imagined as an act of resistance. By designing a series of small devices – as with the tinkering described by Bess Williamson in this volume – the right to sit down in public becomes a 'discrete, if still defiant, kind of adaptive action: to accommodate personal needs where the designed environment fails'.

In the final contribution to the collection, Sara Hendren starts from one of the devices commonly associated with disabled people, the ramp. Her intention is to defamiliarise its simple and 'ordinary' geometry – both to explore alternative potentials that may have been missed, and to open up for study an often overlooked (and thus underrated) technology. Re-thinking and redesigning the ramp as a moveable and multi-use artefact enables it, she suggests, to take on new kinds of poetic life.

The projects and practices here, then, despite their variety and angles of view, are energised by similar concerns. That is, they all make creative interventions that are deeply informed by diverse disabled peoples' experiences, underpinned by the belief that working in this way can challenge some of the simplistic and unspoken assumptions that persistently act to make disabled people marginalised and invisible within 'normal' architectural and built environment design. In a multitude of smaller and bigger ways, they start from the belief that architecture – as a discipline and as built space – has a lot to gain by learning more about how to think and do dis/ability differently.

Recommended further reading

Bates, C., Imrie, R. and Kullman, K. (eds.) (2016) *Care and Design: Bodies, Buildings, Cities*, Hoboken, NJ: John Wiley & Sons, Ltd.

Bauman, H.-D. L. and Murray, J. J. (2014) *Deaf Gain: Raising the Stakes for Human Diversity*, Minneapolis, MN: University of Minnesota Press.

Boys, J. (2014) *Doing Disability Differently: An Alternative Handbook on Dis/Ability, Architecture and Designing for Everyday Life*, London and New York: Routledge.

Cachia, A. (2013) '"Disabling the Museum": Curator as Infrastructual Activist', *Journal of Visual Art Practice* 12(3): 257–289.

Cachia, A. (2013) 'Talking Blind: Museums Access and the Discursive Turn', *Disability Studies Quarterly*, Special Issue on Blindness and Museums 33(3): 257–289.

Davidson, M. (2008) *Concerto for the Left Hand: Disability and the Defamiliar Body*, Ann Arbor, MI: University of Michigan Press.

Edwards, C. and Imrie, R. (2008) 'Disability and the Implications of the Well Being Agenda: Some Reflections from the United Kingdom', *Journal of Social Policy* 37(3): 337–355.

Garland-Thompson, R. (2011) 'Misfits. A Feminist Materialist Disability Concept', *Hypatia Special Issue: Ethics of Embodiment* 26(3): 591–609.

Hamraie, A. (2016) 'Inclusive Design: Cultivating Accountability toward the Intersections of Race, Aging, and Disability', *Age Culture Humanities* 2: 253–262, Spring.

Handler, H. (2014) *An Alternative Age-Friendly Handbook*, Manchester: The University of Manchester Library.

Imrie, R. (2012) 'Universalism, Universal Design and Equitable Access to the Built Environment', *Disability and Rehabilitation* 34(10): 873–882.

Imrie, R. (2013) 'Shared Space and the Post-Politics of Environmental Change', *Urban Studies* 50(16): 3446–3462.

Imrie, R. and Luck, R. (2014) Designing Inclusive Environments: Rehabilitating the Body and the Relevance of Universal Design', *Disability and Rehabilitation* 36(16): 1315–1319.

Keller, J. S. (2016) 'The Politics of Stairs', in *Design Equilibrium*, Atlanta, GA: American Institute of Architects, 42–45.

Kuppers, P. (2014) *Studying Disability Arts and Culture: An Introduction*, London: Palgrave Macmillan.

Lupton, E. (2014) *Beautiful Users: Designing for People*, Princeton, NJ: Princeton Architectural Press.

Nord, C. and Högström, E. (eds.) (2017) *Caring Architecture. Institutions and relational practices,* London: Routledge.

Sandell, R., Dodd, J. and Garland-Thomson, R. (eds) (2010) *Re-presenting Disability: Activism and Agency in the Museum*, London: Routledge.

20

DEAF SPACE

Todd Byrd (2007)

Reprinted from Gallaudet Today: the Magazine, *Spring 2007,*
http://www.gallaudet.edu/university_communications/
gallaudet_today_magazine/deaf_space_spring_2007.html.

A yellow ball bounces down the steps of Clerc dormitory, out the door, and rolls across Hanson Plaza [at Gallaudet University]. Gaining momentum, it careens down the Lincoln Circle sidewalk and takes a turn at the Hall Memorial Building, cutting a trail across campus. The ball symbolizes a Gallaudet student, but it is more accurate to say that it represents any deaf person, whose language and culture are best suited to an environment that, like the ball is spherical and free flowing. Dr. MJ Bienvenu, '74 & G-'83, chair of the Department of ASL and Deaf Studies and co-chair of the James Lee Sorenson Language and Communications Center (SLCC) Planning Committee, calls a three-year, student-centered Deaf Space project to explore the architectural needs of deaf people, "personally and professionally exciting." She asks, "If no one was using sign language, how could a visitor to Gallaudet know it is a university for deaf people?" Not by looking at the buildings. "If you look at Gallaudet and at Harvard [University], both have dignified and prestigious buildings, but the two places are very different," said Bienvenu. So, what about the campus environment represents deaf culture and experience?

The same question was asked earlier by campus constituents serving on the SLCC Planning Committee. "We need a place of identity, so we began looking at what deaf space entails," said Bienvenu. Seeking an answer, the planning committee held workshops to develop a model. Putting a finger on aspects of the campus that are not conducive to deaf sensibilities was easy – a stairway may appear aesthetically attractive, but prove to be a barrier to sign communication. Natural lighting, such as in the Jordan Student Academic Center (JSAC), is pleasing, but can be too harsh on sunny days and too dim when the sky is overcast. In these cases, artificial light can bridge the extremes. Blind spots in hallways at corners, or a door that is opened suddenly can prove hazardous to two signers engrossed in conversation. "So, we had a great understanding of what we wanted," said Bienvenu, "but we needed an architect."

Guidance in interactive design

Identifying exactly what constitutes deaf space proved much more elusive than what does not. So, a quest began for a definition. At one workshop, committee members, deaf faculty, students and administrators took pen and paper and set out across campus.

This inclusive group identified several qualities they would like to see enacted on campus: more facilities like the SLCC that will connect campus groups and encourage interaction; architectural features that retain historical links to the past but incorporate a look to the future and eliminating potential barriers that wouldn't be an issue for hearing people but impede conversation for deaf people – widening narrow sidewalks and, when possible, replacing stairs with ramps.

Plans for a course to further investigate these concepts were first made public by architect Hansel Bauman, a speaker at the 2006 Graduate Hooding exercises. Bauman, whose business is based in California, is one of the architects in the SLCC project due to his expertise in designing academic buildings that foster interaction. Bauman said the class is actually an outgrowth of the SLCC design process: "We began to realize there are a lot of benefits in using the concepts [of open space and a deaf-friendly environment] that are being applied to the SLCC to all new campus facilities and renovations." Bauman said that he and his brother, Dr. Dirksen Bauman, a professor in the ASL and Deaf Studies Department, Dr. Benjamin Bahan, also a professor in the department, and others from the deaf community often have long conversations about the interaction between architecture and cultural studies. From these discussions, they conceived the notion of having these ideas developed through a course at Gallaudet. Former Provost Jane Fernandes and President Emeritus I. King Jordan agreed that the program had great potential and approved adding it to the deaf studies curricula.

Hansel Bauman said it makes sense that this class is offered through the Department of ASL and Deaf Studies. "Architecture is one of the key ways a culture manifests itself in the physical world," he explained. "Deaf culture centers around the language. The language has all the elements of architecture – the spatial kinesthetic of sign language, the desire of deaf people for the visual access that open space affords/lends itself to express the deaf way of being." So, exactly what does that mean when it comes to designing a building with a deaf person's needs in mind? "That's what we're working toward," he replied.

Maluma or takete?

Space that comprises free flowing, circular movements is associated with the anthropological term "maluma," which conjures up images of a soft, flowing aesthetic – the essence of deaf language and culture. The opposite of maluma is "takete," a rigid, sharp, angular aesthetic. When designing homes for a hearing person, for example, the architect is conscious of the desire to create walls that enclose space – takete – which translates into a feeling of security. But in performing the same task for a deaf person, for example, the architect needs to be cognizant of the desire for visual access, which means less walls, and in their place "implied enclosures" – maluma. This can be accomplished through designing partial walls that are less than floor-to-ceiling height, or using building materials such as clouded glass as an alternative to brick, concrete, or drywall to create rooms that afford privacy yet preserve a sense of openness. The strategic placement of skylights and artificial lighting, and installing vertical glass panels next to doors are other ways that enhance the architectural aesthetic embraced by deaf people

The Deaf Space class began in the fall semester with eight graduate students, and for the spring semester expanded to 12 students, two of whom are undergraduates. The fall semester class was six credits and combined two deaf studies classes – one on visual studies, taught by Benjamin Bahan, and the other on cultural studies, led by Dirksen Bauman. Hansel Bauman co-taught in both classes.

The theories on what constitutes deaf space that were discussed by the students and their professors during the fall semester were applied to student life on Kendall Green. Students paired up and analyzed each dormitory, documenting through drawings and photographs what supported interaction and what didn't. The students were given a practical application: the design for the Clerc dormitory, which is slated for an overhaul. They presented their concepts to the architects and design team working on the renovation, and their ideas were incorporated into the design work. "So the students had a very direct and important impact on the project," said Hansel Bauman. They also charted the development of Kendall Green since it was founded in 1864. In addition, they conducted case studies of other universities where students were afforded significant input in the architectural designs of new buildings or renovations, therefore giving them a sense of belonging and ownership of these facilities.

Like many college campuses, academics and day-to-day life lead separate existences on Kendall Green – the cafeteria and dormitories taking up the north sector of campus and academics to the south. While some people think it's a good philosophy to separate the two functions, others feel that the separation detracts from the college experience and that life and study should be intermingled. That concept gives the deaf space class the challenge of creating an environment that is more of a community. Included in the University's current Facilities Master Plan – a list of planned capital improvements projects through 2012 that is on file in the Washington, D.C. Office of Planning and Zoning – is for Ballard North and West to be demolished and replaced with apartment-style housing, and to replace the Hanson parking garage with a campus green, said Hansel Bauman. "So, the University did have some foresight in deaf-friendly space," he said. An idea generated by the students that is not in the Master Plan, he added is an additional student center, separate from the JSAC. "There is a feeling now that there is nowhere on campus that is welcoming," he said. "This would be a hub, a homey touch that would be a common gathering place."

The students were able to test their theories over the spring semester in a studio – a former computer room in the basement of Benson Hall – where they created drawings and models. For example, Hansel Bauman displayed a model of Clerc Hall, based on the students' ideas. The design of the ground floor gives the impression that it is part of the surrounding landscape. A ramp for wheelchair users leads to a second-floor entrance, lending barrier-free access to deaf people walking while engrossed in conversation. The ramp is symbolic of the "third person" in deaf culture – typically, when three deaf people walk together, two converse while the third acts as a guide, looking out for obstacles and charting the course.

Looking beyond the campus

Signing cafes. Movies by deaf filmmakers enjoyed while sipping cappuccino served by ASL-trained wait staff. A visual media center showcasing the works of deaf artists from around the world. Housing for Gallaudet faculty, students with families, and deaf senior citizens. These are just some of the ideas the deaf space students would like to see at "New Town at Capital City Market."

The D.C. City Council enacted legislation last December calling for development of 24 acres immediately west of Kendall Green that is characterized by a market and wholesale businesses. Since Gallaudet owns about 3.7 acres of the parcel, making it the largest landowner in the market project, the class wants to make the deaf community's needs known while development plans are being drawn up.

The students feel that the market – and its close proximity to the New York Avenue/ Florida Avenue/Gallaudet University Metro Station – presents an ideal opportunity to enhance Gallaudet's visibility. They reason that the market is already a glorious potpourri of languages and cultures, and that representation by deaf entrepreneurs should be added to the mix. They foresee deaf-owned businesses, advocacy agencies for the deaf community, restaurants and shops whose staff know ASL, and art galleries and theaters for deaf artists. They also envision deaf-friendly, green buildings that draw their electricity from alternative energy sources.

The deaf space group also investigated ways the market project can meet Gallaudet's housing needs. The results of a survey they conducted show that only 26 of 225 Gallaudet faculty live near the University. This means as soon as their daily teaching duties are done, faculty usually make a hasty retreat from campus. While this may help them beat rush hour traffic, it prevents them from staying for evening events and interacting with the community. Gallaudet students who are married and/or have families face a housing shortage. The 36 apartments at the University are full and have a waiting list of 40. And what about a place near Gallaudet for deaf senior citizens to live with their peers? The solution, the deaf space students say, can be found by incorporating housing into the market's planning.

Visualizing the possibilities

While defining deaf space is a work in progress, there is no question that the concept has jolted the imaginations of the students who have taken the course. It has inspired them to consider the possibilities, using the power of architecture as a catalyst. At presentations to the campus, where they share their ideas, the atmosphere is electric with the excitement they exude. And it is contagious, as members of the audience come forth time and again to fuel their ideas. They envision a new Gallaudet – a model place that will further its global role as the leader in deaf education by becoming the leader in language, culture, the arts, and international development.

What began as a study on deaf space has evolved into thesis projects for some students. For example, Matthew Malzkuhn is writing his master's thesis on deaf space in deaf people's homes. Another graduate student, Thomas Halseth, completed his thesis on the Gallaudet Library and its lack of deaf space design principles.

Malzkuhn's research focuses on deaf homeowners who are designing new homes or renovating existing ones, to document the ways they make their home environment "fit their deaf ways of being," he said. "Up until now, deaf people usually were understood through two categories – education and language," said Malzkuhn. "Do these categories fully explain how we live our lives? Do they tell us about deaf people's cultural values? They barely even scratch the surface. ... These are some of the questions that I am addressing through my thesis."

The Deaf Space project has given Malzkuhn food for thought about the deaf community and the ways it expresses itself. "When we look at other cultures and their habitats, we can learn a lot from just exploring the space they occupy. How would that be different with deaf people? We have such uniqueness in how we form our spaces." He added that when classmates Robert Arnold and Ryan Commerson suggested a sign for deaf space that comes from the French Sign Language sign for three-dimensional, it dawned on him that deaf people are "spherical people," he said. "I hadn't put much thought to that. ... it (the deaf space symbol) shows that we communicate in a spherical way, using sign language.... We converse in a circle, we arrange ourselves in a circle – the list goes on. It blew my mind."

For other students, the Deaf Space project offers a welcome chance to get in on a new study on an important yet overlooked aspect of deaf people's lives. When Commerson first learned about the Deaf Space project, he was anxious to become involved. "Deaf people have never had a place of their own in terms of architectural ownership, so my interest was piqued by an opportunity to create a space that reflects our identity," he said.

Commerson, a graduate student whose concentration is in cultural studies, finds it serendipitous that the program began last fall when the University was embroiled in protest. "The protest was about leadership and university philosophy. As a result, we were faced with a challenge to revisit the academic rigor, shared governance, and history of isolation from the academic community, so this project served as a perfect model to emulate in its innovative research and collaboration of administrators, faculty, staff, and students," he said.

What struck Commerson after getting involved in the project was how deaf people "intuitively and collectively know what kind of space reflects our identity and being." He said it was only a matter of weeks before the class developed a set of principles to guide it in its research. "Personally, I've come to a conclusion that the deaf space principles would benefit everyone all over the world, not just deaf people, because humans are naturally collective and tactile," said Commerson. "For me, the Deaf Space project is just one more validation that being deaf is truly a great thing; that being a visual-tactile oriented member of a collectivist culture has something of value that can be shared with the world." Malzkuhn shares Commerson's viewpoint on why the architectural principles of deaf space make sense in almost every design project, and adds, adamantly, "They are beyond practical. They are absolutely necessary."

Winston Churchill said, "We shape our buildings, and afterwards our buildings shape us." If the spark that has started with the students in the Deaf Space project becomes a flame, then the rising generation of deaf leaders will certainly play a role in molding the future of the deaf community.

Will these ideas be implemented? Who will invest in these projects? Will they change the world? Today, there are no answers, but the vision had been formed, and a dialogue has begun.

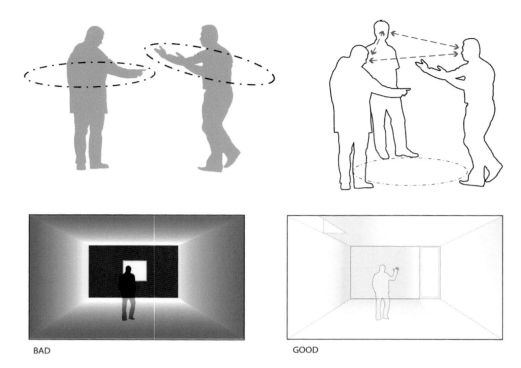

FIGURE 20.1 Examples from the DeafSpace Design Guidelines. Reprinted by permission of Hansel Bauman

In 2005 architect Hansel Bauman (hbhm architects) starting working with Gallaudet's ASL (American Sign Language) Deaf Studies department to create the DeafSpace Project, an initiative that sought to develop architectural guidelines based on how deaf people interact with their built surroundings.

Over the next five years, the DSP developed the DeafSpace Guidelines, a catalogue of over one hundred and fifty distinct DeafSpace architectural design elements that address the five major touch points between deaf experiences and the built environment: space and proximity, sensory reach, mobility and proximity, light and colour, and finally acoustics. Common to all of these categories are the ideas of community building, visual language, the promotion of personal safety and well-being.

These are being developed by Dangermond Keane Architecture (DKa). http://dangermondkeane.com/deafspace-design-guide

21

ALONG DISABLED LINES

Claiming spatial agency through installation art

Amanda Cachia (2016)

This essay explores how contemporary artists, Wendy Jacob (http://wendyjacob.net) and Corban Walker (www.corbanwalker.com), configure a new disabled geometry of space through their site-specific art installations that examine experiences of autism and dwarfism, where the ubiquitous line is the primary mode of engagement. The artists capture how disabled bodies uniquely move through space in order to claim spatial agency over public environments that commonly serve "normative" audiences and art works. Specifically, through the design of custom-made installations and objects, they call into question how to look, and offer the viewer the opportunity to re-think the traditional and ostensibly normative way their own embodiments move through a three-dimensional installation in a gallery or public space. By discussing Wendy Jacob's *Between Spaces* tightrope performances (2007), her collaboration with an autistic boy in *Explorers Club* (2009), and Corban Walker's *Trapezoid* installation (1997), I will suggest that their works offer experiences that shed light on complex embodiment in a bid to politically re-orient the viewer's perceptions of disabled subjectivity that is rarely addressed in contemporary art theory and praxis. Additionally, offering alternative accounts of spatiality through the phenomenology of the disabled body offers new perspectives on architecture itself: on its simultaneous limits and possibilities, and how it might be disrupted and transformed to account for a wider variety of body types and movements. Through the contemporary work discussed in this paper, architecture is re-imagined and re-built.

Following this, I am interested in how audiences might become more aware of what Tobin Siebers calls "disability aesthetics" (2006, this volume). He defines disability aesthetics as a complex embodiment, where the atypical body is marked by nuance rather than deficiency or deviancy. If installation itself, then, is characterized by a viewer's embodied experience with the art and the spaces it creates, how can complex embodiment add new layers to this framework, especially where disabled viewers and/or artists' bodies bring this explicitly to our notice? If installation art has always challenged the so-called normative embodied experience through work that helps us to see in new ways, how might it also offer perceptions of disabled corporeality that add rich new layers to this lineage? Ultimately, I will suggest that the disability aesthetics – and geography – that Jacob and Walker lay out is one that sets an important new agenda within contemporary art practices and architectures, where their unique user perspectives of space should be applied to, as Aimi Hamraie puts it, "a theory of body-environment relations focused on social justice" (2013, see this volume).

Disability, geography and spatial agency

According to geographer B. J. Gleeson, "disability is a profoundly socio-spatial issue" (1996: 388). Apart from being rooted in the ableism of the medical and social models, disability oppression is also connected to the material forces of architecture and the design and geography of urban space, because disabled people inhabit space that is distorted. By this, Gleeson means that the "physical environment is structured in ways that exacerbate the distorting effect of disability, through careless design and signage, for example, which inhibit the access and mobility of disabled people" (1996: 389). Disabled people must therefore inhabit and endure distorted space, which is the social space of the ostensibly "normal" person. But what would happen if the disabled subject were to create their own idealized, yet practical space to "fit" their complex embodiment, thereby transforming the generally inaccessible geographic landscape in their everyday lives?

Theorist Elizabeth Grosz asks if architecture can construct a better future for our citizens, and suggests that while architects must keep social and political problems in mind, it is better if they dwell on exploration and invention, as architecture is a key mode of experimental practice. She says, "architecture is a set of highly provisional 'solutions' to the question of how to live and inhabit space with others" (2001: 148). If there is an acknowledgement of multiple bodies and complex embodiment, then architecture needs to experiment with how this might become manifest through design. What can we learn about this through exploring art installation inside the normative space of the white cube of an art gallery, or a public art installation outside the walls of a gallery or a museum? Can artists "disable" normative space by obstructing or offering new modes of mobility or other multi-modal, architectural sensations?

In *Spatial Agency: Other Ways of Doing Architecture* (2011) Awan, Schneider and Till offer numerous art installation projects where contemporary artists are challenging normative models of how urban space is designed. Referencing Henri Lefebvre's 1974 book, *The Production of Space*, they suggest that social space must draw on the contribution of others, rather than relying on a fixed template of expert authorship. Social space is dynamic and evolving, where multiple actors can contribute to its progress at different stages. Social space is also not neutral, and indeed, nor is the gallery. Instead, it is political, and so charged with the binaries of power/empowerment, interaction/isolation, control/freedom and more. As the authors of *Spatial Agency* note, "…every line on an architectural drawing should be sensed as the anticipation of a future social relationship, and not merely as a harbinger of aesthetics or as an instruction to a contractor" (2011: 30). How, then, can transformation be achieved with lines beyond those that are drawn on architectural plans? Engaging with how Jacob and Walker use line offers one way of thinking and designing differently.

Awan et al. suggest that it is through the concept of spatial agency that artists and architects might find opportunity to contribute new thinking around oppressive or marginalizing spaces, and in ways that need to be articulated in a broader spatial field, beyond artwork or building as product. I will suggest that Jacob and Walker enact this very spatial agency for the benefit of disabled subjectivity through their practices. While it is true that altering the embedded socio-spatial dynamics in the environment or in the gallery will not necessarily lift all that oppresses disabled people at large, it is a beginning in order to think about how spatial agency may contribute to challenging the "normative" user experience of contemporary art and even architecture. Spatial agency as it applies to disability will insist on a type of mapping of disabled corporeality, tracing the complex embodiment of multiple disabled experiences, ranging from autism to dwarfism. How do the bodies of an autistic child or a man with dwarfism push back against spaces that are prohibitive to them, or inaccessible? The body–environment interactions of Jacob's project with an autistic boy, and Walker's engagement with scale and architecture in his combat against the "staturization" of space ("the dominant preference for able bodies of an average height" (Kruse 2010: 184)) both speak to how these engagements can be political sites and contribute to the lexicon of spatial agency, and revised spatial identities. I'd like to explore how the flesh of the complex body in conversation with architecture, the environment and its spatial elements and qualities can also contribute to knowledge production in art theory and praxis, and perhaps more broadly in terms of lived architectural space (Seamon 2010).

Disembodying the gallery: applying the Corban rule

Contemporary Irish artist Corban Walker's work often relates to architectural scale and spatial perception, utilizing industrial materials such as steel, aluminum and glass, drawing on minimalism to highlight different perspectives in relation to height and scale. Walker has anchondroplasia, the most common type of dwarfism. He is four feet tall and creates his sculpture stacks in direct proportion to his body using the "Corban rule," a precise mathematical calculation he devised, wherein he uses his own height as measure of his art. This spurs viewers to think about the built environment in different terms. Walker has talked about how he tries to get viewers to bend, crouch, twist or turn as they encounter his works from new positions. For example, in his *Trapezoid* installation (Figure 21.1) the viewer sees several rows of stainless steel wire lines strung from one side of a gallery wall to the other, suspended approximately four feet above the ground. Then upon walking to another section of the gallery, the lines begin again, and repeat themselves, threading from one side of the room to the next, using the standard dimension of four feet as an elevation point from the ground, reaching up to the lowest row of the steel lines. Walker is using his height as a measuring point for the elevation of the lines, so that he is disrupting the average-height viewer's spatial flow as they walk through a gallery space.

Walker thus provides a point of view that refuses the typical, normal or average. Bending down to see the installation shifts "standard-sized" audiences from their usual, unthought about looking straight-on viewpoint of an artwork. Walker wants to focus on drawing people downwards, closer to the ground, into a dimension equivalent to the "Corban scale." As Walker is four feet tall, he usually has to crane his neck to look up at people's

FIGURE 21.1 Corban Walker (1997) *Trapezoid*, Ridinghouse Editions, London, March 6th – April 19th (catalogue)

Photos courtesy of the artist.

faces or reach up to shake someone's hand in his everyday reality. *Trapezoid* reverses this "staturization of space" (Kruse 2010: 184). As the name implies, the artist is hoping to ensnare the visitor into this throng of lines, disrupting their smooth path so that they are forced to consider an alternative perspective in viewing space at a different scale – a re-staturization through spatial disorientation for average-height visitors.

Walker disembodies the gallery frame through this disruption in space by the effective use of lines, therein claiming an alternative spatial agency in a domain that usually privileges the average-height viewing position, where paintings are hung at a so-called universal and standard eye-level. Walker's work critically intersects with many conventions in art history and exhibition curation, such as Rudolf Arnheim's belief that "the viewer creates a decisive center," and thus that average height is the idealized viewing position that affects everything around him or her (1982: 16). But how and what is seen by a viewer depends on their spatial position and their orientation towards an art object or event. For Arnheim when paintings or objects are seen head-on within the vertical dimension, they are seen well because they are viewed at a comfortable distance. He says this comfort is disrupted when works of art are engaged along the horizontal plane, because "this is the dimension of most of our actions in space" (1982: 13). If our feet "get in the way of our eyes," it will cause a strange optical situation, because:

> the eyes are meant to look forward, to scan the environment in search of whatever shows up vertically as friend or foe. For the eyes to look down, the head or body has to bend, and even then the object underfoot cannot be viewed perpendicularly. It will be seen at an angle and therefore distorted, and that angle changes continuously as the person, engaged in his business, moves across the floor. The viewer's eyes are too close to encompass and analyze any extended horizontal pattern as a whole. Different portions present themselves in the visual field as the viewer changes position.
>
> (1982: 116)

Indeed, Arnheim's discussion fits squarely within the realm of visual and optical sensations experienced by the dwarf, who is positioned at an alternative height from the average-height person and gazes upon different portions of the visual field in comparison to others. Arnheim here also perfectly (and unintentionally) describes Walker's strategy and therefore his spatial agency in *Trapezoid*: for Walker is already aware of the spatial disorientation that ensues when one is forced to look downward, bend, crouch or twist in order to look upon a fixed object or move without visual or physical obstruction. By forcing his "normal" viewers to encounter some discomfort, or at least, temporary distortion, he asks them to take notice of the daily realities of disabled people's geographies.

Through the lines of string or stainless steel, the ideal of the framed painting is also negated as there are now additional conceptual and multi-modal layers to consider. The viewer is forced to reflect on the physical context and "their own participation in the production or experience of any meaning in the encounter with art objects" (1982: 116). This is the axis in which the work of Walker spins, as his work provides embodied encounters to the public that act to reveal the artificial construction of conventional gallery spaces and "normal" viewing experiences. Here the aesthetics of disability renders alternative meanings that make explicit and expressive the often hidden inter-relationships between body size, art object and movements through space. The Corban rule adds a fascinating and evocative intervention and juxtaposition with other human scale devices, such as Leonardo da Vinci's *Vitruvian Man* (1487) and Le Corbusier's *Modulor* (1943). The *Modulor*, in particular, is an anthropometric scale of proportions devised by the Swiss-born French architect. It is based on the six-foot height of an English man with his arm raised. These measurements do not represent the diversity, form and shape of all bodies, and these measurements translated into architecture and our built environment create barriers for disabled people. These art historical aesthetic ideals of perfection, proportion and beauty are found in classical and modernist art, and in architecture through concepts such as the Golden Section. This is "an average measure conforming to man" (Wolfflin 1994: 169). Michael Davidson has talked about how for eighteenth century German art historians and writers Gottfried Lessing and Johann Winckelmann, "a realistic depiction of a 'misshapen man' is less important

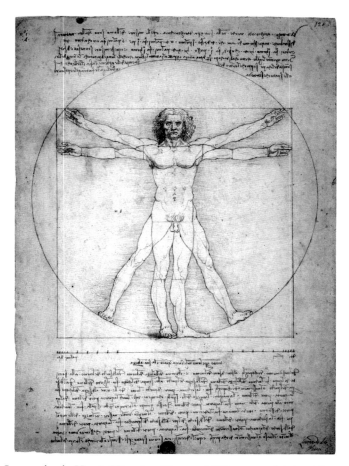

FIGURE 21.2 Leonardo da Vinci, *Vitruvian Man*, c. 1487, pen and ink with wash over metal point on paper

Collection of Gallerie dell'Accademia, Venice

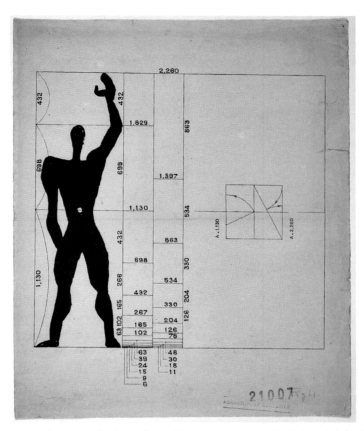

FIGURE 21.3 Le Corbusier (Charles-Edouard Jeanneret, 1887–1965) *Le Modular* 1945.

© ARS,NY. Le Modulor. 1945. Drawing. Photo Credit: Banque d'Images, ADAGP / Art Resource, New York

for its verisimilitude than for its demonstration of artisanal superiority. What is clear …is that the ability of aesthetics to define affective and sensory response depends on – indeed, is constituted by – bodily difference" (Davidson 2015: 26). Regretfully, the widespread representation of a bodily ideal in *Vitruvian Man* (Figure 21.2) and the *Modulor* (Figure 21.3) in art history and architecture contributes to ableist attitudes and discrimination against the disabled minority. This is because there is an internalized, almost unconscious assumption of able-bodiedness in art and architecture theory and praxis – if the assumption becomes "disrupted" by non-normative corporeal forms, then these forms have historically been rejected, and marked as pathological, diseased, and "other." Walker's own Corban rule works as an antithesis to these deeply entrenched ideals.

Tracing a line: minimalism, post-minimalism and Jacob

Wendy Jacob is an American artist whose work bridges traditions of sculpture, invention and design, and explores relationships between architecture and perceptual and bodily experience. Given Jacob's interest in body and space, she has said it was natural for her to find a way into disability studies. Recent projects have involved collaboration with architects, engineers, circus performers, and working with deaf and autistic individuals. In 2007, Jacob developed a project entitled *Between Spaces*, which involved a professional tightrope walker (whom she recruited from a local circus company) balancing and walking on a thirty-eight-foot practice tightrope wire. The tightrope walker moved from a third floor gallery by stepping out the window and crossing six feet to the stacks of an Massachusetts Institute of Technology (MIT) library next door, which involved traversing over a thirty-foot drop (Figure 21.4). The performance only lasted minutes, and it was only by chance if a visitor happened to be in the space to witness it.

A precursor to this project, *Line, Cambridge* (2005), was when Jacob ran a tightrope wire through the living room of a home in Cambridge and had a performer cross it while the family dined in the next room during Thanksgiving (Figure 21.5). Jacob's lines are effectively cutting through public and private space by way of open windows, thus demonstrating the permeability of assumed borders, but also slicing through any "normal" neutrality of architectural and social space.

These projects led Jacob to focus on *Explorers Club* in 2009, which was a series of photographs documenting two years of explorations through the meandering logic of a line, and chronicling the adventures of a twelve-year-old autistic boy named Stefano Micali, as he shapes and defines urban space according to his particular visual and spatial perspective. According to a discussion I had with Jacob in November 2013, Stefano found it reassuring to trace public and private space with string or tape, given his concern around how space is ordered. Jacob has said that "although his sight is perfectly fine, [Micali] has challenges integrating visual spatial information, particularly large, open spaces. He has devised tactics for framing or subdividing space, such as wearing eyeglass frames, even though he doesn't need corrective lenses, and running string around his room" (Badger and Jacob 2011: 4). Given Jacob had been working on projects where she was altering space with lines as discussed above, it made sense for her to work with Micali, who had a similar interest. He decided to call their project and its ensuing activities *Explorers Club*.

They spent the next two years travelling all over Boston and Cambridge by laying down and unrolling long lines of vinyl marking tape and temporarily restructuring and organizing the city with florescent orange lines. Jacob explains that her project was not about the condition of autism per se, but rather "the experience of being with a particular person (Stefano) and his particular way of organizing the world" (2011: 4). What is it to re-imagine the world through an alternative perspective? What new ways of thinking about space might develop? At first, Jacob had Micali divide up her studio with tape to create smaller rooms, which eventually led to the division of space with masking tape at the MIT gym, followed by going outdoors, including even the subway system. While Micali laid out the tape, Jacob attempted to document the process, and another friend would go behind reeling in the yards and yards of tape (Figure 21.6).

Through Jacob's projects involving line, the artist is conveying how bodies in space can be expressed differently. She does this by using tightropes and vinyl tape as modes of interruption, definition and spatial agency. In her projects where lines cut through architecture, the artist effectively "disables" any assumptions that built space has a

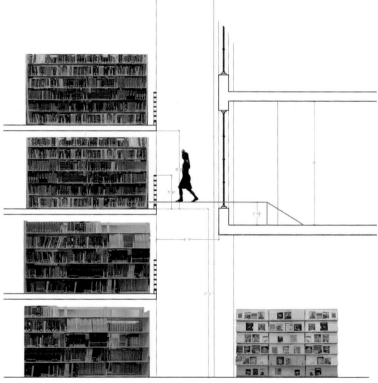

FIGURE 21.4 Wendy Jacob (2007) *Between Spaces*, Wolk Gallery and Rotch Library, MIT, September 20, 2007

Source: Photos courtesy of the artist.

FIGURE 21.5   Wendy Jacob (2005) *Line, Cambridge,* Performance at 21 Bowdoin St, Cambridge, Massachusetts

Source: Photo courtesy of the artist.

definitive form or function. Through the interjection of bodies moving unusually or atypically from one space to another, we come to understand that architecture is malleable and open to manipulation and even political ends. In Micali's negotiation of space and his urban environment, he finds it useful to lay down lines as a means to manage his spatial anxiety and, in the process, he offers opportunities for his non-autistic collaborators to experience a familiar space differently. Weaving through and under miles of tape, the participants began to understand how passages through space can be experienced through an alternative complex embodiment. Like Duchamp in *First Papers of Surrealism*, Jacob is reinforcing the rupture of the generalized or universalized "we" in the habitation of

FIGURE 21.6   Wendy Jacob with Stefano Micali (2009) *Explorer's Club*, Boston, MA

Source: Photos courtesy of the artist.

space, and instead reminds us of bodies as singular and independent entities, traversing many paths (Demos 2001). She says that the more typical pedestrian who cuts through space likely doesn't think about alternative "non-normal" patterns of mobility, and while Jacob's intent is not politicized from the outset, she realizes that making work from the perspective of one who is autistic comes with connotations of otherness that is steeped in histories of oppression and invisibility. Echoing Duchamp's project of displacement via his twine spiderweb, Jacob destabilizes conventional codes of path-making and way-finding in the division and splitting up of space with Micali (Kachur 2001) (Figure 21.7).

In "Topological Pathways of post-Minimalism," Eric de Bruyn expresses how important it became for minimalist artists to develop a different geometry in order to "map this multidirectional, intensive experience of space" (2006: 34). De Bruyn was referring to artist Dan Graham's observation that some post-minimalist sculptural practices were deviating from the Euclidean geometry so readily found in Minimal sculpture during the 1970s. Graham called this geometrical shift a topological "process of alteration," where the artist is "composing the composition" rather than starting with an authorial template

FIGURE 21.7 John D. Schiff (1907–1976). Installation View of Exhibition 'First Papers of Surrealism' Showing String Installation. 1942. Gelatin silver print. 7 5/8 × 10 inches (19.4 × 25.4cm). Gift of Jacqueline, Paul and Peter Matisse in memory of their mother Alexina Duchamp. 13-1972-9(303) Philadelphia Museum of Art. Marcel Duchamp: © Succession Marcel Duchamp / ADAGP, Paris / Artists Rights Society (ARS), New York 2016

Photo credit: The Philadelphia Museum of Art / Art Resource, NY.

or frame (de Bruyn 2006: 34). Within this space, de Bruyn proposes that there are no fixed boundaries, and "no central position of focus are available to the observer" (2006: 35). Following this, I am particularly interested in the question that de Bruyn poses – "what critical relevance does this history of the topological pathways of postminimalism yield for us today?"(2006: 37). I would suggest that the topological pathways of post-minimalism has yielded rich ground in which artists like Jacob and Walker can explore the subjectivity of disability. Jacob and Micali's *Explorers Club* and Jacob's *Between Spaces* have clearly constructed an "other" topological pathway that has similar scope and vision to the work of post-minimalism in their aspirations to compose, and stay connected to, a "deterritorialized space of drifting signs and bodies" (2006: 40). Like the work of Dan Graham, Jacob and Micali are transgressing the "striated space of an institutional practice of art" (de Bruyn 2006: 40) because their line-making is not contained to the minimalist, Euclidean grid of the white cube gallery space. Instead, the florescent wobbly lines and the tightropes are harnessing a more complex relationship to the public spaces of full networks of information and spatial encounters. From a Foucaultian perspective, de Bruyn says that Graham's (and I'll add Jacob's) topology moves "outside the spatial matrix of disciplinary power," essentially liberating the disabled subject from reductive frameworks and models that aim to confine and constrain" (2006: 41).

By placing art works into urban space, Jacobs releases them to a larger and more public world than the gallery. Rudolf Arnheim says that the frame "defines the reality status of works of art as distinguished from the setting of daily life." It has a visible detachment from reality, and "confines the range of the picture" (1982: 52). But if for Arnheim, such a distancing is central to artistic appreciation, for Jacob the art is challenging precisely *because* it cannot necessarily be distinguished from daily life, and nor can the viewer be certain that they are looking at this work from the outside. The viewer is now implicated in the work, blurring the lines between inside/outside, control/freedom and more. Both *Between Spaces* and *Explorers Club* also offer the "lived reality of the urban milieu" that happens to include complex embodiment (De Bruyn 2006: 45), and so the works both talk back to normative attitudes to space and its average occupation.

Conclusion

In the contemporary art installations of Corban Walker and Wendy Jacob, a new disabled geometry of space is configured, that starts from "non-normal" experiences expressed and interrogated through the power of lines that rupture, interrupt and decenter. Most critically, Jacob and Walker's works powerfully contribute to a theory of body–environment relations, where disabled subjectivity can offer new experimental modes of thinking and being through art, architecture and space that is never neutral, always political, and always dynamic. There can no longer be an assumed "average" or normative uniformity in how to engage or respond to a work of art when we remember all the variegated forms of knowing and being in space; just as there can be no one universal design in architecture or single-point perspective to buildings and public spaces. These artists disrupt any certainty of an aesthetic or spatial given, by revealing that the juxtaposition between bodily relations in space is much more heterogeneous than typically assumed. The participant conditions of both artists and audiences are now mediated and individualized through psychological, sensory and social modes that do not claim homogeneity or standardization. Rather, making work based on corporeal complexity offers a form of critical artistic practice centered on experiential engagements with viewers that insists on revealing the particularities of different embodiments-in-space. In these processes the potentialities of material space are also opened up, to re-orientation and radical interpretation.

22

THE RAMP HOUSE

Building inclusivity

Thea McMillan with Katie Lloyd Thomas (2016)

Isabella has known her friend Greta, an eleven-year-old girl who is a wheelchair user, since they were little. She remembers the traditional two-storey terraced house Greta grew up in their friendly seaside neighbourhood of Portobello, Edinburgh, where Greta attends mainstream school, and is a familiar presence. When a neighbour noticed it was getting harder for Greta's architect parents, Thea Chambers and Ian McMillan, to manage the stairs with her she suggested they take a look at a backstreet lane nearby where it might be possible to build their own home. Thanks to the generosity of Arthur who had run the garage at the end of the lane for many years, they were able to purchase a plot and started to design the Ramp House – an inclusive family home for Greta and her sister Bea, where the whole house would enable Greta to lead a barrier-free included life.

> *Isabella: The Ramp House is really thoughtful, it doesn't feel unusual that it has a big ramp instead of stairs and it's very well designed because it has everything that Greta needs and all the equipment she needs, but it's not in the way. There's a wee hidey bit that has a beanbag and little fairy lights – somewhere for Greta to chill out which is really cool. The house is really interesting. It has lots of things you wouldn't think of like the hot tub. It's really bright and spacious and I don't think any room feels tight. Even the small chill-out room feels nice because it's bright and colourful. I think Greta likes it because her mum and dad can do less for her, and they don't need to carry her up stairs or move furniture to let her move around the place. It's probably easier and less stressful.*

This essay comes out of a series of conversations between Thea and co-writer Katie Lloyd Thomas, and many others, like Isabella, who have been and are involved with the house. We present the planning, building and inhabitation of the house as an ongoing process of inclusivity, and we endeavour also to construct an inclusive piece of writing that welcomes and is structured around the voices and responses to the house of those who use it. We suggest that making the experience of a disabled child the starting point of a design process transforms the way she and the family live, and opens up potential rather than limiting expectations. The house physically embodies an alternative spatial experience. For visitors, moving through and around it challenges their own perceptions of disability as they too use space differently. Importantly too, the designing, building and inhabiting of the house has opened up new possibilities for catalysing and including wider communities, even transforming social relations – for local people who participated in making the building happen, and for support workers, friends and relatives who use it with the family.

Designing and inhabiting an inclusive home

Thea: We are often confronted with the physical barriers that the built environment presents; in our own home we were able to design a fully inclusive place. Using a ramp to access all levels provides an equality of space to us all. We have designed spaces along the ramp, connecting both horizontally and vertically, so that the experience of the house changes as it unfolds. As we inhabit the house, we can see how this provides variation, complexity and flexibility in the everyday use of the house, how many spaces can be used concurrently and how it reaches its potential when it is inhabited: movement around it, by foot or on wheels brings the experience to life.

The design process started as soon as Thea visited the plot and started imagining how a house could be built there which would be inclusive both in terms of its spatial organisation and in the process of its coming into being. From the beginning, the whole family were involved in envisaging the arrangement of future spaces and activities. Greta and her sister participated in the design process straight away; working with models to test out and understand different spatial arrangements, and once the project was on site they visited it regularly.

Thea: The models were especially important for Greta's understanding of the space; we made them large enough that Greta could easily look into them, which gave a sense of how it might be to be in there, and of all the connections between the different spaces [Figure 22.1]. They also helped us discover the most important connection that we wouldn't otherwise have seen; making a balcony between our bedroom on the 'first level' and the living space on the 'ground floor'. (We noticed how habitual our use is of the terms up 'stairs' and down 'stairs' and tried to find other ramp-oriented terms that could describe inhabitation as happening at different 'levels' instead.) Now that we are in the house this connection enables a lot more independence for Greta, as she can be in the sitting room with friends and I can see that she is fine and happy, without anyone realising.

The design process consisted of regular Sunday family sessions around the kitchen table, and included everything from the initial concept (the ramp) right down to choosing materials. Bea designed the coursing of the Caithness stone walls for the ground floor of the house, learning to use Microstation Computer Aided Design (CAD) so that she could compare the different possibilities and choose one. She and her friend Jessica even built the IKEA wardrobes just before they all moved in. This involvement of the whole family in the design process has continued into the occupation of the house when Bea

FIGURE 22.1   Greta with one of the development models for the Ramp House

Source: Photo by Thea McMillan.

will sometimes start talking about ways to redesign parts of the house. Greta hearing this reminds the family to include her in these conversations, and so the house keeps evolving, around the everyday of its very specific occupants as they all find different ways to use it.

Just before they moved in the family had a design session writing notes on a large exploded model (Figure 22.2). It showed them how different each of their perceptions was about how the spaces would be used. Now they are inhabiting the spaces, Thea says she can see that it is quite possible for each member of the family to use each space differently. This may have come about from the reversed design process with which they designed. First they got the ramp to work on the site. Then they designed spaces off the ramp for all the different things they wanted to do. This has led to a house that encompasses many different ideas and ways of being.

> *Thea: Something we didn't fully appreciate until the house was built and we were occupying it was how important all the connections – visual, audio, as well as the physical – would be for our everyday life. Greta cannot follow us independently so being able to understand where we are going around the house, and to hear us talking with her from many different places keeps her involved, and shows her an expectation of being part of everything. It is the thing that most chimes with other families with wheelchair-users, who have experienced the difficulties of limitations to their children's independence, and are delighted to see spatial solutions to this.*

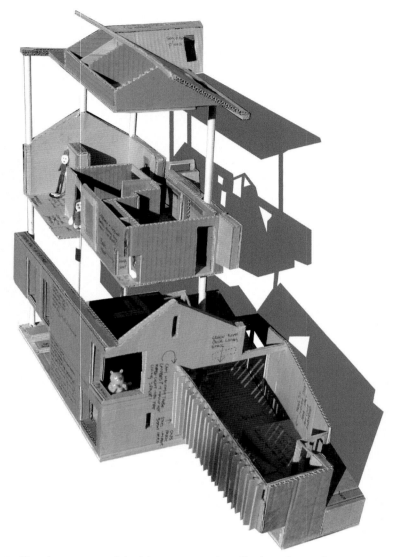

FIGURE 22.2 Development model with comments inscribed on the surfaces

Photo by Thea McMillan

The house caters for the many dimensions of family life, but it also provides transformative spaces for Greta's other activities with people from outside the family.

> *Greta's music teacher Francesca has been doing music sessions with her for the past 5 years. She visits the house once a week and sees Greta becoming increasingly confident about making music and more willing to express herself by trying different music technologies (on iPad and Eyegaze).*

Francesca: Music is a very important part of Greta's life and making music gives her an opportunity to feel connected to other people, to engage in conversations while manifesting her curiosity and liveliness. Greta is growing fast and with that her capacity and desire to be part of a community, to be heard and make a contribution to the people around her. Music is encouraging this growth and we all need a space in order to continue growing. The Ramp House gives Greta this space, in the same way as Greta and her music give meaning to that space and bring it to life.

With its echo and acoustic, the house aims to acknowledge and honour Greta's musical input, which is genuine, generous, not holding anything back. In this respect, Greta can teach all us a huge amount and inspire us to reconsider the value of sharing.

It's just so important having a space for ourselves, in order to develop trust, intimacy and connection in that relationship. I can see how Greta is comfortable in that space, she is safe and at ease, and I'm not sure this is always the case within a school. There's also something about the music we share and the space we are in… being able to play in an open space allows new possibilities and a desire to take different paths within music. It feels relaxed, without time constrictions or a timetable to follow.

The potential of the Ramp House's spaces often exceed the uses originally anticipated in the design, including and enabling a wide range of activities and experiences, which alter everyday living and perception both for the family and its visitors.

The Ramp House as an accessible and equalising experience of space for all

When Greta's friend Neve was asked what she thought Greta liked about the Ramp House her mum thought her answer 'was a bit literal'. She 'was hoping for something more profound'. Neve simply said, 'It's just easier for Greta to get about.' On reflection, though, her mum thinks, 'Perhaps she's judging it from the perspective of a child (her and Greta being the same in this regard) i.e., "You wouldn't ask me about my house and why I like it, would you?"'

From the viewpoint of a child like Neve who knows Greta and her house well, there is nothing exceptional about being able to freely navigate your own home. But accessible space can be about more than getting around without obstacles, it is also about making spaces that invite access and encourage new perceptions of how space can be used. For support workers, carers, friends and visitors, the Ramp House can alter perceptions of what a disabled person can do, replacing limitations and practicalities with possibilities and dreams. The design was shortlisted for architectural awards, bringing judges and journalists into the house, and all the publicity has meant that the house is hugely popular on Open Door Days, with over 900 visitors, encompassing a great range of people including some who use different kinds of wheelchairs, who all come to try out the spaces. Seeing Greta using these spaces, and experiencing them themselves allows people to understand inclusion and accessibility differently, and informs anew how they view the relationship between bodies, space and movement. The house communicates this directly through the visitor's body, extending their notions of how space should and could be used and often encouraging ideas of spatial play and experimentation.

> *One visitor to the house on a Doors Open Day wrote in the comments book, 'Stunning example of imaginative problem-solving and architecture as an expression of / enabler of life. It put the biggest smile on my face!'*
>
> *Nye who is in Greta's class at school and was her neighbour at the old house says the new house is 'fun for everyone… You can race down the ramp in a wheelchair or run down it.'*
>
> *Sarah (who visits the house to clean) comments, 'This would be a great place for roller-bladers.'*

Thea has noticed how much easier the house makes it to welcome people. Even on Scotland's Doors Open Day – when the house is opened to the public for one weekend – it never feels too full. The ramp makes a natural route that enables a flow through the spaces for everyone, whether by wheelchair or on foot. The house welcomes people in, starting at the front door that is rarely locked. Although you arrive straight into the kitchen, the slowing down of the ramp and the variety of articulated spaces coming off the ramp mean that it doesn't feel as if people arrive directly into a private space. Although access is physically meandering, it is visually direct, and for Greta this gives her a chance to get ready to greet people while they make their way through the spaces and up to where she sits at the heart of the house. Just as importantly, the house enables Greta to work and play with her friends in an inclusive way, where there is an equality of their movement and occupation of space.

> *Thea: Last time Greta's friends came round they played Forty Forty Home where Greta and one of the others were 'it'. Spatially this worked really well, as there are lots of opportunities to catch glimpses of people trying to creep down the ramp or stair, and because of this it works especially well for Greta when she sits in one place.*
>
> *Isabella: We love playing that game [Forty Forty Home] – it's really fun! On the main ramp, half way up there's a bookcase and you start there and Greta and another person are at the bottom. You have to get to the pole that splits the kitchen and the living room without Greta and another friend catching you. You have to be really sneaky because if Greta blinks or makes a noise, she's seen you and you're out.*

Thea sometimes wonders how this makes Greta feel, not being able to run the circuit with the other children in the house, but she senses that Greta feels just as involved in all this activity and motion – because it is 'her spaces' and the connections between them that make these activities possible. In this house Greta gets to have a spatial experience equivalent to that of others around her, which is often impossible in the everyday environments beyond that she encounters. The inclined architectural language of the ramp provides, in fact, a levelling of spatial experience. It acts as a platform on which Greta and others share a common ground, changing their perspectives and giving value to her own sense of self as well.

Including the local community in realising and building the house

As a built object – a set of spatial relationships – the Ramp House is inclusive in the way that it is used and in so far as it challenges and transforms perceptions and assumptions of disability. But when the family designed the building, they – and their neighbours – also constructed something else. The building of the house – in the long protracted timespan from seeing that design could offer them a better way to live as a family, to finding a plot, raising money, getting permissions, making it work, living in it, and establishing a place for the house in the imagination of those too distant to visit it – also afforded an opportunity for those outside the immediate family to act, and be included in the process of realising the house. For each actor who became part of this collective process, their involvement was at the same time a moment of understanding accessibility and inclusivity differently.

> *Greta was one of the first to visit the plot and meet its owner, Arthur, who has run the garage at the end of the lane for many years. He could see how much the family needed a more accessible home, in the heart of their community, and he agreed to sell it to them with a handshake. 'Greta moved me,' he says to Thea, 'once when I was telling you about the troubles we were having, she started to cry. It brought me up sharp. Of course disabled people are also taking things in.'*

When Chambers McMillan submitted the planning application for the Ramp House there were fifteen objections – even from some who knew Greta and her family. It was Arthur who alerted his customers to the situation and suggested that planners might accept their letters of support (not just the usual objections). And those letters, from local judges, architects, headmistresses, nurses, engineers amongst others, finally ensured the planning committee's unanimous approval of the scheme.

> *Arthur explains that people from all walks of life, influential and ordinary, bring their cars into his garage, and as good listeners, they have become the local citizens advice bureau. So all he had to do was tell them that, 'there's a wee girl who needs to have an accessible house in Portobello, and we can help her'. He had drawings and the description of the project pinned up on the wall, and because of this planners received around seventy letters of support from people who didn't even know the family. 'To tell the truth,' says Arthur, 'I enjoyed the fight'.*

Galvanising of the local community not only contributed to the planning committee's eventual decision, but also provided Arthur, and others who might not even know the family, to get involved in the project of realising an inclusive space. Others found more direct ways to participate in the process. As construction was coming to an end, and the family were exhausted, they knew they were going to run out of money for the finishes, floors, storage and kitchen. At their wits' end, now they were so near to finally moving in they put out requests for a bit of help on Facebook, and were amazed to discover how many volunteers turned up to help out with laying floors (Jon, Andrew and Geoff), building the IKEA kitchen (Francesca and Rowan), bedroom wardrobes (Jess and Bea), shelving (Paul and Geoff) and concrete pouring for the reflective pool (Roddy).

> *Thea: A lot of the people who turned up I only vaguely recognised, although I later found out they knew Greta very well as their children were in her year at school. Many of these people have become good friends, and they and their children have come to parties and enjoyed using the ramp.*

Thea says that when she sits in the house and looks around she sees the people who helped build it. People wanted to get involved, to be part of making this project happen even if in small ways – the building work was a conduit that enabled them to take part in the realisation of the Ramp House. Unable to be directly involved with Greta, or to achieve change on an individual basis, the many letter writers, floor layers and furniture fixers formed temporary collectives that could together make a difference – building an inclusive *social* environment as well as a *physical* one.

Shifting relations of expertise

The building of the Ramp House has also allowed wider networks of people to become involved in building Greta's world and be transformed by it, even if just in small ways. Its ongoing presence as an accessible hub in the community has changed the way specialist support workers are involved with Greta and the family; and the house has helped to alter conventional hierarchies that too often sideline the specialist knowledges of disabled people and their families. By putting Greta at the centre of the space, and physically embodying different connections between disabled and able-bodied, amateur and professional expertise, family and institutional support, the house changes social relationships. It demonstrates that new alliances and new kinds of relationship are possible, and as such it takes part in a broader political project towards goals of more equal involvement between families with a disabled member and professional experts, support workers and state agencies.

There is a lot of discussion in the Scottish National Health Service (NHS) about inclusion and patient-centred care but this can be difficult to achieve in the spaces of hospitals and institutions: so Greta's family has always invited people to work with her in their house. The spaces of the house are designed out of the family's expertise and deep understanding of Greta's experience and desires. The house therefore embodies and communicates that expertise and puts family and professionals on equal footing. It 'teaches' experts about possibilities not limitations. This space puts Greta at the centre, shifting professionals' emphasis away from what they can do for Greta, to what Greta can do and how they can support this.

> *Thea: Using the house every day, we have many people who work with Greta coming into her space, a space that has been designed to offer her limitless possibilities, when so often our physical environment is about obstacles and difficulties. When we talk with and work with health professionals and educators in Greta's inclusive environment, I think it makes them see her differently. It also makes them see us differently: the house embodies our expertise and understanding of Greta, as well as offering the open-ended approach to her potentials and possibilities that has always been our philosophy living with Greta.*

In the house it is easier for Greta and others to work together as a team, ensuring that she is seen as an equal in their collective efforts. When the team around Greta work on a level basis, the typical, if sometimes subtle, hierarchy of the NHS and educators is transformed into an equality of working.

Filip is Greta's Bobath physiotherapist, which is a specific type of physio/occupational/speech therapy that enables the family to learn to work with their children and to take that knowledge and experience back, to practice in their everyday homes. He has known Greta since she was a baby.

Filip: In terms of emotions, it definitely felt different treating Greta in her own space. At the [Bobath] Centre I feel in charge. In Greta's space I felt an enormous amount of respect somehow… and was almost waiting for suggestions from Greta and any of you. I guess if I am honest, my senses were more ready to invite messages from Greta compared to meeting and treating her in my 'familiar' environment at Bobath Scotland where I feel I am taking the lead much more.

Conclusion: expanding definitions of inclusivity

The British Standards Institution (2005) defines inclusive design as: 'the design of mainstream products and/or services that are accessible to, and usable by, as many people as reasonably possible … without the need for special adaptation or specialised design'. Rather than creating a 'normal' house and then adding on (or 'retrofitting', see Dolmage, this volume) elements that would make it 'work' for Greta, designing *from* a ramped route gives an equality of access to almost all of its spaces as a matter of principle. (This includes a decision to make one space – reached by a ladder-like stair with a window framing a sea view – that is knowingly designed as a kind of retreat from the otherwise fully accessible openness; Figure 22.3).

However, the Ramp House also demonstrates a wider definition of inclusivity in its procurement, design and building, because of the large range of people involved. Persuading the planning committee or literally helping to finish the building work became a vehicle through which the local community could include themselves in supporting the family and demonstrate the extent to which they valued the project of inclusivity and wanted to be part of it.

Equally crucial has been the inclusivity generated through the house's ongoing occupation and use. The Ramp House does not just aim to include disabled 'others'. It *starts from* a positive engagement with the lived experiences of disability as an inherently shared enterprise – and so generates spaces that affect all visitors and residents directly through their diverse bodily registers. This, in turn, opens up our understandings of space beyond 'normal' use and users to other perspectives and new possibilities for occupation. This produces the 'levelling' that Thea describes, that is experienced both by Greta and the visitors who come to the house, and that is also demonstrated in the way the house got built. To appreciate that these aspects of the Ramp House are also inclusive, we need to consider space as more than an object and container for functions and activities. Greta is not just 'included' by being able to move easily around; rather the house enables more inclusive social and spatial encounters between *all* its occupants and visitors, and was a catalyst for including a wider community during the processes of construction. Inclusivity, then, is not simply a property that can be achieved by following guidelines and building regulations, ensuring that a space is 'step-free' for example. Inclusivity is always spatial, social and physical all at once, and the project of making inclusive spaces offers an opportunity for multiple modes of inclusive practice that might involve the building of

FIGURE 22.3 Chambers McMillan Architects (2011). Interior view, Ramp House, Portobello, Edinburgh 2011

Source: Photography: David Barbour.

temporary collectives, or alternative forms of encounter with each other, as much as new spatial visions.

For its visitors (and Katie includes herself here) the house embodies and communicates a particular open-ended approach to the possibilities and potentials for a disabled person. It makes use of the capacity of spaces and objects to 'stand in for' human actions and encounters in ways that have been explored by Actor-Network theorists such as Bruno

Latour. He gives the example of a speed bump on a university campus, as a permanent physical 'translation' of a sign or a policeman standing by the side of the road asking drivers to slow down (1999: 187); and similarly, in its spatial and material configuration, the Ramp House 'performs' what would otherwise have to be constantly communicated and explained by the family 'on behalf of' Greta.

Using the example of a mechanical door closer fixed to the hinge that is 'delegated' the job of shutting the door after you have gone through, Latour also suggests that there can be an affective tone or manner to such performance. Just like a doorman holding the door open, the door closer can do the job graciously, giving you plenty of time to go through, or 'rudely' by closing it too quickly so that it almost catches you on the bottom (Latour 1999). The Ramp House delegates movement to the ramp, making it easy for everyone to navigate their way through the house. But it does more than this – through the variety and richness of spatial relationships, views and materials it communicates accessibility in a certain manner – joyful, playful, witty. The house wears so very lightly, its serious and radical challenge to conventional normative ideas about bodies and inhabitation. Even when its occupants are weary and impatient with some of the assumptions and attitudes they encounter, or during times when health is not so good, the house retains its open optimistic breezy outlook, refusing, perhaps, to be worn down.

> *Katie: As we move round the ramp there is a collage of materials, pink, light and bright, spacious, shiny… here the house looks back at itself, there at a peaceful pool, here at a worn stone wall with gardens beyond, there at a desk just a minute ago abandoned, just here at a round chair still rocking where Greta was playing, there is Bea's school bag dropped off in a corner, and over there at the sky and even beyond, up there, the sea.*

The house is all about the ongoing process of occupation: each space becomes what it is through use, but these varied and changing uses have been made possible by a design which doesn't limit or stereotype space (kitchen, living room, bedroom), but opens up possibilities and potentials for every member of the family. It started with the plan to build a house around a ramp, but it continues to act through its inhabitation and those who encounter it. The house is experienced and performed by many people, in many different ways – all because Greta is enabled to occupy the centre with her family and others.

> *Thea: We remember when Greta was a couple of weeks old, and we were in intensive care, a nurse told us: 'You will have to bring the world to Greta.' Our life feels as if not only have we done this, but also through the Ramp House we have changed the perception of the world.*

23

RESISTANT SITTING

Sophie Handler (2008)

Reprinted from 'Resistant Sitting: The Pensioner's Alternative Street Furniture Guide' Project Report: RIBA/Ice McAslan Bursary, pp 33–37, 39–41.

Public seating

There is a basic generosity in the idea of furnishing a street. A seat, for instance, that is set outdoors as a freely available, public resource generously opens up that street to the passer-by, turns it into a place for sitting in as much as a place for simply passing through. This is the hospitable face of street furniture: furniture that openly invites the leisurely occupation of public space, not only functional passage through it.

Early versions of street furniture (in Paris) are light and flexible: a set of fold-away chairs are laid out in the city's public parks, set out in the morning, tidied away at the end of the day. Street furnishing now (here, in Newham) extend into the streetscape as permanent fixtures of public space: robust, heavy benches and chairs on pavements, in squares, that are rooted physically into the ground as an immoveable public resource, resourced and maintained by the local authority. Borough-wide design guides formalise the language of this provision, carefully codifying the placement, design and appearance of public furnishings, generating a recognisably uniform (or limited?) vocabulary for what are publicly designated spaces for sitting in. Formalised sitting.

There are limits though to this practice of formally codifying street furniture. To generate, for instance, a uniform type of public seat is to, by implication, mark out all other spaces that might be used for sitting in (objects, places, things not explicitly designed for sitting in, but that are sat on all the same) as a mis-use of space, e.g. sitting on a set of steps, on a ledge, on a wall. *See Resistant Sitting below.* Here, the necessarily limited dimension of design coding narrows down and limits the potential for the creative, impromptu (mis) use of urban space (the use of an alternative seat... a low-level wall, a streetside bollard).

Is this the point where the basic generosity behind the idea of furnishing a street reveals itself as a subtle regime of social regulation and control? A bench, for instance, is designed with a bare minimum of comfort to ensure not only adherence to the more mundane municipal ambitions of robustness, durability, low maintenance (value for money) but to also exert subtle degrees of social control (designed-in discomfort will deter the 'undesirable' presence of rough sleepers, etc.). The barely comfortable seat quietly limits and controls the length of the sitter's stay – a precisely pitched ledge of a bus stop seat tolerates a precarious, therefore, temporary perching posture only.

This is the inhospitable extremity of street furniture design: that there are specified pitches and calculated comfort levels designed to determine and curtail the length of a stay on a seat. ... Which is another way of saying that there is, in these local authority design codes, a calculation for both public provision (generosity) but an equal calculation for limiting that provision: for controlling it, taking it away. *i.e. what is generously provided with one hand is, with the other also, carefully guarded, monitored, occasionally (arbitrarily) taken away.*

Upton Lane (c. 2009)

A set of bus stop seats on Upton Lane are, without warning, removed sometime this last year to discourage anti-social behaviour ('drunken Poles' have, allegedly, been congregating on the seat, according to David (from the 50+year old dance class) within what is the technically alcohol-free zone of Forest Gate). In its extreme literalism, local authority logic reasons that it is the bus stop seat that supports the anti-social behaviour – the seat is, therefore, removed leaving David to act out the tragic-comic scenario: of the unwitting passer-by turning up at the bus stop ready to sit down on an accustomed seat, only to encounter the empty space of *a ghost of a bench.*

Sitting as an ordinary, benign act turns into sitting as a uniformly suspect act; gracefully degrading (through official misconstrual) as lingering, loitering ...

In its extreme (neurotic) form, the suspicion of sitting extends into an elaborate typology of sitting deterrents that attempt to establish norms of public behaviour: training, regulating and correcting all forms of bad sitting (in the wrong place). Like the operation of a Pavlovian mechanism (in reverse), the typology of the urban streetscape is designed to effect the psychological internalisation of its physical deterrents:

- a set of stick-down strips of metallic spikes strategically positioned on sittable-height ledging (engendering a bed-of-nails effect)
- otherwise sittable steps washed down at regular intervals (deterrent masquerading as regular 'maintenance')
- commercial seating authorised 'for customer use only' (verbal deterrent of signage/surveillance)
- sittable-height boundary walls finished with hard-angled brickwork (deterrent masquerading as ornament).

Resistant sitting (or how to sit differently)

DATE: 14.05.2009
Location: Cundy Road Recreation Ground

A group of schoolgirls are sitting the wrong way round on top of a park bench i.e. not according to the designed use of the bench (their feet rest, 'improperly' on its seat). To sit the wrong way round (to sit contrary to the designed shape of a public seat) is to resist the behavioural norms that govern the intended use of objects of public space, challenging, implicitly, the design coding that determines the correct posture for the use of street furniture.

In adolescence the territorial appropriation of objects in public space (a wrongly sat-on bench) becomes a public marker of adolescent difference, a deliberate statement of resistance to (paternal) authority (the correct way of sitting). This is the self-conscious aesthetics of mis-use. Sitting the wrong way round as a visible, public statement of emerging (adolescent) identity in space: a generational marker of difference.

DATE: last Monday
Location: Prince Regent Lane

Joan, on the way to the post office and back home, 'plonks' herself down on the boundary wall (of no. 139 Prince Regents Lane). There are no other seats to sit on.

The territorial appropriation of a mis-used/sat-on boundary wall is the creative response to changing physical need in older age: the ageing body as it feels and adapts to the absence of enough seats to sit on when out and about, resisting self-consciously, defiantly even, the limits, or rather these deficiencies, imposed by the urban environment.

Resistant sitting (tactics of resistance in older age)

Doreen Massey describes older age as 'a closing in again', an increasingly curtailed kind of existence that is the inevitable by-product of diminished mobility in older age: a narrowing down of movement, of experience (increasing confinement indoors) that implies, in turn, diminishing levels of flexibility – both physical and psychological. There is, however, a way in which diminished mobility forces, paradoxically, a greater kind of flexibility in older age: adapting to an environment, adapting it in turn, developing a creative relationship to a space as a way of both dealing with and resisting this limiting notion of an increasingly curtailed kind of existence, of a 'closing in' again... working out ways of navigating a place more comfortably, more easily, developing tactics, ways of using a space that bend the environment to aid and accommodate personal desires and needs.

Derek and Joan talk (in a domestic setting) with intimate knowledge about ways of navigating about their own homes, using the radiator (in the front hall) as a walking aid, moving things about the house in order to minimise the need for unnecessary exertions of movement. Joan brings the kettle in from the kitchen into her front living room to limit the number of times she needs to get up out of her armchair to make herself a cup of tea, Derek uses the radiator in the front hall as his improvised handrail, in the absence of a walking stick. The intimate knowledge and sense of personal ownership of domestic space allows for an easy, flexible appropriation of space.

To a degree, that easy appropriation of space extends, outwards into the public space of the street, though more tentatively perhaps. Joan's low wall, that, like the radiator turned into a handrail, transformed into an impromptu, wished-for seat (the sat-on wall). Eileen calls this: *adapting*, a resourcefulness that becomes increasingly necessary in older age: having to adapt the urban environment to the needs of a changing-ageing body, mapping out the urban 'landmarks' (the small features of public space) that affect the body in older age (a dizzyingly sloping section of pavement, for instance), adapting more generally to the sensation that diminished mobility expands space. The longer it takes to get from a to b (with arthritic knees, failing hips, stiffening joints etc.) the lengthier the feeling of that space between a and b, and the journey becomes more tiresome...

PLEASE NOTE: Public provision for resting, in the form of a designated public seat/ bench, cannot always be found to be available at the precise moment when a rest stop is required (the point of tiredness is a variable, subjective point somewhere between a and b)... As public provision fails to meet up with personal need impromptu improvisation follows: in the casual, ad hoc appropriation of found features of the street (non-seats) as seats.

Ambiguous seating (or sitting somewhere between what is permitted and what is not)

Joan sits on 'her' boundary wall, in legal limbo, on the borderlines of what is officially designated as public/private space, perched in between public and private zones (her feet set down on public territory, while the rest of her is sitting on the private realm of a residential wall).

Derek sits on a bollard, on the borderlines of a pedestrian/vehicular zone, perched somewhere in between the two (his feet set down on the public territory of the street, while the rest of him sits on a bollard – an anonymous feature of the street – that is not, technically speaking, actually intended for public use).

In a way it is the ambiguity of the streetscape object – the ambiguous rules of ownership governing these borderline objects (a wall, a bollard), their anonymity in terms of function (as technically non-useable objects, versus the more obviously useable bench) that makes their appropriation possible. Here, a dividing marker of space (a boundary wall, a borderline bollard) turns into an inhabited, thickened out line as a dividing border, an interstitial space is expanded, temporarily, into an occupied place.

This double ambiguity/anonymity of the streetscape object tolerates more easily a subversive attitude of appropriation in older age, mitigates the inhibiting effects of self-consciousness (politeness/reticence), in favour of a more spontaneous and robust confidence in the mis-use of space:

- sitting in full public view (on a bollard) in the obviously wrong place knowing that people might stare
- asking (is this too much?) to sit on a seat, in a shoe stall, just for a rest, knowing that the seat is 'for customer use only', for trying on shoes

- overcoming a slight (but real) feeling of tentativeness in using a wall that belongs to someone else
- self-consciousness (to being moved on), to remain sitting on bus stop seat (just resting) while everyone else has got up to get on the bus.

To borrow space in this way is, in a sense, like the adolescent, to step over a threshold of impertinence, challenging the public etiquette and behavioural norms that govern the 'proper' use of public space. Like sitting on the backrest of the bench, your feet on the seat, sitting the wrong way round...

There is a different tenor, though, to this kind of mis-use of space in older age that does not quite fit the demonstrative pattern of adolescent mis-use of space (as a marker of adolescent difference, as a territorial rite of passage). Here, in older age, mis-use of space is not an explicit attempt to mark out elderly autonomy and difference but rather a discrete, if still defiant, kind of adaptive action: to accommodate personal needs where the designed environment fails. In an altogether more subtle vocalisation of identity, of elderly difference, quietly testing out, pushing beyond the limits of public space.

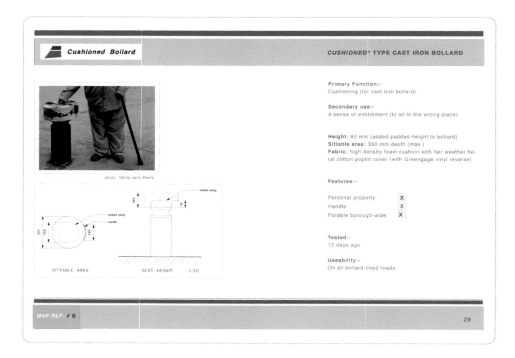

FIGURE 23.1 Cushioned Bollard: technical drawing. Ageing Facilities: diagram from *Resistant Sitting: The Pensioner's Alternative Street Furniture Guide* www.ageingfacilities.net

Source: Photo: Verity-Jane Keefe.

FIGURE 23.2   Cushioned Bollard; completed project

Source: Photo: Verity-Jane Keefe.

24

NOTES ON AN INCLINED PLANE – SLOPE : INTERCEPT

Sara Hendren (2016)

> Not only do disabled people have experiences which are not available to the able-bodied, they are in a better position to transcend cultural mythologies about the body, because they cannot do things the able-bodied feel they must do in order to be happy, "normal", and sane… If disabled people were truly heard, an explosion of knowledge about the human body and psyche would take place.
>
> (Wendell 1996)

A ramp is a machine. It is the "inclined plane" – one of Galileo's six "simple machines". An inclined plane is an elegance of physics that alters the behavior of force across a surface. It transforms the possibilities of load-bearing by its degrees of slope, doing machinic work with a simple geometry that belies its historical importance.

Slope : Intercept is a material and digital social design project organized around the ramp, intended to de-familiarize this simple geometry from its modest, daily work and to show its physics in new ways. Part architectural installation, part digital archive, and part collaborative events, the project uses the ramp to cast both city architecture and city users in a new light. The work creates ramped elevations that enact a literal physics for bodies seeking elevations in the built environment. But its extended life as an archive and series of collaborative events also creates a "political physics" in the form of cultural elevations and activism.

In this chapter and accompanying photographs, I lay out some history for the ramp, suggesting that its machinic simplicity wrongly relegates it outside the usual connotations of "technology" and "innovation" that so preoccupy contemporary cultures. I argue that understanding the ramp as an overlooked technology has powerful implications for a broadened definition of "technology" in general, and that looking for the influence of hidden technological artifacts helps to recover things and politics that otherwise get overlooked or suppressed. I also explore briefly the little-known late 1960s architectural partnership between Paul Virilio and Claude Parent, called Architecture Principe, a practice entirely organized around the inclined plane (Virilio 1996). Their utopian notion of the "oblique function" of the ramp has been an inspiration for my own fascination with inclined planes and their physics. Finally, I describe *Slope : Intercept*'s component parts – its material design, archive, and events – and the work I have done so far with those various elements.

The ramp as a historical technology

The ramp has been historically used for its machinic qualities long before its physics were understood. Sites like Stonehenge in the UK are thought to have been built using the mechanical advantage of the inclined plane formed in the earth as "on-ramps" to structural building. The celebrated Roman causeways made use of the ramp's physics as well, and "siege ramps", like the one that survives at a fortress site in Masada, Israel, created a defensive advantage in battle by its elevations. The historical list goes on. But it took Galileo in the sixteenth century to codify its predictable mathematics, after which he formally classified it as one of six simple machines. Along with the lever, the pulley, the screw, the wedge, and the wheel-and-axle, an inclined plane forms an elemental grammar of mechanics in the built environment – a deceptively humble set of relationships that change the conditions of physics reliably and mathematically, making it possible to multiply and augment those mechanics in complex configurations for industrial work. Pressed into the service of modern labor, those machinic combinations make up the modern modes of manufacturing that have so powerfully structured contemporary global and industrialized cultures.

If a ramp is a machine, then, it may also be understood as a technology – though it most often hides as a thing, as a mere surface, a commonplace geometry, a topographical experience that's often invisible. But it is a technology nonetheless. Seeing a ramp *as a technology* changes it's meaning in key ways.

The historian David Edgerton, in his book, *The Shock of the Old* (2007), has claimed that the ways cultures talk about technology – in history, and in the present day – tend to run along predictable and erroneous lines. Edgerton writes that cultural obsessions with the technological standouts of the twentieth century – flight, nuclear power, the birth control pill, the internet – are shaped by the myopic futurology of our own age: that is, our persistent sense that innovation is just around the bend, proceeding at an ever-faster pace, and by definition "ahead" of culture. And this is despite the fact that that "futurology" has been a cultural mythology in industrialized cultures for more than a hundred years at least. As scholars tell stories of technology in history, Edgerton writes, they link "technology" almost exclusively with "invention" (the creation of a new idea) and "innovation" (the first use of a new idea). Talk about technology centers on research and development, patents and early stages of use – and so the story about historical change is too often hung upon these same timelines. But Edgerton shows how a history of technology-*in-use* yields a far different picture of technological importance. How would historians alternately measure the long arc of impact around such technologies as the rickshaw, corrugated iron, the sewing machine, the hydrogenation of coal, or the bicycle, if use is the key criterion? "In use-centered history," he writes, "technologies do not only appear, they also disappear and reappear, and mix and match across centuries" (2007: xii). So we should look not only at an "absolute value" tied to a moment of technological change, but also a highly situated and relative value of a technology, evolving across time and culture. This view asks those interested in technologies to expand the canopy of where they might look for impact, influence, or importance.

To try to get at a more refined and dispersed sense of technology in use, moreover, Edgerton suggests that we alter our language, doing away with the false hierarchy between "technologies", on one hand, and mere "things" on the other. Edgerton writes that

> [t]hinking about the use of things, rather than of technology, connects us directly with the world we know, rather than the strange world in which "technology" lives. We speak of "our" technology, meaning the technology of an age or whole society. By contrast "things" fit into no such totality and do not evoke what is often taken as an independent historical force.
>
> (2007: xvii)

Slope : Intercept is a project about the inclined plane as an overlooked technology – a technology that is also a thing, and a thing that is a technology – an object whose impact of use extends far back into history.

How, then, might one see it again, take its measure of form, of engineering, of poetics? What metrics would apply? In both material and digital designs, *Slope : Intercept* is an attempt to waken this sleeping technology and its metaphors. The project is a networking of ramps: an attempt at sensory estrangement, in the manner Svetlana Boym (2012) has used the term – through cognitive ambivalence and play, to gain a provisional freedom to see it again. In my case, the project is to estrange oneself from this ubiquitous and banal form and instead to multiply its geometries, its designated and un-designated users.

Precedent work: the "function of the oblique" in Architecture Principe

Ramps can be found in much of architectural history, but the inclined plane took on a distinctive prominence in Architecture Principe, a partnership between the cultural theorist Paul Virilio and the architect Claude Parent, with the painter Michel Carrade and sculptor Morice Lipsi (Virilio and Parent 1996). Theirs was a short-lived, experimental practice in Paris begun in 1966 – a design partnership organized around the inclined plane and what it made possible for the body. The inclined plane, they proposed, would animate the topographical experience of the ground. A ramp provides resistance going up, and acceleration going down – literal and phenomenological. This experience, they thought, was a necessary corrective to the crisis of the "ordered city" – the relentless conformism wrought by the early twentieth century's legacy of verticals and horizontals. The resulting drawings and models for architectural structures bear out this conviction, each featuring the inclined plane at various scales: long and shallow, short and steep, for residences and for public spaces, including the Parent family house in Neuilly (Figure 24.1).

Looking back on that time many years later, Virilio said of his partnership that: "At the time, the tower was the most exalted type of architecture." But as for "Architecture Principe," he writes: "Our opposition to towers was absolute." He wrote: "The idea was to work with gravity in a new way; to create a vision of instability while the perspective is stable…You could call it a kind of 'eroticization' of the ground" (1996: 4). Their opposition was realized in the "function

FIGURE 24.1   Claude and Naad Parent with guests, in their Neuilly house, 1973

Photo Gilles Ehrmann. Reprinted by permission from Ehrmann Estate and with thanks to Chloe Parent. Copyright: Photo Gilles Ehrmann.

of the oblique" – the sideways approach, the diagonal cut, the deforming of the horizontal and vertical grid, and all the ways it rigidly organizes social relations (see also Koolhaas and AMO 2014). I have sought that mystery of the oblique function both in the design of a set of material ramps and in a form of networked architecture that extends the meaning and the reach and the multiplicity of its uses. And, again, I am doing that by deploying a kind of sensory estrangement in material and digital forms – exploring a new design for this simple machine in material space, while letting it live and be in conversation with its many multiple counterparts, wherever they may be found. I'll explore more about such estrangement below.

First the material

In this material design, I am fracturing and dispersing the inclined plane, breaking it free of its architectural scale and finding in it a multiple and *multiplied* set of uses (Figure 24.2). It's a low profile bit of geometry that's designed to nest and stack, to attach side-by-side, to maneuver about with wheels. So it's a suite of objects for installation in public space.

Muted but present in its design are features that make affordances for specific users. So it becomes less an extended architectural form at the urban scale, and instead more a social technology, a nimble and portable tool for both scripted and unscripted uses. I have labored to keep its iconic form but seek its multiplicity as a technology.

FIGURE 24.2   Sara Hendren; suite of objects for ramp design

Source: Photographs by Justin Knight.

Skateboarders have long sought elevations among the verticals and horizontals of cities everywhere. And while skateboarding is still an under-theorized phenomenon as a use of urban space, the architectural historian Iain Borden has posed some ideas about the critical subjectivity of the skater in the otherwise rationalized, economically-ordered city. He writes that skateboarding offers "both an apparently non-commercial realm of compensation and a confrontation of the instructive mechanics of 'signals'" – the ordinary signals in architecture, he means, of what to do with a sidewalk or a curb. He writes that "skateboarding counters signal architecture with a body-centric and multi-sensory performative activity, and with an indifference to function, price, and regulation, creating new patterns of space and time, and turning the signals of the city into ephemeral symbols of everyday meaning and duration" (2001a, 2001b: 256). So here too, with this design, I've been thinking about a structure that could extend and counter verticals and horizontals in a number of different configurations, and with portability built in, since skaters are often unwelcome in center-city plazas. They're engineered to take a lot of force from a skater, to stack securely, and they have this metal angle stock that allows a skater to grind across the surface, especially when locked together.

FIGURE 24.3   Ramps configured for skateboarding

Source: Photograph by Justin Knight.

And while skateboarding – according to Borden – does have an inherent criticality built into it, there's also a legible virtuosity that is achieved by this athletic use of ramp configurations. It's not hard to see the elevations here. It's harder to see other kinds of virtuosity, which brings me to another set of users for this design (Figure 24.3).

These ramps are also made to address a grey area in the architectural code established by the Americans with Disabilities Act (ADA) (Figure 24.4). Single-step entrances at small storefronts are quite common in cities like Boston and New York; you can see the prevalence of these entrances on Cambridge Street here in Cambridge alone. Businesses with single step entrances are not required by law to overhaul their structures unless they're already significantly re-modelling; so they're added in with their steps as they are. Instead the law exhorts these businesses to find "readily achievable" ways to remove barriers to entry. But enacting these changes tends to be complaint-driven, and in many cases ignored. So this material ramp has levelling feet that adjusts its height from a single standard step to varying degrees of height beyond that – taking into account the historic architecture of older cities and their idiosyncratic structures.

While you're likely to see particular ramp forms used by skateboarders and wheelchairs users, you're unlikely to create a kind of Venn diagram of elevations – to see them seeking the same thing; to see these as unlikely bedfellows with different kinds of marginalized status. In this way, the ramp here is also designed to be the same kind of cultural technology as that of a skateboard user – that is, it might well be used by a skateboarder and a wheelchair user

FIGURE 24.4   Ramp configured for single-step entrances

Source: Photograph by Justin Knight.

in a single afternoon, and several others as well, in as-yet-unimagined ways, depending on its site of installation. Mixing uses and users is meant to upend notions of single-minded virtuosity and function, and to instead make a multiplied poetics of a single form. By finding the overlapping elevations sought by these users, I want this design to provide a kind of sensory estrangement from the expected cultural ideas of the form: where and how it appears, how its performers use it, what kinds of virtuosities might lie in its potentials. When one uncouples a technology from its obvious assignments, both a technology and its user can take up a newly unfixed narrative. All ramps are attached to their shared simple machinic history as inclined planes, and the physics they afford; and there are referents to its iconic status in architecture. But the work of this ramp un-tags itself from specific users, from easy identity politics, and indeed from rigid notions of use altogether.

Second the digital

A project about ubiquitous spatial phenomena also begs for a digital life, in the co-extensive site of the public commons online. I have also built this web site (Figure 24.5), wherein a large collection of ramps live side-by-side with each iteration of my material designs – ramps in grand architectural spaces alongside much more modest or surprising ones. It's a selective and enigmatic collection, organized to further strain the edges of likeness among its individual ramps, to see what new connections might be found. From the home page, you can either jump to a long form blog essay laying out the historical and cultural context as in this chapter, or you can begin by navigating through a database, where ramps are found in categories like TRANSVERSALS or ACCELERATIONS or VANTAGES. In

FIGURE 24.5   Homepage, www.slopeintercept.org

VANTAGES, for example, you'll see, side-by-side, the ramp that forms the only access to a hilltop fortress in Masada, Israel; a stunning, elegant beachfront walk in Norway; the access ramp shared by users of a contested religious site; a park for penguins; and my own design, providing a vantage of another kind. Testing my instincts against these categorical abstractions is also how I can further test my model in physical space.

In the item view, you'll find a simple set of descriptors, the other categories that characterize that image, and links to the sources of those ramps. There's no extended commentary except in the alternate text, so that the associations among these forms and their contexts can be constructed at will. If you want to know more, you can click through and find the source and some context for where this ramp is, how it's been written about. The spaces of web architecture therefore allow the reach of a material practice to be amplified and to evolve. And since this project is about the multiplicity one gets with the oblique function, only in tandem with a digital environment can my material models find a commons, an imaginary, and perhaps become some next iteration. Just as in the splintering of scale and use in the material models, online I am piecing together these forms as idiosyncratic and unlikely bedfellows to allow our perceptual forms, broadly conceived – again, both of the uses of the technology and its users – to be redistributed. And above all, the entirety of the project is designed to ask: What counts in the design of technologies, technologies that are things? Whose use matters?

Ramps and critical making

This project, finally, has both reflected and constituted my larger disposition as a maker and thinker in general – that is, the uncoupling of technologies and prosthetics from strictly scientific and medical research designations; a determination to design modes of research in those domains alongside their professionalized expert cultures; an interest in design for disability and marginalized bodies in public spaces.

In *Slope : Intercept* and my other projects, which are brought together on the *Abler* web site I seek a practice that is somewhere between the "autonomous experimentation" of art making and the "direct action" approach of the activist. I am influenced by the "discursive design" strategies employed by designers Anthony Dunne and Fiona Raby (2005, 2013), artist–engineer Natalie Jeremijenko (Jeremijenko and Thacker 2004), the collective Wochenklausur (Jackson 2011), and others who use the language of design for conceptual *and* practical ends, for those ends to be mixed and conflated in unexpected ways – deploying estrangement and de-familiarity for productive, formative, propositional ends. This follows Svetlana Boym (2012) who distinguishes an artistic estrangement *"from the world"* – as in the avant-garde strategy of alienation, shock, and dislocation – from an artistic estrangement that returns a viewer *"to the world"* – a redoubling back to the conditions of political and civic life with new eyes. The language of design may be particularly advantageous for such a return to the world, with its history of problem-solving, practicality, and transparency. *Slope : Intercept* seeks the critical conceptuality of art with the vernacular and consequence of design – an arrangement and re-arrangement of physics for an altered built environment, an altered interpretation of ability and wheeled physics, and an altered future polis.

REFERENCES

Introduction

Agrest, D., Conway, P. and Weisman, L. K. (eds) (1996) *The Sex of Architecture*, New York: Harry N. Abrams.

Barton, C. E. (ed.) (2001) *Sites of Memory: Perspectives on Architecture and Race*, Princeton, NJ: Princeton University Press.

Betsky, A. (1997) *Building Sex: Men, Women, Architecture and the Construction of Sexuality*, New York: William Morrow & Co.

Borden, I., Penner, B. and Rendell, J. (eds) (1999) *Gender Space Architecture: An Interdisciplinary Introduction*, London and New York: Routledge.

Boys, J. (2014) *Doing Disability Differently: An Alternative Handbook on Dis/ability, Architecture and Designing for Everyday Life*, London and New York: Routledge.

Colomina, B. (ed.) (1992) *Sexuality and Space*, Princeton, NJ: Princeton Architectural Press.

Davidson, M. (2008) *Concerto for the Left Hand: Disability and the Defamiliar Body*, Ann Arbor, MI: University of Michigan Press.

Davis, L. J. (2002) *Bending Over Backwards: Disability, Dismodernism and Other Difficult Positions*, New York: NYU Press.

Garland-Thompson, R. (2011) 'Misfits. A Feminist Materialist Disability Concept', *Hypatia Special Issue: Ethics of Embodiment* 26(3), 591–609.

Hughes, F. (ed.) (1998) *The Architect: Reconstructing Her Practice*, Boston, MA: MIT Press.

Levin, M. (2010) 'The Art of Disability: An Interview with Tobin Siebers', *Disability Studies Quarterly* 3(10), available at http://dsq-sds.org/article/view/1263/1272

Lokko, L. N. N. (ed.) (2000) *White Papers, Black Marks: Architecture, Race, Culture*, Minneapolis, MN: University of Minnesota Press.

Massey, D. (1994) *Space, Place, and Gender*, Cambridge: Polity.

Matrix (eds) (1984) *Making Space: Women and the Man-Made Environment*, London: Pluto Press.

Mintz, S. (2007) *Unruly Bodies: Life Writing by Women with Disabilities*, Chapel Hill, NC: University of North Carolina Press.

Sanders, J. (ed.) (1996) *Stud: Architectures of Masculinity*, Princeton, NJ: Princeton University Press.

Weisman, L. (1994) *Discrimination by Design: A Feminist Critique of the Man-Made Environment*, Illinois, IL: University of Illinois Press.

Wilkins, C. L. (2007) *The Aesthetics of Equity: Notes on Race, Space, Architecture and Music*, Minneapolis, MN: University of Minnesota Press.

Part I Histories/narratives

Ben-Moshe, L., Chapman, C. and Carey, A. (eds) (2014) *Disability Incarcerated: Imprisonment and Disability in the United States and Canada*, New York: Palgrave Macmillan.

Campbell, F. K. (2009) *Contours of Ableism: The Production of Disability and Abledness*, Basingstoke and New York: Palgrave Macmillan.

Davis, L. J. (1995) *Enforcing Normalcy: Disability, Deafness, and the Body*, London: Verso.

Davis, L. J. (1997) 'Constructing Normalcy: The Bell Curve, the Novel and the Invention of the Disabled Body in the Nineteenth Century', in L. Davis (ed.) *The Disability Studies Reader*, New York: Routledge, 9–28.

Ervelles, N. (1996) 'Disability and the Dialectics of Difference', *Disability & Society* 11(4): 519–537.

Ervelles, N. (2011) *Disability and Difference in Global Contexts: Enabling a Transformative Body Politic*, London: Palgrave Macmillan.

Galis, V. (2011) 'Enacting Disability: How Can Science and Technology Studies Inform Disability Studies?' *Disability & Society* 26(7): 825–838.

Garland-Thomson, R. (1996) *Freakery: Cultural Spectacles of the Extraordinary Body*, New York: NYU Press.

Imrie, R. (2012) 'Auto-Disabilities: The Case of Shared Space Environments', *Environment and Planning A* 44(9): 2260–2277.

Imrie, R. (2013) 'Shared Space and the Post-politics of Environmental Change', *Urban Studies* 50(1): 3446–3462.

Kafer, A. (2013) *Feminist, Queer, Crip*, Bloomington, IN: Indiana University Press.

Lambert, L. (2012) 'Architectural Theories: A Subversive Approach to the Ideal Normalized Body', April 29, http://thefunambulist.net/2012/04/29/architectural-theories-a-subversive-approach-to-the-ideal-normatized-body/

Lambert, L. and Pham, M.-H. T. (2015) 'Spinoza in a T-shirt', July 1st http://thenewinquiry.com/essays/spinoza-in-a-t-shirt/

Michalko, R. (1998a) *The Mystery of the Eye and the Shadow of Blindness*, Toronto: University of Toronto Press.

Michalko, R. (1998b) *The Two in One Walking with Smokie, Walking with Blindness*, Philadelphia, PA: Temple University Press.

Michalko, R. (2002) *The Difference that Disability Makes*, Philadelphia, PA: Temple University Press.

Sanchez, R. (2015) *Deafening Modernism: Embodied Language and Visual Poetics in American Literature*, New York and London: New York University Press.

Silberman, S. (2015) *Neurotribes. The Legacy of Autism and How to Think Smarter About People Who Think Differently*, Sydney: Allen and Unwin.

Soldatic, K., Morgan, H. and Roulstone, A. (eds) (2014) *Disability, Spaces and Places of Policy Exclusion*, London and New York: Routledge.

Stephens, E. (2011) *Anatomy as Spectacle: Public Exhibitions of the Body from 1750 to the Present*, Liverpool: Liverpool University Press.

Stiker, H.-J. (2000) Translated by Sayers W. *A History of Disability*, Ann Arbor, MI: University of Michigan Press.

Wolff, J. (1985) 'The Invisible Flaneuse. Women and the Literature of Modernity', *Theory, Culture & Society* 2(3): 37–46.

Wolff, J. (2008) 'Gender and the Haunting of Cities (Or, The Retirement of the Flâneur)' in D'Souza, A. and McDonough, T. (eds) *The Invisible Flaneuse? Gender, Public Space and Visual Culture in Nineteenth Century Paris*. Manchester: Manchester University Press, 18–29.

1. David Serlin, Disabling the *flâneur*

Baudelaire, C. (1972 [1863]) 'The Painter of Modern Life', in P.E. Charvet (ed.) *Baudelaire: Selected Writings on Art and Literature*, pp. 395–422. New York: Viking.

Benjamin, W. (1978 [1936]) *Charles Baudelaire: A Lyric Poet in the Era of High Capitalism*, London: New Left Books.

Breckenridge, C. A. and Vogler, C. (2001) 'The Critical Limits of Embodiment: Disability's Criticism', *Public Culture* 13(3): 349–58.

Buck-Morss, S. (1985) 'The Flaneur, the Sandwichman and the Whore: The Politics of Loitering', *New German Critique* 39: 99–140.

Buck-Morss, S. (1991) *The Dialectics of Seeing: Walter Benjamin and the Arcades Project*, Cambridge, MA: MIT Press.

Burgin, V. (1996) *In/Different Spaces: Place and Memory in Visual Culture*, Berkeley, CA: University of California Press.

Chadwick, W. and Ladimer, T. T. (eds) (2003) *The Modern Woman Revisited: Paris Between the Wars*, New Brunswick, NJ: Rutgers University Press.

Charney, L. and Schwartz, V. (eds) (1996) *Cinema and the Invention of Modern Life*, Berkeley, CA: University of California Press.

Crary, J. (2001) *Suspensions of Perception: Attention, Spectacle, and Modern Culture*, Cambridge, MA: MIT Press.

Feld, S. (2005) 'Places Sensed, Senses Placed: Toward a Sensuous Epistemology of Environments', in D. Howes (ed.) *Empire of the Senses: The Sensual Culture Reader*, pp. 179–91. New York: Berg.

Ferguson, P. P. (1994) 'The Flâneur On and Off the Streets of Paris', in K. Tester (ed.) *The Flâneur*, pp. 22–42. London: Routledge.

Friedberg, A. (1994) *Window Shopping: Cinema and the Postmodern*, Berkeley, CA: University of California Press.

Fuss, D. (2004) *A Sense of the Interior: Four Writers and the Rooms that Shaped Them*, New York: Routledge.

Garland-Thomson, R. (2002) 'The Politics of Staring: Visual Rhetorics of Disability in Popular Photography', in S. L. Snyder, B. J. Brueggemann and R. Garland-Thomson (eds) *Disability Studies: Enabling the Humanities*, pp. 56–75. New York: Modern Language Association of America.

Hammergren, L. (1994) 'The Re-turn of the Flâneuse', in S. L. Foster (ed.) *Corporealities: Dancing, Knowledge, Culture, and Power*, pp. 53–69. New York: Routledge.

Keller, H. (1938) *Helen Keller's Journal*, London: Michael Joseph.

Levin, D. M. (ed.) (1993) *Modernity and the Hegemony of Vision*, Berkeley, CA: University of California Press.

Mirzoeff, N. (1995) *Bodyscape: Art, Modernity, and the Ideal Figure*, New York: Routledge.

Nesbit, M. (1992) 'In the Absence Of the Parisienne . . .', in B. Colomina (ed.) *Sexuality and Space*, pp. 307–26. New York: Princeton Architectural Press.

Nielsen, K. E. (2004) *The Radical Lives of Helen Keller*, New York: NYU Press.

Panchasi, R. (1995) 'Reconstructions: Prosthetics and the Male Body in Post WWI France', *Differences* 7(3): 109–40.

Parsons, D. (2000) *Streetwalking the Metropolis: Women, the City, and Modernity*, New York: Oxford University Press.

Pollock, G. (1988) *Vision and Difference: Femininity, Feminism, and Histories of Art*, New York: Routledge.

Prost, A. (1992) *In the Wake of War: 'Les Anciens Combattants' and French Society*, Providence, RI: Berg.

Roberts, M. L. (1994) *Civilizing the Sexes: Reconstructing Gender in Postwar France, 1917–1927*, Chicago, IL: University of Chicago Press.

Scales, R. P. (2006) 'Creating a Listening Body: Radio, Disability, and the Politics of Citizenship in Interwar France', paper presented at the annual meeting of the American Historical Association, Philadelphia, January. Used with permission of the author.

Schwartz, V. (1999) *Spectacular Realities: Early Mass Culture in Fin-de-Siècle Paris*, Berkeley, CA: University of California Press.

Serlin, D. and Lerner, J. (1997) 'Weegee and the Jewish Question', *Wide Angle* 19(4): 95–108.

Sherman, D.J. (1999) *The Construction of Memory in Interwar France*, Chicago, IL: University of Chicago Press.

Stewart, M. L. (2001) *For Health and Beauty: Physical Culture for Frenchwomen, 1880s–1930s,* Baltimore, MD: Johns Hopkins University Press.

Tester, K. (ed.) (1994) *The Flâneur,* New York: Routledge.

Vidler, A. (1992) *The Architectural Uncanny: Essays in the Modern Unhomely,* Cambridge, MA: MIT Press.

Walker, I. (2002) *City Gorged with Dreams: Surrealism and Documentary Photography in Interwar Paris,* New York: Manchester University Press.

White, E. (2001) *The Flâneur: A Stroll through the Paradoxes of Paris,* New York: Bloomsbury.

Wilson, E. (2001) *The Contradictions of Culture: Cities, Culture, Women,* Thousand Oaks, CA: Sage.

Wolff, J. (1985) 'The Invisible Flâneuse: Women and the Literature of Modernity', *Theory, Culture & Society* 2(3): 37–46.

2. Rob Imrie, The body, disability and Le Corbusier's conception of the radiant environment

Ann Hall, M. (1996) *Feminism and Sporting Bodies: Essays on Theory and Practice,* Champaign, IL: Human Kinetics.

Banham, R. P. (1960) *Theory and Design in the First Machine Age,* London: Architectural Press.

Bordo, S. (1995) *Unbearable Weight: Feminism, Western Culture, and the Body,* Berkeley, CA: University of California Press.

Caygill, H. (1990) *Architectural Postmodernism,* London: AA.

Colomina, B. (1994) *Privacy and Publicity: Modern Architecture as Mass Media,* Cambridge, MA: MIT Press.

Crawford, M. (1991) 'Can architects be socially responsible?', in Ghirardo, D. (ed.) *Out of Site: A Social Criticism of Architecture,* Seattle, WA: Bay Press, 27–45.

Crowe, N. (1995) *Nature and the Idea of a Man Made World,* London: MIT Press.

Curtis, W. (1986) *Le Corbusier: Ideas and Forms,* London: Phaidon.

Davies, C. and Lifchez, R. (1987) 'An open letter to architects', in Lifchez, R. (ed.) *Rethinking Architecture,* Berkeley, CA: University of California Press, 35–50.

Dickens, P. (1980) 'Social science and design theory', *Environment and Planning B: Planning and Design,* 6:105–17.

Frampton, K. (1980) *Modern Architecture: A Critical History,* London: Thames and Hudson.

Frampton, K. (1991) 'Reflections on the autonomy of architecture: a critique of contemporary production', in Ghirardo, D. (ed.) *Out of Site: A Social Criticism of Architecture,* Seattle, WA: Bay Press.

Ghirardo, D. (ed.) (1991) *Out of Site: A Social Criticism of Architecture,* Seattle, WA: Bay Press.

Gray, E. (1929) 'De l'eclectisme au doute, l'architecture vivante', translated by Nevins, D., 1981, 'From Eclecticism to Doubt', *Heresies,* 11, 3:71–2.

Grosz, E. (1992) 'Bodies-Cities', in Colomina, B. (ed.) *Sexuality and Space,* New York, 241–54.

Grosz, E. (1994) *Volatile Bodies: Towards a Corporeal Feminism,* Bloomington, IN: Princeton Architectural Press.

Grosz, E. (1995) *Space, Time, and Perversion,* London: Routledge.

Hayden, D. (1981) 'What would a non-sexist city be like: speculations on housing, urban design, and human work', in Stimpson, C., Dixler, E., Nelson, M. and Yatrakis, K. (eds) *Women and the American City,* Chicago, IL: University of Chicago Press.

House Builders Federation (1995) 'The application of building regulations to help disabled people in new dwellings in England and Wales', unpublished paper.

Imrie, R. (1996) *Disability and the City: International Perspectives,* London and New York: Paul Chapman Publishing and St Martin's Press.

Jencks, C. (1987) *Le Corbusier and the Tragic View of Architecture*, London: Penguin.

King, R. (1996) *Emancipating Space*, New York: Guildford.

Knesl, J. (1984) 'The powers of architecture', *Environment and Planning D: Society and Space*, 1, 1:3–22.

Knox, P. (1987) 'The social production of the built environment – architects, architecture, and the post modern city', *Progress in Human Geography*, 11, 3:354–78.

Laws, G. (1994a) 'Oppression, knowledge, and the built environment', *Political Geography*, 13, 1:7–32.

Laws, G. (1994b) 'Aging, contested meanings, and the built environment', *Environment and Planning A*, 26, 11:1787–802.

Le Corbusier (1900) *La Peinture Moderne*, Paris: Cres.

Le Corbusier (1925a) *The Decorative Art of Today*, London: Architectural Press.

Le Corbusier (1925b) *Urbanisme*, Paris: Cres.

Le Corbusier (1927) *Towards a New Architecture*, Trowbridge: Butterworth Architecture.

Le Corbusier (1947) *The Four Routes*, London: Denis Dobson Ltd.

Le Corbusier (1948) *The Home of Man*, London: Architectural Press.

Le Corbusier (1967) *The Radiant City*, London: Faber and Faber Ltd.

Le Corbusier (1980) *Modular I and II*, Cambridge, MA: Harvard University Press.

Lefebvre, H. (1968) *Dialectical Materialism*, London: Jonathan Cape.

Lester, R. (1997) 'The (dis) embodied self in anorexia nervosa', *Social Science and Medicine*, 44, 4:479–89.

McAnulty, R. (1992) 'Body troubles', in Whiteman, J., Kipnis, J. and Burdett, R. (eds) *Strategies in Architectural Thinking*, London: MIT Press, 181–97.

Merleau-Ponty, M. (1962) *The Phenomenology of Perception*, London: RKP.

Mumford, L. (1962) 'The case against modern architecture', *Architectural Record,* April 155–62.

Mumford, L. (1968) *The Urban Prospect*, London: Secker and Warburg.

Nevins, D. (1981) 'From eclecticism to doubt', *Heresies*, 11, 3:71–2.

Probyn, E. (1993) *Sexing the Self: Gendered Positions in Cultural Studies*, London: Routledge.

Sennett, R. (1994) *Flesh and Stone*, London: Faber and Faber.

Shilling, C. (1995) *The Body and Social Theory*, London: Sage.

Sullivan, L. (1947) *Kindergarten Chats and Other Writings*, New York: Wittenborn Shultz.

Tschumi, B. (1996) *Architecture and Disjunction*, Cambridge, MA: MIT Press.

Venturi, R. (1966) *Complexity and Contradiction in Architecture*, New York: Museum of Modern Art.

Vitruvius (1960) *The Ten Books of Architecture*, Dover Publications, New York.

Ward, A. (1993) 'Resistance or reaction? The cultural politics of design', *Architecture and Behaviour*, 9, 1:39–68.

Weisman, L. (1992) *Discrimination by Design*, Champaign, IL: University of Illinois Press.

Whiteman, J., Kipnis, J. and Burdett, R. (eds) (1992) *Strategies in Architectural Thinking*, London: MIT Press.

Wigley, M. (1992) 'The translation of architecture: the production of Babel', in Whiteman, J., Kipnis, J. and Burdett, R. (eds) *Strategies in Architectural Thinking*, London: MIT Press, 240–54.

Wolfe, T. (1981) *From Bauhaus to Our House*, New York: Farar, Straus, Giroux.

4. Liz Crow, Lying down anyhow: disability and the rebel body

Bullivant, S. (2011) 'Sweeping the Homeless – and Charity – From Westminster's Streets', *The Guardian* [Online]. Accessed 04.03.12. Available: http://www.guardian.co.uk/commentisfree/belief/2011/mar/04/homeless-victoria-london-westminster-bylaw (paragraph 4)

Frank, T. (6 July 2011) 'Untitled, Nothing into Something; A Blog About Light' [Online]. Accessed 26.05.12. Available: http://www.nothingintosomething.com/blog/james-turrell-celestial-vault

Herrera, H. (1983) *Frida: A Biography of Frida Kahlo*, New York: Perennial Library/Harper & Row, 406

Lockton, D. (2008) 'Anti-Homeless "Stools": Design with Intent Blog' [Online]. Accessed 26.05.12. Available: http://architectures.danlockton.co.uk/category/benches/

Municipal Code (2011) San Bruno, California. *Title 5 Public peace, Morals and Welfare; Chapter 6.12 Trespassing and Loitering; 6.12.060 Sitting or lying down in designated zones prohibited*, Quality Code Publishing [Online]. Accessed 26.05.12. Available: http://qcode.us/codes/sanbruno/view.php?topic=6-6_12-6_12_060&frames=on

Newell, C. (2002) in Goggin, G. (2008) 'Bioethics, Disability and the Good Life: Remembering Christopher Newell: 1964–2008', *Bioethical Inquiry*, 5, 235–238, 237

Newell, C. (2006) 'Moving Disability from Other to Us', in O'Brien, P. & Sullivan, M. (Eds) *Allies in Emancipation: shifting from providing service to being of support*, Melbourne: Thomson/Dunmore, ix–xi, ix.

Tophoff, M. (2006) 'Mindfulness-Training: Exploring Personal Change through Sensory Awareness', *Internet Journal for Cultural Studies* (Internet-Zeitschrift für Kulturwissenschaften, in translation) [Online]. Accessed 26.05.12. Available: http://www.inst.at/trans/16Nr/09_2/tophoff16.htm (paragraph 5)

Vassi, M. (1984) *Lying Down: The Horizontal Worldview*, Santa Barbara, CA: Capra Press, 14

Visbeek, B. (2009) A Sign of Enlightenment and Beauty (photograph) [Online]. Accessed 26.05.12. Available: http://www.flickr.com/photos/visbeek/4002506546/

Wilkinson, A. (Ed) (2002) *Henry Moore: Writings and Conversations*, Berkeley, CA and Los Angeles, CA: University of California Press

Wright, F.S. (1947), 'Henry Moore: Reclining Figure', *The Journal of Aesthetics and Art Criticism*, 6:2 95–105, 104

5. Rod Michalko, Blinding the power of sight

Jameson, F. 2003. "Future City" in *New Left Review*. 21(May–June): 65–79, 76.

King, T. 2003. *The Truth about Stories*. Massey Hall Lecture Series and Anansi Press Inc. Dead Dog Café Productions Inc. and the Canadian Broadcasting Corporation Page 10.

Part II Theory and criticism

Butler, R., and Parr, H. (eds) (1999) *Mind and Body Spaces: Geographies of Illness, Impairment and Disability*, London and New York: Routledge.

Chouinard, V., Hall, E., and Wilton, R. (eds) (2010) *Towards Enabling Geographies: 'disabled' bodies and minds in society and space*, London and New York: Routledge.

Corker, M., and Shakespeare, T. (eds) (2002) *Disability/Postmodernity: Embodying Disability Theory*, London and New York: Continuum.

Davis, L.J. (1995) *Enforcing Normalcy: Disability, Deafness, and the Body*, London: Verso.

Davis, L. (2002) *Bending Over Backwards. Disability, Dismodernism and Other Difficult Positions*, New York: NYU Press.

Davis, L. (2014) *The End of Normal: Identity in a Biocultural Era*, Ann Arbor, MI: University of Michigan Press.

Garland-Thomson, R. (1996) *Freakery: Cultural Spectacles of the Extraordinary Body*, New York: NYU Press.

Gleeson, B. (1998) *Geographies of Disability*, London and New York: Routledge.

Haller, B. (2010) *Representing Disability in an Ableist World: Essays on Mass Media*, Advocado Press Inc. (epublisher).

Imrie, R. (1996) *Disability and the City: International Perspectives*, London: Sage.

Imrie, R., and Edwards, C. (2007) 'The geographies of disability: reflecting on the development of a sub-discipline', *Geography Compass*, 1(3): 623–640.

Imrie, R. (2012) 'Universalism, universal design and equitable access to the built environment', *Disability and Rehabilitation,* 34(10). Published online at http://www.tandfonline.com/doi/full/10.3 109/09638288.2011.624250?src=recsys

Imrie, R., and Kumar, M. (1998) 'Focusing on Disability and Access in the Built Environment', *Disability and Society,* 13(3). Published online at http://www.tandfonline.com/doi/abs/10.1080 /09687599826687

Kafer, A. (2013) *Feminist, Queer, Crip,* Bloomington, IN: Indiana University Press.

Michalko, R. (2002) *The Difference that Disability Makes,* Philadelphia, PA: Temple University Press.

Siebers, T. (2008) *Disability Theory,* Ann Arbor, MI: University of Michigan Press.

Siebers, T. (2010) *Disability Aesthetics,* Ann Arbor, MI: University of Michigan Press.

Titchkosky (2008) 'To pee or not to pee? Ordinary Talk about Extraordinary Exclusions in a University Environment' *Canadian Journal of Sociology.* 33(1): 37–60, available online at: http://ejournals.library.ualberta.ca/index.php/CJS/article/view/1526/1058

Titchkosky, T. (2011) *The Question of Access: Disability, Space, Meaning,* Toronto: University of Toronto Press.

6. Tobin Siebers, Disability aesthetics

Allan Poe, E. (1978) 'Ligeia,' in Ollive Mabbott, T. (ed) *The Collected Works of Edgar Allan Poe*, 3 vols 2: 305–34. Cambridge: Harvard University Press.

Auerbach, E. (1953) *Mimesis: The Representation of Reality in Western Literature*, trans. Willard R. Trask, Princeton, NJ: Princeton University Press.

Bacon, F. (2007) 'Of Beauty,' in *The Essays*. New York: Cosimo Classics, pp. 111–112.

Baumgarten, A. (1954) *Reflections on Poetry*, trans. William Holther, Berkeley, CA: University of California Press.

Breton, A. (1960) *Nadja,* trans. Richard Howard, New York: Grove Press.

Crow, T. (1996) *The Rise of the Sixties: American and European Art in the Era of Dissent* New Haven, CT: Yale University Press.

Dornberg, J. (1987) 'Art Vandals: Why do They Do It?' *Art News* 86 (March):102–9.

Domberg, J. (1988) 'Deliberate Malice,' *Art News* 87 (October): 63–65.

Foucault, M. (1973) *Madness and Civilization: A History of Insanity in the Age of Reason*, trans. Richard Howard, New York: Vintage.

Gamboni, D. (1997) *The Destruction of Art: Iconoclasm and Vandalism Since the French Revolution* New Haven, CT: Yale University Press.

Mosse, G. L. (1991) 'Beauty without Sensuality / The Exhibition Entartete Kunst, in *"Degenerate Art": The Fate of the Avant-Garde in Nazi Germany*, ed. Stephanie Barron, New York: Los Angeles County Museum of Art and Harry N. Abrams, 25–31.

Quinn, M. (2004) *The Complete Marbles* New York: Mary Boone Gallery.

Siebers, T. (2000a) 'The New Art,' *The Body Aesthetic: From Fine Art to Body Modification* Ann Arbor, MI: University of Michigan Press.

Seibers, T. (2000b) 'Hitler and the Tyranny of the Aesthetic,' *Philosophy and Literature* 24.1: 96–110.

Siebers T. (2002) 'Broken Beauty: Disability and Art Vandalism,' *Michigan Quarterly Review* 41.2: 223–45.

Siebers, T. (2003) 'The Return to Ritual: Violence and Art in the Media Age,' *JCRT* 5.1: 9–32.

Siebers, T. (2004) 'Words Stare Like a Glass Eye: From Literary to Visual to Disability Studies and Back Again,' *PMLA* 119.5: 1315–24.

Wimsatt, W. K. and Beardsley, M. C. (1954) 'The Intentional Fallacy,' in W. K. Wimsatt, *The Verbal Icon* Lexington, KY: University of Kentucky Press, 3–18.

7. Tanya Titchkosky and Rod Michalko, The body as a problem of individuality: a phenomenological disability studies approach

Abberley, P. (1998). 'The Spectre at the Feast: Disabled People and Social Theory,' Shakespeare, T. (ed.) *The Disability Reader: Social Science Perspectives*. London: Cassell Academic, pp. 79–93.

Accessibility Services (AS). (2010). University of Toronto. Viewed July 29th, 2010, http://www.accessibility.utoronto.ca/about/rightsandresp.htm.

Ahmed, S. (2004a). *The Cultural Politics of Emotion*, New York: Routledge.

Ahmed, S. (2004b). 'Collective Feelings: Or, the Impressions Left by Others.' *Theory, Culture & Society*. Vol. 21(2): 25–42.

Bauman, Z. (2004). *Identity*, Malden, MA: Polity Press.

Butler, J. (2009). *Frames of War: When is Life Grievable?*, New York: Verso Press.

Butler, J. (1999). *Gender Trouble: Feminism and the Subversion of Identity*, New York: Routledge.

Butler, J. (1993). *Bodies that Matter: On the Discursive Limits of Sex*, New York: Routledge.

Garfinkel, H. (1967). *Studies in Ethnomethodology*, Upper Saddle River, NJ: Prentice-Hall, Inc.

Heidegger, M. (1962). *Being and Time*, New York: Harper & Row.

Hughes, B. (2007). 'Being Disabled: Towards a Critical Social Ontology for Disability Studies.' *Disability & Society*. Vol. 22(7): 673–684.

Hughes, B. and Paterson, K. (1997) 'The Social Model of Disability and the Disappearing Body: Towards a sociology of impairment.' *Disability and Society* Vol 12(3). Available online at http://www.tandfonline.com/doi/abs/10.1080/09687599727209

Husserl, E. (1970). *The Crisis of European Sciences and Transcendental Phenomenology: An Introduction to Phenomenological Philosophy*, Evanston, IL: Northwestern University Press.

Merleau-Ponty, M. (1958 [1945]). *Phenomenology of Perception*, London: Routledge and Kegan Paul.

Michalko, R. (2002). *The Difference that Disability Makes*, Philadelphia, PA: Temple University Press.

Michalko, R. (1999). *The Two in One: Walking with Smokie, Walking with Blindness*, Philadelphia, PA: Temple University Press.

Michalko, R. (1998). *The Mystery of the Eye and the Shadow of Blindness*, Toronto: University of Toronto Press.

Sacks, H. (1984). 'On Doing "Being Ordinary",' Maxwell, J. and Heritage, J. (eds) *Structures of Social Action: Studies in Conversation Analysis*. Cambridge: Cambridge University Press, pp. 413–30.

Schutz, A. (1973). *Collected Papers I: The Problem of Social Reality*, The Hague: Martinus Nijoff.

Stiker, H.-J. (1999). *The History of Disability*, Ann Arbor, MI: University of Michigan Press.

Titchkosky, T. (2011). *The Question of Access: Disability, Space, Meaning*, Toronto: University of Toronto Press.

Titchkosky, T. (2008). '"To Pee or Not to Pee?" Ordinary Talk about Extraordinary Exclusions in a University Environment.' *Canadian Journal of Sociology*. Vol. 33(1): 37–60. http://ejournals.library.ualberta.ca/index.php/CJS/article/view/1526/1058.

Titchkosky, T. (2001). 'Disability – A Rose by Any Other Name? People First Language in Canadian Society.' *Canadian Review of Sociology and Anthropology*. Vol. 38(2): 125–40.

Titchkosky, T. and Aubrecht, K. (2009). 'The Power of Anguish: Re-mapping Mental Diversity with an Anti-colonial Compass,' Kempf, A. (ed.) *Breaching the Colonial Contract: Anti-Colonialism in the US and Canada*. New York: Springer, pp. 179–99.

Titchkosky, T. and Michalko, R. (2009). *Rethinking Normalcy: A Disability Studies Reader*, Toronto: Canadian Scholars/Women's Press.

Weiss, G. (2008). *Refiguring the Ordinary*, Bloomington, IN: Indiana University Press.

8. Aimi Hamraie, Designing collective access: a feminist disability theory of universal design

Barad, K. 2007. *Meeting the Universe Halfway: Quantum Physics and the Entanglement of Matter and Meaning*. Durham: Duke University Press.

Brown, L., ed. 2011. *Feminist Practices: Interdisciplinary Approaches to Women in Architecture*. Surrey: Ashgate.

Center for Universal Design. 1997. "The Principles of Universal Design, Version 2.0." North Carolina State University. Available at: http://www.ncsu.edu/www/ncsu/design/sod5/cud/about_ud/udprinciplestext.htm. Accessed on: March 20, 2013.

Chouinard, V., E. Hall, and R. Wilton, eds. 2010. *Toward Enabling Geographies: 'Disabled' Bodies and Minds in Society and Space*. Burlington, VT: Ashgate.

Code, L. 2006. *Ecological Thinking: The Politics of Epistemic Location*. New York: Oxford University Press.

Corker, M. 2001. "Sensing Disability." *Hypatia: A Journal of Feminist Philosophy* 16.4: 34–52.

D'Souza, N. 2004. "Is Universal Design a Critical Theory?" In *Designing a More Inclusive World*, edited by S. Keates and J. Clarkson, 3–9. London: Springer.

Dyck, Is. 2010. "Geographies of Disability: Reflecting on New Body Knowledges." In *Toward Enabling Geographies: 'Disabled' Bodies and Minds in Society and Space*, edited by V. Chouinard, E. Hall, and R. Wilton, 253–264. Burlington, VT: Ashgate.

Eiseland, N. 1994. *The Disabled God: Toward a Liberatory Theology of Disability*. Nashville, TN: Abington Press.

Garland-Thomson, R. 1996. *Extraordinary Bodies: Figuring Disability in American Culture and Literature*. New York: Columbia University Press.

Garland-Thomson, R. 2005. "Feminist Disability Studies: A Review Essay." *Signs: A Journal of Women and Culture* 2:1557–1587.

Garland-Thomson, R. [2002] 2011a. "Integrating Disability, Transforming Feminist Theory." In *Feminist Disability Studies*, edited by Kim Q. Hall, 13–47. Bloomington, IN: Indiana University Press.

Garland-Thomson, R. 2011b. "Misfits: A Feminist Materialist Disability Concept." *Hypatia: A Journal of Feminist Philosophy* 26.3:591–609.

Glesson, B. 1999. *Geographies of Disability*. London and New York: Routledge.

Grasswick, H. 2011. (ed) *Feminist Epistemology and Philosophy of Science: Power in Knowledge*. Rotterdam: Springer.

Hamraie, A. 2012. "Universal Design Research as a New Materialist Practice." *Disability Studies Quarterly* 32.4. Available at: http://dsq-sds.org/article/view/3246/3185. Accessed on: March 20, 2013.

Hannson, L. 2007. "The Power of Design – Allies Fighting Design Exclusion." In *Little Monsters: (De)Coupling Assemblages of Consumption*, edited by H. Brembeck, K. Ekstrom, and M. Morck, 15–28. Berlin: Lit Verlag.

Hayden, D. 2000. "What Would a Non-Sexist City Be Like? Speculations on Housing, Urban Design and Human Work." In *Gender Space Architecture: An Interdisciplinary Introduction*, edited by I. Borden, B. Penner, and J. Rendell, 266–281. London: Routledge.

Imrie, R. 2002. "Architects' Conceptions of the Human Body." *Environment and Planning D: Society and Space* 21.1:47–65.

Imrie, R. 2010. "Disability, Embodiment, and the Meaning of Home." In *Toward Enabling Geographies: "Disabled" Bodies and Minds in Society and Space*, edited by V. Chouinard, E. Hall, and R. Wilton, 23–44. Burlington, VT: Ashgate.

Imrie, R. 2012. "Universalism, Universal Design, and Equitable Access to the Built Environment." *Disability and Rehabilitation* 34.10:873–882.

Lifchez, R. 1987. *Rethinking Architecture: Design Students and Physically Disabled People*. Berkeley, CA: University of California Press.

Mace, R. 1985. "Universal Design: Barrier-Free Environments for Everyone." *Designer's West* 33.1:147–152.

Matrix. 1984. *Making Space: Women and the Man Made Environment*. London: Pluto Press.

Mills, C. 1997. *The Racial Contract*. Ithaca, NY: Cornell University Press.

Mingus, M. 2010a. "Reflections from Detroit: Reflections on An Opening: Disability Justice and Creating Collective Access in Detroit." *INCITE Blog*. Available at: http://inciteblog.wordpress.com/2010/08/23/reflections-from-detroit-reflections-on-an-opening-disability-justice-and-creating-collective-access-in-detroit/. Accessed on: December 15, 2012.

Mingus, M. 2010b. "Changing the Framework: Disability Justice." *RESIST Newsletter* November/December. Available at: http://www.resistinc.org/sites/default/files/NovDec10NL_sm.pdf. Accessed on: December 15, 2012.

Mueller, J. 1997. *Case Studies on the Principles of Universal Design*. Raleigh, NC: Center for Universal Design, North Carolina State.

Mullick, A., S. Agarwal, A. Kumar, and P. Swarnkar. 2011. "Public Bathroom for Universal Access: An Article." *The Trellis* 2.7:117–126.

Nielson, K. E. 2012. *A Disability History of the United States*. Boston, MA: Beacon Press.

Ostroff, E., M. Limont, and D. Hunter. 2002. *Building a World Fit for People: Designers with Disabilities at Work*. Boston, MA: Adaptive Environments.

Rose, G. 1993. *Feminism and Geography: The Limits of Geographical Knowledge*. Cambridge: Blackwell Publishers.

Sandhu, J. 2011. "The Rhinoceros Syndrome: A Contrarian View of Universal Design." In *Universal Design Handbook: Second Edition*, edited by W. Preiser and K. Smith, 44.3–44.11. New York: McGraw-Hill.

Sanford, J. 2012. *Universal Design as a Rehabilitation Strategy*. New York: Springer.

Sarkissian, W. 1987. "How the Students Saw It." In *Rethinking Architecture: Design Students and Physically Disabled People*, edited by R. Lifchez, 123–134. Berkeley, CA: University of California Press.

Silvers, A. 1998. "Formal Justice." In *Disability, Difference, and Discrimination*, edited by A. Silvers, D. Wasserman, and M. Mahowald, 13–146. Oxford: Rowman & Littlefield Publishers.

Steinfeld, E. 1979. *Access to the Built Environment: A Review of the Literature*. Washington, DC: U.S. Department of Housing and Urban Development Office of Policy and Development Research.

Steinfeld, E. and B. Tauke. 2002. "Universal Designing." In *Universal Design: 17 Ways of Thinking and Teaching*, edited by Jon Christophersen, 165–189. Husbanken: Council of Europe.

Steinfeld, E. and J. Maisel. 2012. *Universal Design: Creating Inclusive Environments*. Chichester: John Wiley & Sons.

Steinfeld, E., V. Paquet, C. D'Souza, C. Joseph, and J. Maisel. 2010. "Final Report: Anthropometry of Wheeled Mobility Project." *Report of the Center for Inclusive Design and Environmental Access for the U.S. Access Board*. Buffalo, NY: Center for Inclusive Design and Environmental Access.

Titchkosky, T. 2011. *The Question of Access*. Toronto: University of Toronto Press.

Tuana, N. and S. Sullivan, eds. 2007. *Race and Epistemologies of Ignorance*. Albany, NY: State University of New York Press.

Weisman, L. K. [1981] 1999. "Women's Environmental Rights: A Manifesto." *Heresies* 11 (1981) Vol 3 No 3. Reprinted in *Gender Space Architecture: An Interdisciplinary Introduction*, edited by Borden, I., Penner, B. and Rendell, J. (1999), 1–5. London and New York: Routledge.

Weisman, L. K. 1989. "A Feminist Experiment: Learning from WPSA, Then and Now." In *Architecture: A Place for Women*, edited by E. Berkley and M. McQuaid, 125–133. Washington DC: Smithsonian.

Weisman, L. K. 1992. *Discrimination by Design: A Feminist Critique of the Man-Made Environment*. Champaign, IL: University of Illinois Press.

Weisman, L. K. 1999. "Redesigning Architectural Education." In *Design and Feminism: Re-visioning Spaces, Places, and Everyday Things*, edited by J. Rothschild, 159–174. Camden, NY: Rutgers University Press.

Weisman, L. K. 2012. "The Environment is Political: Universal Design and Social Sustainability," *Universal Design Newsletter* April. Available at: http://www.universaldesign.com/interest/sustainability/531-the-environmental-is-political-universal-design-and-social-sustainability-with-leslie-kanes-weisman.html. Accessed on: January 1, 2013.

Welch, P. 1995. "What Is Universal Design?" In *Strategies for Teaching Universal Design*, edited by P. Welch. Boston, MA: Adaptive Environments Center and MIG Communications. Available at: http://www.udeducation.org/resources/62.html. Accessed on: March 18, 2013.

Welch, P. and S. Jones. 2002. "Universal Design: An Opportunity for Critical Discourse in Design Education." In *Universal Design: 17 Ways of Thinking and Teaching*, edited by J. Christophersen, 191–216. Husbanken: Council of Europe.

Wendell, S. 1996. *The Rejected Body: Feminist Philosophical Reflections on Disability*. New York: Routledge.

9. J. Kent Fitzsimons, More than access: overcoming limits in architectural and disability discourse

Aymonin, D. (2008). "D-475 days, on the way towards the Library of the Rolex Learning Center of the Ecole Polytechnique Fédérale de Lausanne, Switzerland" (Abstract) conference presentation *21st Century Libraries: Changing Forms, Changing Challenges, Changing Objectives: 8th Frankfurt Scientific Forum* 3–4 November.

Breckenridge, C., and Vogler, C. (eds) (2001). *The Critical Limits of Embodiment: Reflections on Disability Criticism. (Special Issue of Public Culture.)* Durham, NC: Duke University Press.

Centre Suisse pour la construction adaptée aux handicapés (2005). "L'art d'une architecture discriminatoire." *Info: Bulletin du Centre Suisse pour la construction adaptée aux handicapés*, November 42, 2–4.

Eisenman, P. (2006). *Feints*, Milan: Skira.

Hockenberry, J. (1995). *Moving Violations: War Zones, Wheelchairs, and Declarations of Independence*, New York: Hyperion.

Kristeva, J. (2003). *Lettre ouverte au président de la République sur les citoyens en situation de handicap, à l'usage de ceux qui le sont et ceux qui ne le sont pas*, Paris: Fayard.

McNeill, W. (1995). *Keeping Together in Time*, Cambridge, MA: Harvard University Press.

Wölfflin, H. (1886). *Prolegomena zu einer Psychologie der Architektur*, Munich: Kgl. Hof- & Universitäts-Buchdruckerei, 1886; translated as Prolegomena to a Psychology of Architecture (1994). In R. Vischer et al., H.F. Mallgrave and E. Ikonomou (Transl.) *Empathy, Form and Space: Problems in German Aesthetics, 1873–1893*. Santa Monica, CA: Getty Center for the History of Art and the Humanities.

10. Jay Dolmage, From steep steps to retrofit to universal design, from collapse to austerity: neo-liberal spaces of disability

Berlant, L. (2011) *Cruel Optimism*, Durham, NC: Duke University Press.

Blyth, M. (2013) *Austerity: The History of a Dangerous Idea*, Oxford: Oxford University Press.

Dolmage, J. (2006) 'Mapping Composition,' in Brueggeman, B. and C. Lewiecki-Wilson (eds.) with J. Dolmage *Disability and the Teaching of Writing: A Critical Sourcebook*, pp. 14–27. Boston, MA: Bedford St. Martin's.

Dolmage, J. (2015a) 'We Need To Talk About Universal Design,' *Cripping the Computer*, Unpublished Edited Collection. http://ncte.connectedcommunity.org/wlu/ourlibrary/viewdocument?DocumentKey=5caa9259-7e61-453b-b958-c409c8200d10

Dolmage, J. (2015b) 'Disabling Studies, Disability Studied, and Disability Studies,' Keynote, Canadian Disability Association Conference, Ottawa, Ontario, 3 June.

Duggan, L. (2003) *The Twilight of Equality: Neoliberalism, Cultural Politics, and the Attack on Democracy*, Boston, MA: Beacon.

Fitzgerald, F. S. (1996 (1920))*This Side of Paradise*, New York: Modern Library.

Gleeson, B. (1999) *Geographies of Disability*, New York: Routledge.

Hamraie, A. (2013) *Designing Collective Access: A Feminist Disability Theory of Universal Design,* online http://dsq-sds.org/article/view/3871

Harvey, D. (1993) 'From Space to Place and Back Again: Reflections on the condition of postmodernity,' In Bird, J., Curtis, B., Putnam, T., Robertson, G., and Tickner, L. (eds) *Mapping the Futures: Local Cultures, Global Change,* pp. 3–29. London: Routledge.

Harvey, D. (2005) *A Brief History of Neoliberalism,* Oxford: Oxford University Press.

Kerschbaum, S. L. (2014) 'Toward a New Rhetoric of Difference,' Urbana, IL: Conference on College Composition and Communication/National Council of Teachers of English.

Mace, R. L. (1985) 'Universal Design, Barrier Free Environments for Everyone,' *Designers West* 33.1: 147–152.

Mackey, E. (1999) *The House of Difference: Cultural Politics and National Identity in Canada,* London: Routledge.

Mayer, A. (2008) 'Architecture in an Age of Austerity,' *New Geography.* 29 Nov, online http://www.newgeography.com/content/00444-architecture-age-austerity.

McRuer, R. (2015) *Crip Times,* Unpublished manuscript.

Mitchell, J. (2014) 'Graves' Discovery Affects Miss. Medical School's Plans,' *The Jackson Mississippi Clarion Ledger,* 9 February. http://www.usatoday.com/story/news/nation/2014/02/09/mississippi-medical-school-graves-found/5320995/.

Mosby, I. (2013) 'Administering Colonial Science: Nutrition Research and Human Biomedical Experimentation in Aboriginal Communities and Residential Schools, 1942–1952,' *Histoire sociale/Social history* 46.1: 145–172. *Project MUSE,* Web. 1 Jun 2015. https://muse.jhu.edu/.

Price, M. (2011) *Mad At School: Rhetorics of Mental Disability and Academic Life,* Ann Arbor, MI: University of Michigan Press.

Price, M. (2012) 'Access: A Happening,' Featured session, in collaboration with J. Dolmage, Q.-L. Driskill, C. Selfe, et al. Conference on College Composition and Communication. St. Louis, MO. March 23, 2012.

Stuckler, D. and S. Basu. (2013) *The Body Economic: Why Austerity Kills,* London: Allen Lane.

Titchkosky, T. (2011) *The Question of Access,* Toronto: University of Toronto Press.

Trent, J. W. (1994) *Inventing the Feeble Mind,* Berkeley, CA: University of California Press.

Welsome, E. (1999) *The Plutonium Files: America's Secret Medical Experiments in the Cold War,* New York: Dial Press.

Wilder, C. S. (2013) *Ebony and Ivy,* New York: Bloomsbury Press.

Zarfas, D. E. (1963) 'The Formation and Function of the Children's Psychiatric Research Institute, London, Ontario.' *Canadian Medical Association Journal* 88.4:192–195.

Part III Education

Afacan, Y. (2006) 'Integrating Universal Design into the Main Stream of Architectural Design Education', *Proceedings of the 1st International CIB Endorsed METU Postgraduate Conference, Built Environment and Information Technologies,* Ankara.

Basnak, M., Tauke, B. and Weidemann, S. (2015, April) 'Universal Design in Architectural Education: Who is Doing It? How is it being done?' paper accepted to ARCC's conference, Chicago.

Boys, J. (2014) *Doing Disability Differently: An Alternative Handbook on Dis/ability, Architecture and Designing for Everyday Life,* London and New York: Routledge.

Boys, J. (2016) 'Architecture, Place and the "Care-full" Design of Everyday Life', in C. Bates, R. Imrie and K. Kullman (eds) *Care and Design: Bodies, Buildings, Cities,* Chichester: John Wiley & Sons Ltd, 153–179.

CEBE Special Interest Group (2002) *Building and Sustaining a Learning Environment for Inclusive Design.* Edited by Ruth Morrow. Online. Available for free download at http://www.cebe.heacademy.ac.uk/ learning/sig/inclusive/report.php.

Centre for Excellence in Universal Design (2010) *Integrating Universal Design into the Third Level Curriculum*, National Disability Authority, Dublin, Ireland. http://universaldesign.ie/What-is-Universal-Design/Education/Integrating-Universal-Design-Content-in-Third-Level-Curriculum/

De Cauwer, P., Clement, M., Buelens, H. and Heylighen, A. (2009) 'Four Reasons Not to Teach Inclusive Design', paper presented at *'Include'* conference, Helen Hamlyn Centre, Royal College of Art, UK, 5–8 April.

Dolmage, J. (2005) 'Disability Studies Pedagogy, Usability and Universal Design', *Disability Studies Quarterly* Fall 25: 4. Available at: http://dsq-sds.org/article/view/627/804

Dolmage, J. (2008) 'Mapping Composition: Inviting Disability in the Front Door', in C. Lewiecki-Wilson, B. J. Brueggemann and J. Dolmage (eds) *Disability and the Teaching of Writing: A Critical Sourcebook*, Boston, MA: Bedford/St. Martin's, 14–27.

Dolmage, J. (2009) 'Disability, Usability, Universal Design', in S. K. Miller-Cochran and R. L. Rodrigo (eds) *Rhetorically Rethinking Usability: Theories, Practices, and Methodologies*, New York: Hampton Press. Available for download at: https://www.academia.edu/1569909/Disability_Usability_Universal_Design

Dolmage, J. (2013) *Disability Rhetoric*, Syracuse, NY: Syracuse University Press.

Dolmage, J. (2015) 'Disabling Studies, Disability Studied, and Disability Studies', Keynote, Canadian Disability Association Conference, Ottawa, Ontario, 3 June.

Goggin, G. (2010) '"Laughing with/at the Disabled": The Cultural Politics of Disability in Australian Universities', *Discourse: Studies in the Cultural Politics of Education* 31: 4, 469–481.

Heylighen, A. and Bianchin, M. (2013) 'How Does Inclusive Design Relate to Good Design?' *Design Studies* 34: 93–110.

Kennig, B. and Ryhl, C. (2002) 'Teaching Universal Design: Global Examples of Projects and Models for Teaching in Universal Design at Schools of Design and Architecture', *AAOutils Design for All* report. http://anlh.be/aaoutils/

Kerschbaum, S., Garland-Thomson, R., Oswal, S., Vidali, A., Ghiaciuc, S., Dolmage, J., Meyer, C., Brueggemann, B. and Samuels, E. (2013) 'Faculty Members, Accommodation and Access in Higher Education', *Profession* (online). Available at: https://profession.commons.mla.org/2013/12/09/faculty-members-accommodation-and-access-in-higher-education/

Lifchez, R. (1986) *Rethinking Architecture: Design Students and Physically Disabled People*, Berkeley, CA: University of California Press.

Mintz, S. B. (2007) *Unruly Bodies. Life Writing by Women with Disabilities*, Chapel Hill, NC: The University of North Carolina Press.

Morrow, R. (2001a) 'The Draware Project.' Online at *Universal Design Education Online*: http://www.udeducation.org/teach/program_overview/program_infused/morrow.asp

Morrow, R. (2001b) 'Universal Design as a Critical Tool in Design Education', in W. Preiser and E. Ostroff (eds.) *The Universal Design Handbook*, McGraw-Hill, 54.1–54.16.

Newall, C. (2008) 'Flourishing Rhetorically: Disability, Diversity and Equal Disappointment Opportunity' *Vance* 117–127. Available for download at: http://scia.intersearch.com.au/sciajspui/bitstream/1/332/1/Newell%202008.pdf

Price, M. (2009) 'Access Imagined: The Construction of Disability in Conference Policy Documents', *Disability Studies Quarterly* 29:1 online http://dsq-sds.org/article/view/174/174

Price, M. (2011) *Mad at School. Rhetorics of Mental Disability and Academic Life*, Ann Arbor, MI: University of Michigan Press.

Tauke, B., Steinfeld, E. and Basnak, M. (2014) 'Challenges and Opportunities for Inclusive Design in Graduate Architecture', in Caltenco, H.A., Hedvall, P.-O., Larsson, A., Rassmus-Gröhn, K. and Rydeman, B. (eds) *Proceedings of the International Conference on Universal Design*, UD 2014, Lund, Sweden, June 16–18 Amsterdam: IOS Press.

Titchkosky, T. (2003) *Disability, Self and Society*, Toronto: University of Toronto Press.

Titchkosky, T. (2007) *Reading and Writing Disability Differently: The Textured Life of Embodiment*, Toronto: University of Toronto Press.

Titchkosky, T. (2008) '"To pee or not to pee?" Ordinary Talk about Extraordinary Exclusions in a University Environment', *Canadian Journal of Sociology/Cahiers canadiens de sociologie* 33:1, 37–60.

Yergeau, M., Brewer, E., Kerschbaum, S., Oswal, S. K., Price, S. M., Selfe, M. J. and Howes, F. (2013) 'Multimodality in Motion: Disability and Kairotic Spaces' (online), *Kairos: A Journal of Rhetoric, Technology, and Pedagogy* 18.1. August. View at: http://kairos.technorhetoric.net/18.1/coverweb/yergeau-et-al/index.html

11. Stefan White, Including architecture: what difference can we make?

Deleuze, G. (1988). *Spinoza, Practical Philosophy*, San Francisco, CA, City Light Books.

Deleuze, G. (1992). *Expressionism in Philosophy: Spinoza*, New York: Zone Books.

Deleuze, G. (1994). *Difference and Repetition*, London, Continuum.

Deleuze, G. (2003). 'The three kinds of knowledge.' *Pli: The Warwick Journal of Philosophy* 14: 1–20, Warwick.

Eisenman, P. (1995). 'Eisenman (and company) respond: The politics of formalism.' *Progressive Architecture* 76(2): 88–91

Evans, R. (1995). *The Projective Cast: Architecture and Its Three Geometries*, Cambridge, MA, MIT Press.

Evans, R. (1997). *Translations between Drawing and Building and Other Essays*, London, Architectural Association.

Ghirardo, D. (1994). 'Eisenman's bogus avant-garde.' *Progressive Architecture* November, 70–73.

Naess, A. (1989). *Ecology, Community and Lifestyle*, Cambridge, Cambridge University Press.

Nussbaum, C. M. (2011). *Creating Capabilities: The Human Development Approach*, London, Harvard University Press.

OECD (2015). *Ageing in Cities*, Paris, OECD Publishing. DOI: http://dx.doi.org/10.1787/9789264231160-en

Rawes, P. E. (2013). *Relational Architectural Ecologies: Architecture, Nature and Subjectivity*, New York, Routledge.

Sen, A. (1999). *Development as Freedom*, Oxford, Oxford University Press.

Spinoza, B. (1677 [1996]) *Ethics*, London, Penguin Classics.

White, S., Phillipson, C. and Hammond, M. (2012). 'Old Moat in an Age-Friendly Manchester Research Report (AFOM).' http://www.southwayhousing.co.uk/your-neighbourhood/age-friendly-neighbourhoods.aspx (accessed 2016).

White, S. R. (2014). 'Gilles Deleuze and the project of architecture: an expressionist design-research methodology.' PhD thesis. University College London.

World Health Organisation (2002). *Active ageing: a policy framework*. Geneva: WHO Press. Downloadable from http://apps.who.int/iris/bitstream/10665/67215/1/WHO_NMH_NPH_02.8.pdf

World Health Organization (2007). *Global Age-friendly Cities: A guide*, Geneva: WHO Press.

12. Jos Boys, Diagramming for a dis/ordinary architecture

arq (2012) Diagramming Architecture, *Architectural Research Quarterly*, 16, 3–4

Artemel, A. J. (2013) 'Peter Versus Peter: Eisenman and Zumthor's Theoretical Throwdown,' 1st August, http://architizer.com/blog/peter-versus-peter/

Borden, I., Kerr, J., Pivaro, A., and Rendell, J. (1996) *Strangely Familiar: Narratives of Architecture in the City*, London: Routledge

Boys, J. (1996) 'Neutral Gazes and Knowable Objects. Challenging the Masculinist Structures of Architectural Knowledge,' in Wigglesworth, S., Ruedi, K., and McCorquodale, D. (eds) *Desiring Practices: Architecture Gender and the Interdisciplinary*, London: Black Dog Publishing

Boys, J. (1998) 'Beyond Maps and Metaphors. Re-thinking the Relationships between Architecture and Gender,' in Ainley, R. (ed.) *New Frontiers of Space, Bodies and Gender*, London and New York: Routledge

Boys, J. (2014) *Doing Disability Differently: An Alternative Handbook on Architecture, Dis/ability and Designing for Everyday Life*, London and New York: Routledge

Boys, J. (2016) 'Architecture, place and the "care-full" design of everyday life,' in Bates, C., Imrie, R., Kullman, K. (eds) *Care and Design: Bodies, Buildings, Cities*, Hoboken, NJ: Wiley-Blackwell

Deleuze, G., and Guattari, F. (1980 [2013]) *A Thousand Plateaus: Capitalism and Schizophrenia*, London: Bloomsbury Academic

Eisenman, P. (1987) *Houses of Cards*, New York: Oxford University

Eisenman, P. (1999) *Diagram Diaries*, New York: Universe Architecture Series

Eisenman, P. (2007) Diagram. 'An Original Scene of Writing', in *Writing into the Void: Selected Writings 1990 – 2004*, New Haven, CT: Yale University Press

Evans, R. (2000) *The Projective Cast: Architecture and its Three Geometries*, Boston, MA: MIT Press

Fedorchenko, M. (2008) 'Beautiful Apparatus: Diagrammatic Balance of Forms and Flows,' *Architectural Theory Review*, 13:3, 288–305

Frank, S. (1994) *Peter Eisenman's House VI: The Client's Response*, New York: Watson-Guptil Publications

Garfinkel, H. (1967) *Studies in Ethnomethodology*, Upper Saddle River, NJ: Prentice-Hall

Garland-Thompson, R. (2011) 'Misfits: A Feminist Materialist Disability Concept,' *Hypatia Special Issue: Ethics of Embodiment*, 26:3, 591–609, Summer

Ghirardo, D. (1994) 'Eisenman's bogus avant-garde,' *Progressive Architecture*, November. 70–73.

Gins, M. and Arakawa (2002) *The Architectural Body*, Tuscaloosa: University of Alabama Press

Goldberger, P. (1989) 'The Museum That Theory Built' *The New York Times* November 5th. http://www.nytimes.com/1989/11/05/arts/architecture-view-the-museum-that-theory-built. html?src=pm&pagewanted=1

Henry Dreyfuss Associates (1974) *Body Measurements*, Boston, MA: MIT Press

Kafer, A. (2013) *Feminist, Queer, Crip*, Bloomington, IN: Indiana University Press

Lambert, L. (2012) 'Architectural Theories: A Subversive Approach to the Ideal Normalized Body,' April 29, http://thefunambulist.net/2012/04/29/architectural-theories-a-subversive-approach-to-the-ideal-normatized-body/

Lambert, L. and Pham, M-H. T. (2015) 'Spinoza in a T-shirt', July 1st, http://thenewinquiry.com/essays/spinoza-in-a-t-shirt/

Le Corbusier (2004) [First published in two volumes in 1954 and 1958.] *The Modulor: A Harmonious Measure to the Human Scale, Universally Applicable to Architecture and Mechanics*. Basel & Boston: Birkhäuser.

Michalko, R. (2002) *The Difference that Disability Makes*, Philadelphia, PA: Temple University Press

Neufert, E. and Neufert, P. (2012) *Architects' Data 4th Edition*, Hoboken, NJ: Wiley-Blackwell

Price, M. (2015) 'The Bodymind Problem and the Possibilities of Pain,' *Hypatia Special Issue: Conversations in Feminist Disability Studies*, 30:1, 268–284, Winter

Reiser, J. and Umemoto, N. (2006) *Atlas of Novel Tectonics* Princeton, NJ: Princeton University Press

Rowe, C. (1947) 'The Mathematics of the Ideal Villa: Palladio and Le Corbusier Compared,' *Architectural Review*, March 101: 101–104

Somol, R. E. (1999) 'Dummy Text, or the Diagrammatic Basis of Contemporary Architecture,' Introduction to *Diagram Diaries*, by Peter Eisenman, New York: Universe Publishing, 7–25.

Titchkosky, T. (2002) 'Cultural maps; which way to disability?', in Corker, M. and Shakespeare, T. (eds) *Disability/Postmodernity: Embodying disability theory*, London: Continuum

Titchkosky, T. (2008) 'To Pee or Not to pee?' Ordinary Talk about Extraordinary Exclusions in a University Environment, *Canadian Journal of Sociology/Cahiers canadiens de sociologie*, 33(1): 37–60

Titchkosky, T. (2011) *The Question of Access: Disability, Space, Meaning*, Toronto: University of Toronto Press

Vidler, A. (2000) 'Diagrams of Diagrams: Architectural Abstraction and Modern Representation,' *Representations*, 72, 1–20, Autumn

Virilio, P. and Parent, C. (1966 and 1996) *Architecture Principe*, Les Editions de Imprimeur

Wittkower, R. (1949) *Architectural Principles in the Age of Humanism*, London: The Warburg Institute

Zumthor, P. (2006) *Atmospheres*, 5th Edition, Basel: Birkhauser Architecture

Zumthor, P. (2010) *Thinking Architecture*, 3rd Edition, Basel: Birkhauser Architecture

13. Margaret Price, Un/shared space: the dilemma of inclusive architecture

Abramson, K. (2014). 'Turning up the lights on gaslighting,' *Philosophical Perspectives* 28.1: 1–30.

Ahmed, S. (2012). *On being included: Racism and diversity in institutional life*, Durham, NC: Duke University Press.

Alaimo, S. (2008). 'Trans-corporeal feminisms and the ethical space of nature,' *Material feminisms*. Ed. Stacy Alaimo and Susan Hekman. Bloomington: Indiana University Press.. 237–264.

Barad, K. (2003). 'Posthumanist performativity: Toward an understanding of how matter comes to matter,' *Signs* 28.3: 801–831.

Barad, K. (2007). *Meeting the universe halfway: Quantum physics and the entanglement of matter and meaning*, Durham, NC & London: Duke University Press.

Blankmeyer Burke, T. and B. Nicodemus. (2013). 'Coming out of the hard of hearing closet: Reflections on a shared journey in academia,' *Disability Studies Quarterly* 33.2. http://dsq-sds.org/article/view/3706/3239

Boys, J. (2014). *Doing disability differently: An alternative handbook on architecture, dis/ability and designing for everyday life*, London & New York: Routledge.

Charlton, J. I. (1998). *Nothing about us without us: Disability oppression and empowerment*, Berkeley, CA: University of California Press.

Crowley, S. (2006). *Toward a civil discourse: Rhetoric and fundamentalism*, Pittsburgh, PA: University of Pittsburgh Press.

Dadas, C. (2017) 'Interview Practices as Accessibility: The Academic Job Market' *Computers and Composition*. Ed. Melanie Yergeau and Elizabeth Brewer. Digital Press.

Dolmage, J. (2008). 'Mapping composition: Inviting disability in the front door,' *Disability and the teaching of writing: A critical sourcebook*. Ed. C. Lewiecki-Wilson and B. J. Brueggemann, with J. Dolmage. Boston, MA: Bedford/St. Martin's. 14–27.

Dolmage, J. (2013). *Disability rhetoric*, Syracuse, NY: Syracuse University Press.

Dolmage, J. (2015). 'Universal design: Places to start,' *Disability Studies Quarterly* 35.2. http://dsq-sds.org/article/view/4632

Dunne, A. and F. Raby. (2013). *Speculative everything: Design, fiction, and social dreaming*, Cambridge, MA & London: MIT.

Eligon, J. (2016, February 3). 'Diversity is one thing, inclusion another: After racist episodes, blunt discussions on campus,' *New York Times*. 'Education Life.'

Fox, C. (2002). 'The race to truth: Disarticulating critical thinking from whiteliness,' *Pedagogy* 2.2: 197–212.

Hamraie, A. (2013). 'Designing collective access: A feminist disability theory of universal design,' *Disability Studies Quarterly* 33.4. http://dsq-sds.org/article/view/3871/3411

Hawhee, D. (2002). 'Kairotic encounters,' *Perspectives on rhetorical invention*. Ed. J. M. Atwill and J. M. Lauer. Knoxville, TN: University of Tennessee Press 16–35.

Kafer, A. (2013). *Feminist, Queer, Crip*, Bloomington, IN: University of Indiana Press.

Kafer, A. (2016). 'Un/safe disclosures: Scenes of disability and trauma,' *Journal of Literary & Cultural Disability Studies* 10.1: 1–20.

Keller, J. S. (2016). 'The politics of stairs,' *Design Equilibrium*. American Institute of Architects, Atlanta, GA: 42–45.

Kerschbaum, S. (2014). *Toward a new rhetoric of difference*, Urbana, IL: National Council of Teachers of English.

Konrad, A. (2016). 'Access as a lens for peer tutoring,' *Another Word*. Feb 22. http://writing.wisc.edu/blog/?p=6454

Lefebvre, H. (1974 (trans. 1991)). *The production of space,* Trans. Donald Nicholson-Smith. Oxford: Blackwell.

Massey, D. (1994). *Space, place and gender*, Minneapolis, MN: University of Minnesota Press.

McLaren, P. (1988). 'Schooling the postmodern body: Critical pedagogy and the politics of enfleshment,' *The Journal of Education* 170:3, 53–83.

Mingus, M. (2011). 'Access intimacy: The missing link,' *Leaving Evidence*. May 5. https://leavingevidence.wordpress.com/2011/05/05/access-intimacy-the-missing-link/

Newell, C. (2007). 'Flourishing rhetorically: Disability, diversity, and equal disappointment opportunity,' *Disabled faculty and staff in a disabling society: Multiple identities in higher education*. Ed. Mary Lee Vance. Huntersville, NC: AHEAD. 117–127.

Pratt, M. B. (1984). 'Identity: Skin blood heart,' *Yours in struggle: Three feminist perspectives on anti-Semitism and racism*. Ithaca, NY: Firebrand, 1984. 11–63.

Price, M. (2009). 'Access imagined: The construction of disability in conference policy documents,' *Disability Studies Quarterly* 29.1. http://dsq-sds.org/article/view/174/174

Price, M. (2011). *Mad at school: Rhetorics of mental disability and academic life*, Ann Arbor, MI: University of Michigan Press.

Price, M. (2016). 'Access statement for presentations'. https://margaretprice.wordpress.com/access-statement-for-presentations/

Price, M. and Kerschbaum, S. L. (2016). 'Stories of Methodology: Interviewing Sideways, Crooked and Crip,' *Canadian Journal of Disability Studies* 5.3: 18–56.

Reynolds, N. (2004). *Geographies of writing: Inhabiting places and encountering difference,* Carbondale, IL: Southern Illinois University Press.

Rickert, T. (2007). 'Invention in the wild: On locating kairos in space-time,' *The locations of composition*. Ed. C. J. Keller and C. R. Weisser. Albany, NY: SUNY P. 71–89.

Rickert, T. (2013). *Ambient rhetoric: The attunements of rhetorical being*, Pittsburgh, PA: University of Pittsburgh Press.

Ruíz, E. F. (2014). 'Musing: Spectral phenomenologies: Dwelling poetically in professional philosophy,' *Hypatia* 29.1: 196–204.

Schalk, S. (2013). 'Coming to claim crip: Disidentification with/in disability studies,' *Disability Studies Quarterly* 33.2. http://dsq-sds.org/article/view/3705

Smith, W. A. (2004). 'Black faculty coping with racial battle fatigue: The campus racial climate in a post-civil rights era.' Ed. D. Cleveland. *A long way to go: Conversations about race by African American faculty and graduate students*, New York: Peter Lang. 171–190.

Titchkosky, T. (2007). *Reading and writing disability differently: The textured life of embodiment,* Toronto: University of Toronto Press.

Titchkosky, T. (2011). *The question of access: Disability, space, meaning*, Toronto: U of Toronto P.

Ventola, E., C. Shalom, C, and S. Thompson (eds) (2002). *The Language of Conferencing*, Frankfurt am Main: Peter Lang

Wilson, S. (2012). 'They forgot Mammy had a brain', *Presumed incompetent: The intersections of race and class for women in academia*, Ed. G. Gutiérrez y Muhs, Y. Flores Niemann, C. G. González and A. P. Harris. Boulder, CO: Utah State University Press. 65–77.

Wood, T., J. Dolmage, M. Price and C. Lewiecki-Wilson. (2014). 'Moving beyond disability 2.0 in composition studies,' *Composition Studies* 42.2: 147–150.

Yergeau, M., E. Brewer, S. Kerschbaum, S. Oswal, M. Price, M. Salvo, C. Selfe and F. Howes. (2013). 'Multimodality in motion: disability and kairotic spaces,' *Kairos: A Journal of Rhetoric, Technology and Pedagogy* 18.1. http://kairos.technorhetoric.net/18.1/coverweb/yergeau-et-al/index.html

14. Aaron Williamson, The collapsing lecture

Barber, S. (2003) *Blows and Bombs. Antonin Artaud: The Biography,* London: Creation Books

Butt, G. (2005) Introduction to *After Criticism – New Responses to Art and Performance,* Oxford: Blackwell.

Dillon, B. (2007) 'Slapstick Theory' *Frieze,* Issue 110, October.

Thody, P. and Read, H. (1998) *Introducing Sartre,* London: Icon Books.

Williamson, A. (2008) *Performance / Video / Collaboration,* The Bancroft Library, University of California, Berkeley 44–45.

Part IV Technologies/materialities

Davis, L.J. (1995) *Enforcing Normalcy: Disability, Deafness, and the Body,* London: Verso.

Sobchack, V. (2006) 'A leg to stand on: prosthetics, metaphor, and materiality', in M. Smith and J. Morra (eds) *The Prosthetic Impulse: From a Posthuman Present to a Biocultural Future,* Cambridge, MA: MIT Press.

Wigley, M. (1991) 'Prosthetic theory: The disciplining of architecture', *Assemblage* 15, 7–29.

15. Peter Anderberg, Where does the person end and the technology begin?

Akrich, M. & Latour, B. (1992) 'A Summary of a Convenient Vocabulary for the Semiotics of Human and Nonhuman Assemblies'. In: W. E. Bijker & J. Law (Eds.), *Shaping Technology/Building Society: Studies in Socio-Technical Change,* Cambridge, MA: MIT Press, 259–264.

Bateson, G. (1972) *Steps to an Ecology of Mind: A Revolutionary Approach to Man's Understanding of Himself,* New York: Ballantine.

Callon, M. (1986) 'Some Elements of a Sociology of Translation: Domestication of the Scallops and of the Fishermen of St. Brieuc Bay'. In: J. Law (Ed.), *Power, Action, and Belief: A New Sociology of Knowledge?,* London, UK: Routledge & Kegan Paul, 196–229.

Haraway, D. (1991) 'A Cyborg Manifesto: Science, Technology, and Socialist-Feminism in the Late Twentieth Century'. In: D. Haraway, *Simians, Cyborgs and Women: The Reinvention of Nature,* New York: Routledge.

Hernwall, P. (2001) *Barns digitala rum. Berättelser om e-post, chatt & Internet,* Stockholm, Sweden: Pedagogiska institutionen, Stockholms universitet.

International Standardization Organization (2002) 'ISO 9999:2002.' *Technical Aids for Persons with Disabilities – Classification and Terminology,* Central Secretariat, Geneva Switzerland, http://www.iso.ch/iso/en/ISOOnline.frontpage

Jain, S. (1999) 'The Prosthetic Imagination: Enabling and Disabling the Prosthesis Trope.' *Science, Technology, & Human Values,* 24(1), 31–54.

Landow, G. P. (1992) *Hypertext. The convergence of contemporary critical theory and technology,* Baltimore, MD & London: Johns Hopkins University Press.

Law, J. (1987) 'Technology and Heterogeneous Engineering: the Case of the Portuguese Expansion.' In: W. E. Bijker, T. P. Hughes & T. Pinch (Eds.), *The Social Construction of Technical Systems: New Directions in the Sociology and History of Technology,* Cambridge, MA: MIT Press, 111–134.

Law, J. (1992) *Notes on the Theory of the Actor Network: Ordering, Strategy and Heterogeneity,* Lancaster: Centre for Science Studies, Lancaster University.

Moser, I. & Law, J. (1999) 'Good Passages, Bad Passages.' In: J. Law & J. Hassard (Eds.), *Actor Network Theory and After,* Oxford: The Sociological Review and Blackwell, 196–219.

Radabaugh, M. P. (1988) *Study on the Financing of Assistive Technology Devices and Services for Individuals with Disabilities: A Report to the President and the Congress of the United States*, March 4, 1993, 1. Washington, D.C.: National Council on Disability.

Seelman, K. D. (2001) 'Science and Technology Policy: Is Disability a Missing Factor?' In: G. L. Albrecht, K. D. Seelman & M. Bury (Eds.), *Handbook of Disability Studies*, Thousand Oaks, CA: Sage, 663–692.

Sobchack, V. (1995) 'Beating the Meat/Surviving the Text, or How to Get Out of the Century Alive.' In: M. Featherstone & R. Burrows (Eds.), *Cyberspace/cyberbodies/cyberpunk: Cultures of Technological Embodiment*, London: Sage, 205–214.

Stone, R. A. (1995) *The War of Desire and Technology at the Close of the Mechanical Age*, Cambridge, MA: MIT Press.

Winance, M. (2006) 'Trying Out the Wheelchair.' *Science, Technology & Human Values*, 31(1), 52–72.

16. S. Lochlain Jain, The prosthetic imagination: enabling and disabling the prosthesis trope

Bateson, G. (1971). 'The cybernetics of 'self': A theory of alcoholism.' *Psychiatry* 34:1–18.

Brahm, G. and M. Driscoll, eds. (1995). *Prosthetic territories: Politics and hypertechnologies*. Boulder, CO: Westview.

Freud, S. ([1930] 1962). *Civilization and its discontents*, translated by James Strachey. New York: W. W. Norton.

Gray, C. H., ed. (1995). *The cyborg handbook*. New York, London: Routledge.

Grosz, E. (1994). *Volatile bodies: Toward a corporeal feminism*. Bloomington, IN: Indiana University Press.

Scarry, E. (1994). 'The merging of bodies and artifacts in the social contract.' In *Culture on the brink: Ideologies of technology*, edited by Gretchen Bender and Timothy Druckery, 85–98. Seattle, WA: Bay Press.

Seltzer, M. (1992). *Bodies and machines*. New York, London: Routledge.

Sobchack, V. (1995). 'Beating the meat/surviving the text, or how to get out of this century alive.' *Body & Society* 1:205–214.

Stone, R. A. (1995). *The war of desire and technology at the close of the mechanical age*. Cambridge, MA: MIT Press.

Virilio, P. (1995). *The art of the motor*, translated by Julie Rose. Minneapolis, MN: University of Minnesota Press.

Wiener, N. (1985). *Cybernetics, science, and society: Ethics, aesthetics, and literary criticism*, edited by P. Masani. Cambridge, MA: MIT Press.

Wigley, M. (1991). 'Prosthetic theory: The disciplining of architecture.' *Assemblage* 15:7–29.

Wills, D. (1995). *Prosthesis*. Stanford, CA: Stanford University Press.

17. Bess Williamson, Electric moms and quad drivers: people with disabilities buying, making and using technology in postwar America

Brandt, E. N. and MacPherson Pope, A. (eds) (1997) *Enabling America: Assessing the Role of Rehabilitation Science and Engineering*. Washington, DC: National Academy Press.

Breslin, M. L. (2000) "Cofounder and Director of the Disability Rights Education and Defense Fund, Movement Strategist," in Disability Rights and Independent Living Movement Oral History Project, an oral history conducted in 1996–1998 by Susan O'Hara. Regional Oral History Office.

Brinkman, I. (1958) "The Home and I," *Toomeyville Jr Gazette*, Winter 1958, 13.

Bruck, L. (1978) *Access: The Guide to a Better Life for Disabled Americans*, 1st ed. New York: Obst Books.

Clark, C. E. (1986) *The American Family Home, 1800–1960*. Chapel Hill, NC: University of North Carolina Press.

Colson-Cleveland Co.(nd) *Colson Ball-Bearing Rubber-Tired Steel Wheels,* Cleveland.

Crawford, M. (1995) "Scarcity and Promise: Materials and American Domestic Culture During World War II," in *World War II and the American Dream,* Albrecht, D. and Crawford, M. (eds) Washington, DC: National Building Museum, 42–89.

Eglash, R. (2004) "Appropriating Technology: An Introduction," in *Appropriating Technology: Vernacular Science and Social Power.* Minneapolis, MN: University of Minnesota Press.

Flink, J. J. (1988) *The Automobile Age.* Cambridge, MA: The MIT Press.

Goldstein, C. (1998) *Do It Yourself: Home Improvement in 20th-Century America.* New York and Washington, DC: Princeton Architectural Press and The National Building Museum.

Grimley Mason, M. (2000) *Life Prints: A Memoir of Healing and Discovery.* New York: Feminist Press at the City University of New York.

Hounshell, D. A. (1984) *From the American System to Mass Production, 1800–1932: The Development of Manufacturing Technology in the United States.* Baltimore, MD: Johns Hopkins University Press.

Jordan, J. (1951) "Hand Controlled," *Paraplegia News,* January, 7.

Kline, R. and Pinch, T. (1996) "Users as Agents of Technological Change: The Social Construction of the Automobile in the Rural United States," *Technology and Culture* 37, no. 4 (October 1): 763–795

La Michle, V. (1959) "The Home and I," *Toomey J Gazette,* Fall–Winter 1959, 17.

Longmore, P. L. (2003) *Why I Burned My Book and Other Essays on Disability.* Philadelphia, PA: Temple University Press.

Lowman, E. W. and Rusk, H. A. (1962) *Self-Help Devices, Part 1.* New York: Institute of Physical Medicine and Rehabilitation, New York University Medical Center.

Mee, C. L. (1999) *A Nearly Normal Life: A Memoir.* Boston, MA: Little, Brown and Co.

Meikle, J. L. (1995) *American Plastic: A Cultural History.* New Brunswick, NJ: Rutgers University Press.

Oshinsky, D. M. (2005) *Polio: An American Story.* New York: Oxford University Press.

Ott, K. (2002) "The Sum of Its Parts: An Introduction to Modern Histories of Prosthetics," in *Artificial Parts, Practical Lives: Modern Histories of Prosthetics,* ed. Ott, K., Serlin, D. and Mihm, S. New York: New York University Press.

Percy, S. L. (1989) *Disability, Civil Rights, and Public Policy: The Politics of Implementation.* Tuscaloosa, AL: University of Alabama Press.

Roberts, Z. (2000) "Counselor for UC Berkeley's Physically Disabled Students' Program, Mother of Ed Roberts," Oral History conducted in 1994–1995 by Susan O'Hara. Berkeley, CA: Regional Oral History Office, The Bancroft Library, University of California, 63–65.

Rusk, H. A. and Taylor, E. J. (1953) *Living with a Disability.* Garden City, NY: Blakiston Co.

Stiker, H-J. (1999) *A History of Disability.* Ann Arbor, MI: University of Michigan Press.

Toomey J. Gazette (1960) "Mouthsticks," Spring, 8–9.

Toomey J. Gazette (1961) "Travel by Respos," Spring, 18–19.

Toomey J. Gazette (1968) "Wheelchairs: Accessories, New Models, Oddments and Endments," 60

Wajda, S. T. and Shuemaker, H. (eds.) (2008) *Material Culture in America: Understanding Everyday Life.* Santa Barbara, CA: ABC-CLIO.

White, R. B. (2000) *Home on the Road: The Motor Home in America.* Washington, DC: Smithsonian Institution Press.

Wilson, D. J. (2005) *Living with Polio: The Epidemic and Its Survivors.* Chicago, IL: University of Chicago Press.

18. David Serlin, Pissing without pity: disability, gender and the public toilet

Bérubé, A. (1984) 'The History of Gay Bathhouses', reprinted in Dangerous Bedfellows, eds, *Policing Public Sex: Queer Politics and the Future of AIDS Activism,* Boston, MA: South End Press, 187–220.

Bettison, S. (1982) *Toilet Training to Independence for the Handicapped: A Manual for Trainers*, Springfield, IL: Charles C. Thomas.

Breckenridge, C. A. and C. Vogler (2001) 'The Critical Limits of Embodiment: Disability's Criticism,' *Public Culture* Special Edition 13.3 Durham, NC, Duke University Press.

Carter, J. B. (2007) *The Heart of Whiteness: Normal Sexuality and Race in America, 1880–1940*, Durham: Duke University Press.

Charlton, J. I. (2000) *Nothing about Us without Us: Disability Oppression and Empowerment,* Berkeley, CA: University of California Press.

Chess, S. A. Kafer, J. Quizar, and M. U. Richardson (2004) 'Calling All Restroom Revolutionaries!' in Matt Bernstein Sycamore, *That's Revolting! Queer Strategies for Resisting Assimilation,* Brooklyn, NY: Soft Skull Press, 189–206.

Ervin, M. (2002) 'Johnny Crescendo, British Balladeer for Disability Rights,' *Disability World* 14 June–August.

Goffman, E. (September 1977) 'The Arrangement Between the Sexes,' *Theory and Society* 4:3, 316.

Goldsmith, S. (2001 [1997]) *Designing for the Disabled: The New Paradigm*, Oxford, UK: Architectural Press.

Igo, S. E. (2008) *The Averaged American: Surveys, Citizens, and the Making of a Mass Public*, Cambridge: Harvard University Press.

Johnson, R. A. (1983) 'Mobilizing the Disabled', in J. Freeman and V. Johnson, eds, *Waves of Protest: Social Movements since the Sixties,* New York: Rowman & Littlefield, 1999, 25–45.

Joyce, P. (2004) *The Rule of Freedom: Liberalism and the Modern City*, New York: Verso.

Kittay, E. F. (1999) *Love's Labor: Essays on Women, Equality, and Dependency*, New York: Routledge.

Levi, J. and B. Klein (2006) 'Pursuing Protection for Transgender People through Disability Laws,' in P. Currah, R. M. Juang, and S. P. Minter, eds, *Transgender Rights*, Minneapolis, MN: University of Minnesota Press.

Lifchez, R. and B. Winslow (1980) *Design for Independent Living: The Environment and Physically Disabled People,* Berkeley, CA: University of California Press.

Longmore, P. (1997) 'Conspicuous Contribution and American Cultural Dilemmas: Telethon Rituals of Cleansing and Renewal,' in D. T. Mitchell and S. L. Snyder, eds, *The Body and Physical Difference: Discourses of Disability*, Ann Arbor, MI: University of Michigan Press, 134–158.

Mairs, N. (1996) *Waist-High in the World: A Life among the Nondisabled*, Boston, MA: Beacon Press.

Ogle, M. (2000) *All the Modern Conveniences: American Household Plumbing, 1840–1890*, Baltimore, MD: Johns Hopkins University Press.

Schweik, S. (2009) *The Ugly Laws*, New York: New York University Press.

Serlin, D. (2004) 'Bathhouses,' in Marc Stein, ed., *The Encyclopedia of American Lesbian, Gay, Bisexual, and Transgender History in America,* New York: Charles Scribner's Sons, 122–125.

Serlin, D. (2004) *Replaceable You: Engineering the Body in Postwar America*, Chicago, IL: University of Chicago Press.

Serlin, D. (Winter 2006) 'Making History Public: An Interview with Katherine Ott,' *Radical History Review* 94, 197–211.

Serlin, D. (2006) 'Disability, Masculinity, and the Prosthetics of War, 1945 to 2005,' in M. Smith and J. Morra, eds, *The Prosthetic Impulse: From a Posthuman Present to a Biocultural Future,* Cambridge: MIT Press, 155–183.

Shapiro, J. P. (1993) *No Pity: People with Disabilities Forging a New Civil Rights Movement,* New York: Three Rivers Press.

Stiker, H-J. (2000) *A History of Disability*, trans. William Sayers, Ann Arbor, MI: University of Michigan Press, 128.

Terry, J. (1999) *An American Obsession: Science, Medicine, and Homosexuality in Modern Society*, Chicago, IL: University of Chicago Press.

Wilson, D. J. (2004) 'Fighting Polio Like a Man: Intersections of Masculinity, Disability, and Aging,' in B. G. Smith and B. Hutchison, eds, *Gendering Disability*, New Brunswick, NJ: Rutgers University Press.

White, P. (2003) 'Sex Education, or How the Blind Became Heterosexual,' *GLQ: A Journal of Lesbian and Gay Studies* 9:1–2, 133–148.

Zames Fleischer, D. and F. Zames (2001) *The Disability Rights Movement: From Charity to Confrontation*, Philadelphia, PA: Temple University Press.

Part V Projects and practices

Anthony, K. (2001) *Designing for Diversity: Gender, Race, and Ethnicity in the Architectural Profession*, Champaign, IL: University of Illinois Press.

Bauman, H-D. L. and Murray, Joseph J. (2013) 'Deaf Studies in the 21st Century: "Deaf-Gain" and the Future of Human Diversity', in Lennard J Davis (ed.) *Disability Studies Reader*, 4th ed. London: Routledge, 246–260.

Bauman, H-Dirksen. L. and Murray, Joseph J. (2014) *Deaf Gain: Raising the Stakes for Human Diversity*, University of Minnesota Press.

Davis, L. J. (1995) *Enforcing Normalcy: Disability, Deafness, and the Body*, London: Verso.

Goldsmith, S. (2001) *Universal Design*, Oxford: Reed Educational and Professional Publishing.

Goldsmith, S. (2012) *Designing for the Disabled: A New Paradigm*, London: Routledge.

Mace, R. (1985) 'Universal Design: Barrier-Free Environments for Everyone', *Designer's West* 33.1, 147–152.

O'Connell, K. (2012) 'Designing a City for the Deaf', May 27 *CityLab* (online), http://www.citylab.com/design/2012/03/designing-city-deaf/1600/

Pullin, G. (2011) *Design Meets Disability*, Boston, MA: MIT Press.

Silberman, S. (2015) *Neurotribes. The Legacy of Autism and How to Think Smarter about People Who Think Differently*, Sydney: Allen and Unwin.

Tauke, B., Smith, K. and Davis, C. (2015) *Diversity and Design: Understanding Hidden Consequences*, London and New York: Routledge.

21. Amanda Cachia, Along disabled lines: claiming spatial agency through installation art

Arnheim, R. (1982) *The Power of the Center: A Study of Composition in the Visual Arts*, Berkeley, CA: University of California Press.

Awan, N., Schneider, T., and Till, J. (2011) *Spatial Agency: Other Ways of Doing Architecture*, Abingdon, Oxon, England & New York: Routledge.

Badger, G. and Jacob, W. (2011) 'In the Presence of another Being: A Conversation with Wendy Jacob,' *Scapegoat: Architecture/Landscape/Political Economy*, Issue 01: 4–5.

Davidson, M. (2015) 'Keywords in Disability Studies: Aesthetics,' *Keywords in Disability Studies*, Edited by Rachel Adams, Benjamin Reiss and David Serlin, New York: New York University Press.

De Bruyn, E. (2006) 'Topological Pathways of Post-Minimalism,' *Grey Room*, 25, Fall 33.

Demos, T. J. (2001) 'Duchamp's Labyrinth: First Papers of Surrealism 1942,' *October*, Vol. 97 (Summer), 91–119.

Gleeson, B. J. (1996) 'A Geography for Disabled People?', *Transactions of the Institute of British Geographers*, New Series, Vol. 21, No. 2, 387–396.

Grosz, E. (2001) *Architecture from the Outside: Essays on Virtual and Real Space*, Cambridge, MA and London, England: The MIT Press.

Hamraie, A. (2013) 'Designing Collective Access: A Feminist Disability Theory of Universal Design,' *Disability Studies Quarterly*, Vol. 33, No. 4. Special Issue: Improving Feminist Philosophy and Theory by Taking Account of Disability. http://dsq-sds.org/article/view/3871/3411. Accessed October 28, 2013.

Kachur, L. (2001) *Displaying the Marvelous: Marcel Duchamp, Salvador Dali, and Surrealist Exhibition Installations*, Cambridge, MA and London, England: The MIT Press.

Kruse II, R. J. (2010) 'Placing Little People: Dwarfism and the Geographies of Everyday Life,' *Towards Enabling Geographies: 'Disabled' Bodies and Minds in Society and Space.* Edited by V. Chouinard, E. Hall, and R. Wilton, Farnham: Ashgate Publishing Ltd.

Lefebvre, H. (1974) *The Production of Space,* Hoboken UK: John Wiley & Sons.

Seamon, D. (2010) 'Merleau-Ponty, Perception, and Environmental Embodiment: Implications for Architectural and Environmental Studies,' available at: https://www.academia.edu/948750/Merleau-Ponty_Perception_and_Environmental_Embodiment_Implications_for_Architectural_and_Environmental_Studies_forthcoming_

Siebers, T. (2006) 'Disability Aesthetics,' *Journal for Cultural and Religious Theory* (JCRT) 7.2 Spring/Summer, 63–72.

Wolfflin, H. (1994) 'Prolegomena to a Psychology of Architecture,' in *Empathy, Form, and Space: Problems in German Aesthetics, 1873–1893*, Introduction and Translation by Harry Francis Mallgrave and Eleftherios Ikonomou, Los Angeles, CA: The Getty Center for the History of Art and the Humanities.

22. Thea McMillan with Katie Lloyd Thomas, The Ramp House: building inclusivity

British Standards Institution (2005) BS7000–6: 2005 *Guide to Managing Inclusive Design*, London: BSI Publications.

Star, L. (ed)(1995) *Ecologies of Knowledge – Work and Politics in Science and Technology*, Albany, NY: SUNY Press, 257–280.

Latour, B. (1999) *Pandora's Hope: Essays on the reality of science studies*, Cambridge, MA: Harvard University Press.

24. Sara Hendren, Notes on an inclined plane – Slope : Intercept

Borden I. (2001a) 'Performing the City' reprinted in Gelder, K. (ed.) (2005) *The Subcultures Reader.* London and New York: Routledge.

Borden, I. (2001b) *Skateboarding, Space, and the City.* Oxford and New York: Berg.

Boym, S. (2012) *Another Freedom: The Alternative History of an Idea.* Chicago, IL: University of Chicago Press.

Dunne, T. and Raby, F. (2005) *Hertzian Tales: Electronic Products, Aesthetic Experience and Critical Design.* Boston, MA: MIT Press.

Dunne, T. and Raby, F. (2013) *Speculative Everything: Design, Fiction and Social Dreaming.* Boston, MA: MIT Press.

Edgerton, D. (2007) *The Shock of the Old: Technology and Global History Since 1900.* Oxford: Oxford University Press.

Jackson, S. (2011) *Social Works, Performing Art, Supporting Publics.* New York: Routledge.

Jeremijenko, N. and Thacker, E. (2004) *Creative Biotechnology: A User's Manual.* Newcastle-Upon-Tyne: Locus+.

Koolhaas, R. and AMO (2014) *Elements: Ramp.* Venezia, Italy: Marsilio Editions.

Virilio, P. (1996) 'Architecture principe.' In: *The function of the oblique: the architecture of Claude Parent and Paul Virilio, 1963–1969.* London: AA Publications.

Virilio, P. and Parent, C. (1966) *Architecture Principe.* Joue les Tours: Les Editions de Imprimeur 27.

Wendell, S. (1996) *The Rejected Body: Feminist Philosophical Reflections on Disability.* New York: Routledge.

INDEX

Page references in *italic* indicate figures.